Cotton City

Cotton City

URBAN DEVELOPMENT
IN ANTEBELLUM
MOBILE

*

Harriet E. Amos

THE UNIVERSITY OF ALABAMA PRESS

COPYRIGHT © 1985 BY

THE UNIVERSITY OF ALABAMA PRESS

UNIVERSITY, ALABAMA 35486

ALL RIGHTS RESERVED

MANUFACTURED IN THE UNITED STATES OF AMERICA

Publication of this book has been assisted by a grant from
the Andrew W. Mellon Foundation through the American Council of
Learned Societies.

Library of Congress Cataloging in Publication Data

Amos, Harriet E.
Cotton City.

Bibliography: p.
Includes index.
1. Mobile (Ala.)—Economic conditions.   2. Mobile
(Ala.)—History—19th century.   3. Port districts—
Alabama—Mobile—History—19th century.   4. Cotton
trade—Alabama—Mobile—History—19th century.
5. Cities and towns—United States—Growth—Case studies.
I. Title.
HC108.M8A66   1985   338.9761′22   84-189
ISBN 0-8173-0218-2

TO MY PARENTS,

BEVIL T. AND NONA S. AMOS

Contents

ILLUSTRATIONS   viii

TABLES   ix

ACKNOWLEDGMENTS   xi

INTRODUCTION   xiii

1. OLD TOWN, YOUNG CITY   1

2. COTTON CITY   18

3. CITY FATHERS   48

4. WORKING PEOPLE   80

5. MUNICIPAL FINANCE AND DEFAULT   114

6. CITY SERVICES   136

7. SOCIAL SERVICES   168

8. PURSUIT OF PROGRESS   193

9. TEST OF LOYALTY   222

APPENDIX: CLASSIFICATION OF OCCUPATIONS   241

NOTES   243

ESSAY ON SOURCES   287

INDEX   299

Illustrations

View of Mobile in 1842   27

Mobile Harbor in 1851   27

Christ Church   66

Fire in 1839   125

City Hall and New Market in 1857   133

Barton Academy   181

MAPS

Plan Profil et Elevation du Fort Condé de la Mobile, c. 1725   8

Plan of Mobile, 1760   9

Mobile in 1765   10

Mobile in 1815   14

Mobile in 1824   15

Distribution of Cotton Production in Alabama in 1860   19

Mobile Bay Area, 1861   25

Mobile in 1860   69

Location of Railroads in Alabama, 1861   201

Tables

2-1	Cotton Crop of South Alabama, 1818–59	21
2-2	Cotton Bales Exported from Mobile, 1829–59	21
2-3	Value of Exports and Imports for the Port of Mobile, 1821–60	23
2-4	Exports and Imports of Major U.S. Ports, 1860	23
2-5	Bank Capital of Major U.S. Exporting Centers, 1860	39
2-6	Local Insurance Companies, 1861	41
3-1	Comparison of Geographical Origins of Urban Leaders of Antebellum Mobile, Richmond, and Norfolk	51
3-2	Region of Birth by Group	52
3-3	Most Frequently Listed Birthplaces of Urban Leaders and Sample Males, 1860	52
3-4	Occupational Category by Group	57
3-5	Total Wealth by Group	57
3-6	Real Estate by Group	60
3-7	Personal Estate by Group	60
3-8	Number of Slaves Held by Group	61
3-9	City Residence by Group	68
3-10	Age by Group	71
3-11	Age of Wife by Group	71
3-12	Number of Children by Group	71
3-13	Age of Youngest Child by Group	72
3-14	Age of Eldest Child by Group	72
3-15	Nativity of Business Leaders in Mobile	73
3-16	Nativity of Government Leaders in Mobile	74
4-1	Male Employment in Manufacturing in the City of Mobile, 1860	82
4-2	Population of Mobile by Racial Group and Sex, 1830–60	86
4-3	Percentage of Decennial Population Growth by Racial Group in Mobile, 1830–60	86

4-4	Whites, Free Blacks, and Slaves as Percentages of the Population of Mobile, 1830–60	86
4-5	Occupations of White Male Heads of Household and Free Black Male Heads of Household, 1860	92
4-6	Occupations of White Female Heads of Household and Free Black Female Heads of Household, 1860	98
4-7	Residence of Racial Groups by Wards, 1860	100
4-8	Real Estate Holdings of Heads of Household by Race and Sex, 1860	102
4-9	Personal Estate Holdings of Heads of Household by Race and Sex, 1860	102
4-10	Increase of the Foreign-Born Population, 1850–60	106
5-1	Property Holdings of Government Leaders of Antebellum Mobile	119
5-2	Occupations of Government Leaders of Antebellum Mobile	119
5-3	Value of Taxable Property in Mobile, 1820–37	128
5-4	Value of Taxable Property in Mobile, 1838–60	129
5-5	Value of Classes of Taxable Property in Mobile, 1820–37	130
5-6	Value of Classes of Taxable Property in Mobile, 1838–60	131
6-1	Percentages of Annual Expenditures for City Departments, 1852–58	138
8-1	Manufacturing Enterprises in Mobile County, 1860	214
8-2	Manufacturing in Mobile County, 1860	215
8-3	Population and Manufactures of Major Southern Cities, 1860	217

Acknowledgments

Preparation of this book has extended over a number of years, during which I have benefited from the help, advice, and encouragement of many people. Three who guided my studies of Mobile deserve special recognition. Bernadette Loftin introduced me to the study of Mobile's history; John L. Gignilliat of Agnes Scott College directed my independent study of Mobile in the 1850s; and James Z. Rabun of Emory University directed my dissertation on the social history of antebellum Mobile, which laid the foundation for this book.

A host of people cooperated with me in my research, often by going beyond the call of duty to help me find materials. These people include, in Mobile, Caldwell Delaney, director of the Museum of the City of Mobile; Mrs. Carter C. Smith, then archivist of the Historic Mobile Preservation Society; Richard Smith, city clerk; Barbara Kleinschrodt, then curator of the City of Mobile Archives; and Edith Richards, holder of the Horton Family Papers. Staff members at numerous libraries and manuscript repositories cheerfully aided my research. Virginia Jones and Miriam Jones of the Alabama State Department of Archives and History provided special assistance, as did Robert Lovett, then curator of manuscripts in the Baker Library, Graduate School of Business Administration, Harvard University. Staff members in the Special Collections Division of the Mobile Public Library conscientiously handled my requests for information. Librarians at the University of Alabama in Birmingham helped me find hard-to-locate materials. Alan S. Thompson of Louisiana State University in Shreveport shared some political identification data from his own research with me. Rod Clark of the Center for Urban Affairs at the University of Alabama in Birmingham expertly drafted several of the maps for this book.

Graduate students at the University of Alabama in Birmingham contributed research assistance for certain aspects of this study, particularly census data regarding the urban leaders. Graduate assistants Michael Breedlove, Jane E. Keeton, Edward S. Mudd, Jr., and Lynn H. Smith helped with research assignments. Norma Walter assisted with tabulations of certain data. Henry F. Inman generously gave his time to help design and run the computer programs for analyzing data on the urban leaders.

Colleagues and friends kindly read some or all of the manuscript to offer helpful comments and criticisms. Grace H. Gates of Anniston, Caldwell Delaney of Mobile, and E. Jane Bellamy, Mary E. Frederickson, and Laura Jarnagin Pang, all of the University of Alabama in Birmingham, contributed suggestions for improvement of selected chapters. J. Mills Thornton III of the University of Michigan read a late draft of the manuscript to give me advice. My colleagues Margaret Armbrester and Virginia V. Hamilton carefully read the entire manuscript and revisions to help me strengthen the work. Two anonymous readers for The University of Alabama Press offered extremely valuable suggestions on the manuscript. Numerous improvements resulted from their advice.

The University of Alabama in Birmingham provided aid in research and preparation of the final manuscript. University College Faculty Research Grants in 1978–79 and 1979–80 facilitated research travel. Dean George E. Passey of the School of Social and Behavioral Sciences contributed funds to pay for typing the manuscript. Debra Givens and Katharine Watson helped prepare the manuscript for final typing. Jeanne Holloway cheerfully and conscientiously typed the manuscript. I am pleased to acknowledge each of these contributions to my work. And I wish to thank Malcolm MacDonald, director, and the staff of The University of Alabama Press for their encouragement, patience, and cooperation in this project.

Introduction

> *Mobile—a pleasant cotton city of some thirty thousand inhabitants— where the people live in cotton houses and ride in cotton carriages. They buy cotton, sell cotton, think cotton, eat cotton, drink cotton, and dream cotton. They marry cotton wives, and unto them are born cotton children. In enumerating the charms of a fair widow, they begin by saying she makes so many bales of cotton. It is the great staple—the sum and substance of Alabama. It has made Mobile, and all its citizens.*[1]

THIS description penned by a British visitor, Hiram Fuller, in 1858 accurately depicts the integral part the cotton trade played in the urban development of antebellum Mobile, although it doubtless exaggerates the local obsession with cotton. Fuller conveys the impression that cotton secured the prosperity of all Mobilians, yet the export trade benefited only some residents directly, more indirectly, and others, mainly slaves, not at all. While Fuller's portrait is not completely accurate, there can be no question that cotton is the key to the history of antebellum Mobile.

Concentration on the exportation of one staple crop did not in itself set Mobile apart from other southern cities, but the extent of the commitment to the cotton trade made Mobile the southern port with the most extreme position of colonial dependency within the national economy. This colonial relationship helped to shape for southern cities a course of development that made them different from cities in other regions.[2] Economic dependency upon the North created by the cotton trade controlled urban development in antebellum Mobile. Mobile developed an export trade that placed the city third, after New York and New Orleans, in total value of exports for the nation by 1860. Since these exports consisted almost entirely of cotton destined for northern and foreign textile factories, Mobile, like other cotton ports, depended upon northern businessmen for marketing services. Furthermore, Mobile relied on New York for almost all imports. Mobile had the worst export-import imbalance of all antebellum ports.[3]

As the volume of cotton exports increased, so did the population of Mobile, from 1,500 in 1820 to 30,000 in 1860. Although Mobile was the least populous of all major southern cities in 1860, its growth rate throughout the antebellum period remained exceptional. Urban growth proceeded rapidly throughout the nation during the antebellum years, and cities everywhere dealt with growth in similar ways. As certain quantitative and qualitative indicators of urbanism in the largest southern cities suggest, urban development in the antebellum South resembled that throughout America.[4] This study attempts, in part, to delineate the basis for Mobile's growth and the ways in which residents and their government promoted and adapted to growth. In so doing this work should fill a void in the scholarship dealing with southern cities.

Specialization in the cotton trade led to a reliance upon northern marketing, shipping, and banking firms, some of which maintained their own local agencies. Large numbers of northern-born businessmen in Mobile attended to the export trade and participated widely in civic affairs. For this reason this study also explores the North-South relationship in economic and personal terms in the microcosm of one city during a period of increasing sectional tensions.

Even though the town was settled in the early eighteenth century, it became a city only in the nineteenth century. Rather than define *city* in a particular way, I have approached the subject by analyzing the process of urban growth, which implies change. A definition of a city according to population and function can be constraining, since urban growth has repeatedly changed the size and function of cities.[5]

If, however, some basic distinction among antebellum cities must be made on the basis of size and function, a guideline based on population, function, and influence of an urban place serves the purpose. By this standard Mobile was a "small" city in 1820, meaning that its population fell between 1,000 and 2,500 and it carried on some wholesaling and perhaps basic processing industries, with its market influence extending beyond its immediate hinterland but short of the entire region. By 1850 Mobile's population of some 20,000 clearly raised it above the maximum size of a "small" city, which at that time was 4,000.[6] In addition, Mobile's export trade and railroad projects extended the city's influence beyond the South.

Antebellum Mobile illustrates the role of fresh leadership in integrating an old, stagnating colonial port into the market economy of nineteenth-century America. New Yorkers supplied the catalyst that stimulated the economic development of Mobile after Americans occupied it during the War of 1812. In the resettled town local residents apparently welcomed anyone, regardless of birthplace, whose activities boosted the cotton trade that burgeoned in the port. Leaders in Mobile, in contrast to other southern cities, came from a wide variety of places, indicating citizens' receptivity to enterprising newcomers. Enterprise indeed became the characteristic most admired by the populace.

The ethnic makeup of Mobile's population changed considerably between 1813 and 1860. When Americans occupied the town during the War of 1812, they found immigrants from the British Isles, France, and American states as well as black Creoles. During the rapid expansion of the boom 1820s and 1830s, many northerners and Englishmen migrated to Mobile to launch commercial firms. In the 1840s and 1850s large numbers of Irishmen and Germans arrived in Mobile to seek their fortunes. By that time many of the major businesses in the city were well established, and opportunities for newcomers were thus reduced. Destitute immigrants took low-paying unskilled labor positions anywhere they could find them in the city. Their entry into the work force displaced some free blacks and slaves from menial jobs. With customs and religion often at variance with those of the Protestant Anglo-Saxon leaders of the city, Irish and German immigrants encountered a number of conflicts with local decision makers.

Government served basically to foster commercial growth. As the city grew at a phenomenal rate in the boom 1830s, municipal services expanded to sustain prosperity. When the boom collapsed in the Panic of 1837, the city faced bankruptcy. This crisis mandated rigid economy and fiscal responsibility from officials who had formerly often neglected to supervise budgetary matters as they conducted their own private pursuits of wealth.

A decade after the onset of the panic, Mobile's growth rate slowed and, by contrast to the pre-panic era, the city appeared to stagnate. This "stagnation" came at a time when Mobile's growth, in relative terms, still exceeded that of some major southern cities. Nonetheless, urban leaders of Mobile began to question the economic system of cotton marketing that had provided the financial base for the city. Not only did they implore southerners to build railroads to expand their markets and to open direct import trade to offset their dependence upon New York, but they also encouraged manufacturing to diversify the economy.

In this process southerners stressed sectional loyalty as never before, casting suspicions upon any persons dwelling among them who were not natives of the region. Northern-born leaders, many of whom had resided in Mobile for twenty to thirty years, faced criticism solely on the basis of their birthplaces, regardless of whether their actions in Mobile benefited the South or the North. Native southerners, who were anxious to judge loyalty to their own city and region, conveniently ignored past or current contributions to the city's development made by nonsoutherners in their midst.

In their quest for southern independence from northern commercial domination, urban boosters apparently thought that reducing the influence of native northerners among them would reinforce their larger effort to strengthen southerners' control of their own economy. The regional specialization within the national economy that had led the South to produce raw materials and the North to provide manufacturing and marketing services was, by the 1850s, too well established to change substantially. Southerners, particularly in Mobile, had profited from this system so that they in essence had almost as much interest in maintaining the arrangement as northerners. Thus, as the secession crisis developed, Mobile's national and international commerce dictated moderation, while sectional loyalty promoted separation.

Cotton City

✳ I ✳

Old Town, Young City

M OBILE is becoming a place of great importance," reported *Niles' Register* in 1822, "and it is possible, may soon be one of the most populous of our southern cities." *Niles' Register* based this prediction on the town's growth from 300 at the time of American occupation in 1813, to 809 at the city's incorporation by the new state of Alabama in 1819, and to 2,800 in 1822.[1] Hope of financial gain lured most newcomers to the Alabama port as the Cotton Kingdom pushed into the Southwest. News of Mobile's growth as a young American city attracted the attention of "distant adventurers of every description," including attorneys, doctors, merchants, and mechanics, who, according to a local physician, "have fled hither as to an Eldorado."[2]

After years of stagnation under foreign rulers, could Mobile capitalize on its geographical and historical advantages to become not just a resettled boom town but a major seaport? This question intrigued new residents and visitors from other parts of the United States and foreign countries. Both groups remarked on current conditions and future prospects of Mobile by drawing comparisons between the Alabama port and other cities. In the early 1820s neither the architecture nor the society built by Mobilians equaled that of older American ports, yet appearances improved throughout the decade.

With its multinational population, American Mobile initially lacked community cohesion. Legacies remained of foreign colonial rule: French, 1702 to 1763; British, 1763 to 1780; and Spanish, 1780 to 1813. After 1813 a "new population" headed to Mobile "to make money."[3]

These inhabitants, according to an American officer of occupation in 1817, were generally "a mixture consisting of the Creoles (principally coloured), and emigrants from England, Scotland, Ireland, and different parts of the United States who are governed entirely by personal interest; and exhibit very little of what may be termed *National feeling*."[4] Adam Hodgson, a merchant from Liverpool, found Mobile in 1820 "an old Spanish town, with mingled traces of the manners and language of the French and Spaniards."[5]

Mobile appeared to many visitors in the 1820s as more of a rough frontier town than a long-established city. "Indeed, for a place that has been so long settled, more than a hundred years," observed Welcome Arnold Greene from Rhode Island in 1824, "there is little evidence of improvement in the way of polish and refinement as I suspect of any town of but half that age, in our country, would display." At the time of Greene's visit, Mobile had 240 houses, 110 stores and warehouses, 30 brick buildings, 2 churches, 3 hotels, and several buildings used for other public purposes, certainly all the structures expected in a small city then.[6] However, neither the construction of homes nor cultivation of gardens created a settled appearance for Mobile, according to the standards of visitors from the eastern United States.

In architecture Mobile displayed a hodgepodge of styles, some used by Creoles during the colonial era and others introduced by recently arrived New Englanders. Construction of early residences and public buildings apparently was more often controlled by utility and expediency than by aesthetics and durability. Creole-style wooden houses suited to the hot, humid climate, with long, sloping roofs and galleries on the front, predominated in the older sections of the city. Most private homes were made of wood, while most public buildings such as the theater, bank, and federal and county courthouses were built of brick. When contractors tried to use brick for townhouses, they sometimes were not able to get enough to complete the construction. Thus newly built brick houses might have a layered look, with the first two stories of red brick and the third of yellow brick.[7] It is no wonder that their appearance failed to make a favorable impression upon visitors from New England and Britain.

Even more than their makeshift architecture, Mobilians' behavior offended British visitors in the 1820s. Portraits drawn by these Englishmen corroborated observations European tourists generally made of the habits of Jacksonian Americans. Boorishness received particular attention in visitors' journals. Adam Hodgson reported that he "saw much more of *men* than of *manners*" at a Mobile tavern where he took his meals with thirty or forty other men, mainly assorted agents and clerks. He began to believe the story he had been told, that travelers proceeding westward in America might take their longitude by observing the decreasing amounts of time spent at meals. Five to six minutes was the average time in Mobile, Hodgson estimated. Margaret Hall confirmed Hodgson's observations. At a "noisy, bustling public table" in a boarding house she watched while "sixty persons dispatched their unchewed dinner in the course of twenty minutes." A private dinner in the home of a prominent local attorney failed to make a much more favorable impression upon Mrs. Hall, who considered the dining table overloaded with badly cooked food.[8]

In their materialistic value system, Mobilians, like other Jacksonian Americans, stressed above all the pursuit of wealth. Refinement in social manners mattered little while newly established merchants competed furiously for business. Business opportunities attracted a large number of merchants to Mobile; in 1817, for instance, 42 merchants competed for the patronage of 600 residents plus settlers headed for cotton lands upstate or elsewhere in the Southwest.[9] By 1822, when the city was, according to the *Mobile Register*, assuming a settled character, merchants who leased stores or rented warehouses from year to year still scrambled for business. Some shopowners actually beckoned people from one store to another, even ones across the street from each other. Trying to dissuade merchants from these unseemly practices, the *Mobile Register* urged them to adopt self-restraint for the sake of the good image of the city.[10]

Opportunity seekers initially came alone to the port city, so Mobile abounded with young single men. The disproportionate male-female ratio retarded urban growth and social development. Throughout the 1820s young white males outnumbered white females in Mobile more than two to one.[11] Many of the young men worked as itinerant agents of cotton firms based in New York. As one local resident described them, they were "mere birds of passage—here in the winter and off in the summer." An "occasional epidemic . . . frightened away the unacclimated," he added.[12] The sexual imbalance in the population, plus the itinerant habits of the cotton merchants, retarded urban growth in Mobile as elsewhere in the cotton South before 1830.[13]

Social development also proceeded slowly while single males predominated in Mobile. One young physician found companions for card games and supper parties among bachelor merchants from the North. "The want of female society is sensibly felt in Mobile," Dr. Solomon Mordecai reported in 1823, "as it would be in all places where the population as here consists of single gentlemen."[14]

Recognizing the potential of Mobile to become more than a rough frontier town, some residents supported social activities found in established cultural centers of the South. They attended horse races and theatrical productions. They organized Masonic lodges that gave balls.[15] Sponsors of these activities soon emerged as social leaders. While the common people of Mobile were as coarse and rough as the buildings in their city, according to one visitor from New England, "the better class who have come here to seek their fortunes" included "a few whose gentlemanly manners, united to a full share of natural talents and acquired intelligence, would be creditable to any place."[16] Solomon Mordecai, one of these gentlemen, predicted in 1825 that Mobile would become "the Charleston of Alabama."[17]

Mobile's future as a city depended in part upon the fate of a rival city across Mobile Bay, Blakeley. This boom town was the brainchild of Josiah Blakeley, a native of Connecticut who had moved to Alabama during the late Spanish period. When he eventually concluded that the port of Mobile had only limited possibilities for business, he decided to establish his own seaport to produce greater financial returns for his investment. In 1813 Blakeley bought a site for his town on the Tensaw River on the east side of Mobile Bay, opposite the town of Mobile. He obtained permission the next year from the Mississippi Territorial Legislature to lay out a town on his land. Following the plan of New England townships transplanted to the Southwest, Blakeley reserved two parcels of land for public use, one for a park and one for public buildings. A few lots may have been sold as early as 1813, but most sales occurred in 1817 and 1818. Blakeley, who died in 1815, never witnessed the settlement of his town.[18]

As a boom town from 1817 until 1820, Blakeley, in direct competition with Mobile, attracted entrepreneurs from across the United States. Town promoters in early Alabama usually did not employ a booster press, but Blakeley published its own, the *Blakeley Sun*. In 1818 the *Sun* boasted that 100 houses had been built in the area, which had had only one the previous year. Reprints of this claim appeared in newspapers as far away as Dayton, Ohio. New Yorkers and New Englanders in particular moved to Blakeley to open commercial firms or businesses that served commerce. Twenty-one merchants from seventeen firms petitioned the United States Congress in December 1818 to establish Blakeley as a port of entry and delivery. They reminded Congress that the town's population of 300 people had all moved there since November 1817, a fact that indicated to them a great potential for growth. Congress did not grant the petition until 1822, but the Alabama General Assembly did pass an act in 1820 to regulate the port and harbor of Blakeley. Commerce between Blakeley and Mobile increased enough by early 1819 to justify ferry service between the two ports.[19] By 1820 a visiting merchant from Liverpool observed that Mobile and Blakeley were "contending violently for the privilege of becoming that great emporium which must shortly spring up in the vicinity of this outlet for the produce of the young fertile state of Alabama."[20]

Alabama's "great emporium" became Mobile instead of Blakeley. After 1824 Blakeley declined quickly as a port. While Mobile exported most of the cotton produced in south Alabama, Blakeley exported 4 percent of the crop in 1825 but only 1 percent the next year. In 1827 the collector for the new port moved his records to Mobile. Blakeley remained as an official United States port of entry until 1831, when Congress repealed the 1822 legislation that had established the customs district of Blakeley.[21] Blakeley became a ghost town that never again challenged the commercial preeminence of Mobile in south Alabama.

As a port, Blakeley had initially appeared to offer geographic advantages superior to those of Mobile. For this reason historians have had trouble explaining Blakeley's decline in conventional terms of natural advantages. One theory maintained that Blakeley declined while Mobile thrived because improvements in approaches to the harbor of Mobile eventually made it more accessible to the bay than Blakeley. According to this view, the dredging of the Choctaw Pass allowed vessels of the size that had been going to Blakeley to proceed directly to Mobile. That made the wharves of Mobile more convenient to the bay than those of Blakeley. But the Choctaw Pass was not dredged until 1831, several years after Blakeley was virtually defunct as a port, so the dredging could have had no appreciable effect on Blakeley's demise. Besides that, the harbor at Blakeley was not as easy to reach from the bay as town promoters suggested. Vessels sometimes had to remain in

Mobile Bay for a week to get winds strong enough to propel them up the Tensaw River to Blakeley.[22] Geographic determinism, as it turns out, does not explain the failure of Blakeley.

Another theory explained Blakeley's decline in terms of its reputation for unhealthiness as yellow fever ravaged the town in 1819, 1826, and 1828. Although the epidemic of 1819 prompted temporary evacuation, survivors returned to Blakeley. Before the outbreaks of yellow fever in 1826 and 1828, commerce had already declined drastically.[23]

Runaway land speculation has also been suggested as an explanation for Blakeley's demise. As speculators drove up land prices in the frontier seaport, the lower and more stable prices for land in Mobile attracted an increasing number of the merchants who came to south Alabama. The *Mobile City Directory* for 1855–56 subscribed to this view. So did the nineteenth-century journalist Bernard Reynolds, who presented Thomas Hallett as an example of an ambitious merchant who headed for Blakeley only to settle ultimately in Mobile. Hallett, according to Reynolds, arrived in Mobile Bay "determined to open a commercial house" at Blakeley. When Hallett tried to secure a location for his business, he found such extravagantly high prices placed on lots in Blakeley that he "determined to try his fortune in Mobile." Reynolds interpreted the arrival of Hallett as "the signal for a complete change in the relative positions, in point of importance, of the two places" since "trade soon flourished in Mobile and languished in Blakeley."[24] Certainly land speculation contributed both to Blakeley's rise and to its decline. Deflation in land values caused by the Panic of 1819 halted Blakeley's growth, yet the same thing happened to other towns that eventually recovered and grew even faster in the 1820s than they had before 1819.

Blakeley declined and Mobile survived ultimately because of Mobile's earlier founding. As the *New York American* noted in 1823, "Blakeley has every advantage over Mobile, except that of being begun when this was already established." Urban growth may be explained by factors other than site and situation, and urban historians and urban geographers now agree that the case of Mobile illustrates this fact. Nineteenth-century America's largest cities tended to be the long-established ones, which took advantage of their early leads.[25] In the final analysis, that first century of Mobile's existence, even under colonial rule and in relative commercial stagnation, laid the foundation for the city's survival and growth.

With the demise of Blakeley, Mobile dominated settlements on Mobile Bay. Yet Mobile ranked second among ports on the Gulf of Mexico to New Orleans. From its position of superiority, New Orleans complimented Mobile in a patronizing way. For instance, in 1822 the *Louisiana Gazette* of New Orleans noted that, after almost a century "buried in obscurity and little esteemed," Mobile had dramatically become "a sea-port of the second order." Responding to this description, the *Mobile Argus* maintained that Mobile had "all the characteristics of one of the first order." Not only did Mobile have a large, rich hinterland, but its residents reportedly felt "no servile imitation, no mark of colonial dependence." In other words, Mobilians had the attitudes of citizens of a first-class port. The *Argus* recognized that Mobile was "destined to carry on a large foreign trade" as well as to maintain close trading relationships with New York and New Orleans, both first-class ports.[26] Mobile, striving to become a first-class port, competed with New Orleans in a rivalry that intensified over the years as gaps in development narrowed between the two Gulf cotton ports. In this process Mobile sought release from the colonial dependency that had characterized the city's first century.

Since its founding in 1702, Mobile had remained basically a trading outpost for successive French, British, and Spanish colonial rulers. Commercial and security advantages had persuaded a French Canadian soldier named Pierre Le Moyne d'Iberville to select Mobile Bay as the site for a French colony in southern Louisiana. Mobile Bay possessed an adequate harbor at Massacre Island and resources in timber and inland water connections that appeared superior to those of Biloxi Bay or the lower Mississippi River, which had been considered as alternative sites. Mobile suited the security considerations of French officials, who wished to found a settlement to protect their interests in Louisiana against European colonial rivals and to make inroads into Britain's monopoly on trade with the Indians of the Southeast. Not only was Mobile Bay located close to the path of the British advance southward from Carolina, but it also provided a communication link with major Indian nations in the interior via the Alabama-Tombigbee River system that flowed into the Mobile River on its way to the bay.[27] The name Mobile came from the French rendering of "Movile," the Spanish version of "Mobila," which was the name that the natives gave to the bay. In French and English, *mobile* serves as an adjective meaning "capable of moving or being moved."[28]

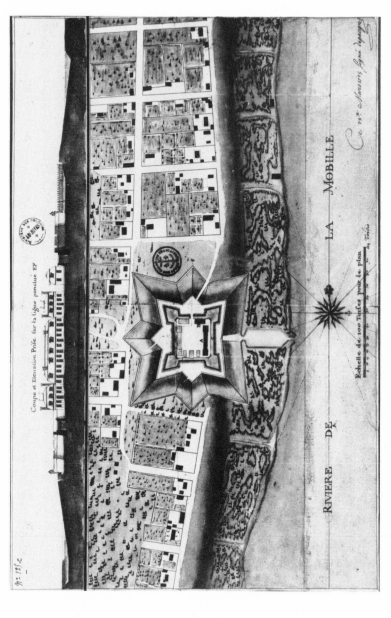

Plan Profil et Elevation de Fort Condé de la Mobile, c. 1725 (Courtesy of Special
Collections Division, Mobile Public Library)

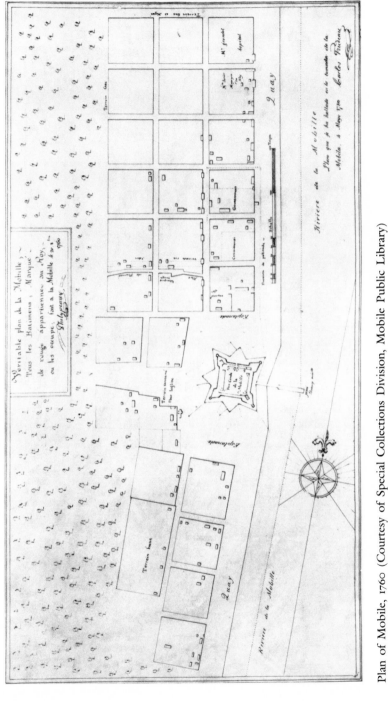

Plan of Mobile, 1760 (Courtesy of Special Collections Division, Mobile Public Library)

Mobile in 1765 (Courtesy of Special Collections Division, Mobile Public Library)

This description suited the settlement that became the city of Mobile, for it moved from its original site to a permanent one. In 1702 the French Canadians led by Jean-Baptiste Le Moyne de Bienville established Fort Louis de la Louisiane on a bluff twenty-seven miles north of the mouth of the Mobile River. Built in the French colonial style of a fort surrounded by a town, Fort Louis served as capital of the French colony on the Gulf. After seven years of problems caused by poor drainage at the upriver site, the French founded their permanent settlement in 1711 on a plain along the west bank of the Mobile River delta.[29] Fort Condé served to protect settlers who lived on the streets surrounding it.

As a French settlement Mobile never claimed more than a few hundred inhabitants, an indication of its relative insignificance in the ultimate colonization of Louisiana. In 1718 Biloxi replaced Mobile as capital of the colony, and in 1720 the newly founded city of New Orleans supplanted Biloxi. By the middle of the eighteenth century, New Orleans had superseded Mobile as the most important town in the Gulf region. Mobile served basically as the main center for trade with the Muscogee Indians. Colonists also exported animal skins and engaged in forestry and lumbering, but their trade did not seriously challenge the commercial primacy of New Orleans.[30]

Mobile grew slowly under the colonial rule of the British, who claimed the town as part of the settlement of the French and Indian War arranged by the Treaty of Paris of 1763. Major Robert Farmar, the British commandant, gave French residents several months to choose allegiance to George III or emigration. According to Farmar, about forty of the one hundred French families remained in Mobile. Many of the remaining Frenchmen moved their homes from the town to sites along the river and bay where they could raise cattle.[31] Other colonists continued to trade with the southeastern Indians and to export skins and furs.

Economic conditions changed little if any under the new Spanish rulers, who occupied Mobile in 1780 during the American Revolution and gained formal title to British West Florida in the Treaty of Paris of 1783. Mobile reportedly had 746 residents in 1785 and 1,468 three years later, yet the population, exclusive of the garrison, dropped to perhaps 300 by the end of the Spanish occupation in 1813.[32]

Shortly after the Louisiana Purchase in 1803, the United States claimed that its title to Louisiana included West Florida to the Perdido

River, which flowed to the east of Mobile Bay. According to the treaty of cession, the province of Louisiana had the same boundaries as it had had under French possession and Spanish control. This provision was ambiguous since the boundaries differed under the two rulers. Under the French the eastern boundary of Louisiana had been the Perdido River. In 1763 when England received Florida from Spain, the territory was divided into East and West Florida with a western boundary of the Mississippi River. When Spain regained the Floridas in 1783, the boundaries remained the same as under England. At the time of the Louisiana Purchase, the Mississippi River served as the boundary between West Florida and Louisiana, except for New Orleans. When France had settled the Gulf Coast, however, the eastern boundary of Louisiana extended to the Perdido River. After the cession of Louisiana, the United States claimed that the Perdido River was the eastern boundary of that portion of Louisiana located south of the thirty-first parallel.[33]

Mobile, located in the disputed territory between the Perdido and Mississippi rivers, was placed into a United States Customs district in 1804. Spain protested this action and refused to surrender West Florida to the United States on the grounds that West Florida was not part of Louisiana. In 1810, after large planters in the western part of West Florida declared their independence from Spain, President James Madison issued a proclamation that annexed parts of the province between the Mississippi and Pearl rivers and along the Gulf coast to the Perdido River. Even though the town of Mobile was included in this proclamation of annexation, Spain maintained the garrison there.[34]

The Spanish occupation finally ended during the War of 1812. Since the Spanish allowed British naval vessels to rendezvous in Mobile and other Gulf ports in their possession, the American government decided to occupy Mobile in order to stop this indirect Spanish aid to the British. In February 1813 Madison ordered Major General James Wilkinson, the commander at New Orleans, to take possession of Mobile. Wilkinson moved effectively in mid-April to cut off the land and sea communications from the Spanish garrison in Fort Charlotte (formerly Fort Condé). He informed the commander of the garrison that he was simply relieving the forces occupying a post considered within the legitimate boundaries of the United States. The Spanish forces, who were out of provisions, surrendered the fort without bloodshed.[35] As

Spanish civilians departed along with the troops, Americans moved into the town, situated in the only territory that the United States acquired as a result of the war. Thus the United States effectively annexed West Florida by military force, while it obtained East Florida by diplomacy in the Adams-Onis Treaty signed in 1819 and consummated in 1821.

Americans soon provided government for the town of Mobile. Under the provisions of an act of the Mississippi Territorial Legislature passed in January 1814, the white male landholders, freeholders, and householders within the town elected seven commissioners and a town treasurer, collector, and assessor. These new officers, chosen in March, included relative newcomers and long-time residents. Among the leaders were Commissioners James Innerarity, a partner in the large commercial house of John Forbes and Company; Lewis Judson, a merchant from Connecticut; Samuel H. Garrow, a refugee from Santo Domingo; and the assessor Miguel Eslava, a former Spanish official. At their first meeting in a private home, the commissioners outlined the boundaries of the town and divided it into three wards. Ward designations followed those used by the Spanish: South for the area south of the fort, Middle for land from the fort to Dauphin Street, and North for land north of Dauphin Street. French, rather than Spanish, was the predominant language besides English in early American Mobile, as indicated by the commissioners' decision to translate their resolutions into French and post three copies in public places.[36]

Territorial town government operated with severe financial constraints. Commissioners had authority to raise sums they considered necessary "for the well regulation" of the town, provided that the maximum annual assessment never exceeded 12½¢ per $100 worth of property subject to taxation. License taxes on stores, liquor dealers, carriages, and billiard tables augmented the town's meager resources. To conserve these funds, the commissioners contracted with private individuals to construct a public market house and wharf in 1815. Fees on transactions at the market apparently paid for its maintenance in the early years. Commissioners auctioned off the lease for the public wharf to the business partner of Commissioner S. H. Garrow. This wharf builder had to build the wharf to town specifications, collect proceeds from tolls for nine years to recoup his construction costs, and then sell the property back to the town. Town expenditures were kept low. To

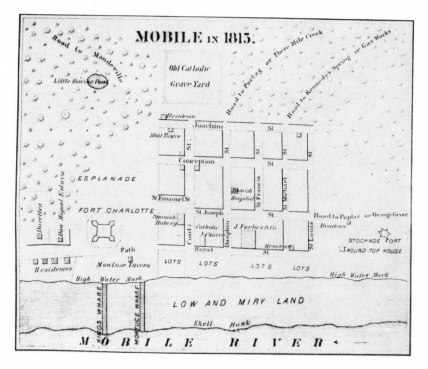

Mobile in 1815 (Courtesy of Special Collections Division, Mobile Public Library)

save money, the board of commissioners rented a room for its meetings. Even so, the first board of commissioners handed a balance in the treasury of less than $70 to its successor.[37]

Conventional civil government for Mobile began under an act of incorporation passed by the General Assembly of the new state of Alabama on 17 December 1819. As usual for the early nineteenth century, the charter was a simple document, containing only fourteen sections. According to its provisions, the electorate consisted of free white male adult residents who owned freehold property within the city or who had lived in the city for one year and paid taxes during the year before the election and had rented a tenement or separate rooms for six months just before the election. Voters directly selected seven aldermen, who in turn chose one of their number as mayor. The aldermen and mayor appointed other city officers and levied poll taxes and property taxes, which were not to exceed the maximum property tax rate of 40¢ per $100.[38]

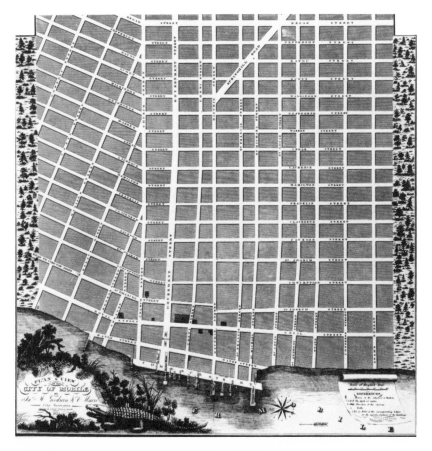

Mobile in 1824 (Courtesy of Special Collections Division, Mobile Public Library)

American Mobile expanded as private developers purchased the Fort Charlotte property in 1820. Congress had authorized the sale because the fort was no longer needed for defense. A locally formed syndicate, the Mobile Lot Company, purchased the bulk of the property. This real-estate development company had the land platted to conform to adjacent streets before selling building lots. City funds paid for the demolition of the fort's walls to clear new streets laid to the river through the site of the fort. Debris from the demolition was used to fill private lots as well as the easily flooded Water and St. Francis streets. Location of the former fort was not even marked on the Goodwin and Haire map of the city drawn in 1823, which emphasized the harbor and public buildings developed by the Americans.[39]

Settlement during the 1820s clustered primarily along the banks of the Mobile River. The river front and wharves from the foot of Dauphin Street to the foot of Government Street, a new one-hundred-foot-wide thoroughfare, made up the downtown commercial core of the city. The heart of the business district was the corner of Conti, the main east-west street, and Water, the front street of the town. Most businesses were located on one of these streets. New businesses located south of Government Street after Henry Stickney built a block of brick stores on the southwest corner of Water and Church streets in the late 1820s. Conception Street was the favorite residential address. Building lots for homes opened on the former site of Fort Charlotte.[40]

Private interests controlled the development of Mobile for commercial and residential purposes in the 1820s. Government served to facilitate that process. Expediency often influenced the actions of real-estate promoters, who, in their haste to open new development, sometimes neglected drainage problems caused by poor grading of new streets and fire hazards resulting from wooden construction of buildings. During the early part of the decade, town government hardly assumed an activist role in regulating and supervising private interests, for those interests essentially demanded noninterference from government. In the second half of the decade, however, disaster prompted government to take on the regulation and coordination of private concerns. This development did not in itself change the course of urbanization in Mobile, but it set precedents for greater government responsibilities in the maturing city.

New regulation of citizens' activities truly began to develop after a fire in October 1827 consumed two-thirds of the business district bounded by Conti and St. Michael streets. Flames destroyed numerous businesses along with their books and merchandise, and 169 private homes. Property losses exceeded $1,000,000. Since seven-eighths of the buildings razed were wooden, Mobilians realized the necessity of rebuilding with more durable materials. Within three months of the fire, insurance companies settled the losses that they covered (about half of the total), and people again invested in real estate, this time in brick buildings as required by a new city ordinance for the fire district.[41] By 1831, four years after the conflagration, Mobile looked like a new city. Few discernible traces of the fire remained as brick houses replaced log huts.[42] In 1833 the *Mobile Register* boasted that the city had "risen in all the vigor and beauty of a phoenix."[43]

Disaster graphically reminded Mobilians of the destruction that could result from the pursuit of private interests without regard to the community welfare. It had the immediate, direct result of promoting construction with brick instead of wood. It had the longterm, indirect result of encouraging organizations for civic purposes. In the decade after the fire Mobilians formed six fire companies to protect their property. They also supported three charitable groups that organized in 1829: the Female Benevolent Society; the Auxiliary Tract Society, an affiliate of the American Tract Society; and the Temperance Society. These groups augmented services that had been provided by the Hibernian Benevolent Society since 1822 and the Mobile Bible Society, an auxiliary to the American Bible Society, since 1825. Such voluntary associations provided more avenues for linking together the heterogeneous elements of Mobile's new American population than the one institution that had survived from the colonial era, the Roman Catholic church. Many of the Americans were Protestants who wanted their own churches instead of the one preferred by the Creoles. In 1822 they erected a small church, which served Protestants until various denominations formed their own congregations later in the decade.

By the end of the 1820s Mobile differed markedly from the town occupied by Americans in 1813. Some of the changes might be traced to the permanent removal of colonial governments that tended to control commerce for the benefit of imperialist powers. Americans committed to private enterprise purchased the fort that had dominated the town and its commerce and used the site for new streets leading to a dozen new private wharves. They developed the waterfront property to provide the wharves and terminal facilities needed by the steamboats that had just begun to ply the Mobile River en route to the cotton districts of southern Alabama and southeastern Mississippi. The advent of steamboats provided an important stimulus to local development. Commerce in cotton would ultimately make Mobile "a place of great importance," as predicted by *Niles' Register*. Ironically, however, commerce continued in the colonial dependency pattern established with the founding of Mobile. Mercantile interests in the North simply replaced foreign imperialist governments.

✳ 2 ✳

Cotton City

MOBILIANS and visitors reiterated the same theme: the local economy depended upon cotton. A clergyman described cotton as "the circulating blood that gives life to the city." As such it generated profits to merchants who in turn met payrolls, financed construction projects, and purchased consumer goods and services.[1] Because prices set on the world market determined profits made from cotton sales, local merchants carefully monitored foreign cotton exchanges. A British visitor observed that when news arrived from Europe, merchants turned "instinctively to the Liverpool cotton report." They knew that a tiny rise or fall in cotton prices made "the difference between ease and embarrassment—between riches and poverty—between a good speculation and a bad one." As merchants' incomes depended upon fluctuations in cotton prices on the world market, so did incomes for their employees and suppliers of goods and services. Thus it was hardly an exaggeration for the British traveler to report that all Mobilians "directly or indirectly live[d] . . . by the cotton trade."[2]

Export trade provided the major economic endeavor of antebellum Mobile as it had of the colonial settlement. Cotton, the main commodity for export, required a new superstructure of transportation and financial services. Virtually all local commercial activities, from marketing cotton to obtaining goods for planters in the interior, served the cotton trade. Local banking and insurance facilities, for instance, provided financial exchanges, credit, and security for property, respectively, rather than loans or risk capital for enterprises not directly related to the cultivation or sale of cotton. Local hotels and theaters made jaunts to the city attractive for upcountry planters and itinerant

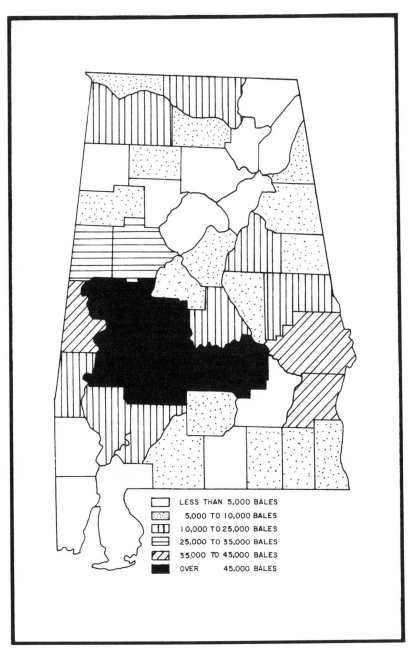

Distribution of Cotton Production in Alabama in 1860 (Adapted from Charles S. Davis, *The Cotton Kingdom in Alabama* [Montgomery: Alabama State Department of Archives and History, 1939], p. 199)

merchants who wished to combine business with pleasure. Commercial and service institutions undergirded the cotton trade, which in turn shaped the city's development.

Mobile's hinterland encompassed some of the richest cotton-producing areas in Alabama and Mississippi, which were known as the Black Belt. By 1850 Alabama surpassed Mississippi, formerly the leader among cotton-growing states, in cotton production. Alabama maintained its top rank as a cotton state throughout the 1850s. Planters in counties in both Alabama and Mississippi with access to the Alabama-Tombigbee River system that flowed into the Mobile River used Mobile as their cotton market.[3]

Navigable waterways circumscribed Mobile's hinterland, which included only southern Alabama and southeastern Mississippi. Alabama river systems flowing into the Mobile River were navigable just as far north as central Alabama, so only cotton growers in Shelby, Tuscaloosa, Fayette, and counties to the south of them could use Mobile as their seaport. Planters in northern Alabama sent their cotton via the Tennessee and Mississippi rivers 1,500 miles to New Orleans. North Alabama's commercial estrangement from south Alabama resulted in limited identity of interests between the two sections. As early as 1819 Governor William Wyatt Bibb recognized the negative implications of this intrastate sectionalism and suggested offsetting it by constructing a turnpike or canal from the Tennessee River to the headwaters of the Alabama River. These projects, and railroads proposed later for a similar route, never came to fruition, so the whole state of Alabama could not serve as Mobile's hinterland.[4]

Cotton exports from Mobile grew in proportion to the production of the crop in south Alabama (see Tables 2-1, 2-2). Increasing quantities of cotton shipments permitted Mobile to eclipse all other southern ports but one as a cotton exporter. In the 1830s Mobile surpassed Savannah and Charleston in terms of exports. By 1840 Mobile ranked second only to New Orleans as a cotton exporter. Mobile remained in the economic orbit of New Orleans, which received cotton from northern Alabama as well as from Mississippi and Louisiana.[5]

Planters usually sent their cotton to Mobile on flatboats or steamboats. They hauled cotton from the plantation to the nearest river bluff, from which bales were slid down an incline to a steamboat or barge. Planters on the rivers had their own private landings, while those in the country used either public landings or private ones owned

COTTON CITY

Table 2-1. Cotton Crop of South Alabama, 1818-59

Year	Bales	Year	Bales	Year	Bales
1818	7,000	1832	125,605	1846	421,669
1819	10,000	1833	129,366	1847	322,516
1820	16,000	1834	149,513	1848	438,324
1821	25,390	1835	197,847	1849	517,846
1822	45,423	1836	237,590	1850	350,297
1823	49,061	1837	232,685	1851	451,697
1824	44,924	1838	309,807	1852	549,777
1825	58,283	1839	251,742	1853	546,514
1826	74,379	1840	445,725	1854	538,110
1827	89,779	1841	317,642	1855	454,595
1828	71,155	1842	318,315	1856	659,738
1829	80,329	1843	482,631	1857	503,177
1830	102,684	1844	468,126	1858	522,843
1831	113,075	1845	517,550	1859	704,406

SOURCES: Mobile Register, 3 October 1836; Mobile Advertiser, 3
September 1859; DeBow's Review 7 (1849): 446; and Weymouth T. Jordan,
"Ante-Bellum Mobile: Alabama's Agricultural Emporium," Alabama Review
1 (1948): 187, 190, 196, 198.

NOTE: According to Jordan, south Alabama in the 1820s included the
counties of Shelby, Tuscaloosa, and Fayette, and counties south of
them. For the next three decades those regions that traded directly
with Mobile constituted south Alabama.

Table 2-2. Cotton Bales Exported from Mobile, 1829-59

Year	Bales	Year	Bales
1829-30	103,065	1844-45	521,996
1830-31	112,354	1845-46	415,581
1831-32	126,695	1846-47	306,907
1832-33	129,358	1847-48	439,561
1833-34	149,264	1848-49	539,642
1834-35	197,770	1849-50	373,046
1835-36	238,014	1850-51	436,228
1836-37	230,772	1851-52	574,650
1837-38	310,021	1852-53	541,201
1838-39	249,635	1853-54	515,631
1839-40	440,102	1854-55	453,103
1840-41	319,876	1855-56	681,321
1841-42	319,038	1856-57	489,044
1842-43	481,894	1857-58	515,045
1843-44	465,205	1858-59	514,952

SOURCES: Hunt's Merchants' Magazine 8 (1845): 422, 21 (1849): 442;
and DeBow's Review 18 (1855): 239, 27 (1858): 473, 28 (1860): 210.

by their neighbors. Downriver traffic on streams flowing into the Alabama and Tombigbee rivers often used flatboats; transport thus depended upon adequate water levels in the streams. Planters on rivers navigable by steamboats used these vessels to ship their bales to market. Several enterprising local businessmen, John B. Hogan, Lewis Judson, and T. L. Hallett, organized two companies as early as 1821 to utilize the new means of transportation. By the mid-1840s steamboat lines connected Mobile with Montgomery, Wetumpka, Gainesville, and Selma, among other places. These steamboats carried cotton downriver and imported goods upriver.[6] By 1850 most Alabama cotton reached Mobile by either the Alabama or the Tombigbee River. Of the 350,952 bales received in Mobile that year, 187,130 bales came down the Alabama and 101,208 came down the Tombigbee. Only 56,276 bales arrived in Mobile via the Warrior River. Wagons carried 6,314 bales.[7]

Oceangoing commerce followed a triangular pattern evolved by shipping lines in New York that handled most of the trade. Elisha D. Hurlburt, a New Yorker, instituted a packet line between New York and Mobile in 1825, when he also opened a connection with Appalachicola, Florida. Service proceeded irregularly until 1830, when Hurlburt set a bimonthly schedule for departures from both ports. The line did not actually operate as a shuttle between New York and Mobile but as a triangular link for Mobile with Liverpool or Le Havre and New York. Ships typically transported cotton from Mobile to Liverpool, emigrants and general freight from Liverpool to New York, and general cargoes of domestic manufactured and foreign imported items to Mobile. One other New York concern, Ripley, Center and Company, provided packet service for Mobile but never attained even the degree of regularity managed by Hurlburt's ships. Both lines served Mobile only from fall to spring. Because Mobile's intense specialization in cotton offered few alternatives for export, coastal runs between Mobile and New York were not economically feasible unless cotton was ready for the northward voyage.[8] Cotton usually made up 99 percent of the total value of exports from antebellum Mobile. Lumber and lumber products, the export ranking second to cotton in value, accounted for only 1 percent of the total value of exports. Thus, during the summer when cotton was not yet ready for market, the export trade virtually stopped.

Triangular arrangements for major shipping in and out of Mobile explained some of the severe local imbalance between the value of exports and imports (see Table 2-3). Compared to other major American

COTTON CITY

Table 2-3. Value of Exports and Imports for the Port of Mobile,
1821-60

Year	Imports ($)	Exports ($)	Year	Imports ($)	Exports ($)
1821	-------	108,960	1841	530,819	10,981,271
1822	36,421	209,748	1842	363,871	9,965,675
1823	125,770	202,387	1843a	360,655	11,157,460
1824	91,604	460,727	1844	442,818	9,907,654
1825	113,411	692,635	1845	473,491	10,538,228
1826	179,554	1,527,112	1846	259,607	5,260,317
1827	201,909	1,376,364	1847	390,161	9,054,580
1828	171,909	1,182,539	1848	419,396	11,927,749
1829	233,720	1,693,958	1849	657,147	12,823,725
1830	144,823	2,294,594	1850	865,362	10,544,858
1831	224,435	2,413,894	1851	413,446	18,528,824
1832	306,845	2,736,387	1852	588,382	17,385,704
1833a	265,918	4,527,961	1853	809,562	16,786,913
1834	395,361	5,670,797	1854	725,610	13,911,612
1835	525,955	7,574,692	1855	619,764	14,270,565
1836	651,618	11,184,166	1856	793,514	23,734,170
1837	609,385	9,658,808	1857	709,090	20,576,229
1838	524,548	9,688,244	1858	606,942	21,022,149
1839	895,201	10,338,159	1859	788,164	28,933,662
1840	574,651	12,854,694	1860	1,050,310	38,670,183

SOURCE: U.S. Secretary of the Treasury, Reports on Commerce and Navigation, 1821-60.

a Nine-month period; shift from 30 September to 30 June as of end of fiscal year.

Table 2-4. Exports and Imports of Major U.S. Ports, 1860

Port	Exports ($)	Imports ($)
New York	120,600,000	233,600,000
New Orleans	107,800,000	22,900,000
Mobile	38,600,000	1,000,000
Charleston	21,100,000	1,500,000
Savannah	18,300,000	700,000
Boston	13,500,000	39,300,000
San Francisco	7,300,000	9,500,000
Baltimore	8,800,000	9,700,000
Philadelphia	5,500,000	14,600,000

SOURCE: Robert Greenhalgh Albion, The Rise of New York Port [1815-1860] (New York: Charles Scribner's Sons, 1939), pp. 400-401.

NOTE: Foreign reexports are not included in export totals.

exporting centers, Mobile had the worst disparity between exports and imports (see Table 2-4). No other cotton port was more of a colonial dependent of New York than Mobile.

Mobile maintained a closer trading relationship with New York than even with its nearest southern port, New Orleans. Yet the two Gulf ports, alone among southern ports, established significant commodity flows between them. When cotton could not be sold directly to northeastern or foreign ports, Mobile shipped it to New Orleans for sale. New Orleans shipped flour, corn, and other western produce along with sugar and molasses to Mobile. Trade between Mobile and New Orleans increased in the late antebellum period. Between 1849 and 1860 cotton dealers in Mobile sent 35 to 50 percent of their domestic shipments to New Orleans annually for foreign or domestic re-export. Cotton shipments from Mobile to other southern cities during the same period usually amounted to less than 2 percent of the total. Even the relatively high volume of commodities traded between Mobile and New Orleans remained confined almost exclusively to staples. For other items each major southern port, including Mobile, functioned basically as a colonial outpost of a northeastern regional city-system rather than as a part of a southern regional city-system.[9]

Mobile's port and harbor facilities were adequate but less than ideal for a large export trade. The city is located on the southwestern side of the Mobile River on an extended plain fifteen feet above the highest tide. Major downriver traffic in agricultural produce from the interior reached Mobile through the Alabama and Tombigbee rivers, which form the Mobile River forty miles north of the city. This river enters Mobile Bay by two channels: a western, called the Mobile River; and an eastern, called the Tensaw River. Mobile Bay, about thirty miles long and twelve miles wide, connects the city with the Gulf of Mexico. Vessels enter the bay on either side of Dauphin Island, located at its mouth. The channel on the west side of the island was five feet deep; the eastern one was twice as deep. In the 1840s the amount of water carried over the bar at the entrance to Mobile Bay increased from thirteen feet to twenty feet. While the depth of water in the lower part of the bay increased, the upper part of the bay remained eleven feet deep. Vessels drawing over eleven feet of water could not proceed directly to the city; they had to pass six miles up the Spanish River, around a marshy island into the Mobile River, and down to the wharves at the city.[10]

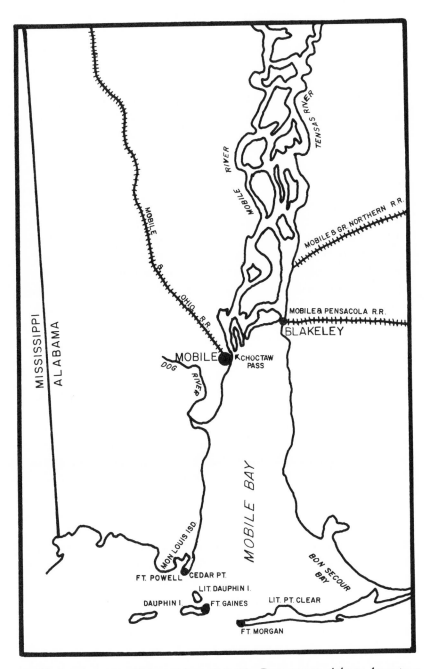

Mobile Bay Area, 1861 (Adapted from U.S. War Department, *Atlas to Accompany the Official Records of the Union and Confederate Armies, 1861–1865* [Washington, D.C.: Government Printing Office, 1891], plate 147)

Because it was virtually impossible for large ships to reach the wharves in Mobile, most of them anchored at Mobile Point in the lower bay. There they received and discharged cargoes. Lightering involved transferring cargoes from oceangoing ships with deep draughts anchored at Mobile Point to smaller vessels with shallow draughts. These lighters, as the small vessels were called, then carried cargoes thirty miles through Mobile Bay to the city wharves. In the late 1850s nearly one hundred local tug steamers or bay boats lightered cotton to what was called the Lower Fleet and imports from the Lower Fleet to city docks.[11]

To avoid the expense of lightering, progressive businessmen in 1835 projected a railway to connect the city with the lower bay. They proposed a route to proceed from Mobile to Cedar Point with an extension to Mon Louis Island on the west side of Mobile Bay, twenty miles south of the city. Thus shippers might send cotton by rail to deep water at a cost lower than lightering. Among the organizers of the Mobile and Cedar Point Railroad Company were William R. Hallett, a banker; Philip McLoskey and James Innerarity, both merchants; and William R. Robertson, M. D. Eslava, and Joseph Krebs, real estate developers. Promoters estimated construction costs at $134,405. They opened subscription books for 500 shares of stock at $100 each. Soon they sold enough shares to finance construction of the rail line running parallel to the bay five miles from the city to Dog River. Service began on this first section of the route in 1837 with one locomotive. Much of the route was graded south of the river, but a bridge needed to cross Dog River was not built before the Panic of 1837 disrupted work on the line. Bankrupted, the company never completed the railroad.[12] Shippers thus continued to use lightering, a procedure that added inconvenience and expense to commerce. Lighterage charges for shipping in and out of Mobile harbor in 1846 were estimated to be $200,000. These charges, of course, provided income to owners of the vessels involved in the operation. Cox, Brainerd and Company operated one of the most prosperous lightering services in the 1850s.[13]

Local businessmen slowly provided facilities sufficient for receiving, storing, and compressing cotton bales before their sale and reshipment. They built a dozen private wharves in the early 1820s and four times that number by the 1850s. Even though the City of Mobile acquired title to the waterfront property by an act of Congress in 1824, the city did not take over the privately owned wharves in the ante-

View of Mobile in 1842 (Courtesy of The New-York Historical Society, New York City)

Mobile Harbor in 1851 (Courtesy of the Museum of the City of Mobile)

bellum period. Most of the wharves were owned by individuals, yet a number were controlled in the 1850s by the wharfinger combine of D. W. Goodman and C. P. Gage. Four dozen wharves lining the waterfront from One Mile Creek on the north to the foot of Government

Street on the south were arranged so that 42,000 bales of cotton could be landed simultaneously without interfering with space needed for shipping and receiving goods.[14]

Local merchants eventually constructed enough cotton warehouses and presses to handle the volume of bales received by the port. In the 1830s, as cotton production from south Alabama quadrupled, construction of warehouses did not keep pace with demand. Storage facilities were so poorly arranged that it was difficult to move cargoes quickly. These problems were remedied by the 1850s, when forty-two fireproof brick warehouses could store 310,000 bales, more than half of the number exported during an entire six-month season. Operating in conjunction with the warehouses were a dozen cotton presses capable altogether of compressing seven thousand bales daily. *Hunt's Merchants' Magazine* accepted the judgment of the *Mobile Journal of Commerce, Letter Sheet Price Current* that Mobile had better facilities for storing and compressing cotton, in proportion to the amount received, than any other American cotton port.[15]

Even more important to the cotton trade than the physical facilities for handling the staple were the factors who marketed it. While some planters sold their own cotton, a majority employed the services of factors as professional middlemen. Technically a factor was an agent hired to sell produce for a principal, that is, a planter. A commission merchant, on the other hand, purchased various types of supplies, such as farm implements, household items, and foodstuffs, on commission for his customers. In practice the factor and the commission merchant were frequently the same person. A business circular sent out in 1832 by a local factor illustrated the dual nature of the occupation. He announced his services "as a Seller of Cotton and other produce of the country, better known as a (Factor)—also of purchasing the Planters' supplies, and of receiving and forwarding country Merchants' and Planters' goods, and executing all orders from Merchants and Planters."[16]

Factors charged fairly standard commissions for their services. The usual fee throughout the South for selling cotton was 2½ percent of the sale price, a continuation of the rate charged by London factors who received consignments of American tobacco in the seventeenth and eighteenth centuries. For procuring various goods for planters, factors earned commissions equal to or greater than those for the sale of cotton. For additional fees they extended credit by making advances to planters who were short of cash. Factors charged 8 to 12 percent interest on advances plus perhaps a brokerage fee of ½ to 2½ percent. For 1 percent or less of the amount of the transaction, factors obtained bills of exchange, discounted notes, and remitted specie for their clients. Factors sometimes came to know their clients so well that they acted as personal agents, proffering advice about investments, stocks, and real estate.[17]

Since fees for services of factors remained standard throughout the South over time, their employment frequently depended on friendships or personal connections with their planter clients. Successful factors in Mobile often maintained close personal and professional ties to planters in Black Belt counties. Six local firms—Rives, Battle and Company; Boykin and McRae; James Crawford; Malone and Foote; Hartwell Davis; and Alexander Pope and Son—conducted extensive business in the interior counties of Wilcox, Dallas, Marengo, and Greene in the 1830s and 1840s. Alexander Pope, formerly a clerk in the state land office in Cahaba, moved to Mobile in 1829 to open a cotton commission business. Soon after his arrival in Mobile, Pope requested an old friend at Black's Bend to inform their friends in the vicinity of Claiborne of his wish to handle sales of their cotton. Pope communicated a great deal with his clients by mail, while Colin McRae of Boykin and McRae solicited business from cotton planters in Clarke and Wilcox counties part of each winter. McRae and Boykin each had many relatives in Dallas County who helped their businesses.[18]

Throughout the antebellum era, itinerant factors or agents from northern firms provided many of the commercial services required by the marketing of cotton. As in other southern ports, regional specialization of the cotton trade developed in Mobile in the 1820s as New York merchants sent their agents to purchase cotton directly from planters or their factors. Agents provided the market as well as freight and credit arrangements. Business records of major New York firms that dealt in cotton verify the appearance of this institutionalized system in early American Mobile. Ogden Day and Company (later Ogden Ferguson and Day) purchased cotton from local factors Robertson and Barnewall and Peters and Stebbins (later Russel Stebbins and Company) in the 1820s. The New York company relied upon some of the local factors to visit the upcountry planters to solicit their business.

Brown Brothers and Company, one of the largest international merchant banking houses in the nineteenth century, used local factors on an ad hoc basis in the 1820s and 1830s. Two of the Mobile firms that traded with the Browns of New York were McLoskey Hagan and Company, a branch of John Hagan and Company of New Orleans, which served as the Brown agent there, and John Boyd and Company. After the Panic of 1837 Brown Brothers and Company adopted a policy of establishing resident agents in southern ports. Charles D. Dickey headed the highly successful agency in Mobile from 1847 through 1859, when he was made a partner of the firm.[19]

Some cotton dealers specialized as buyers for British and French traders or manufacturers. George Martin and Company bought cotton for English houses and eventually served as an agent for an insurance company in Liverpool. Martin reportedly made a fortune and retired to Liverpool in the mid-1850s but retained the commission house in Mobile. Gwathmey, Forbes and Company and D. Wheeler and Company also served English accounts primarily. Harleston Broun, who represented French mill interests, became one of the most successful cotton buyers in Mobile. With authorization to purchase a set number of bales of a specific grade of cotton, buyers placed their orders with brokers, who in turn traded with commission merchants. These factors supplied the order from cotton stocks in their warehouses.[20]

This significant representation of northern and foreign firms in the cotton trade did not preclude southerners from opening their own factorage businesses. Southern-born Mobilians showed none of the disdain for commerce that characterized Charlestonians of the early nineteenth century. In the old South Carolina city, northern- or foreign-born businessmen controlled the majority of leading commercial houses.[21] That was not the case in Mobile, although nonsoutherners managed significant cotton-trading concerns. Southerners readily entered the cotton trade. Experienced factors from southern ports where the cotton trade was declining, such as Duke W. Goodman from Charleston, relocated to the rapidly growing cotton capital of Mobile. Other native southerners capitalized on their visibility in fields other than commerce within the state to open a commission house in Mobile. Robert A. Baker, a five-term state legislator from Franklin County, and John A. Winston, a plantation owner from Sumter County who served multiple terms as a state representative and senator and two terms as governor, each opened commission houses in Mobile in the 1840s.[22]

All cotton merchants, whether they were agents of large nonlocal firms or independent entrepreneurs, faced similar problems in their dealings with planters. The cotton trade provided many opportunities for unscrupulous actions. Neither factors nor planters were uniformly circumspect. Factors complained loudest about the "false-packing" of cotton bales. This deception appeared in several forms: thin strips of prime cotton on the two sides of the bale usually sampled with inferior grades in the middle; layers of successively poorer grades proceeding from the outside to the core of the bale; and stones, dirt, or water inside the bale to increase weight. Planters false-packed more extensively in Alabama than was generally recognized, according to the *Alabama Planter* in 1853. The extent of the fraud increased annually and depreciated the value of Mobile cotton in the English market. Dishonest packing damaged the reputation of the whole planter community, although it was usually difficult to determine whether the cotton producer or the ginner perpetrated the fraud. When factors discovered falsely packed bales, they often preferred to reach compromise agreements with the planters rather than go to the effort and expense of prosecuting the guilty.[23]

In 1858 the state legislature passed a law benefiting factors by stating that certain actions by planters involved in the cotton trade carried with them implied warranties. When a planter sent his bales to his factor for sale, his action implied that the bales were not packed fraudulently. When cotton was sold to a purchaser on the basis of a sample, the action implied that the sample was drawn fairly. If these assumptions proved wrong, then factors could sue for damages by filing within one year of the date of sale.[24] This law dealing with frauds helped to redress some if not all of the factors' grievances against planters.

Planters registered a number of their own complaints against factors. Even before shipping their crops to market, many planters suspected the accuracy of crop forecasts and cotton statistics issued by factors. This suspicion was linked to the slow pretelegraphic communication between Liverpool and major American cities. Planters frequently claimed to ship more cotton to market than their factors credited to their accounts. Sales then brought what planters considered insufficient prices, which were the result of the unpredictability of the market, bad luck, poor strategy, factors' violation of contract or instructions, or some combination of these problems.[25]

Most of the planters' grievances related to their perception that the cotton marketing system tended to give the factor too much control over the cotton. One observer charged that in Mobile and cotton centers on the Mississippi River "swarms of cotton brokers usurp the market; the planters are mere babes in their hands."[26] Planters tried to change the situation by issuing detailed instructions to their factors. These attempts appeared most frequently during financial crises, such as the Panic of 1857. In October 1857 one planter in Mississippi advised his factor in Mobile, Joel W. Jones of John A. Winston and Company, that he was shipping cotton "which I wish you to sell at your own Discrition [sic]." The client wrote a week later to order that his bales be held for sale until cotton prices reached a set amount or until he issued further instructions. Another planter who did business with Winston and Company issued similar instructions, saying that he wanted the highest price on his cotton so that he could pay his factors what he owed them.[27]

Even though many Alabamians in the Jacksonian era ordinarily opposed state intervention in the economy, dissatisfied planters made several attempts through the state legislature to increase regulation of the cotton trade in Mobile. Under ideal circumstances "Commerce must regulate it Self," as the factor Duke W. Goodman observed to his client Richard Singleton in 1841. "[T]he Planter Should Carefully and Closely attend to his interest: and the merchant do the same," according to Goodman. "[T]hereby a balancing power would be exerted—and both parties would be equally bennifitted [sic]."[28] When planters thought that they had received inequitable treatment from factors, they sought to redress the balance in various ways. In 1832 representatives of planter interests introduced a bill in the state legislature to regulate commissions of merchants in Mobile and to levy heavy penalties on anyone who took more than 1 percent as commission, even by contract. The bill passed the Alabama house but failed in the senate. *Niles' Register* sarcastically wondered why the supporters of the bill refrained from attempting to regulate the prices also of lands, slaves, and cotton.[29] Legislators never mustered enough votes to pass a bill regulating commissions, so the controversy over charges lingered for many years.

Critics of Mobile factors in 1837 proposed the erection of a public warehouse with state agents to take over the cotton storage. Representatives from counties in the interior, where planters felt victimized by factors, sponsored bills in the legislature to counteract alleged abuses in the sale of cotton. One act designed to suppress misconduct by factors, carriers, and others allowed them to be charged with a misdemeanor for unauthorized selling of property entrusted to them for safekeeping or for appropriating for themselves merchandise entrusted to them for sale. The other act regulated the sampling of cotton in Mobile. It also ordered the governor to appoint three commissioners to study "the expediency and practicality" of the state's establishing one or more public warehouses in Mobile to store cotton sent there from the interior.[30]

These acts obviously insulted merchants in Mobile. Their state representative, Joseph Bates, Jr., protested against the bill regarding sampling "for the reason that it assumes to place the planting interests of this State under the especial privelege [sic] of the Legislature."[31] He reminded legislators of the fraud practiced upon factors by planters who resorted to false packing or deceptive sampling of cotton bales. Over Bates's protest, the legislators passed the bill. The committee appointed by the governor to study the feasibility of the state warehouse submitted a plan for the proposed building, but the legislature never pressed the plan to fruition. William Garrett, a state official at the time, viewed the attack on the factors as a response to the commercial problems caused by the Panic of 1837. The sudden financial depression after a period of unparalleled prosperity disturbed people so much that they sought a scapegoat, Garrett argued.[32] Factors in Mobile served as that scapegoat, yet they were not to blame for the complicated economic ills of the times.

Lawsuits occasionally settled disagreements between planters and factors. Either party might file suit. When Austill and Marshall of Mobile sold an upstate planter's crop in 1845 as part of a larger lot that brought an average of 13¢ per pound, they paid the planter 12¢ per pound, the price his crop would have brought had it been sold separately. The planter sued successfully for the balance owed him. His factors appealed the verdict unsuccessfully to the Alabama Supreme Court on the grounds that their practice conformed to the "usages of trade" in Mobile. "Usages of trade" also figured in the case involving alleged misrepresentation of the quality of cotton. In 1853, on the strength of his own samples, a planter named P. Chaudron sold factor O. Eustis 802 bales of cotton at 9⅝¢ per pound for a total of $14,783. When the factor did his own sampling, he found some cotton of lesser quality than claimed by the planter. Yet Eustis accepted the cotton, reshipped it, and paid Chaudron the sale price minus a $283 indemnity for the loss resulting from the discrepancy in sampling. Chaudron sued in city court in 1855 for the amount of the indemnity plus interest. After hearing conflicting testimony from experts in the cotton trade on customs observed in Mobile, the jury rendered a verdict in favor of the planter, but for a reduced amount of damages.[33]

Planters' ignorance of commerce in the city often explained their misunderstandings with factors. Planters considered factors' profits exorbitant, yet they overlooked the interest on loans and office overhead costs that had to be deducted from the gross profits. Shortly before the Panic of 1837 the *Mobile Register* estimated that the average local factor sold 10,000 bales of cotton annually and earned a commission of $16,000 based on prevailing prices. Expenses reduced the net profit considerably. A factor normally paid $6,000 annually for rent, taxes, and salaries for employees. Furthermore, the factor often had to obtain personal loans at high interest to make sizable advances to his clients, thus consuming much of his commission on the advances. As a creditor, the factor assumed risks for drought, disaster, and planters' insolvency. In light of the factor's own risks, the interest usually charged on advances, the possible brokerage fee added to the interest, and the commission charged on goods obtained by the factor for the planter appeared less outrageous. The Alabama Supreme Court decided in 1850 that the legality of the commissions charged by Mobile factors both for accepting planters' notes and for advancing cash depended on their purpose. Commissions that simply served to evade the statute on usury were illegal; those levied to cover the merchants' risks or inconvenience in paying bills were legal. A jury rather than a court had to draw the distinction.[34]

Transactions in cotton demanded extensive credit and other financial services offered by banks. Close ties between banking and commerce often meant that banks suffered from the fluctuations of the cotton market as much as any other segment of the economy. The only local bank that successfully withstood all financial crises in the antebellum era was the Bank of Mobile. An unusual charter granted by the state legislature in 1819 allowed the Bank of Mobile to open with reserves in gold and silver of only $8,750, a liberal provision designed for a period of financial stringency when specie was scarce. In the summer of 1819 before the bank was open for business, a thief absconded with much of the cash used as capital. This loss of funds delayed the opening of the bank until 1820. Realizing that a new bank in a rejuvenated town had to stand on its own completely, the merchant directors of the Bank of Mobile adopted cautious policies of management. They increased the bank's capital as permitted by the charter amended in 1833. Within the first hour that commissioners opened subscription books for the first major public offering of bank stock in 1834, Mobilians pledged the entire $200,000.[35]

Conservative management directed by William R. Hallett, who was president of the bank for nearly thirty years, earned the Bank of Mobile a remarkable record for solvency. As the lone survivor in Alabama of the Panic of 1837, the Bank of Mobile provided the only banking services in the state by 1845. In 1848, amid many business failures, a rumor that the bank was unsafe caused a run on it, but officials employed a "formidable array of extra persons . . . ready to shell out the specie."[36] Recognizing both the need for an expansion of banking capital in the state and the soundness of the Bank of Mobile, the legislature approved raising its capital stock from $1,000,000 to $1,500,000 in the 1850s.[37]

The Bank of Mobile maintained an outstanding rating with the major antebellum credit-reporting firm of R. G. Dun and Company. Its agent observed in 1858 that the "condition [of the bank was] considered the best of any Southern Bank, certainly the best of any in this state." According to the Dun investigator, the Bank of Mobile was not only "the strongest Bank in Alabama," but it was "in fact as good as any in the United States." With its ample capital and "very cautious business," the Bank of Mobile was "good as Gold" in 1860.[38]

During a period of rapid growth in the cotton trade, local merchants lobbied for a branch of the Second Bank of the United States to expand financial services provided by the Bank of Mobile. Nicholas Biddle, President of the BUS, agreed with local merchants that growing business operations in Mobile justified the branch. Yet Governor John Murphy considered the chartering of the branch in 1826 a threat to all banks in Alabama, especially the State Bank. In 1830 the Alabama Senate fell just one vote short of passing a resolution declaring that establishing the branch of the BUS in Mobile violated the state's sovereignty. Governor Gabriel Moore opposed renewal of the BUS charter by Congress in 1832. He and other opponents of the national bank overlooked the excellent record achieved by the Mobile branch from 1826 to 1833. In 1832 the Mobile branch of the BUS ranked third in the total amount of business conducted in the South and eighth in the nation. That year the branch handled discounts for notes worth more than $1,000,000 and bills of exchange for $5,000,000. Yet business concluded at the branch after the BUS charter expired in 1836.[39]

The state of Alabama belatedly established a branch of the State Bank in Mobile. In 1826 some Mobilians argued unsuccessfully for a State Bank branch to offset the influence of the BUS branch on the cotton business of south Alabama. Under the state constitution, the legislature might establish just one branch during any one session. Other towns won branches of the State Bank well before Mobile. In the spring of 1832, when the legislature chose Montgomery as the site for another branch of the State Bank, Mobilians increased their efforts to secure their own branch from the next General Assembly. They reminded the legislators that a city with trade valued at $11,000,000 annually needed more banking facilities than those offered by one local bank and a branch of the BUS. Late that year the legislators approved a charter for Mobile's branch of the State Bank of Alabama, and it opened its doors for business in 1833. Respected businessmen made up the board of directors, who were elected by the state legislature. The secretary of the treasury of the United States chose the Mobile branch of the State Bank as a pet bank, the only one in the state, to receive federal deposits removed from the national bank. As a depository the State Bank branch proved less than secure. In late 1834 Alabamians learned that the president and directors of the Mobile branch of the State Bank had liabilities to it in an amount equal to nearly half of its capital.[40]

The Panic of 1837 further undermined the State Bank. After the panic directors of the bank decided to increase their holdings of specie by entering the cotton trade. New state laws in 1841 allowed the bank to establish agencies, issue notes, and advance money to planters on their cotton crops. Bank officials hoped that bills of exchange would draw in specie. Agents for the bank accepted cotton, shipped it at the owner's risk, and sold it for repaying the planter's bill with interest to the bank. Factors in Mobile protested competition from cotton agents for the bank. Even with investigations by the legislature, the bank's speculation in cotton got out of hand. Directors of the State Bank made unsound loans secured by future cotton crops. The Mobile branch of the State Bank finally was terminated by the legislature in 1844. Sales of real estate belonging to the branch continued for fifteen years.[41] The branch of the State Bank had eased the shortage of banking facilities during the flush times but had failed to withstand the hard times.

Another bank followed a path very similar to that of the branch of the State Bank. Prosperity-minded citizens argued in 1835 that a large increase in local banking capital seemed "imperiously" demanded by the growth of the city. In response, the Alabama General Assembly chartered the Planters and Merchants Bank in January 1836. Soon a number of local commissioners launched a subscription drive for $3,000,000 in bank stock. These commissioners, men like William R. Hallett and Henry Hitchcock, were commercial and financial leaders with experience as officers or directors of at least one bank in Mobile. The Planters and Merchants Bank opened its newly built office for business in May 1838 and closed a little more than four years later, in October 1842. A stockholders' investigating committee listed several causes of the failure: extravagant loans made to individuals in 1836 and 1837, general monetary stringency of the time, excessive salaries paid to bank officers, stiff annual bonuses paid to the state for the banking privilege, and the enormous cost of the banking house. Liquidation of the bank's assets continued into 1850.[42]

With the demise of all but one bank in Alabama in the 1840s, Mobilians struggled to meet the shortage of banking facilities. Local merchants finally succeeded in convincing the state legislators to grant a charter to a new bank, the Southern Bank of Alabama, in 1850. Soon after it opened in 1851, it helped to stabilize financial services in the city. As *Rowan's Directory* boasted, "The exchange market no longer flickers as a sickly flame—its movements are no longer regulated by the necessities of buyers, but by the necessities of sellers, or by the equitable rule of supply and demand." The Southern Bank, like others in the city, basically facilitated exchange transactions and loans. None paid interest on deposits except the Mechanics Savings Company, which was incorporated in 1852. It credited interest to accounts of $25 or more from "the earnings and savings of working people and others." As if to broaden its appeal to commercial as well as individual depositors, the institution soon changed its name to the Mobile Savings Company.

The bank temporarily suspended payments on deposits during the Panic of 1857 but resumed full service shortly afterward. No other incorporated banking institutions opened in the 1850s. The Bank of Alabama, which was incorporated in 1860, launched a subscription drive for $500,000 of capital stock but failed to institute service before the onset of war.[43]

Even the new banks that opened in the 1850s failed to supplement capital in the Bank of Mobile enough to meet the commercial needs of the city. According to a study conducted in 1848 by *Bankers' Magazine* of the number of banks and amount of banking capital in selected American cities, Mobile ranked near the bottom of cities with $1,000,000 of banking capital. Mobile then had one bank, the Bank of Mobile, with capital of $1,500,000. No other American city with comparable commerce had only one bank. *Bankers' Magazine* called the amount of banking capital in Mobile "very small" for the export trade that exceeded $10,000,000 annually.[44] The situation grew steadily worse by 1860, when Mobile had two conventional banks with combined capital of $2,000,000 and one savings bank with capital of $100,000 to serve an export trade of nearly $40,000,000. Of all major American exporting centers, Mobile had the worst shortage of banking capital (see Table 2-5). Limited local banking facilities forced businessmen to deal directly with nonlocal banks or to use the services of local private bankers.

Private bankers conducted much of the exchange business in Mobile as in other southern cities that lacked sufficient local banking facilities. These exchange brokers competed with each other and with banks for the fees earned from buying and selling notes drawn on foreign and domestic banks and mercantile houses.[45] St. John, Powers and Company, the oldest and strongest local private banking firm, handled the bulk of local financial business not conducted by banks. The senior partner, Newton St. John, a native New Yorker who moved to Mobile in the 1830s, maintained banking ties with Duncan Sherman and Company and August Belmont in New York. St. John faced competition in the exchange business from the Bank of Mobile and two local agencies of major international banking houses. After the Panic of 1837 Brown Brothers and Company opened permanent branches in Mobile and New Orleans to compete for the extensive exchange business conducted in the Gulf cotton ports. By the 1850s Charles Dickey, the man-

Table 2-5. Bank Capital of Major U.S. Exporting Centers, 1860

Port	Exports ($)	Bank Capital ($)
New York	120,600,000	72,390,475
New Orleans	107,800,000	24,551,666
Mobile	38,600,000	2,100,000
Charleston	21,100,000	11,124,251
Savannah	18,300,000	3,735,400
Boston	13,500,000	33,710,000
Baltimore	8,800,000	10,328,243
Philadelphia	5,500,000	11,963,260
Richmond	5,000,000	3,959,450

SOURCES: Export figures in Robert G. Albion, Rise of New York Port, pp. 400-401; bank capital figures in Allan Pred, Urban Growth and City-Systems in the United States, 1840-1860 (Cambridge, Mass.: Harvard University Press, 1980), p. 220; for Savannah in U.S. Congress, House Executive Documents, 36th Cong., 2d sess., 1861, H. Ex. Doc., 10: 205.

ager of the Brown agency, and Archibald Gracie, the local agent of the international banking firm of Baring Brothers, contested the market for sterling bills with St. John and the Bank of Mobile. Attempting to increase their volume of business, St. John, Powers and Company and Brown Brothers and Company lowered their rates of profit on transactions. Charles Dickey, manager of the Brown agency, indeed handled some transactions in 1852 without a commission to stop his customers from going to his competitors. Yet he declined to accept bills from firms that were judged unable to pay their debts.[46] Dickey, a newcomer to Mobile, marvelled at the fact that St. John, Powers and Company and the Bank of Mobile handled bills for customers "frequently even *without B[ills] o[f] Lading* on *first class names!*"[47] Local firms, whose partners likely knew their clients personally, conducted business casually as compared to international firms like Brown Brothers and Company. This pattern put Dickey in a very awkward position when he insisted upon reading certain "letters of authority [from potential clients] which to say the least is not a pleasant thing to require of any one especially here, where it is hardly ever done."[48]

Competition among the private bankers peaked in 1859. "St. John acts as if he was resolved to do the business regardless of all consequences," Dickey complained. What bothered Dickey the most was

St. John's disregard for the bill-of-lading system. St. John actually preferred not to have the bills of lading for cotton shipments used as collateral for exchange transactions. Rivalry was so intense that brokers no longer routinely counted on the business of regular customers. Rumors circulated, according to Dickey, that St. John had hired his own agent "to scour the Town daily & tempt parties to his office!"[49] Not content to lose business, Dickey reduced profit on transactions to little or nothing. Brown Brothers and Company's profits on exchange negotiations in their southern agencies dropped from between 1 and 1½ percent of turnover in 1820 to ⅛ percent in 1860. Nonetheless, the volume of business in all transactions still grew so that the Brown agency in Mobile handled a $900,000 exchange trade in 1840, $2,900,000 in 1845, and $3,100,000 in 1855.[50] Figures from rival firms are not available, but they doubtless conducted large amounts of business as well.

Besides banking, Mobile's commercial activities required insurance services. At least ten local insurance companies opened during the antebellum era (see Table 2-6). Most of the companies offered basic protection against marine and river mishaps and fires. The Mobile Marine Railway and Insurance Company (later called simply the Mobile Insurance Company), the Merchants Insurance Company, the Alabama Life Insurance and Trust Company, and the Firemen's Insurance Company began to issue policies in the 1830s. In the late 1840s and 1850s the City Insurance Company, Fulton Insurance Company, Alabama Life Insurance Company, Mobile Navigation and Mutual Insurance Company, Marine Dock and Mutual Insurance Company, Alabama Mutual Insurance Company, and Southern Insurance Company added to the local coverage available against fire, marine, and river risks. With nine local insurance companies offering policies in 1852, the *Alabama Planter* remarked that Mobilians had only themselves to blame for losses resulting from fires "for every faculty is now at hand for insurance."[51]

Agencies of nonlocal insurance companies augmented the services offered by local insurance institutions with relatively meager resources. Nonlocal firms, often with very large assets, maintained agencies in Mobile. By 1833 companies from Augusta, New Orleans, and Hartford operated offices in Mobile. By 1845 three companies from New York and one each from Hartford, Boston, and Augusta employed local agents. In the 1850s companies from Charleston and Columbia, South Carolina; Aberdeen, Mississippi; Athens, Georgia; and Liverpool, En-

Table 2-6. Local Insurance Companies, 1861

Name	Capital ($)
Alabama Life Insurance and Trust Company	275,000
Alabama Mutual Insurance Company of Mobile	125,000
City Insurance Company	200,000
Firemen's Insurance Company of Mobile	100,000
Fulton Insurance Company of Mobile	100,000
Merchants' Insurance Company of Mobile	250,000
Mobile Insurance Company	200,000
Mobile Navigation and Mutual Insurance Company	100,000
Southern Insurance Company	200,000

SOURCE: Directory of the City of Mobile (Mobile: Farrow & Dennett, 1861), p. 18.

gland maintained agencies also.[52] Sometimes there were as many or more such agencies as there were local companies.

The presence of numerous agencies of nonlocal insurance companies provided just one indication that local merchants failed to produce pools of investment funds adequate to handle the needs of their own cotton trade. Local banks and insurance companies, it is true, absorbed and reinvested some of the profits from the cotton trade. But a considerable portion of the profits, sometimes estimated at 40 to 75 percent of the total, left Mobile for the northern firms that supplied extensive credit, insurance, and shipping services. *Rowan's Mobile Directory* (1850) routinely observed that profits mainly went "to the owners of the money, who are generally non-residents." "This simple fact," noted the directory, "lies at the foundation of all the affairs in the history of local progress of Mobile."[53] In other words, the chronic drain of funds away from the city limited all facets of local development.

Merchants attempted to further their own prosperity and that of Mobile by forming a chamber of commerce to regulate certain business practices among members for the good of their local, national, and international reputations. In 1823 businessmen formed a chamber of commerce that established a schedule of rates and regulations for various phases of cotton marketing and an arbitration committee to adjust disputes between tradesmen. Regular lists of officers do not appear in local newspapers until 1836. By then the chamber reportedly included two-thirds of local merchants among its members. The association attempted regulation of its members so that the reputation of Mobile could be preserved in outside markets. In 1841, for instance, the chamber adopted resolutions regarding procedures for fair sampling and weighing of cotton. In 1842 the Mobile Chamber of Commerce criticized the officers of the State Bank branch for buying cotton, "thus departing from their legitimate sphere of action and interfering with the business of the merchants."[54] The president of the bank, Jacob Magee, promised to curb the practice, which had cut the business of local factors at a time of severe depression in the economy. Records of concerted action by the Chamber of Commerce are absent from newspapers from 1844 to 1854. During the late 1840s merchants may have been so preoccupied with their own individual problems lingering from the Panic of 1837 that they had little interest in collective organization.

By 1854 local merchants argued that they needed a state-chartered chamber of commerce "to diminish litigation and to establish uniform and equitable charges." They convinced the state legislature that the chamber might benefit Alabamians in general as well as commercial interests. The "Constitutional Rules and Regulations" of the Mobile Chamber of Commerce detailed procedures for settling disputes among members and between members and other merchants. An arbitration committee served to arbitrate and assign settlement awards for "all disputed accounts or other matters" submitted to its consideration. Fees for arbitration and appeals were scaled to the amount of the sum under dispute; charges doubled for local merchants who did not belong to the Chamber of Commerce. In addition to the committees for settling grievances, the chamber organized others to oversee various economic matters and to suggest guidelines for certain practices. These committees included commerce; manufactures; banks and currency; customs, usages, and charges; internal improvements; inland trade; cotton trade; and accounts.[55] Together they sought to "unite the voice of the commercial classes, and establish a thorough reform of all abuses that have crept into the channels of trade."[56] The Chamber of Commerce ultimately aimed to use collective action of merchants to increase local trade.

Shortly after the reorganization of the Chamber of Commerce, local businessmen formed the Merchants' Exchange to collect commercial information for themselves. The exchange provided a reading room stocked with newspapers from American and foreign cities, commercial magazines and reports, and business reviews. For the first year of operation, 1856–57, 166 merchants subscribed to the exchange.[57] As members kept themselves abreast of the latest business news, they also became better acquainted with their associates and competitors in commerce. Perhaps they even transacted business at the exchange.

As an aid to commerce, merchants supported the production of business directories. The first one, a modest guide, appeared in 1837. Publication by a variety of authors and printers continued sporadically; no regular annual or biennial schedule was established before the Civil War. As Mobile grew, strangers and residents alike increasingly needed assistance to locate commercial houses. As late as the early 1850s few street names were posted at corners and few buildings displayed numbers. Instead of using meaningless street addresses in his *Comprehensive Mobile Guide and Directory* (1852), William R. Robertson identified business locations by section letters and numbers keyed to his own map. In 1854 the city passed an ordinance requiring that names of streets be posted conspicuously on corners, which helped to remedy at least some of the confusion for visitors.[58] The lack of house numbers continued throughout the decade, although prominent businessmen eventually persuaded the aldermen to enact an ordinance requiring the systematic numbering of buildings within the city. In 1858 Robert S. Bunker, a New York-born insurance agent and former president of the common council, presented the aldermen with a petition for building numbers signed by sixty merchants. Aldermen responded favorably to the petition because "it would be vastly beneficial to our business men of all classes, and great[ly] facilitate strangers in their intercourse with our citizens."[59] Owners of businesses in the prescribed area seemed more inclined than householders to display the numbers assigned to them.

Besides business directories and building numbers for the convenience of visitors, local merchants championed facilities to house and to entertain their clients who frequented Mobile during the business season. Soon after Mobilians who had spent their summers in northern resorts returned home each fall, planters from the interior of Alabama began flocking to Mobile. During business hours planters made yearly purchases of supplies and consulted with their factors. At night they attended balls, parties, or the theater. The soirées where Mobilians mingled socially with other Alabamians produced "an excellent effect," observed the *Mobile Register*: "Under the influence of bright smiles, and cheerful faces, Mobile takes the place which its position ought to give it, the point of reunion and enjoyment for the state."[60] Thus, besides being the commercial capital of Alabama, Mobile served as its leading winter resort.

Mobile struggled for much of the antebellum era to offer housing adequate in quantity and quality for the influx of visitors. In the 1820s, when Mobile might still be considered a frontier town, hotels provided plain accommodations and few services to guests, yet they fulfilled their function as a focal point of community activity. Karl Bernhard, duke of Saxe-Weimar-Eisenach, and his party lodged in 1826 at Smooth's Hotel, a typical establishment of the time described by the duke as "a wooden building the barroom of which is at the same time the post office, and therefore somewhat lively."[61]

Fires repeatedly destroyed hotels and consequently caused overcrowding of visitors. For instance, when the English travelers Captain and Mrs. Basil Hall arrived in Mobile in April 1828, they acutely felt the pinch of hotel space after the gigantic fire of the previous October. They secured one bedroom for their entire party at a "nasty, dirty house," which had no private suite available for them. Between 1835 and 1845 when the winter population of Mobile frequently was three times the number of year-round residents, hotel shortages persisted. A new hotel, begun in 1836, was nearly ready for opening in 1839, when arsonists burned much of the downtown area. With most large hotels and 500 houses burned, lodging facilities were meager for the 200 visitors who were flocking into Mobile daily that season. The scarcity of hotels led to inflation of costs. One planter found visiting the commercial capital so expensive in 1840 that he vowed to make less frequent trips there. He thought that hotels should lower their rates since agricultural products brought such low prices in the depression-stricken economy.[62]

The situation slowly improved during the 1840s. In 1842 the American Hotel opened under a new manager from New York who offered lodging to thirty single men and boarding to others. By the mid-1840s the larger Waverly Hotel and Mansion House provided more comforts for the general public. One observer called the Mansion House "the Southe [*sic*] Tremont House—which is as good a Hotel probably as the Union affords."[63] Alexander Mackay, a British visitor, thought the hotels in Mobile "on a most extensive and sumptuous scale, scarcely surpassed by any of those in New York, Boston, or Philadelphia." Both the Waverly Hotel and Mansion House succumbed to fires in the summer of 1850. The destruction of the two major hotels of course inconvenienced visitors, but residents responded as usual by building another, even larger, hotel.[64]

A "decided epoch" in local development began with the opening of the Battle House in 1852. As noted by the *Mobile Register*, Mobile had previously had "a good, but never a fine hotel." The Battle House was truly a first-class hotel comparable to those in major American cities. A group of local businessmen led by James, Samuel, and John A. M. Battle engaged the services of Isaiah Rogers, a nationally renowned architect who had designed hotels in Bangor, Maine; New York City; Charleston, South Carolina; Richmond, Virginia; Cincinnati, Ohio; and New Orleans, Louisiana. The local corporation built the five-story hotel designed by Rogers on the site of the Waverly Hotel, the southeast corner of Royal and St. Francis streets, convenient to the business district. The Battle House Company leased the hotel to Paran Stevens, an entrepreneur who also participated in the ownership or management of famous hotels in Boston, New York, and Philadelphia. Stevens hired a manager, A. B. Darling, who met his responsibilities at the Battle House so well from 1852 to 1859 that Stevens promoted him to the management of a hotel he had leased on Fifth Avenue in New York.[65] The involvement of a nationally known architect and hotel entrepreneur helped to ensure that the Battle House reflected and catered to the bustle and excitement of life in the city.

The Battle House offered many attractions for guests, who invariably praised the excellence of the lodgings there. As the largest hotel in Mobile, it had 240 guest rooms plus dining rooms and shops. Soirées followed by suppers became regular weekly events during the winter season. City and country dwellers mingled at dances that provided "the Battle House the very cream and champagne sparkle of its excellent cheer," according to the *Mobile Register*. A quiet private room at the rear of the bar afforded friends seclusion to "meet and drink, talk over the past, or arrange the future." The bridal chamber was one of the most popular rooms in the Battle House. If an old bachelor who examined the room did "not go immediately and pop the question for the especial purpose of occupying these apartments," the *Register* warned, "he ought to be made to support ten orphans for the balance of his life." Planters from the cotton districts of southern Alabama and Mississippi often selected the Battle House for their honeymoons.[66] Because few visitors came to Mobile during hot weather, the Battle House waited for the first frost to open for guests.[67]

Theaters also served to entertain the hundreds of visitors who journeyed to Mobile each winter. In fact, three-fifths of theatergoers in Mobile reportedly hailed from outside the city. This situation made it extremely important to the local economy that theaters be available for the use of professional troupes. Many of the visitors had traveled extensively and cultivated a taste for good theater, so they demanded professional performances.[68]

Newspaper columns encouraged fundraising for the construction of theaters and employment of good managers. In 1840, when the city lacked a theater, "Many Citizens" launched a subscription drive in the *Mobile Register* for a place of "rational amusements." According to the sponsors, "all classes of society" should recognize that Mobilians needed to make stays in their city pleasant for planters and strangers who transacted business there in the winter so that they would not rush away for home or for New Orleans. In 1849 the *Alabama Tribune* also justified support for the theater in economic terms. After extolling the intellectual benefits theatrical amusements offered to civilization, the editor focused on meeting the demands of strangers who came to Mobile during the winter season "principally on a double errand— business and pleasure." The editor argued that visitors who found "an intense and refined gratification" in the theater would seek it elsewhere if it were unavailable locally. Or they might launch into unspecified "excesses infinitely gross, demoralizing and expensive." Thus, the *Tribune* concluded, "a pecuniary and moral evil results to the city." For these reasons a well-managed theater providing good entertainment constituted "a public benefit."[69]

Advantages that accrued to the city from the theater help to explain the repeated success of public subscription drives to build theaters. In 1824 public subscriptions financed the construction of a theater with a seating capacity of 600 to 700 for Noah Miller Ludlow's professional touring company. Five years later when Ludlow's theater burned, a public meeting quickly obtained $2,000 in pledges to erect a new building, which Ludlow used for the rest of the season. This structure burned the next year, and for a brief period Mobilians had no theater. Sol Smith used a hall over a billiard parlor for his dramatic troupe in 1832. Two years later J. Purdy Brown built his own 1,500-seat Mobile Theater on the west side of St. Emanuel Street near Dauphin. Brown died soon after the end of the season.[70]

Ludlow and Smith formed a partnership through which they dominated theatrical management in Mobile for twenty years with much public support. In the mid-1830s Ludlow and Smith used the Mobile Theater, which burned at the opening of the season in 1838. The managers had to use other rented facilities for the remainder of the season. Before the Panic of 1837 local businessmen and theater patrons subscribed funds to Ludlow and Smith for another theater, which was not built after the onset of the financial crisis. In 1841 James Caldwell of New Orleans, a competitor of Ludlow and Smith, opened the Royal Street Theater in Mobile. Caldwell retired from business in Mobile in 1843, leasing his theater to Ludlow and Smith for the next decade. They operated simultaneously in Mobile and New Orleans during the winter and performed in St. Louis in the summer and early fall. After Ludlow and Smith ceased operations in Mobile in 1853, other managers ran the Royal Street Theater. Shortly after it burned in 1860, Mobilians subscribed funds for a new theater to seat nearly 1,700 people.[71] They never wished their city to lack adequate facilities for theatrical performances.

With cotton as the basis for its economy, Mobile, as much as any other southern port, remained essentially undiversified. Many people provided services directly related to the marketing of cotton or entertaining of planters and their factors, while few entered other economic pursuits. As capital in plantation districts was tied up in land and slaves used to produce cotton, so capital in Mobile most likely supported business institutions that catered to the cotton trade. A substantial portion of profits from transactions in cotton undoubtedly left Mobile for northeastern American cities as well as for Liverpool and Le Havre, where international firms handled many of the transport, insurance, and market arrangements for Alabama cotton. The representatives of these firms who made their homes in Mobile exercised much influence over local affairs. Along with other entrepreneurs, they opened the way to considerable commercial development for Mobile. In so doing they made Mobile, more than any other southern city, dependent upon New York for its economic welfare.

✳ 3 ✳

City Fathers

MOBILE'S transformation from sleepy hamlet to busy city demanded fresh leadership, preferably from its newer residents. The cultivation of a city required a vision often absent in people accustomed to viewing Mobile as an obscure outpost. American newcomers, who arrived as foreign officials departed at the end of colonial rule, supplied this vision as they filled the power vacuum. Realizing that their prosperity depended upon that of their town, they assumed decision-making positions in local government, business institutions, and voluntary associations from which they could supervise Mobile's growth. From these influential posts they provided the initiative needed for the city's development.

Leaders did not simply join civic groups; they directed them. Most influenced local progress by holding important posts in at least two different organizations that affected Mobile's development.[1] Offices with this scope included the mayoralty, board of aldermen, common council, school board, local banks, local insurance companies, the Mobile and Ohio Railroad Company, the Chamber of Commerce, and major voluntary associations—fire companies, benevolent societies, fraternal lodges, and military companies.

Urban leaders made up a select group among officeholders in business, government, and voluntary associations. Culling names of officers from contemporary newspapers and minutes of various boards produced a pool of some 650 men who served as general officers, directors, or chairmen or members of important committees between 1820 and 1860. Of this group, 256 who held offices in two or more different organizations met the strict criteria for urban leadership used in this study. For instance, someone who held office in several insurance companies was included only if he also held office in an endeavor besides insurance. To be classified as an urban leader, an alderman had to have an important position on another board. This method of selection should ensure that leaders indeed served in positions from which they could shape city development. Biographical information was obtained from contemporary newspapers, manuscript census returns, credit reports, and published biographical dictionaries.[2]

Leaders were analyzed both in terms of their characteristics as a group and in terms of their relationship to their constituents, adult white male householders. Leaders listed in the 1860 census, 112 of the 256 cases, were compared to a sample group of 437 white male heads of household representing approximately 10 percent of the white male heads of household in the city of Mobile. Quantitative comparisons of the leader and sample groups were derived from tables generated by computer analyses. Packaged computer programs available in the Statistical Analysis System (SAS) greatly facilitated study of the census data.[3]

Most of the 256 urban leaders in Mobile, like their counterparts in Richmond, Norfolk, Cincinnati, and elsewhere, were not very active in positions of local leadership.[4] In other words, the largest proportion of leaders (55.5 percent) held posts in only two of the twelve activities counted for this analysis. Fewer (39.1 percent) were moderate activists who led three or four civic endeavors. A select group of activists (5.5 percent) committed themselves to five or more activities. No one held positions of power in all twelve categories; the highest number recorded for any one person was six.

No single urban leader directed more civic activities than anyone else. Three led six different activities each. These enterprising merchants came to Mobile from northern states or England in the 1820s or 1830s and remained throughout the antebellum era. Thaddeus Sanford, a Connecticut Yankee, opened a mercantile establishment in 1822. He soon won election to three terms on the board of aldermen (1824–26). In 1828 he sold his business in order to publish and edit the Democratic newspaper, the *Mobile Register*, which he continued to manage almost without interruption until 1854. From his editorial post Sanford made political contacts that helped to influence his appointment as one of the state's directors of the Bank of Mobile (1836, 1838–43). The directors elected Sanford to four terms as president of the bank (1839–43). He also sat on the board of trustees of the Alabama Life Insurance and Trust Company (1836–38, 1841–43). Sanford was reportedly "esteemed for his social qualities and admired for his rectitude in business." His loyalty to the Democratic party earned him an appointment as U.S. customs collector for the port of Mobile in 1853, when Sanford sold his newspaper to devote himself to his new duties. Although Sanford's main concerns appear to have revolved about political and financial matters, he served Mobilians in several other areas. He held offices in the Mobile Bible Society (1825) and the Auxiliary Tract Society (1829). He supported public education as a school commissioner (1852–63) and president of the board that inaugurated the first genuine public school system in Mobile and the state of Alabama.[5]

Two successful cotton merchants, William John Ledyard from New York and Jonathan Emanuel from England, also became maximum activists. Ledyard, who had arrived by the mid-1830s, operated a commission-merchant business that maintained a good credit rating throughout the 1850s. Ledyard was reportedly "much respected" in Mobile. He helped to direct the boards of the Mobile Insurance Company (1850–53, 1855–60), the Mobile branch of the Alabama State Bank (1840), the Mobile and Ohio Railroad Company (1856), and the Chamber of Commerce (1836, 1854–56). He gave of his time as a school commissioner (1843–45) and an officer of the Samaritan Society (1845, 1847, 1856–58). He belonged to Government Street Presbyterian Church, the church of that denomination favored by urban leaders.[6]

The other most active leader, Jonathan Emanuel, belonged to the most prestigious Episcopal congregation in the city, Christ Church. Emanuel came to Mobile in the 1820s as a cotton broker. He retired from that business in 1856 to work full time as president of the Mobile Insurance Company, where he had served as a director since 1832 and president since 1841. Emanuel served on the directorates of other business institutions: the Alabama Life Insurance and Trust Company (1836–38), Bank of Mobile (1832, 1838–44, 1846–49, 1851, 1854), the Mobile branch of the Second Bank of the United States (1828), and the Mobile and Ohio Railroad Company (1848–54, 1858–59). He also held office in the Chamber of Commerce (1854–56). In government Emanuel won election to the common council (1840, 1844, 1846, 1852) and

Table 3-1. Comparison of Geographical Origins of Urban Leaders of
Antebellum Mobile, Richmond, and Norfolk

Region	Mobile, 1860 %	Richmond, 1850 %	Norfolk, 1850 %
South[a]	49.5 (includes 7.2 Alabama)	89.8 (includes 88.1 Virginia)	84.9 (includes 69.8 Virginia)
North[b]	36.9	8.5	7.5
Foreign	13.5	1.7	7.6
Number of Cases[c]	111	59	53

SOURCE: Richmond and Norfolk figures in David R. Goldfield, Urban
Growth in the Age of Sectionalism: Virginia, 1847-1861 (Baton Rouge:
Louisiana State University Press, 1977), p. 42.
[a]Slaveholding states.
[b]Free states.
[c]Includes cases for which place of birth was located in the U.S. census.

the board of school commissioners (1843–47).[7] The fact that the most active leaders held more elected offices in business than in government institutions underscores their preoccupation with commerce. Decisions they made as directors of insurance companies or banks could have as much or more impact on local development than could the resolutions of municipal officials.

These city fathers hailed from a wide variety of places. In a newly settled or, as in the case of Mobile, newly resettled city, many residents came from long distances. Rapidly growing cities attracted people from a wider variety of birthplaces than did slowly developing ones. The geographic or ethnic backgrounds of urban leaders, who emerged from these new residents, reflected both the age and rate of growth of their respective cities. Thus the elite in the booming metropolis of mid-nineteenth-century Chicago represented a great diversity of birthplaces, as did the elite of Mobile, which burgeoned twenty-fold in population between 1820 and 1860.[8] By comparison the urban leaders of Richmond and Norfolk, older cities in the South Atlantic region with a slower rate of growth than in the Southwest, were less varied in their geographic origins (see Table 3-1). Mobile and New Orleans, the fastest-growing cotton ports, attracted many northern-born businessmen who readily assumed positions of leadership in civic activities. Their influ-

Table 3-2. Region of Birth by Group

Region of Birth	Leader		Sample	
	N	%	N	%
South	55	49.6	134	31.0
North	41	36.9	69	16.0
Foreign	15	13.5	229	53.0
Total[a]	111	100.0	432	100.0

[a]Cases for which place of birth was reported in 1860 census: 111 (99.1%) leaders and 432 (98.9%) sample males.

Table 3-3. Most Frequently Listed Birthplaces of Urban Leaders and Sample Males, 1860

Leader		Sample	
Place	%	Place	%
New York	17.1	Ireland	21.3
Virginia	11.7	German States	11.1
Georgia	9.9	Alabama	10.2
South Carolina	9.9		
Alabama	7.2	New York	5.6
England	6.3	France	5.3
Number of Cases[a] 111		Number of Cases[a] 432	

[a]Cases for which place of birth appeared in 1860 census.

ence in Mobile and New Orleans exceeded that of their counterparts in Richmond, Norfolk, and Charleston.[9]

The diverse geographic origins of Mobile's leaders reflected the city's cosmopolitan heritage, new influx of population, and critical trade ties to New York. Few of Mobile's leaders had been born in Alabama (see Tables 3-2 and 3-3). The small proportion (7.2 percent) of Alabamians among the leaders can be partially explained by the age of the state compared to the median age of the leaders. While Alabama was forty-one years old in 1860, the median age of the leaders was forty-nine. In the Virginia cities with long American histories, the overwhelming majority of urban leaders were natives of their state. As befitted its different historical circumstances, Mobile counted as many nonsoutherners as southerners among its leaders. Throughout the antebellum era northern-born and foreign-born men made up approximately three-eighths and one-eighth, respectively, of all leaders.

The proportion of nonsoutherners among these leaders contrasted sharply with their representation among the sample of white male heads of household. More than twice as many northerners appeared in the leadership group as in the sample, confirming the contemporary impression that northerners in major cotton ports exercised power far in excess of their numbers in the citizenry. Because of their trade ties with Mobile, New Yorkers were the single largest contingent of urban leaders, appearing more than three times as often as in the sample. Only about one-fourth as many foreign-born appeared among the leaders as among the sample, reflecting the difficulty that new immigrants had in accumulating the requisite wealth and contacts to win election to places of urban leadership. In Mobile large numbers of destitute immigrants who arrived from Ireland and central Europe in the late 1840s and 1850s had virtually no chance of entering the urban leadership by 1860. The newly arrived Irish held the lowest-paying jobs, often serving as domestics, waiters, and laborers. Natives of northern and western Europe who emigrated before the mid-1840s were the likeliest of foreign-born candidates to become urban leaders. The most numerous foreign contingent within the population by the 1850s was markedly underrepresented among the leaders, while one of the smaller groups was overrepresented: more than three times as many Englishmen as Irishmen were urban leaders.

Ambitious newcomers to this port city found that, as in many other antebellum American cities, they could win positions of leadership soon after their arrival by taking an active part in local affairs. Within ten to fifteen years they were considered distinguished, long-time citizens of the town.[10] Addin Lewis, the first American mayor of Mobile, was one such newcomer. Lewis, a native of Connecticut, moved south after his graduation from Yale in 1803 to serve as a tutor at the University of Georgia in Athens. Appointed as the first collector of U.S. customs for the port of Mobile, he assumed his post in 1813. Lewis worked energetically on civic improvements as collector (1813–29), postmaster (1818–24), president of the Bank of Mobile (1818) and mayor (1820–22). His health eventually deteriorated so much that his annual summer vacations in Connecticut could not restore his vitality. In 1829 Lewis, then forty-nine years old, retired from civic affairs. At a public dinner in his honor, Lewis contrasted the "forlorn" condition of Mobile upon his arrival in 1813 with its improved circumstances in 1829. He observed that he had done his duty for fifteen years in Mobile with the aid of other leaders, whom he expected to continue their efforts for local improvement after his retirement to New Haven. Prominent Mobilians lauded Lewis as "one of their oldest and most respected citizens."[11]

Death, relocation, financial failure, and retirement made the ranks of urban leaders ever changing. Even in the 1840s relative newcomers could win multiple positions of power. New Yorker Charles D. Dickey moved to Mobile in the late 1840s as a cotton buyer for Brown Brothers and Company of New York.[12] By the middle of the next decade he was a director of two insurance companies and an officer in the Chamber of Commerce. Another New Yorker, Francis B. Clark, moved from New York via Augusta, Georgia, to Mobile in 1843 to manage Haviland, Clark and Company, a branch of the New York-based drug firm of Haviland, Kesse and Company, which had other stores in Charleston and Augusta. In late 1851, when Haviland withdrew from the firm, Clark took in a local partner who had already been successful in the drug business. By the end of the decade Clark, George and Company was reputed to be the largest wholesale dealer in the city. Meanwhile, Clark had become an officer in the Chamber of Commerce, a director of an insurance company, the chairman of the executive committee of the board of directors of the Mobile and Ohio Railroad Company, and a director of the Mobile and Great Northern Railroad Company. His younger brother Willis also moved to Mobile, where in the 1850s he edited the *Mobile Daily Advertiser* and served on the executive committee of the Board of School Commissioners.[13]

In a city experiencing its first stage of major expansion anyone, whether a new or an old resident, could win positions of local power if he met the community's expectations of leaders: accumulation of wealth; service on the boards of business and government institutions, and voluntary associations; and good manners and advantageous social contacts. Money enabled individuals to buy stock in local banks, insurance companies, and railroad companies whose stockholders elected their officers. Sizable personal incomes allowed these leaders to serve in major municipal offices that paid little or no salaries.[14] Extra capital supplied dues for or donations to voluntary associations of a benevolent, fraternal, or social nature. Ample funds also provided tickets to the balls, theater, concerts, and lectures enjoyed by those in well-to-do circles.

In the acquisition of wealth and positions of leadership, family background counted for little in antebellum Mobile, which had no previous generations of American residents. Neither did Mobile have a significant Creole presence. Before America gained title to Mobile, many of the respectable Creole families had left the area. Creole kinship ties remained few in Mobile, in contrast to New Orleans, where a notable representation of prestigious Creole families stayed in the city after the colonial era. Despite its long history, early antebellum Mobile had almost no residents whose families had lived there before the nineteenth century. Aspiring leaders in Mobile, then, could not count on the prestige of family names and kinship networks that were well established in a city like Charleston, where ninety families dominated the upper class from the eighteenth century into the nineteenth century.[15]

Intergenerational ties mattered little, yet kinship ties among generational peers helped some newcomers acquire the financial security and contacts necessary for election to important local boards. Assistance from relatives, whether in the form of a job, a marriage settlement, an introduction to fashionable society, or another favor, boosted the careers of some who became urban leaders. Among the 256 men examined for this study were 10 sets of brothers, 21 cases in all. Family ties did, it seems, influence the migration of certain individuals to the Alabama port and their attainment of positions of power there. Some leaders augmented their own fortunes by advantageous marriages. Reports on the credit status of Mobile's leaders include comments about property owned by their wives or the financial condition of rich fathers-in-law.[16]

William R. Hallett's career illustrates the family connections that helped to advance one newcomer from New York on the path to leadership in Mobile. In 1817 he moved to the Alabama port to join his brother Thomas, who had arrived from New York three years earlier with the merchandise for a large retail business, frames for partially prefabricated houses, and Yankee workmen to assemble them. Thomas Hallett soon became a director of the Bank of Mobile and a state representative from Mobile County. His brother enjoyed a similar rise to prominence. William Hallett married Catherine Susan Judson in 1824. By that time her brother Lewis Judson had already served as a town commissioner during the territorial period, an alderman, and a director and a president of the Bank of Mobile. Two years after his marriage to Catherine Judson, William Hallett became a director of the Bank of Mobile. In the early 1830s he also served as an alderman, state representative from Mobile County, and a director of the Bank of Mobile, the Mobile branch of the Second Bank of the United States, and the Mobile Insurance Company. In 1836 he became president of the Bank of Mobile, a post he held almost continuously until his death in 1860. His sound management practices helped the bank to withstand the Panics of 1837 and 1857. At his death the *Mobile Register* mourned, "Mobile has lost one of her strong men and one who has exercised in his day and generation vast influence in his sphere."[17]

Family connections did not always explain an individual's success. Some, like Moses Waring, made fortunes by personal initiative and enterprise. Waring moved from Connecticut to Mobile several years after the War of 1812. He made his living as a commission merchant and cotton factor as well as a steamboat agent. According to the credit investigator for R. G. Dun and Company, Waring amassed his own fortune through speculation. He reportedly made nearly $20,000 from trade during the Mexican War. Waring involved himself heavily in civic affairs, winning election as an alderman (1838), a common councilman (1841), a director of the Mobile Marine Dock and Mutual Insurance Company (1852–56), and a director of the Mobile and Ohio Railroad Company (1848–55). In addition, he belonged to a militia company and to the most prestigious Episcopal church in Mobile.[18] Waring, in short, marshalled his own business skills and personal contacts toward achieving multiple positions of local power.

Commerce provided the path to prominence chosen most often by leaders in Mobile. In this respect Mobile conformed to a pattern common in early nineteenth-century America, leadership by mercantile elites. The preponderance of leaders who made their living in commerce, some 75 percent, reflected Mobile's extreme dependence on mercantile activities (see Table 3-4). Southern cities with relatively diversified economies like Richmond counted a greater proportion of professionals and industrialists among their leaders than did Mobile.[19] Since Mobile was, as one contemporary described it, "a strictly com-

CITY FATHERS

Table 3-4. Occupational Category by Group

Occupational Category[a]	Leader		Sample	
	N	%	N	%
Agriculture/fishing	1	0.9	10	2.4
Building	3	2.8	43	10.3
Transport	1	0.9	29	6.9
Commerce, employee[b]	9	8.3	77	18.4
Commerce, proprietor[c]	73	67.6	72	17.2
Manufacturing	7	6.5	68	16.3
Professions/gentlemen	9	8.3	15	3.6
Services/labor[d]	5	4.6	104	24.9
Total[e]	108	99.9*	418	100.0

[a]Occupations included in each category are listed in the Appendix.
[b]Includes, besides clerks, etc., merchants with less than $500 worth of property.
[c]Includes various merchants with $500 or more of property.
[d]Combines nonprofessional and public services with semiskilled and unskilled labor.
[e]Cases with occupations listed in 1860 census.
*Rounding error.

Table 3-5. Total Wealth by Group

Total Wealth ($)[a]	Leader		Sample	
	N	%	N	%
1-4,999	6	5.7	97	51.6
5,000-24,999	25	23.8	52	27.7
25,000-49,999	21	20.0	18	9.6
50,000-99,999	23	21.9	10	5.3
100,000+	30	28.6	11	5.9
Total[b]	105	100.0	188	100.1*

[a]The sum of real estate and personal estate reported in the 1860 census.
[b]Cases that reported some property: 93.8% of leaders, 43.0% of sample males.
*Rounding error.

mercial metropolis," its "aristocracy . . . consists of its merchant prin-ces and their families." While wealthy planters with estates in the inte-rior resided in and led society in southern cities like Charleston and Savannah, the pursuit of commerce in Mobile dictated that business-men there were "the princes of the social empire." Physicians, attor-neys, and clergymen exerted their influence, but their representation among the leaders amounted to only a fraction of that of the commer-cial men.[20]

Leaders' occupations generally ranked higher in status than those of sample males.[21] While some nine-tenths of the leaders engaged in com-merce held proprietary positions, fewer than half of the sample men did. The urban leaders were likely to be commission merchants, cotton factors, retailers, and wholesalers who perhaps employed clerks and storekeepers. Leaders included more than twice the sample group's proportion of professionals and "gentlemen." Representing a broad cross-section of vocations, the sample included sizable numbers of men involved in building and manufacturing enterprises as well as services and labor. Nearly one-fifth of the sample males worked as unskilled (15.1 percent) or semiskilled (4.1 percent) laborers, as compared to none of the leaders.

More than anything else, the leaders' propertyholding distinguished them from the sample male householders. Almost all of the leaders owned some property, while the majority of sample males owned nothing, or at least nothing reported in the 1860 census (see Table 3-5). Thirty leaders were in fact wealthy, according to the mid-nineteenth-century standard of measurement—an estate worth $100,000 or more. The total wealth of individual leaders ranged from $300 to $490,000. The median value of the leaders' total wealth was $47,000, but, be-cause of the large number of considerable estates, the average value was even higher, $77,572. The median value of the sample males' wealth was $4,000, although the average, again because of some large estates, was greater, $9,555.

The wide disparity between the property holdings of the leaders and sample males in Mobile was typical of many other mid-nineteenth-century American cities, where inequitable distribution of wealth was the rule.[22] Aggregate holdings of Mobile's urban leaders were substan-tial, making up 18 percent of the value of real estate and personal estate reported in the 1860 census for Mobile County. Urban leaders who resided in the city of Mobile owned 21 percent of the real estate and 27 percent of the personal estate in the city in 1860. Those leaders made up less than 1 percent of the property holders, yet they as a group claimed about one-fourth of the city's property.[23]

A substantial number of leaders invested in local real estate, which not only increased their fortunes but also tied their financial interests to the progress of their city. Building lots and housing units rarely kept pace with demand during the city's growth in the antebellum years, so property sales and rentals proved lucrative, especially in boom periods. "No one gets rich who does not embark in speculation in real estate, which has turned into gold in the hands of all who have touched it," pronounced one established resident in the 1830s, the decade in which Mobile quadrupled in population.[24] Because the demand for housing could not be satisfied, the price of lots, new residences and commercial buildings, and rents soared to new heights. A similar situation developed in the late 1850s, when another building boom failed to meet the demand. By 1860 more than three-quarters of the leaders owned real estate, and nearly three-tenths of them claimed property worth $50,000 or more. In contrast, just one-quarter of the sample heads of household owned real estate, and less than one-tenth of them had property valued at or in excess of $50,000 (see Table 3-6). The sample males' median real-estate holding was $2,500, slightly more than one-tenth the median for the leaders' real estate, $21,000.

Even more leaders owned personal property (92.9 percent) than real estate (82.0 percent). Personal property included slaves, although it also counted stock in banks, insurance companies, and internal improvement companies. Leaders' total personal estates were considerably larger than their real-estate holdings. Sixteen leaders owned personal property valued at $100,000 or more, yet only seven had real-estate holdings of the same amount. Personal-property holdings of individual leaders ranged from $300 to $440,000; the median was $28,000. The leaders' median personal estate was ten times greater than the median for the sample males, $2,750. Just slightly more than one-third (35.9 percent) of the sample male householders owned any personal estate at all. More than half of those who did own personal property reported estates of less than $5,000 (see Table 3-7).

Property-holding patterns of Mobile's leaders revealed some differences related to their places of birth. Leaders generally, regardless of

Table 3-6. Real Estate by Group

Real Estate ($)	Leader		Sample	
	N	%	N	%
0	19	17.3	320	73.2
1-4,999	7	6.4	68	15.6
5,000-24,999	39	35.4	32	7.3
25,000-49,999	18	16.4	9	2.1
50,000-99,999	20	18.2	3	0.7
100,000+	7	6.4	5	1.1
Total[a]	110	100.1*	437	100.0

[a]Number of cases for whom real-estate ownership could be determined from the 1860 census.
*Rounding error.

Table 3-7. Personal Estate by Group

Personal Estate ($)	Leader		Sample	
	N	%	N	%
0	6	5.4	280	64.1
1-4,999	20	18.2	84	19.2
5,000-24,999	31	28.2	44	10.1
25,000-49,999	20	18.2	13	3.0
50,000-99,999	17	15.4	12	2.7
100,000+	16	14.6	4	0.9
Total[a]	110	100.0	437	100.0

[a]Number of cases for whom personal-estate ownership could be determined from the 1860 census.

their places of birth, invested more of their money in personal property than in real estate. Native southerners, on the average, placed the greatest proportion of their wealth in personal property. The mean percentage of southern-born leaders' wealth in personal property was 59.1 percent. Leaders from outside the South, on the average, invested less than southerners in personal property: 53.5 percent of the foreign-born leaders' wealth, and 51.7 percent of the northerners' assets. Nonsouth-

Table 3-8. Number of Slaves Held by Group

Number of Slaves	Leader		Sample	
	N	%	N	%
0	27	24.5	348	79.6
1	6	5.5	18	4.1
2-4	14	12.7	37	8.5
5-9	29	26.4	23	5.3
10+	34	30.9	11	2.5
Total[a]	110	100.0	437	100.0

[a]Number of cases for whom slaveholding could be determined from the 1860 census.

erners placed more of their wealth in real estate than southerners. The mean proportions of leaders' wealth in real estate was 48.3 percent for the northern-born, 46.5 percent for the foreign-born, and 40.9 percent for the southern-born. The most marked differences related to the place of birth appeared at the highest levels of wealth in both real and personal estate. Of the seven leaders whose real estate was valued at $100,000 or more, four hailed from northern states, one from a foreign country, and two from southern states. Of the sixteen leaders whose personal estates equalled or exceeded $100,000, twelve were southerners and four were northerners.

Slaveholding was prevalent among the leaders generally but most pronounced among the southern-born (see Table 3-8). The median number of bondsmen held was nine, a reflection of the ordinarily small size of urban slaveholdings, even those of leaders.[25] Native southern leaders, on the average, owned more than two times as many bondsmen as nonsoutherners. The average number of bondsmen owned by native southerners was 13, more than twice the average for northern-born, 6, and foreign-born, 5. The largest individual slaveholdings appeared among southern-born leaders: 61 slaves were owned by Allen H. Ryland, a brickmaker from Virginia; 106 by Duke W. Goodman, a commission merchant and commercial wharf operator from South Carolina; and 124 by James E. Saunders, a cotton factor from Virginia.[26] The slight preponderance of males (54.8 percent) among the total of 1037 slaves held by all of the urban leaders indicates some preferred employment of males in certain industrial and commercial labor positions in the city. Yet Mobile was still basically a commercial city in 1860, so that it did not have the same availability of employment for male slaves as did the industrializing city of Richmond.[27]

Ownership of slaves indicated assimilation of southern mores. Native southerners claimed the largest individual holdings of slaves in Mobile County. Of the eighteen persons who owned fifty or more slaves in 1860, only one was born outside the South.[28] Nonsoutherners did not have to purchase large numbers of bondsmen, just enough to illustrate their commitment to the peculiar institution. Southerners' emotional and material commitment to slavery exceeded that of people who were not natives of the Cotton Kingdom, yet all slaveowners had some financial and social stake in the system of bondage.[29]

Opponents of slavery learned to keep their opinions to themselves and even to own slaves in order to accommodate themselves to their adopted society. They came to realize that, probably more than anything else, their attitudes toward slavery determined their reception in the South. For this reason, as Daniel Hundley argued in 1860, northern-born merchants who joined the southern middle class professed proslavery views and perhaps owned slaves acquired by marriage. Either because of their antislavery views or their intention to return eventually to the North, they sometimes preferred to hire rather than buy slaves. Merchants from England also frequently owned or employed slaves without committing themselves to the institution.[30] All slaveowners in Mobile who were not native southerners learned an object lesson in 1856 when two booksellers who had a well-established local business, William Strickland from England and Edwin Upson from Connecticut, were publicly forced from the city for selling abolitionist publications. Both Strickland and Upson had kept their antislavery views to themselves, had formerly owned slaves as domestics, and had sometimes accepted slaves in payment for debts owed to their business. They nonetheless faced exile for selling books considered incendiary by community standards.[31]

Ownership of slaves indicated a leader's accommodation to southern mores; membership and officeholding in voluntary associations indicated his acceptance by other men in Mobile. Whether membership or officeholding in voluntary associations led directly to offices in municipal government or business institutions cannot be determined in any systematic way. It is clear, however, that officers of voluntary associations appeared frequently among the urban leaders and vice versa. Urban leaders generally made up from one-tenth to one-fourth of the rosters of most voluntary associations with extant records. Half of the officers might be urban leaders, although the membership was far less exclusive. Voluntary associations formed for any number of purposes, ranging from social to benevolent. Their direct impact on the development of the city varied greatly, but all exerted indirect influence as they provided opportunities for informal contacts among leaders and other townspeople who belonged to the associations.

For their members, and even more for their officers, voluntary associations improved opportunities for upward mobility. In a mercantile city like Mobile, where commerce depended greatly upon personal contacts for clientele and credit, affiliation with a voluntary association enlarged the circle of personal and business contacts for a businessman. Associations often provided contact with potential business associates in contexts that, by explicit rules or implicit assumptions regarding members' behavior, encouraged ethical business conduct.[32] These subtle benefits of participation in voluntary associations furthered the careers of aspiring urban leaders.

Many leaders joined a fire or militia company or both. Membership not only indicated good citizenship; it offered pleasant social opportunities as well. Individual fire companies met once a month for the washing of engines and checking of equipment, which could be called into service for fighting fires at any time. Mobile's fire companies jointly staged a parade and ball each spring to observe the organization in 1838 of the Mobile Fire Department Association, a benevolent group. These anniversary celebrations provided what the *Mobile Register* called "a kind of city jubilee in which all classes take equal pleasure." Besides social activities of fire companies, members enjoyed rewards for faithful service. Firemen who provided five years of active service became "exempt firemen," that is honorary members with privileges of active members, who were excused from militia duty, road taxes, and jury duty.[33]

Militia companies instilled martial ardor among the members and provided social occasions for them. Each group sponsored target shoots within its own ranks and sometimes challenged companies from New Orleans. Encampments each spring for all companies in the First Volunteer Regiment and excursions to nearby towns afforded other pleasurable activities. Parades and military balls jointly sponsored by the local companies to celebrate the anniversaries of the Battle of New Orleans and of George Washington's birth provided major social occasions.

Most military and fire companies were ethnically varied in membership and leadership. A few accepted only the foreign-born. The Irish Independent Greens, German Fusiliers, Mobile Grenadiers, and Lafayette Guards were ethnically exclusive militia companies for natives of Ireland, German states, and France, respectively. The only fire company with any indication of an ethnic preference for membership was Mechanics Number 7, in which half of the roster of 1860 was composed of men with Irish surnames.[34] Fire and militia companies organized according to nationality provided ample opportunities for naturalized citizens and their descendants to exhibit the American values expected of would-be urban leaders.[35]

Rising leaders also provided their neighbors with evidence of civic spirit by holding offices in charitable associations. Mobilians boasted that they provided as liberal support for public charities as any urbanites in the country "when the claims of a worthy object [were] set forth and pressed by any well-known individual."[36] Who then could better champion benevolent causes than the urban leaders? Their names abounded on lists of officers of such groups as the Can't Get Away Club, Samaritan Society, and Mobile Port Society, which provided relief to yellow fever sufferers, indigent poor, and destitute seamen, respectively.

Mystic societies, secret social groups that celebrated the pre-Lenten carnival, offered fashionable affiliations for urban leaders. Their fêtes may be traced back to Renaissance Europe where masked balls, parades, and feasts observed the time before the beginning of Lent. In America pre-Lenten carnivals developed in parts of the South like Mobile with French or Spanish background. French colonists in Mobile organized the Boeuf Gras Society in 1711 to celebrate Mardi Gras, or Shrove Tuesday, as Bienville recalled it in his native France. He and his associates built a large bull's head and paraded it on wheels through the settlement, following the custom set by the Butchers' Guild in France. Spanish colonists observed the pre-Lenten carnival by forming the Spanish Mystic Society in 1793 to parade on Twelfth Night (January 6) annually for a number of years. American observance of pre-Lenten festivities in Mobile began in 1830 with Michael Krafft, a cotton broker from Pennsylvania, who, with some of his friends, paraded through the streets at dawn on New Year's Day. Gathering up hoes, rakes, gongs, and cowbells from a hardware store, they made their New Year's Day calls.[37] In accord with a custom established in New York City, gentlemen in Mobile called on ladies of their acquaintance on New Year's Day.[38]

Membership rolls of the now-defunct secret mystic societies from the antebellum period are not available. Thus participation in mystic societies cannot be verified for specific men, but it assuredly carried social prestige that would be advantageous to urban leaders. The Cowbellion de Rakin Society, formed by Krafft and his friends, was the oldest and most prestigious mystic society.[39] Cowbellions donned masks and staged parades on New Year's Eve before hosting a ball for invited guests.

Those excluded from the Cowbellions' highly selective membership formed their own societies. Apprentices in the cotton trade organized the Strikers Independent Society in 1841. (The Strikers' name related to the "striking" or marking of cotton bales for shipment.) By 1852 the *Mobile Register* thought that the Strikers Society was "composed, like their elders, of undoubtedly respectable citizens." Other fun-loving young men formed new mystic societies: Calfbellions, Rising Generation, and T.D.S. (The Determined Set or Tea Drinkers Society) in 1844, Jim Oakes in 1845, and the Indescribables in 1846. These secret societies were, according to Charles C. Langdon, editor of the *Mobile Daily Advertiser*, "composed mostly of young men moving in the most respectable walks of life . . . bound together by ties of warmest friendships." "Their association together for the purpose of affording amusement, and oftentimes instruction for themselves and their friends, tends," argued Langdon, "greatly to destroy that acerbity of feeling which the clashing interests of business are always calculated to engender."[40]

In addition to social gatherings sponsored by voluntary associations, leaders enjoyed soirées at salons maintained by prominent local hostesses. Octavia Walton Levert, wife of Dr. Henry S. Levert, assembled the most fashionable guests for her weekly receptions. After touring Europe twice in the 1850s, Madame Levert modeled her salon

Christ Church, 1840 (Courtesy of the Museum of the City of Mobile)

after those of the French. She held open house each Monday from 11 A.M. to 11 P.M. "To be a novelty in fact or reputed, was sufficient to secure *entree* into the salon," observed Thomas C. De Leon. Madame Levert welcomed artists, actors, actresses, and writers along with politicians and filibusterers.[41]

Two other hostesses assembled civic leaders for their own salons. Mary Walker Fearn, wife of Dr. Richard Lee Fearn, gave receptions for such local guests as Governor John A. Winston, the surgeon Claude Mastin, and the writer Theodore O'Hara. Distinguished American and European visitors also found welcome in the Fearn home. Phoebe Desha Smith, wife of commission merchant Murray Smith, gave what De Leon called "costly, but not popular" parties.[42] Fashionable hostesses by no means restricted their guest lists to local leaders. They did, however, provide them with opportunities for prized social contact with each other.

Religious affiliations indicated exclusive tendencies among leaders. In Mobile, as in Montgomery, New Orleans, Savannah, and elsewhere in the South, the elite belonged to the Episcopal church.[43] Most (60.8 percent) of the urban leaders whose religious affiliations are known joined Episcopal congregations.[44] Almost all of these Episcopalians belonged to Christ Church, the oldest and most prestigious Protestant church in town. After Episcopalians, Methodists and Presbyterians (15.5 percent each) accounted for the largest contingents of leaders. Again the leaders favored the oldest congregations in their respective denominations: St. Francis Street Methodist and Government Street Presbyterian. A few leaders belonged to Jewish (5.2 percent) and Catholic (3.1 percent) congregations. None joined Baptist churches. Leaders' religious preferences thus separated them from the masses of Mobile County's 10,355 church members, who in 1855 belonged to Catholic (61.3 percent), Methodist (19.0 percent), Presbyterian (6.6 percent), Baptist (6.5 percent), Episcopal (5.6 percent), and Jewish (0.9 percent) congregations.[45]

Denominations that attracted large numbers of poor immigrants in the late antebellum period did not claim very many urban leaders as members. Without a large representation of prominent families remaining from the French and Spanish colonial periods, the Catholic church in Mobile did not carry the same social prestige that it did in New Orleans. The reputation that the Catholic church had acquired by the late antebellum era as a refuge for the poor Irish and German immi-

Table 3-9. City Residence by Group

Residence	Leader		Sample	
	N	%	N	%
Ward 1	18	18.2	31	7.1
Ward 2	11	11.1	73	16.7
Ward 3	13	13.1	34	7.8
Ward 4	23	23.2	35	8.1
Ward 5	8	8.1	45	10.3
Ward 6	17	17.2	154	35.2
Ward 7	9	9.1	65	14.9
Total[a]	99	100.0	437	100.1*

[a]Those whose residence was within city limits; 13 leaders who lived outside the city are thus excluded.
*Rounding error.

grants who were flocking to Mobile made it a relatively undesirable religious affiliation for the elite.[46] Counting poor immigrants from central Europe as a majority of its members in the 1850s, the local Jewish synagogue also attracted an elite contingent of prominent, affluent Jewish businessmen.[47] Their religious association with poor immigrants did not prevent them from earning positions as urban leaders. Generally, however, Mobile's urban leaders preferred churches with predominantly upper-class congregations.

Leaders in Mobile exhibited some of the exclusive residential tendencies noted among the elite in nineteenth-century cities, although they scattered their residences throughout all of the wards in 1860 (see Table 3-9). Most of the affluent made their homes in the central section of the city bounded by Congress Street on the north, Monroe Street on the south, Royal Street on the east, and Lawrence on the west.[48] This area, which was entirely within the city fire limits, was also the retail business district of stores, hotels, restaurants, government buildings, professional offices, and meeting halls. Some residential concentration of leaders appeared on a few streets—Spring Hill Road, Shell Road, Ann Street, and Government Street. Interspersed among the residential areas of the city chosen by the leaders were the sample males. They clustered in the northern and relatively undesirable part of the city in the sixth ward, although they lived in all of the other wards as well.

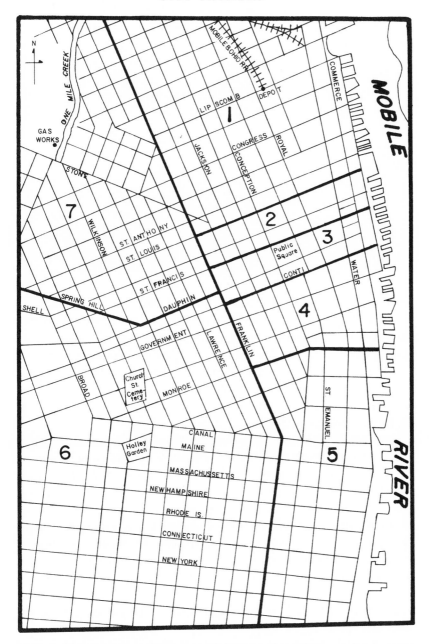

Mobile in 1860 (Adapted from Alan Smith Thompson, "Mobile, Alabama, 1850–1861: Economic, Political, Physical, and Population Characteristics" [Ph.D. diss., University of Alabama, 1979], p. 204)

About one-tenth of the urban leaders lived outside the city limits in the developing suburbs of Summerville and Spring Hill. They commuted to and from the downtown business district by private transportation or by the omnibus line that began service in 1858. Residence outside the city limits barred their election to offices in municipal government although not to posts in other important local institutions.

By their successes in commerce, affiliation with respected voluntary associations and churches, and residence in preferred neighborhoods, leaders established themselves securely in the community. As a group they offered stability and cohesiveness to a heterogeneous and fluid population. Over half (51.8 percent) of the leaders active in 1860 had lived in Mobile for twenty or more years, and their persistence enhanced their positions in Mobile. The leaders' family situations provided evidence of their stability by 1860. While they might have headed to Mobile alone to seek their fortunues, leaders eventually planted roots, so to speak, by marrying and raising families. Most leaders (84.8 percent) had married by 1860. They had typically wed women ten years younger than themselves and had fathered four children. By 1860 the leaders' median age was forty-nine and that of their wives was thirty-nine (see Tables 3-10, 3-11, and 3-12). Leaders' children ranged in age from a median of six for the youngest to eighteen for the eldest (see Tables 3-13, 3-14). Among the leaders' offspring, a notable proportion of young adults lived at home. Young men frequently clerked in their fathers' businesses while young women awaited marriage or taught school.

Families of leaders, perhaps because of the parents' ages, tended to be larger and older than those of the sample males. The median age of the sample heads of household was thirty-seven and that of their wives thirty. As was the case with the leaders, most sample males (77.3 percent) were married and most who were married had children. Perhaps because of the younger parents among the sample families, the median number of children, three, was smaller than that for the leaders. Offspring in the sample families were typically young, with a median age of one for the youngest and eight for the eldest.

Although they had come to Mobile from a wide variety of places, leaders shared common concerns about their new home and their roles there. More than anything else, they were preoccupied with their own individual pursuits of wealth. Their outpourings of energy and enterprise contributed to making money for themselves and developing

Table 3-10. Age by Group

Age in Years	Leader		Sample	
	N	%	N	%
15-19	0	0.0	7	1.6
20-29	3	2.7	89	20.6
30-39	9	8.1	138	31.9
40-49	45	40.5	136	31.4
50+	54	48.7	63	14.6
Total[a]	111	100.0	433	100.1*

[a]Those cases for whom age was reported in the 1860 census.
*Rounding error.

Table 3-11. Age of Wife by Group

Age in Years	Leader		Sample	
	N	%	N	%
15-19	0	0.0	16	4.8
20-29	11	11.6	124	36.8
30-39	31	32.6	125	37.1
40-49	35	36.8	55	16.3
50+	184	19.0	17	5.0
Total[a]	95	100.0	337	100.0

[a]Number of cases that were married.

Table 3-12. Number of Children by Group

Number of Children	Leader		Sample	
	N	%	N	%
1-2	21	22.8	139	49.6
3-4	29	31.5	95	33.9
5+	42	45.7	46	16.4
Total[a]	92	100.0	280	99.9*

[a]Number of cases that reported children in household in 1860 census, whether the male head of household was married or single (presumably widowed).
*Rounding error.

71

Table 3-13. Age of Youngest Child by Group

Age in Years	Leader		Sample	
	N	%	N	%
1-4[a]	36	43.9	146	68.9
5-9	17	20.7	35	16.5
10-14	20	24.4	20	9.4
15+	9	11.0	11	5.2
Total[b]	82	100.0	201	100.0

[a]Includes infants less than one year old.
[b]Number of observations in which household reported at least two children in family, since only one child was counted as eldest for purposes of this study.

Table 3-14. Age of Eldest Child by Group

Age in Years	Leader		Sample	
	N	%	N	%
1-4[a]	5	5.4	73	26.1
5-9	10	10.9	75	26.8
10-14	9	9.8	54	19.3
15+	68	73.9	78	27.9
Total[b]	92	100.0	280	100.1*

[a]Includes infants less than one year old.
[b]Number of households that reported children in family in 1860 census.
*Rounding error.

Table 3-15. Nativity of Business Leaders in Mobile

Position	Southern-born %	Northern-born %	Foreign-born %	Total Number in Position
Director of one insurance company	45.2	38.4	16.4	73
Director of more than one insurance company	55.6	27.8	16.7	36
Director of one bank	51.0	39.6	9.4	53
Director of more than one bank	53.3	26.7	20.0	15
Officer of Chamber of Commerce	39.5	41.9	18.6	43
Director of M & O Railroad	37.5	50.0	12.5	24

SOURCE: Harriet E. Amos, "'Birds of Passage' in a Cotton Port: Northerners and Foreigners among the Urban Leaders of Mobile, 1820-1860," in Class, Conflict, and Consensus: Antebellum Southern Community Studies, ed. Orville Vernon Burton and Robert C. McMath, Jr. (Westport, Conn.: Greenwood Press, 1982), p. 244.

NOTE: This table examines the business leadership positions held by 120 of the urban leaders, some of whom held positions in more than one category listed above. It deals only with business leaders whose places of birth were known. Percentages were subject to rounding.

Table 3-16. Nativity of Government Leaders in Mobile

Position	Southern-born %	Northern-born %	Foreign-born %	Total Number in Position
Mayor	50.0	50.0	0.0	6
Alderman	43.8	43.8	12.5	48
Common councilman	35.9	53.8	10.3	39
School commissioner	48.8	37.2	14.0	43

SOURCE: Amos, "'Birds of Passage' in a Cotton Port," p. 246.

NOTE: This table examines the government leadership positions held by 105 of the urban leaders, some of whom held positions in more than one category listed above. It deals only with government leaders whose places of birth were known. Percentages were subject to rounding.

the port of Mobile and eventually its industrial and railroad interests. Daniel Hundley credited southern Yankees with stimulating southern gentlemen into action designed to increase prosperity in the region. Yet he maintained that southern Yankees acted from selfish, profit-oriented motives, in contrast to southern gentlemen's public spirit and patriotism. Both southern gentlemen and southern Yankees, if one classifies men according to their birthplaces as Hundley did, served among the urban leaders of Mobile.[49] Neither subgroup dominated the other in business directorates or municipal offices.

Despite Mobile's economic subservience to northern and English merchants, they did not dominate the boards of local businesses. Non-southerners generally held positions of business leadership in proportion to their representation among the urban leaders generally (see Table 3-15). In the progressive venture of railroad building, however, northerners clearly took the lead, securing fully half of the offices in the Mobile and Ohio Railroad Company held by urban leaders.

To foster commercial growth of Mobile, many of its leading businessmen took positions in municipal government. Northern-born leaders were heavily represented as mayors, aldermen, and common councilmen (see Table 3-16). The fact that they composed more than half (54 percent) of the common councilmen among the urban leaders provides a clue regarding their main concern with local government: fiscal conservatism. The Common Council was created in the aftermath of the Panic of 1837, during which the city of Mobile went bankrupt, to help the mayor and aldermen increase the efficiency of the collection and disbursement of revenue.[50]

Leadership in partisan politics was not a prerequisite for urban leadership, yet a number of civic leaders led political activities. Their propertyholding provided few clues about their partisan affiliations because in Mobile, as in a number of other cities, party leaders differed little from each other in terms of propertyholding. This conclusion comes from an analysis of a group of partisan leaders drawn from records for 1848 through 1853 of candidates for and officeholders on municipal elected boards and judgeships, state legislative seats, United States Congress (from Alabama's First District), and appointments to major federal patronage positions in the port, such as collector of customs. Men who chaired, addressed, or served as officers of major partisan political meetings were also included for analysis. This leadership group included sixty-four Democrats and fifty-six Whigs, whose propertyholding in the city was checked in the City Property Tax Book for 1850, a more complete and reliable source for that year than the federal census.[51]

The distribution of real-estate holdings among Democrats and Whigs was strikingly similar.[52] Almost the same proportion of leaders of each party owned no real estate: 28.1 percent of Democrats, 30.4 percent of Whigs. Most who owned real estate listed holdings valued at less than $50,000. More Democrats (34.4 percent) owned property worth $5,000–$24,999 than any other amount, while the largest group of Whigs (37.5 percent) owned real estate valued at less than $5,000. Median propertyholding of Democrats, $3,500, slightly exceeded that of Whigs, $3,000. Because of some large estates, means for each group differed more notably—Democrats, $13,354, and Whigs, $6,245.

In comparison to their real-estate holdings, political leaders' ownership of slaves provided more distinction between the parties. Substantial proportions of leaders of both parties listed no slaves in the City Property Tax Book—45.3 percent of Democrats, and 37.5 percent of Whigs. Whig slaveowners claimed more slaves than their Democratic counterparts. Median ownership varied considerably, with 1 slave each for Democrats and 3 for Whigs. Average slaveholding remained close: 3.8 for Democrats and 4.05 for Whigs. No leader of either party listed value of slaves in excess of $25,000. This evidence regarding propertyholding, both in real estate and slaves, indicates more similarities than differences among leaders of both parties.[53]

Party activists not only resembled each other in terms of their propertyholding but also in terms of their age and occupation. Eighty-two percent of Whig and Democrat leaders in 1850 were in their thirties or forties. Median and mean ages for each party group were very close: Democrats' median age was 40 and mean 39.76, Whigs' median age was 41 and mean 41.36.[54] In the mercantile city of Mobile, more party leaders came from commercial occupations than any other field (48 percent of Democrats, and 59 percent of Whigs). Next came professionals, especially attorneys, composing 28 percent of Democrats and 23 percent of Whigs. Almost the same small percentages of men in each group came from building and manufacturing enterprises. This occupational distribution for Mobile's political activists distinguished them from congressmen and state legislators from Alabama who, during the Second Party System, largely came from the ranks of lawyers or planters.[55]

Cosmopolitan Mobile counted more nonsoutherners among its political leaders than did the state as a whole. Most (over 90 percent) of the state's congressmen and legislators were born in the South, with few coming from northern states or foreign countries.[56] Party leaders in Mobile overwhelmingly came from the South, 50 percent of Democrats, more from South Carolina than any other state, and 72 percent of Whigs, more from Virginia than any other state. Yet natives of the North and foreign countries also held prominent political roles in 1850. Democratic leaders included 26 percent northerners and 24 percent foreigners, while Whig leaders included 23 percent northerners and 5 percent foreigners. The relatively small representation of the foreign-born among Whig leaders fit the profile of the party nationally. Aside from this divergence between birthplaces of Democratic and Whig activists, leaders of both parties in Mobile were in fact more alike than different.[57] As a group they differed in certain respects from their associates in the state, mostly because of Mobile's mercantile and cosmopolitan character.

Like members of other commercial elites, leaders in Mobile considered devotion to commerce and acquisition of wealth as evidence of good character.[58] Mercantile success topped the list of qualifications for a "widely known" and "highly esteemed" mayoral candidate in 1855:

> As a merchant he ranks among the first in our city. He possesses a practical knowledge of business, commercial matters, etc., and is thus eminently fitted to preside over a city whose life and hopes are based upon commerce and trade. He is a considerable property holder in the city, and thus will be directly interested in seeing its financial affairs prudently and skillfully administered. He is a man of cultivation, education, and agreeable manners, and thus will be able to discharge the duties of courtesy and hospitality devolving upon the chief Magistrate of a city like ours, with credit to himself and with honor to the city.[59]

Without the aristocratic family backgrounds or inheritances of their counterparts in northeastern or even south Atlantic cities, leaders of Mobile, for the most part, made their money in one generation of residence in the Alabama port.[60] Before the Panic of 1837 many of them profited handsomely from speculation. Then they valued the venturesome spirit associated with speculation, whether in cotton or real estate. When a number of leaders lost substantial amounts of money after the panic, they tended to approach investment more conservatively as private businessmen and municipal officials.

"Hereabouts, our mental atmosphere, like that of the interior of a Gin-room, is impregnated almost entirely with cotton," lamented the local poet, historian, and editor A. B. Meek. Local mercantile leaders constricted their talents, according to *Rowan's Directory*, "within the narrow confines of cotton circulars and counting houses."[61] Their obsession with cotton adversely affected both cultural endeavors and municipal improvements.

In spite of their preoccupation with the cotton business, some leaders joined the Franklin Society, which was formed in 1835 to improve members' knowledge of science and literature. In promotion of its aims, the Franklin Society occasionally sponsored famous speakers such as the Swiss naturalist Louis Agassiz and the British poet Charles Mackay.[62] Leaders' sons helped young businessmen, reportedly "all . . . of good character," who in 1855 organized the Mobile Literary Society for declamation, debate, and oration. As members showed improvement in their speaking abilities, the *Mobile Advertiser* commended them because they were "all engaged in mercantile pursuits, having little time to devote to study and mental improvement, except what is offered by the Society itself." The *Advertiser* hoped that these young men would, by their example, foster general appreciation of intellectual pursuits.[63] Intellectual interests, however, failed to attract general support in the cotton city, partly because leaders never sustained them.

As businessmen committed to some aspect of the cotton trade, many leaders stayed in Mobile only during the months from fall through spring, when commerce demanded their presence. Their long summer absences had a negative effect on urban development. A visitor from the North observed in 1840:

> Mobile might be made a delightful place in Winter and a pleasant one in Summer, but unfortunately like too many of the Southern Towns & Cities but little attention is paid to it by the authorities . . . .[S]o many of the inhabitants leave there in the Summers, that their erratic life forbids them making improvements or paying much attention to these little conveniences & Comforts without which any life & especially a city one is unpleasant.[64]

This description of the vacation habits of Mobilians with money remained true throughout the antebellum period. More than any other residents of Mobile, leaders had the wealth and time to spend on civic improvements, yet they were slow to do so partly because of their annual seasonal absences and their own sense of priorities. Once they had established themselves and guided city government through financial crisis, they did sponsor improvements to make Mobile a more attractive place.

Urban leaders of Mobile respected commerce, class, and consensus. From heterogeneous origins, they perhaps disagreed among themselves openly about politics and secretly about slavery, but they agreed on commercial priorities. While they competed with each other in business, they collaborated on improvements to aid commerce locally. They supported government to establish an environment conducive to commerce, focusing on order rather than regulation. As men who made their own money, they revered enterprise and assumed it earned its own reward in worldly possessions and renown. They tried to shape community consensus on the value of commerce and enterprise, which they considered crucial to the city's development. Bourgeois in origins and outlook, leaders of Mobile represented the concerns of mercantile urban America.

✳ 4 ✳

Working People

MOBILE'S labor force was more heterogeneous, both ethnically and racially, than the city's mercantile leadership.
Various subgroups of laborers competed with each other
for employment in certain occupations. Slaves and free blacks filled a
number of service positions in the city, thus reducing employment op-
tions for whites in these areas. White skilled workers, always scarce,
fared the best, yet even they encountered competition from outsiders
whom employers brought in during hard times after the Panic of 1837.
Competition in the labor force sharpened over the years as increasing
numbers of foreign immigrants came to Mobile in search of jobs in the
1840s and 1850s. Lacking a sense of common identity, workers supported a variety of occupational, benevolent, and religious institutions
that reflected their various interests.

Like other southern cities, Mobile had a shortage of skilled labor
throughout the antebellum period. Skilled white workers remained especially scarce in the building trades, which mechanics claimed were
"connected with every elegance, every comfort, and every convenience
of civilized life."[1] For their own houses some affluent businessmen
brought in their own builders. Thomas L. Hallett brought artisans
from New York in 1814 to erect partially prefabricated houses. William
Dawson, a cotton dealer, imported workers directly from Italy about
1840 to build his residence to his own specifications.

Because of their small numbers, skilled laborers who made the port
city their home generally commanded good wages. Their wages in fact
compared favorably with, and in some cases exceeded, those of their

counterparts in the North. During building booms occasioned either by prosperity or by major fires, wages rose to particularly high levels. For example, after the fire of 1827 the great demand for carpenters drove their daily wages up to five dollars.[2]

For the size of its population Mobile had few tailors, dressmakers, and furniture makers, a circumstance that drove up labor costs in these skilled crafts. Labor costs remained high through the antebellum era, as indicated by residents' comments. In 1823 a young physician who had just located in Mobile ordered his clothes from Philadelphia to save money and to suit his taste. Fifteen years later a cotton clerk who had moved to Mobile from Boston had his clothes shipped from the New England port, where they could be made more inexpensively and attractively than in his new home. When this cotton dealer, Gustavus Horton, sent his son to school in Boston, the boy received advice from home to purchase a handsome winter suit "as you can get it much cheaper there than here, as well as other articles which you will need for Winter."[3] Dressmaking also remained expensive in Mobile, where in the 1840s the cost of having a dress made was twenty dollars. This figure was four times the usual price in London. Since material cost about as much in Mobile as in London and Paris, the additional expense resulted from labor.[4]

Consumers who wanted items of clothing or furniture that remained unusually expensive because of labor costs generally ordered directly from New York firms. Even with the expense of having the purchases made to order and shipped express from New York to Mobile, customers found the items cheaper than those made locally.[5] High labor costs and southerners' preferences for purchasing goods from northern firms contributed to the patronage difficulties of skilled laborers in Mobile.

Shortages of skilled laborers affected industrialization in the 1850s in two ways. First, employers had to pay good wages to workers in order to attract and keep them (see Table 4-1). Second, some industrialists who were introducing operations new to the area could not recruit specialized workers locally. Therefore, they sought both managers and operatives from the North. For example, a textile factory built just outside the city employed a manager from Rhode Island and operatives, including male and female Irish immigrants, who had worked previously in a northeastern mill.[6]

Table 4-1. Male Employment in Manufacturing in the City of Mobile, 1860

Product	Number of Establishments	Average Number Male Hands (Total)	Average Individual Monthly Wage (Range)
Barrels (cooperage)	1	6	$ 50
Boots and shoes	1	3	25
Carving (wood)	1	10	20
Cigars	1	1	--
Gas (Mobile Gas Co.)	1	20	90
Liquor, distilled	1	2	100
Lumber, planed	1	28	34
Lumber, sawed	2	33	27-33
Machinery	3	102	25-75
Marblework	1	30	60
Meal (grist mill)	2	6	20-50
Metalware (tin, copper, iron)	3	14	75
Oil (rosin, gas, refined, coal)	1	5	100
Plaster ornaments	1	4	40
Soap	1	3	50
Wagons, buggies, carts, drays	1	20	30

SOURCES: Eighth Census, Manufacturing, pp. 8-9; and 1860 U.S. Census, Manufactures, Alabama, Mobile County, ASDAH.

With Mobile's underdeveloped manufacturing sector and its overwhelmingly mercantile character, laborers rarely organized themselves for any purpose. Few industrial firms existed, and most of them had few employees. Because firms varied considerably, few journeymen or artisans had similar grievances at the same time.[7] Yet periodically, when skilled laborers in a trade had serious complaints against their employers, they did organize themselves to stage protests.

Two major protests came after the Panic of 1837 as employers cut wages of local workers and brought in laborers from other areas who would accept wages lower than those demanded by permanent residents. After several years' resentment of competition from journeymen carpenters who came to Mobile in the winter to work for low pay, local carpenters resorted to violence in February 1839. Breaking windows and doors and destroying some furniture, protestors attacked a shop that employed "the obnoxious workmen." This "disgraceful riot," as the *Mobile Register* labeled it, dissipated as firemen arrived on the scene to arrest "the spirit of misrule." Volunteer militia companies then guarded other areas threatened by attack because they contained "some buildings erected under the contracts which excited the ire of the other workmen." Reporting that some of "the respectable mechanics of the city" had disavowed any connection with the protest, the *Mobile Register* theorized that "the great body of the intelligent and well-behaved carpenters would themselves turn out and put down any attempt to destroy property or endanger the persons of any one, no matter what may be the offence."[8]

Shortly after the incident mechanics called a meeting to discuss grievances. "We hope every respectable mechanic of the place will make it a sacred duty to attend," the *Register* implored, "and give a correct tone to the direction of the proceedings." According to the newspapers, the carpenters whose work was attacked had committed no crime, for they were pursuing their vocation in a way consistent with natural freedom.[9] The outcome of the mechanics' meeting is unfortunately not known.

Whatever resolution, if any, of the mechanics' problem was reached, employers in at least one other enterprise continued to bring in outsiders whose wages undercut those of local workers. Rather than engage in violence as carpenters did, journeymen tailors ran a notice in the *Mobile Register* in November 1840 to explain their grievances. Contending that they were not "standing out for higher prices" as their employers maintained, tailors argued that they were instead resisting wage cuts. Employers had announced they would no longer pay wages in effect since 1836. Their new schedule of prices reduced wages to journeymen tailors by at least three dollars per week. According to local journeymen, their employers had brought in large numbers of tailors from the North with the promise of plenty of work at 1836 prices, only to inform them about the new wage schedule after their arrival in Mobile. Local tailors wished the public to know about this breach of faith by their employers. Explaining that journeymen tailors did not usually make written contracts with their employers on the assumption that workers were dealing with "high minded and honorable men," journeymen argued that employers in Mobile had failed to meet this standard by practicing deliberate deception.[10] Journeymen ran their notice in the newspaper, yet no evidence exists to show that their protest made their employers halt the practice of importing cheap competitors for the labor force. Tailors and carpenters successfully attracted public attention to their grievances, but both informal groups of skilled laborers apparently failed to get remedies for themselves.

In contrast to journeymen carpenters and tailors, printers succeeded in negotiating a satisfactory settlement of their wage demands, primarily because of their organization and freedom from competition with outsiders. Since Mobile's earliest American days, newspapers had had difficulty engaging an adequate number of journeymen printers. For the mutual benefit of employer and employee, printers organized the Mobile Typographical Association in 1837. According to its constitution, the employer received a promise that employees would not interfere in his business, would secure for him a certain number of apprentices, and would give adequate notice or locate a suitable replacement for an employee leaving his job. Employees gained protection from runaway apprentices and poorly trained printers. Association members won preference for employment. Initially, harmonious relations prevailed between members of the Mobile Typographical Association and their employers, who attended a dinner celebrating Independence Day in 1838.[11]

By 1854 inflation and hard times prompted typesetters in the offices of the *Mobile Register* and *Mobile Advertiser*, the major dailies, to strike for higher wages. Whether or not the strikers belonged to the typographical association is unclear, but they did use organized bargaining to press their demands. Strikers demanded a 25 percent increase in wages paid per amount of type set, which would raise their average daily wage from $2.60 to $3.25. Typesetters in the *Alabama Planter* office did not join the strike. Its editor maintained that the wage demand was too high in comparison to the profits of the local newspaper business. Admitting that prices had risen for food, rent, and clothing, the *Planter* did acknowledge the right of the printer to receive a good livelihood in view of the late hours and few holidays required by his work. The *Planter* nevertheless hoped that its competitors would not yield to strikers' terms.[12]

Journeymen printers and their employers managed to reach "a just settlement" on October 31, nearly eight months after the announcement of the typesetters' demands. Printers won a 12.5 percent increase, or half of what they had originally stipulated. "The increased cost of living and the demand for labor of whatever kind, rendered this movement natural and proper," reported the *Mobile Advertiser* as it an-

nounced the adjustment of the difference of opinion between proprietors and printers.[13] Any other disagreements regarding printers'
wages were apparently resolved without recourse to strikes. Strikes
were viewed as a last resort by the National Typographical Union, with
which the Mobile Typographical Union affiliated in 1857.[14]

If the vast majority of Mobile's skilled workers were white, slaves
supplied much of the city's semiskilled and unskilled labor. They worked
as domestics and body servants, carriage drivers and draymen, mechanics, and press hands.[15] Their representation in the population remained
large throughout the antebellum decades, which indicates their signifi-
cance in the local economy. Slaves increased in numbers each decade,
particularly in the 1830s and 1840s when Mobile experienced its most
rapid expansion (see Tables 4-2, 4-3). Compared to whites and free
blacks, however, slaves declined as a part of the population, dropping
from almost 37 percent of the total in 1830 to almost 26 percent in 1860
(see Table 4-4). This relative decline resulted from a number of factors,
not the least of which were, in the 1850s, the rising purchase prices of
slaves and competition in menial jobs from immigrants.

Until the 1850s Mobile served as the slave-trading center of the
state. Dealers shipped slaves by water from Maryland, Virginia, and
the Carolinas to Mobile. There local residents and planters from southwestern Alabama and southeastern Mississippi made their purchases.
Visitors returned home via the Alabama or Tombigbee River with
their new bondsmen. After rail lines connected Montgomery with the
Atlantic states in the 1850s, the state capital soon equalled and perhaps
surpassed Mobile in the volume of its slave trade. Planters who sold
cotton in Mobile, however, consistently bought and sold slaves there.
For most of the antebellum period, the slave market stood on the west
side of Royal Street between St. Louis and St. Anthony streets. Nearby
a three-story barracks housed slaves between auctions. In an effort to
make this unpleasant aspect of the slave trade less conspicuous, the city
eventually banned slave depots from the downtown area.[16]

Slave trade proceeded virtually unabated throughout the antebellum period. For brief periods, from 1827 to 1829 and for a few months
in 1832, Alabama passed laws prohibiting the introduction of slaves
into the state by professional traders. The Anti-Immigration Act of
1832, passed in response to the Nat Turner slave revolt in Virginia the
previous year, calmed public fears that unscrupulous traders would sell

WORKING PEOPLE

Table 4-2. Population of Mobile by Racial Group and Sex, 1830-60

	White		Free Black		Slave		
Year	Male	Female	Male	Female	Male	Female	Total
1830	1,094	553	172	200	611	564	3,194
1840	5,655	2,607	250	291	1,901	1,968	12,672
1850	7,022	5,975	286	429	3,212	3,591	20,515
1860	11,509	9,345	355	462	3,871	3,716	29,258

SOURCES: Fifth Census, pp. 100-101; Sixth Census, pp. 244-45; Seventh Census, p. 422; and Eighth Census, Population, p. 9.

Table 4-3. Percentage of Decennial Population Growth by Racial Group in Mobile, 1830-60

Racial Group	1830-40	1840-50	1850-60
White	402	57	60
Free Black	45	32	14
Slave	229	76	12
Total	297	62	43

SOURCES: Fifth Census, pp. 100-101; Sixth Census, pp. 244-45; Seventh Census, p. 422; and Eighth Census, Population, p. 9.

Table 4-4. Whites, Free Blacks, and Slaves as Percentages of the Population of Mobile, 1830-60

Year	Whites	Free Blacks	Slaves
1830	51.6	11.6	36.8
1840	65.2	4.3	30.5
1850	63.4	3.5	33.2
1860	71.3	2.8	25.9

SOURCES: Fifth Census, pp. 100-101; Sixth Census, pp. 244-45; Seventh Census, p. 422; and Eighth Census, Population, p. 9.

rebellious slaves from the Upper South to the Lower South. As this anxiety subsided, the intrastate slave trade resumed.[17]

An illicit market in Mobile supported foreign slave trade despite the federal prohibition against it since 1808. Reports appeared occasionally of African natives working in the city. In March 1859, according to the British consul, "twenty wild African Negroes" worked in Mobile. Since these Africans spoke only their native dialect, residents concluded that the slaves were recently imported. Their appearance sparked excitement among the citizens about the foreign slave trade.[18] Later in 1859 the schooner *Clotilde*, owned by the northern-born steamboat builder Timothy Meaher, transported what was reputedly the last cargo of contraband slaves from Africa to the United States. Slavers then transferred 116 survivors of this voyage to John Dabney's plantation on the Alabama River a few miles north of Mobile. Some slaveowners in the area secretly purchased some of the Africans, and the shipowner and captain retained the rest.[19]

Local domestic slave sales slowed somewhat in the 1850s as prices rose to new highs. Sellers could still find buyers, but the process took more time than usual. Early in 1859 Alfred Witherspoon sold two female slaves, apparently dining room servants, in an effort to pay off some debts. He received $1,100 for one woman and $1,140 for the other.[20] By the fall prices rose even higher. "Good men" sold for as much as $1,750 and "good field girls" $1,500. These prices made buyers "very scarce," according to one local observer.[21] In November, male slaves aged eighteen to thirty-three brought prices ranging from $1,410 to $1,875. These costs resembled those in New Orleans, where, as in Mobile, bondsmen sold slowly.[22] Steep prices meant that purchasing slave laborers was increasingly difficult for many.

Slave ownership remained confined to a small proportion of the free population of Mobile, slightly less than 6 percent in 1830 and 1840, 8.6 percent in 1850, and slightly less than 6 percent in 1860.[23] Masters and mistresses came from widely different backgrounds and occupations. In 1860 native New Englanders like Thaddeus Sanford, a newspaper publisher turned farmer; Gustavus Horton, a cotton broker; and William Rix, a merchant, owned slaves. So did foreign-born Mobilians like Israel I. Jones and Jonathan Emanuel, English-born merchants; Ann Yuille, a Scottish baker's widow; and Albert Stein, a German-born hydraulic engineer. The largest numbers of slaves belonged to two native southern businessmen, James E. Saunders (124) and Duke W. Goodman (106). The Factors Cotton Press owned 95 slaves and the brickmaker A. H. Ryland owned 61.[24] Individual wealth and business profits facilitated these large slaveholdings. Averages remained much smaller, 5 per owner in 1850, in keeping with the pattern of urban slaveholding elsewhere in the South.[25]

As costs of purchasing bondsmen increased, slave hiring provided an advantageous option for those who wished to utilize black labor. Employers might pay only for the services they needed rather than commit themselves to the lifetime maintenance of slaves. By hiring out their slaves, owners could generate steady income, employ surplus servants, and spare themselves from some of the responsibility for day-to-day supervision of their bondsmen. Owners attempted to ensure that their slaves would not learn bad habits while working for someone else. In 1828 Dr. Solomon Mordecai placed his "supernumerary" slave Phil with a carpenter, "preferring," he said, "to afford him an opportunity to become useful to himself and me in this way, to hiring him out at the risk of his getting into bad habits." Soon Mordecai received $15 per month as a fee for Phil's services to the carpenter. One of Mordecai's other hired-out slaves brought in $12.50 per month for unspecified work in 1830, but he was "often indisposed" and Mordecai decided to sell him for $400 and invest the money more judiciously.[26] By 1835, with the city expanding rapidly and labor in short supply, some hired slaves could draw $30 to $40 monthly for their masters. A few years later, during the depression that followed the Panic of 1837, hired slaves apparently earned lower wages. For instance, the proprietors of Haviland, Clark and Company, a drug firm, paid $26 per month to the owner of a twenty-one-year-old male slave who worked in the store. By the 1850s, when unskilled labor was especially plentiful, hired slaves earned low wages, sometimes as low as $10 per month for servants on steamboats and in private homes.[27]

Income from renting out slaves helped to support a number of well-to-do widows whose husbands had willed bondsmen to them. In 1850, 191 women owned 807 slaves. Women made up nearly 10 percent of large slaveholders, those with 11 or more slaves, in 1850. By renting some of their slaves to local employers, widows received good incomes. Sarah Barnes, sixth largest slaveowner in Mobile in 1850, presumably rented some of her 52 slaves to others. So did two other women with large slaveholdings in the 1857 city tax book: Eliza Goldthwaite, widow of a former state judge, who claimed 17 slaves, and Sarah Walton, widow of a former mayor of Mobile and mother of Octavia Walton Levert, who owned 20 slaves.[28]

Employers usually hired slaves for the business season in Mobile, from November through May. Work began on 1 November, when "most people engage[d] their servants for the season." During the summer, when many well-to-do residents left the city, slaveowners advertised a number of slaves, mostly domestics, for hire until 1 November. Owners might accept lower wages for their bondsmen during the summer, for they knew that wages rose in the fall.[29]

Arrangements for the hiring of slaves might be made directly with slaveowners or their agents or through clearinghouses established in newspaper or theater offices. Mobilians assisted their relatives elsewhere in the south who wished to hire out their extra slaves in the port city. Solomon Mordecai hired out a slave who belonged to his sister in Virginia. Colin J. McRae assisted his mother in Mississippi with the hiring of three of her slaves in Mobile. Sometimes the management of someone else's slaves vexed the intermediary. Solomon Mordecai, one exasperated agent, wrote his sister Ellen that he had smoothed out another problem between her hired slave Jenny and Jenny's employer "with the premonition that any further complaints would have to be settled by a police officer."[30]

Some masters allowed their slaves to hire their own time and to rent their own places of residence with part of their wages. Failing to halt the "living out" practice with prohibitory ordinances, city government adopted a policy of monitoring it with permits issued for slaves who had their masters' permission to live apart from them. Badges worn by slaves with these permits cost five dollars. Two hundred badges were sold in 1855, when an estimated 1,000 out of 6,900 slaves lived apart from their masters. Slaves who lived away from their owners without permission or compliance with registration rules fell subject to one-dollar fines, while their owners faced fines of ten dollars for neglect. This intervention by the city goverment in residence arrangements made by slaves and their masters failed to curb violations.[31] Furthermore, authorities lacked the power to enforce ordinances against slaves who lived outside the city limits. By the 1850s numerous slaves congregated just outside the city limits, yet many of them found employment within the city.[32]

Besides slaves, free blacks filled labor positions. Their numbers remained small, less than 3 percent of the free labor force in 1860.[33] Opportunities available for work in Mobile attracted increasing numbers of the state's free blacks to reside in the port city. Mobile had about 33 percent of Alabama's free blacks in 1840, 41 percent in 1850, and 50 percent in 1860. There, as in other Gulf Coast ports, free blacks found more respect for their liberty and more occupational opportunity than in other parts of the South.[34]

Free blacks in Mobile came from two backgrounds: Creole and non-Creole. Creoles were descended from early white settlers, mostly French and Spanish single men who formed liaisons with slave women. Most black Creoles in antebellum Mobile were descendants of one of these early settlers: Jean Chastang, Hilaire Dubroca, William Mitchell, Frank Mitchell, Simon L'Andre, Honore Collins, Auguste Collins, Nanette Durette, or Regis Bernody. Born in Alabama, they had French or Spanish surnames. A few came from Louisiana or Florida. Manumitted in the eighteenth century through liberal Spanish laws, they won protection for their freedom in the treaties by which the United States acquired Louisiana in 1803 and Florida in 1819. Other free blacks moved to Mobile in the later antebellum decades from other places in Alabama or from the Upper South. They generally had English or Scottish surnames. Blacks of Creole descent, with longer residence in the area and often higher social status, remained aloof from the American freedmen.[35]

A few free blacks in Mobile were manumitted by their masters locally during the antebellum period with approval by acts of the legislature. Of the 278 slaves legally emancipated in Alabama from 1818 through 1846, 73 lived in Mobile, and most of them were manumitted before 1832.[36] Certainly the most famous manumission was that by popular subscription of Pierre Chastang in 1819. Born in Mobile in 1779, Pierre Chastang was the son of Jean Chastang, a white physician, who sold him to Regis Bernody in 1810 or 1811. During the Indian wars in the Alabama Territory, Andrew Jackson appointed Pierre Chastang to take provisions to troops at Fort Mims and at Mount Vernon. Chastang successfully handled this dangerous mission. During the yellow fever epidemic in the summer of 1819, he provided essential service to the city by caring for the sick, burying the dead, and protecting the property of absentee residents. When merchants returned in the fall to find their stores in order, they quickly subscribed funds to purchase freedom for Pierre Chastang as a reward for his meritorious service. They also bought him a horse and dray so that he could earn his living as a drayman. Upon his death in 1848, the *Alabama Planter* lauded Pierre Chastang, observing, "No person in this community, white or black, was ever more highly esteemed or respected, and no one in his sphere has been a more conspicuous, honest, benevolent and upright man."[37]

Pierre Chastang's manumission provided the only case of civic subscription; other manumissions came from individual owners. Joshua Kennedy, for instance, bequeathed freedom and $5,000 in 1838 to his slave Mary Ann for her faithful service during his long illness. Abraham Shanklin, a free black, arranged for the manumission of his wife Keissey in 1844. Patrick McLoskey freed his slave William the same year. Upon his appointment to the U.S. Supreme Court in 1853, John A. Campbell emancipated his slaves, all of whom were domestics.[38] Each of these manumissions required an act of the legislature to legitimize it.

In whatever manner they acquired their freedom, free blacks, Creole and non-Creole, held a variety of skilled and unskilled labor positions. Listings in the 1839 city directory included five grocers, five barbers, three shoemakers, three butchers, three carpenters, one bricklayer, one blacksmith, one fisherman, one drayman, and one wood merchant.[39] By 1860 the largest numbers of free black male heads of household worked either in building trades (as carpenters, bricklayers, or painters) or as unskilled laborers (see Table 4-5). Compared to their white counterparts, a greater proportion of free black male heads of household held service and labor positions. A smaller percentage of free black male heads of household engaged in commerce than white males, and very few of those who carried on trade did so at the proprietary level, meaning that they had at least five hundred dollars' worth of property. Free black male heads of household reported no gainful employment almost twice as often as their white counterparts.

Stiff competition developed in the labor force of Mobile and other southern ports late in the antebellum period when increasing numbers of white immigrants sought jobs formerly held by slaves and free blacks. By 1860 the free male labor force of Mobile consisted of 50 percent foreign-born, 34 percent southern-born, and 16 percent northern-born workers.[40] In the 1850s visitors repeatedly commented on the large representation of white immigrants, particularly Irishmen and Ger-

Table 4-5. Occupations of White Male Heads of Household and Free Black
Male Heads of Household, 1860

Occupational Category[a]	White Males		Free Black Males	
	N	%	N	%
Agriculture/fishing	10	2.3	2	1.8
Building	43	9.8	24	21.4
Manufacturing	68	15.6	14	12.5
Transport	29	6.6	5	4.5
Commerce, proprietor[b]	72	16.5	2	1.8
Commerce, employee[c]	77	17.6	16	14.3
Professions	14	3.2	0	0
Service (nonprofessional and public)	20	4.6	7	6.3
Semiskilled labor	18	4.1	9	8.0
Unskilled labor	66	15.1	24	21.4
Gentleman	1	0.2	0	0
None	19	4.3	9	8.0
Total[d]	437	99.9*	112	100.0

SOURCE: Eighth Census, Free Population Schedule.

[a] Occupations included in each category are listed in the appendix.
[b] Includes, besides clerks, etc., merchants with less than $500 worth of property.
[c] Includes various merchants with $500 or more of property.
[d] Includes for white males every tenth head of household in the 1860 census drawn for the sample used in chapter 3 and for free black males, a much smaller group, each head of household.
*Rounding error.

mans, among the ranks of unskilled workers in Mobile. "The Irish and the Germans seem to do nearly all the work of the streets," reported John S. C. Abbott. "Here, as in New Orleans," he noted, "I was surprised to see how effectually free labor seems to have driven slave labor from the wharves and streets."[41] Immigrant men assumed many unskilled positions. Of the unskilled laborers among the white male heads of household included in the sample compiled from the 1860 census for Table 4-5, more than three-quarters were foreign-born. Moreover, almost all of the foreign-born unskilled laborers came from Ireland. Their presence in the labor force helped to account for the proportional decline of slaves in the population, from 33 percent in 1850 to 26 percent in 1860.

White women, native-born and foreign-born, became a more prominent part of the gainfully employed population in the late antebellum decades. Nationally, about half of all women never worked for wages. Of the other half, about two-thirds stopped work at the time of marriage while the remaining third continued their wage labor. Increasingly, women in the work force, particularly in cities, tended to come from the ranks of the poor, immigrants, and those without male support. According to estimates, less than 5 percent of married women worked outside their homes for wages. By 1860, according to estimates derived from census figures, no more than 15 percent of all females participated in the wage-labor force at any one time. More women probably worked for wages from their homes, perhaps taking in sewing, laundry, or boarders. Others, influenced by the domestic ideology that exalted homemaking and denigrated employment outside the home, probably failed to report their occupations to census takers.[42] Thus census figures undercount working women.

Before the 1860 census, which for the first time listed occupations of women, information regarding women's employment comes primarily from city directories and secondarily from selected census schedules. City directories basically provided listings of persons in business and thus included at least some of the women engaged in commercial activities. According to the 1839 directory, white women operated twenty-seven boarding houses and eleven shops of various sorts. Listings also appeared for six dressmakers, four milliners, five teachers, and one midwife. The 1852 business directory included twenty-seven female boardinghouse operators, eighteen dressmakers, twelve milliners, and five shopkeepers. Twenty Catholic nuns, eight teachers, and one midwife also appeared in the directory. Three years later another commercial directory listed thirty-three boardinghouse or hotel proprietors, twenty-one storekeepers, fourteen milliners, seven dressmakers, and one regalia worker as well as twenty Roman Catholic nuns, eight teachers and two midwives.[43]

According to the United States Census for Manufactures in 1850, women made up about 8 percent of the industrial labor force, or 42 of 544 workers. Women found jobs in six enterprises, where they made up the following percentages of employees: millinery, 100 percent; clothing making, 41 percent; confectionaries, 14 percent; cabinetmaking, 6 percent; brickmaking, 4 percent; and sawmills, 2 percent. For these tasks milliners earned twenty dollars per month; clothing makers ten to twenty; confectioners, ten to twenty-five; cabinetmakers, twenty-five; brickmakers, ten to fourteen; and sawmill workers, ten. Monthly wages for their male counterparts in industrial work ranged higher: bakers, ten dollars to thirty-three dollars; confectioners, seventeen to thirty; tailors, twenty-five to forty; furniture makers, forty to sixty; and sawmill hands, fifteen.[44]

White women also worked as live-in domestic servants. In 1850 households where Irish women unrelated to the family resided, presumably as servants, included those of Jefferson Hamilton, a Methodist clergyman; Philip Phillips, an attorney; H. A. Schroeder, a merchant; and William Strickland, a bookseller.[45] Opposition to slavery, preference for white servants, limited investment capital, or some combination of these factors explained the employment of Irish female domestics.

In 1860, 873 of 9,807 free females listed an occupation. In other words, 8.9 percent of the free female population of Mobile reported gainful employment. Working women tended to be either heads of households or single women who lived apart from a family unit. Dependent adult women and minors constituted a relatively small number of the total employed females.[46]

Females composed 10.4 percent of the total free work force of Mobile in 1860. They dominated domestic service. Many Irish women found positions as servants at better hotels in Mobile. For instance, of the forty-seven female servants at the Battle House in 1860, forty-five were Irish. Employment of Irish servants conformed to a pattern followed by hotels in New Orleans as well. In Mobile women worked in a number of skilled crafts, particularly as seamstresses, dressmakers, and milliners. In the teaching profession women slightly outnumbered men, with forty-nine females and forty-four males. In addition, several of the nineteen Roman Catholic sisters served as teachers, while others were nurses. Six women provided services as midwives.[47] Women also engaged in commerce, primarily operating boardinghouses but also running various shops.

More than eighty white women supported themselves through prostitution. Only five listed their occupations directly as "ill fame" in the 1860 census. Seventy-four others, identifying themselves as "female lodgers," resided in one of four "female lodging houses" located close to each other in the outlying seventh ward. A "mistress of the house," who claimed considerable property, headed each all-female household.[48] This relatively large proportion of white women prostitutes stemmed in part from limited employment opportunities for white women in a southern city where slave women did many of the jobs that white women claimed in northern cities.

Free children also found gainful employment in Mobile. Some 353, all but two of whom were ages twelve to seventeen, listed employment in the 1860 census.[49] A number of these working adolescents came from households headed by single women. Their sons, usually ages fifteen to seventeen, reported employment as bricklayers, clerks, laborers, and painters. Daughters worked as dressmakers. Young people thus earned wages that were vital to the support of their families.

Local orphanages facilitated child labor by providing that older children who were capable of supporting themselves might be bound out to respectable persons in the community. The Protestant Orphanage Asylum Society required that orphans in its care "must have religious instruction, moral examples and habits of industry inculcated on their minds." Young women volunteers taught lessons to the children in a schoolroom at the asylum. School lasted until the Board of Lady Managers deemed the unadopted children "capable of earning their own living" and bound them out "to some reputable persons or families" for purposes approved by the board. In 1844, for instance, "a respectable carpenter" in Mobile adopted a ten-year-old boy after promising the board that he would teach the boy the trade and give him a good education. This carpenter also pledged to give his adopted son a set of valuable tools when he reached his twenty-first birthday. In 1852 the Protestant Orphan Asylum Society sent four of the largest boys to the "Factory at Fulton," presumably the textile mill developing just outside the city.[50]

Managers of the Catholic Orphan Asylums also placed some of their charges at trades. Of the 191 children in the male and female asylums from December 1854 through December 1855, 14 boys and 18 girls were placed out at trades or otherwise removed from the orphanages. How many of them were adopted cannot be determined from available records. Some of the older girls who remained in the girls' orphanage contributed toward their support by working as dressmakers. In 1860 seven girls ranging in age from fifteen to twenty-one listed occupations as dressmakers.[51]

The relatively limited availability of employment for white adolescents in southern cities like Mobile apparently influenced immigrants with families to choose northern cities over southern ones for their residence. There, without competition from slaves, white adolescents stood better chances of finding employment to augment their families' earnings. Among immigrants who came to America from 1849 to 1855, single men were the ones most likely to head for Mobile. Mobile received 2⅓ males for every female immigrant from 1849 to 1855, while northeastern ports received immigrants in more balanced sex ratios, 1½ males for each female. Men with families apparently recognized that northeastern ports, where they entered the country, offered more job opportunities to their dependents than southern cities.[52] Single people, particularly men, were the immigrants most likely to locate in a port like Mobile, still undergoing its first major wave of expansion.

Even with many new immigrants being single males, Mobile's foreign-born population grew 20 percent more than native-born free population during the 1850s. Free residents born in the United States increased 52.7 percent during the decade (from 9,565 in 1850 to 14,610 in 1860), while the foreign-born increased 72.8 percent (from 4,086 to 7,061). This tremendous growth increased the foreign-born percentage of the free population from almost 30 in 1850 to 32.5 in 1860.[53]

In the 1850s, with Mobile's growing foreign-born population competing for jobs, tensions ran high among laborers. Residents resented newly arrived immigrants who competed for their jobs. White workers resented blacks, slave and free, who they thought took certain jobs away from them. Direct statements on these subjects rarely appeared in local newspapers, for editors wished to portray race relations and labor relations as harmonious. Occasional comments nevertheless provide clues regarding tensions among subgroups of laborers.

In 1850 stevedores, who served an important function in the port city, criticized local merchants who preferred to hire people coming from long distances to do the same job. According to the *Mobile Register*, the city had about twenty resident stevedores, "most of whom have families, and are holders of real and personal estate to a considerable value." They paid their share of taxes as "useful, honest, industrious and worthy members of the community." It seemed logical to the *Register* to urge employment of resident stevedores in preference to non-residents because Mobilians spent their wages within the city.[54] Stevedores then contemplated forming an association for their mutual benefit that would protect them and merchants from incompetent stevedores. In 1851 they formed the Baymen's Society, a benevolent group.

Whites struggled to protect themselves from the competition of blacks in their trades. Skilled white craftsmen in milling and carpentry organized themselves for this purpose, forming the Mobile Carpentry and Joiners' Mutual Benefit Society in 1836. This society, one of a very few of the type in antebellum southern cities, served primarily a benevolent function as a mutual aid association. Secondarily the society lobbied to exclude blacks from competition in milling and carpentry trades. Failing to obtain legislation to get slaves excluded from their trades, white artisans focused their resentment on the slaves rather than on their owners, who had successfully blocked the legislation. Sawmills around the city usually employed whites for skilled jobs and blacks for unskilled jobs. On a seasonal basis mill owners and lumber dealers hired slaves to chop wood.[55]

Free blacks who held skilled jobs or conducted small businesses in the city drew the ire of local editors. According to the editor of the *Alabama Planter* in 1853, "There are now among us free negroes whom the law proscribes holding situations which scores of young white men among us would be glad to get."[56] As a way of reducing competition for themselves, whites sometimes deliberately made it hard for free blacks, including Creoles, to conduct business. One place of direct competition was the city market, where vendors of fruits, vegetables, meat, cakes, and other foodstuffs rented stalls to carry on trade. There, in 1841, a free black Creole woman named Polite Collins, a coffee seller, frequently quarreled with a white female vendor from a nearby stall. Polite Collins maintained that the quarrels, which she said she did not cause, exposed her to injustice and exposed the city to racial turmoil and disorder in the market. She petitioned municipal authorities to refund half of the year's rent that she had paid in advance on her stall. In return, she would remove her business from the market. Authorities granted her petition, and she moved her business elsewhere.[57]

Competition perhaps existed in other areas between free black and white women. Of the thirty-six free black female heads of household who listed occupations in the 1860 census, almost two-thirds offered washing and ironing services (see Table 4-6). Well-to-do white women who did not own or hire domestics shunned washing and ironing for themselves. For example, Caroline Plunkett, a widowed schoolteacher,

Table 4-6. Occupations of White Female Heads of Household and Free
Black Female Heads of Household, 1860

Occupational Category[a]	White Females		Free Black Females	
	N	%	N	%
Commerce, employee[b]	5	2.3	0	0.0
Commerce, proprietor[c]	12	5.5	0	0.0
Manufacturing[d]	24	11.0	9	10.8
Nonprofessional service[e]	6	2.8	22	26.5
Public service[f]	6	2.8	0	0.0
Unskilled labor	0	0.0	3	3.6
Miscellaneous[g]	4	1.8	0	0
None	161	73.9	49	59.0
Total[h]	218	100.1*	83	99.9*

SOURCE: Eighth Census, Free Population Schedule.
[a]Occupational categories were modified from those listed in the appendix to suit women at work. Only categories that had some representation are listed here.
[b]Includes merchants, shopkeepers, and landladies with less than $500 worth of property.
[c]Includes various merchants and boardinghouse operators with $500 or more of property.
[d]Consists primarily of dressmakers and seamstresses.
[e]Includes mostly washers and ironers.
[f]Teachers, nuns, and midwives.
[g]Includes women who were apparently prostitutes, listed as lodger, mistress of the house, or ill fame.
[h]Includes for white females every third head of household and for free black females every head of household.
*Rounding error.

would do all of her own household chores for herself except washing.[58] She and other women in her circumstances, plus single men, provided business for free black female washers and ironers, who dominated that service. Some Irishwomen also worked as washerwomen, thus competing with free black women. While free black women numerically dominated the washing and ironing service, white women predominated as dressmakers and seamstresses. About the same proportion of white and free black female heads of household engaged in dressmaking, but the larger number of white women in the population gave them a numerical advantage in this manufacturing pursuit.[59]

Many free blacks engaged in occupations in which their livelihoods depended on whites' patronage. Therefore, they tried not to cause of-

98

fense if at all possible. They knew that whites viewed their freedom with misgivings. "We can have a healthy State of society," the *Mobile Register* maintained in 1859, "with but two classes—white and slave."[60] Keenly aware of this attitude, free blacks tried not to antagonize whites.

Residential separation provided one way of reducing friction between free blacks and whites as well as between affluent and poor whites. By the 1850s the development of the city had proceeded enough to allocate certain areas suitable for construction to various business and residential purposes. In the 1850s Mobile had the same boundaries set by its act of incorporation in 1819. Encompassing about twelve square miles, the city limits included land in a radius of about three miles from the eastern end of Dauphin Street at its intersection with the Mobile River. With the marshy and swampy Mobile River delta on the east, a swamp north of the city between Three Mile and One Mile creeks, and a swampy area west of the city, only about half of this land was suited for development.[61]

The central core of the city, from Congress Street on the north to Monroe Street on the south and from Royal Street west to Lawrence Street, contained most of the better residential construction in the city. People with property worth at least $10,000—merchants, attorneys, physicians, government officials, bankers, and insurance-company officers—generally made their homes in this central district. This area, plus that between Royal Street and the riverfront, also housed many of the city's retail and service establishments: stores, hotels, restaurants, boardinghouses, professional offices, meeting halls, and some churches. By the 1850s this central core of the city had water service and gas lamps. Since all of the district was placed within the fire limits, construction there had to be brick, stone, or masonry.[62]

North and south of the central core came relatively inexpensive residential construction. Ward 1 included docks and facilities for processing cotton: warehouses, presses, and pickeries. Laborers and slaves employed in these places lived in cheap housing nearby. A number of them lived in the area north of Congress Street. This ward included the largest concentration of slaves in any ward. More than 20 percent of slaves in the city lived there, composing more than 50 percent of the population in the ward (see Table 4-7). South of the central core resided many artisans, clerks, and laborers. In areas south of Monroe Street and between Lawrence and Broad streets, residents generally

Table 4-7. Residence of Racial Groups by Wards, 1860

Ward	White		Free Black		Slave		Total (N)
	% of Ward Total	% of Race Total	% of Ward Total	% of Race Total	% of Ward Total	% of Race Total	
1	47.5	6.8	1.3	4.6	51.1	20.2	2,986
2	77.9	15.3	.4	2.1	21.7	11.7	4,087
3	82.7	9.1	.7	2.1	16.6	5.0	2,307
4	68.8	10.0	.8	2.8	30.4	12.1	3,020
5	82.5	10.0	4.0	12.5	13.5	4.5	2,539
6	72.9	35.2	2.8	34.9	24.2	32.1	10,051
7	66.6	13.6	7.9	41.0	25.6	14.4	4,268
Race Total Number (All Wards)	20,854		817		7,587		29,258
Percentage	71.3		2.8		25.9		100.0

SOURCE: Eighth Census, Population, 1:9.

listed taxable wealth less than $5,000 and homes worth less than $3,000. By the 1850s many residences in this area were, according to the tax assessor, multifamily tenements or single-family shanties.[63]

Development also proceeded west of the central core into the sixth and seventh wards. In the 1850s some residents built their own community at the intersection of Spring Hill Road, Ann Street, St. Stephens Road, and Center Street. This West Ward, as they called it, had its own stores, hotel, public school, and Methodist mission.[64]

By the 1850s three-fourths of free blacks in the city resided in the outlying sixth or seventh wards (see Table 4-7). In the early American period up to 1840, free blacks had scattered their homes throughout the city in racially mixed neighborhoods. During the last two antebellum decades, some free blacks continued to live in the downtown area, but most moved to outlying wards. In the 1850s free blacks clustered on three streets: Monroe near the Church Street Graveyard, St. Michael west of Lawrence Street, and Stone near local hospitals and the gas works.[65] Purchase or rental of property in these areas that whites considered undesirable for residences suited the poor financial condition of many free blacks (see Tables 4-8, 4-9).

Free blacks and ethnic minorities in Mobile helped to preserve some of their separate group consciousness by forming their own social and benevolent associations. Other residents generally accepted these associations along with their activities exclusively for members and guests. Organizations of a racial nature were the ones most likely to draw criticism from the community.

Creole blacks formed one of the first exclusive associations, their own volunteer fire company. In 1829 thirty-four free blacks of Creole ancestry volunteered to form a fire company, and the board of aldermen accepted their offer. Aldermen put the group in charge of engine number one and arranged for fire wardens to supervise operations of the company. Members could select their own officers. Arrangements were settled in April 1830, when "Neptune Number 1 Creole Fire Company" was permanently organized.[66] According to its constitution, adopted in 1846, active membership was limited to seventy-five Creole free males at least sixteen years of age.[67]

Members of the Creole Fire Company, as it came to be called, determined to keep their exclusive status as an elite group by discouraging contact with slaves. Creole firemen considered motions for penalizing members who associated with slaves either by expulsion from the

Table 4-8. Real Estate Holdings of Heads of Household by Race and Sex, 1860

Real Estate ($)	White		Free Black	
	Male (%)	Female (%)	Male (%)	Female (%)
0	73.2	75.2	77.7	90.4
1-4,999	15.6	20.2	20.5	9.6
5,000-24,999	7.3	3.7	1.8	0
25,000-49,999	2.1	0.9	0	0
50,000-99,999	0.7	0	0	0
100,000+	1.1	0	0	0
Number of Cases[a]	437	218	112	83

SOURCE: Eighth Census, Free Population Schedule.

[a]Includes every tenth white male, every third white female, and every free black male and female head of household in the 1860 census.

Table 4-9. Personal Estate Holdings of Heads of Household by Race and Sex, 1860

Personal Estate ($)	White		Free Black	
	Male (%)	Female (%)	Male (%)	Female (%)
0	64.1	76.1	85.7	84.3
1-4,999	19.2	17.0	13.4	15.7
5,000-24,999	10.1	6.4	0.9	0
25,000-49,999	3.0	0	0	0
50,000-99,999	2.7	0.5	0	0
100,000+	0.9	0	0	0
Number of Cases[a]	437	218	112	83

SOURCE: Eighth Census, Free Population Schedule.

[a]Includes every tenth white male, every third white female, and every free black male and female head of household in the 1860 census.

company or fines of five dollars per offense. Members did not pass these motions, probably because of the virtual impossibility of their avoiding all association with slaves.[68] These Creole leaders nonetheless made it clear that they frowned on contact with slaves, with whom they felt little if any identity.

Local newspapers praised the Creole Fire Company and individual members. "The Creole company is one of our worthiest fire companies," the *Alabama Tribune* observed, "and its services are highly esteemed and its members well respected by our citizens." According to the *Alabama Planter*, "The Creole company is an old and useful association, and composed of some of the most exemplary of our citizens." Upon the death of one member of the Creole Fire Company, native Mobilian Joseph Laurendine, the *Mobile Register* reported that he was "very much respected by our citizens."[69]

These laudatory comments about Creole firemen did not change the fact that they encountered racial prejudice from whites. Only one direct statement of this prejudice appeared in local newspapers of the antebellum era, yet it provides telling evidence of racism. According to a letter to the editor of the *Alabama Tribune* in 1849, a fire warden ordered a white man from the crowd of onlookers at a fire to take the brakes of Creole Engine Number 1. "We believe that they have the authority for this," the writer admitted, "but one likes to choose his own company, and if compelled to work amongst the quadroons and darkies, where the perfume is not that of the 'orange blossom,' we think the department should furnish cologne for the VICTIM."[70]

Creole firemen also met prejudice within the Mobile Fire Department. The department permitted only one delegate from Creole Company Number 1 to serve on its governing board, and he served in a nonvoting capacity. Companies with white members sent as many as five or six representatives. This arrangement vexed members of the Creole Fire Company, who elected to parade separately on the anniversary of their company's founding rather than join white companies for a parade on the anniversary of the founding of the Mobile Fire Department Association on 9 April 1838. When officers of the fire department invited the Creole Fire Company in 1852 to take its "proper place" in the annual parade, Creole firemen declined. They unanimously adopted a resolution protesting the unequal representation in the department accorded to their company compared to that of others, even ones with fewer members. Members resolved "that this Company with a pride due alike to themselves & the Department have never ask[ed] any favors of thire [sic] Brethrern [sic] of the Department—all they have ever clamed [sic] is simple justice." Failing to receive justice, the company resolved that it would never accept "anything from the fire Department as a Favor while its [*sic*] theirs by *right* of justice & honor." Members nevertheless agreed to pay their portion of expenses for the fire department, except costs of the annual parade.[71] In so doing they maintained the integrity of their company, while they also assumed their civic obligations.

The Creole Fire Company conducted its own social and charitable activities separately from those of white fire companies. Beginning annually in the 1840s, late each April Creole Fire Company Number 1 staged a torchlight parade from its engine house on Joachim Street between Dauphin and St. Francis streets that wound through nearby streets before returning to the engine house for a ball. This celebration provided the highlight of the company's social calendar and that of the Creole black community. Creole firemen appointed their own relief committee to visit sick members and placed monies from fines and dues that were not needed for repairs to their engine in a separate charitable fund to meet their members' needs. Periodically the Creole Fire Company also aided the Creole Free School in the 1850s by allowing the school to hold a benefit ball in the hall above the engine house.[72] Children of the members, as Creoles, were eligible to attend this school, which provided educational opportunities that were denied by state law to other free blacks and slaves.

No other volunteer fire company had such an exclusive membership as the Creole. Of the eight fire companies for whites, only the Mechanics Fire Company Number 7 provided evidence of any tendencies toward ethnic exclusiveness. Men with Irish surnames made up half of its roster in 1860. The Ancient Order of Hibernians met regularly at the engine house of Mechanics Fire Company in 1860, a fact that further indicates the group's close ties with Irishmen.[73] Merchants Fire Company Number 4 presumably drew its members from men engaged in commerce. Other companies accepted a cross section of men with different ethnic backgrounds and occupations. Members received exemptions from jury and militia duty. They also enjoyed social contacts with fellow members and guests at balls each year.

Several militia companies accepted only members of particular ethnic origins. Black Creoles had no militia company during the antebellum era, although they, like their counterparts in New Orleans, had had a unit during colonial days. In the 1820s Mobile's foreign-born had two militia companies: Irish Independent Greens and Mobile Grenadiers. Exiled Bonapartists founded the latter company, which patterned its uniforms after those worn by Napoleon's troops. By the 1850s Mobile had eleven militia companies, two of which maintained ethnically exclusive rolls.[74] Lafayette Guards accepted natives of France. German Fusiliers accepted natives of German states, the fastest-growing element of the foreign-born population (see Table 4-10). Fusiliers sponsored a ball each winter. They staged a special celebration in June 1858 to accept a flag made by their wives, daughters, and sweethearts. After marching to Holly's Garden for the presentation ceremony and refreshments, German Fusiliers returned to the armory for a grand ball.[75]

Mobile's German-born residents supported the Turners Society, formed in 1851. Following the customs of their homeland, Turners celebrated May Day with gymnastics, singing, and other amusements. Members of the German Turners Society marched from downtown to Holly's Garden for their activities. Their parade made a "becoming show" in 1856, according to the *Mobile Register*. "Their band was splendid—for every German is a musician," contended the *Register*, "and their uniform quite national, being of brown Hollands." As a "quiet, orderly and well regulated body," seventy Turners marched in their annual parade for 1857. For the celebration in 1858, friends from New Orleans joined the Turners in Mobile for the parade, activities at Holly's Garden, and a ball at the Odd Fellows Hall. In 1859 the German Turners Society held its gymnastics activities at Heller's Garden, perhaps a new name for its previously used site.[76]

German-born Mobilians enthusiastically supported the German Dramatic Association, a touring company that visited in 1858 to perform theatricals for natives of Germany, particularly those who had not yet mastered the English language. *Die Deutschen Einwander* (*The German Immigrants*) attracted "an overflowing audience." Performers also staged vaudeville acts that were popular in Europe.[77]

A Schiller festival in 1859 attracted participation from Mobilians without regard to their national origins. The celebration on 10 November coincided with ones in other American cities to commemorate the hundredth anniversary of the birth of the German poet best known to English readers. Two German-born merchants, Jacob Bloch and S. H. Goetzel, took subscriptions for festival activities, which attracted sizable numbers of residents. Nearly 200 people enjoyed a champagne banquet prepared by one of the city's French restaurateurs. Others

Table 4-10. Increase of the Foreign-Born Population, 1850-60

Native Country	Number, 1850	Number, 1860	Percentage of Increase
Ireland	2,009	3,307	64.6
Germany	513	1,276	148.7
England	547	663	21.2
France	303	538	77.6
Scotland	205	318	55.1
Other	509	959	88.4

SOURCES: Seventh Census, Mortality, 2:38-39; and Eighth Census, Population, 1:xxxi.

attended a concert that featured an opening address in German by S. Schlesinger, a speech in English by John Forsyth, a Georgia-born editor, and musical numbers including a duet by J. and S. Schlesinger. "Altogether, the festival was a perfect success," reported the *Mobile Register*, "worthy of the occasion, worthy of our German population, and reflecting the highest credit on those people who took part in the execution of the programme."[78]

From Mobile's earliest American days, Irishmen organized to celebrate St. Patrick's Day and to aid their compatriots in need. "For the relief of natives of Ireland and their descendants," they formed the Hibernian Benevolent Society in 1822. Each year the Hibernians gave a St. Patrick's Day dinner for members and guests. Irishmen who were not members of the Hibernian Benevolent Society formed their own association, the Irish Benevolent and Naturalization Society, in 1837. A deputation from the older, more prestigious society visited the junior association's dinner in 1838. The next year the two societies merged, coordinating their social and charitable activities. Members unanimously elected the former president of the junior society as president of the united association. The Hibernian Benevolent Society continued to sponsor a dinner and a ball on St. Patrick's Day. Proceeds from the ball benefited a relief fund for Irish immigrants, especially widows and orphans.[79]

Like benevolent societies, churches served certain ethnic, class, or racial groups. During the colonial era the Catholic church served French and Spanish settlers, but the religious preferences of residents diversified considerably during the antebellum years. Yet "Catholics, descended from the oldest French and Spanish families," remained "numerous and influential."[80] By 1850, however, Irishmen, many of whom had arrived in the 1840s, constituted the largest single nationality among Catholics. They perhaps attended services at the Cathedral of the Immaculate Conception, which was constructed downtown in the 1840s to replace a small wooden chapel that could no longer hold the congregation. Irish Catholics more likely worshipped in the Parish of St. Vincent de Paul, which was organized for them in 1847. The next year they built a church on Charleston Street in a working-class neighborhood. In 1858 St. Joseph's Church reached out to people living farther west of the core of the city on Spring Hill Avenue.[81]

Episcopalians served no particular ethnic group, yet they formed churches that catered to specific social classes. Affluent Episcopalians most likely joined Christ Church, the oldest congregation. Formed in 1826, Christ Church met in a stone sanctuary that was built from 1835 to 1840 on the southwest corner of Jackson and St. Francis streets. By the mid-1840s Christ Church proved inadequate to serve the city's growing population, so Episcopalian clergymen organized Trinity parish in 1846. Founded as a free church, Trinity Church did not follow the custom of renting pews to members but instead collected free-will offerings for its support. In 1853, when the congregation outgrew its quarters in the Musical Hall on St. Anthony Street, members constructed an English Gothic church on the corner of St. Anthony and Jackson streets.[82] Affluent Episcopalians who lived in the suburbs of Mobile belonged to either St. Mary's Church in Summerville or St. Paul's in Spring Hill, both of which were organized in the 1850s.

St. John's parish grew the fastest of all Episcopalian parishes as it served working-class people in the southern part of the city. After holding services in private homes for some time, priests decided to erect a mission building in 1853. They selected a site on the southeast corner of Dearborn and Monroe streets in a thickly populated area where the 3,000 residents had no church convenient to them. Three members of prestigious Christ Church purchased the building lot and other members of that congregation donated funds to construct a "rural Gothic" style church. The trio of generous benefactors who had bought the building lot resolved to pay the salary of a minister for St. John's Church so that the poor could hear the Gospel free of expense.[83]

Methodists "seem to be incomparable beggars, and press forward where other denominations are afraid to venture, and find success where others find nothing but discouragements," reported one visiting clergyman.[84] Methodists indeed established a number of missions that evolved into churches. From the first mission, established in 1826, developed the Bee Hive Methodist Church, as it came to be called for its members' industriousness. In 1840 members of this congregation organized the Jackson Street Church on the corner of Jackson and St. Michael streets in a rented building. During the next three years these Methodists erected on the corner of St. Francis and Joachim streets a sanctuary that became the St. Francis Street Methodist Church.[85]

Methodists further extended their ministries in the 1840s and 1850s by establishing three missions. One chapel served West Ward. A German Mission reached immigrants in the vicinity of St. Francis and Wilkinson (later Washington) streets. A former college professor and editor of a German-language newspaper, the Reverend George Rottenstein, headed the German Mission, which featured children's Sunday-school classes in the German language. "The cause should commend itself to every good citizen," noted the *Mobile Register*, "and we hope it may receive the encouragement which it merits." Methodists also launched the South Ward Mission or Wesley Chapel in a working-class neighborhood in the southern part of the city, traditionally a stronghold of Catholicism. Organized by established Methodist churches in the early 1850s, this mission was located on the corner of Warren and New Hampshire (later Augusta) streets.[86]

Neither Presbyterians nor Baptists established any missions directed specifically toward immigrants. However, both denominations founded churches in the downtown area and in western areas that were settled in the 1840s and 1850s. As the first church of its denomination in the city, Government Street Presbyterian Church, founded in 1831, attracted the most prestigious congregation. Other Presbyterian churches served the population moving west of Government Street: Second Presbyterian, founded in 1842 on Jackson Street; Third Presbyterian, organized in 1853 and soon located on the northeast corner of Jackson and St. Michael streets; and Fourth Presbyterian, organized as a mission in 1852 and located on the corner of Broad and Dauphin streets.[87]

Financial problems contributed to the organizational problems of

108

Baptists. Of all Protestants, Baptists received the least support from the city's wealthiest people. Most members of the early Baptist churches were women who had no incomes of their own. The few male members had limited means. The failure of efforts to raise enough money to build sanctuaries contributed to the demise of the First Baptist Church, organized in 1835 and disbanded in 1840, and the St. Anthony Street Baptist Church, founded in 1840 and dissolved in 1848. The Second Baptist Church, organized in 1845, managed to survive by soliciting funds for a church building from prominent men of other faiths. In its new house of worship, built on St. Francis Street in 1848, the Second Church became known as the St. Francis Street Baptist Church. This congregation even established a mission on the corner of Broad Street and Spring Hill Avenue in 1855, in response to the movement of people westward from the downtown area.[88]

Congregations formed by Unitarians attracted no laborers. Unitarians, who formed a society in the late 1830s, drew a limited following because of their alleged "unchristian tenets," their association with northerners, and their antislavery views. From 1840 to 1860 the Unitarian Society declined in Mobile, as in other southern cities, while proslavery doctrines and religious fundamentalism gained favor. By 1859 the Unitarian congregation had decreased so drastically that Herbert C. Peabody, one of its northern-born members, called it "the Church of the Deserted."[89]

While the Unitarian society disintegrated, Jews managed to form a small congregation. Some Jews had resided in Mobile since the British occupation, and more came during the early American years from England and the northern United States. German Jews began arriving in the 1830s; their numbers increased during the next two decades. Eking out a marginal living through mercantile enterprises, they found the path to prosperity and assimilation difficult. Leadership for a congregation came from two pairs of brothers who had settled in Mobile in the 1830s and established themselves well in business and voluntary associations. Israel I. Jones, an English-born auctioneer and commission merchant, served as the first president of Shaari Shomayim U-Maskil el Dol (Gates of Heaven and Society of Friends of the Needy), which was formed in 1844. Solomon I. Jones, Israel's elder brother and business partner, served as a trustee of the congregation. Commission merchants David and Ezekiel Salomon, whose family came from Pennsylvania, served as the first vice-president and secretary, respectively, of the congregation. In 1846 members purchased a meeting hall on St. Emanuel Street. With about seventy-five families in the 1850s, the congregation moved to a larger building on Jackson Street and in 1858 built its own synagogue.[90]

Local churches and the synagogue provided both spiritual and social associations for their members. While only two churches were specifically established for immigrants, a number of churches in working-class neighborhoods apparently had predominantly foreign-born congregations. Three churches held services in both English and German: St. Joseph's Catholic, St. Paul's Episcopal, and the (Methodist) German Mission. Some churches occasionally arranged for preaching in French, which was the predominant language in Mobile at the time of its American occupation. Numerous residents still spoke French in the mid-1830s, when a priest delivered a sermon in French at the Catholic chapel, "crowded with Creoles, mulattoes, Indians, and Sailors." A clergyman from Paris preached in French at a special afternoon service at Government Street Presbyterian Church in 1851.[91] These accommodations to French-speaking Mobilians and ministries to the German-speaking indicated the cosmopolitan character of the population in the city.

Some of the churches that were founded by whites accepted black members; others sponsored separate congregations. Whatever the arrangement, whites supervised blacks in their church-related activities. Catholics and Presbyterians admitted blacks as members into predominantly white congregations rather than establish separate churches for blacks. Black Creoles, who descended from French or Spanish Catholics, worshipped at the Cathedral of the Immaculate Conception or at St. Vincent de Paul in the sixth ward, where many of them lived in the late antebellum period.[92] Both Government Street Presbyterian Church and the Second Presbyterian Church received black members, some of whom were slaves of the white communicants and others of whom were freedmen. Laymen in these Presbyterian churches examined members, white and black alike, about their religious knowledge and censured "unchristian conduct."[93]

After ministering to blacks through predominantly white churches, Episcopalians did establish one separate congregation for them. For many years Episcopal churches accepted black members, who usually attended services separate from those for whites. Priests sometimes performed baptisms and nonbinding marriages of slaves in their masters' homes. In 1854 Christ and Trinity Episcopal churches organized the Church of the Good Shepherd for a black congregation that had been meeting in homes for several years. This church then accepted black members from the predominantly white sponsoring churches.[94]

Blacks clearly preferred the evangelical faiths. They flocked to white Baptist and Methodist churches in such large numbers that both denominations established separate African missions for them. In these churches blacks achieved as much autonomy as they could within the state's slave code, which required the presence of a set number of whites at assemblies of slaves and forbade slaves to own property, including church buildings. Evidence regarding black churches indicates that slaves, and perhaps some free blacks, routinely tested the limits of their privileges regarding assembly.

White Baptists established separate congregations for blacks from the outset of their activities in Mobile. The First Baptist Church supervised a hundred-member black congregation from 1835 to 1840, when it surrendered its responsibility to the St. Anthony Street Baptist Church. By 1841, "to the grief of this church, and general & manifest discredit of the cause of Christianity," white sponsors claimed that members of the African Branch had abused their privileges of worship by totally insubordinate actions. Consequently, whites resolved to obtain from members of the African Branch "their due subordination to this church." That goal periodically eluded whites. In 1845, for instance, the St. Anthony Street Baptist Church closed the building set aside for its slave members until they "quietly and in a proper spirit submit themselves to the rules and regulations of the church." These regulations placed the black congregation under the direct supervision of a committee from the sponsoring church and of a white ordained pastor "who respects the laws of our Southern institutions." By 1846 the St. Anthony Street and St. Francis Street churches had smoothed out differences with their black members enough to organize for them the African Baptist Church on Stone Street. In 1859 this black congregation asked the St. Francis Street Baptist Church for its "watchcare and protection," lessons in the laws that "protect us from our enemies . . . which we must obey," and instruction "as children of God . . . to know and obey him, and to worship Jesus Christ as the Savior of all believers."[95]

Black Methodists also received their own churches. For many years blacks attended special preaching services on Sunday evening in the churches where whites had worshipped in the morning. A mission established for blacks in 1835 failed later that year. In 1842 the St. Francis Street Methodist Church founded the African Mission on the northeast corner of Dearborn and Church streets. In "one of the most depraved districts of Mobile, which was wont to be full of gaming and drinking houses," this mission reportedly reformed the habits of residents in its vicinity. White Methodists established another church for blacks. In 1853 members of Franklin Street and St. Francis Street Methodist churches resolved to build a separate house of worship for servant members who had been attending special services in the galleries of whites' churches and using the basement rooms for Bible classes and prayer meetings. The new African Mission on State Street, founded in 1854, attracted many members. They built a brick sanctuary valued at $6,000 and paid their pastor, a white minister, $1,200 in 1859.[96]

For their success black churches needed whites' toleration and protection. When whites who lived near African missions complained about the noise there during services, they often harbored the worry that blacks were using the meetings for plotting conspiracies against whites. Other whites favored using the churches as tools for teaching to black congregations lessons of obedience and subservience. For example, in 1840 Reverend Jefferson Hamilton, Duke Goodman, Charles Gascoigne, and others pledged their "*word* and *standing* in the community" to help teach the ideas of subservience to masters and piety to God to blacks attending the African Church on St. Michael Street. These white leaders justified the existence of the mission on the grounds that it accommodated 400 regular worshippers who could not find places to sit in the galleries of other churches.[97] White churchmen supported separate churches for blacks as a way of segregating the races and removing blacks from the galleries of white churches. Most black churches were located in the sixth or seventh wards, west of the central core of the city. There they existed in neighborhoods not too far removed from churches established as missions for working-class whites.

Churches, fire companies, militia companies, occupational organizations, and ethnic benevolent societies offered foreign-born and native-born Mobilians, white and black, a variety of associations through which they might see their friends for social as well as other purposes. These associations allowed some subgroups of laborers to separate themselves from each other. A few skilled laborers, notably printers, formed occupational associations that helped them to improve their wages and working conditions. Well-established Irish and German immigrants distinguished themselves from their destitute countrymen by forming charitable associations. Black Creoles set themselves apart from other free blacks and from slaves in affiliating with their own fire company. Churches throughout the city, especially ones in areas developed in the 1840s and 1850s, served the varied religious preferences of residents. Not only did these diverse associations formed by members of the labor force suit their needs, but they also suited urban leaders. Editorial praise for activities ranging from Turners' May Day outings to Creole Fire Company parades indicated leaders' acceptance. As long as no laborers' group sought to take economic or political power away from their employers, they found favor with the press and municipal officials.

Workers provided vitally needed labor for the port city. Yet they possessed little economic power because relatively few of them owned property, propertyholding being the key to influence in municipal affairs. Among workers, recent immigrants and free blacks, even with long residence in the area, had little spare capital for purchases of property, and slaves had no legal right to own property. Any of their actions that threatened the property of others reaped harsh reaction from the press and police. Working people generally received the most attention from municipal government if they paid taxes to it or committed actions that somehow threatened to disrupt order or destroy property. Even though they exercised limited direct influence in municipal affairs, workers did contribute to urban development.

* 5 *

Municipal Finance and Default

CITY government in antebellum Mobile faced the blessing and burden of rapid expansion. As the obscure colonial village burgeoned into a major export center, it attracted new residents who clamored for city services. Funds to provide these services came largely from property taxes assessed according to the market value of local real estate and personal property. The inflation of the early 1830s, with its increase in property values, boosted the tax base of the city, while the depression following the Panic of 1837 substantially reduced the sources of municipal revenue. Ambitious public improvements undertaken in the booming 1830s on borrowed capital nearly bankrupted the city government when the boom collapsed. Under the specter of default, municipal government struggled to achieve solvency. Financial disaster forced officials to revise accounting procedures and spending policies. Their corrective actions slowly improved not only the balance sheets for city government but also Mobile's national and international credit reputation.

Local government in Mobile was organized in much the same way as governments in other American cities. The mayor acted as an administrator as well as a judge in cases dealing with infractions of city ordinances. The board of aldermen served as the legislative body for the city. Under the city charter of 1819 this board elected the mayor from among its members. In 1826 a revision of the charter permitted popular election of the mayor, in keeping with a nationwide trend toward direct election of mayors.[1] A second legislative body, the common council, was created in 1839 as a check on the actions of the mayor and aldermen. The mayor's judicial duties lessened in 1850 with the creation of the city-court judgeship for handling serious cases.

Requirements for voting in local elections eventually provided for universal adult white male suffrage, as in other antebellum cities. Voters for mayor, aldermen, and councilmen had to have been adult white male residents of the city for one year as freeholders or as city taxpayers. By the 1850s, when aldermen ran for seats by wards, persons who wished to vote for aldermen in a particular ward not only had to have lived in the city for one year but also in that ward for at least twenty days before the election. The first charter required nonfreeholders to rent a tenement or separate room six months before the local election, although later charters omitted this stipulation. Propertyholding was not an absolute requirement for voting in local elections, since a resident might pay a poll tax or a business tax instead of property taxes. Officers, members, and fire wardens of the fire department were exempted from paying poll taxes.[2] Whether a propertyholder or not, in theory virtually any adult white male could qualify for voting.

The number of popularly elected municipal board members increased along with the number of wards to keep pace with a rapidly growing population. In 1822, when the city had seven aldermen, the *Mobile Argus* suggested increasing the number to thirteen, the same number as in Savannah. Admitting that the city with a population of 2,700 did not then need thirteen aldermen, the *Argus* claimed that the city's rapid growth would soon require the larger number. The population indeed quadrupled during the 1830s. Aldermen commissioned two city censuses in the decade to count their constituents. The first census, which was taken in 1833, was supposed to provide the Mobile County delegation to the state legislature with figures to obtain separate representation for the city as permitted by the state constitution. The aldermen failed to win the extra representation, but they obtained an accurate count of the 5,901 residents in four wards (labeled West, North, Middle, and South) drawn in March 1833. The city grew so quickly that the municipal government conducted another census in 1838, which counted 13,621 residents. This increase in population spurred the aldermen to raise the number of wards from four to seven, which were simply identified by number. In 1842 the number of aldermen was raised to fourteen, two from each of the city's seven wards. By 1852, when the city's population exceeded 20,000, an amended charter raised the number of aldermen to twenty-one, three from each ward. The common council consisted of seven members, who were elected at large as long as one came from each of the city's wards.[3]

Elections for city officials invariably occurred during the cotton-marketing season, which lasted from fall through spring. During that time, both the businessmen who resided in the city only to engage in the cotton trade and the permanent residents participated in civic affairs. They elected their mayor and city legislators during the peak of the cotton-trading season, between November and March.[4]

Because the cotton trade usually ended by June, many associated with it left for vacations in July or August. Indeed each summer, particularly when an epidemic threatened or appeared, anyone who could afford to leave the steamy city did so. Seasonal population shifts characterized Mobile.[5] As one visitor observed, "The richer inhabitants . . . , as at New Orleans, steam away to the north every summer, as soon after June as they can, and never stop till they reach the rocky shores of Boston, or the springs of Saratoga."[6] "Blessed are the poor," asserted one Mobilian, "for they shall enjoy the comforts of home."[7] Those who could not travel to distant resorts perhaps moved to Spring Hill or to another suburb from which they could commute to the city if necessary. Others tried resorts along the eastern shore of Mobile Bay or the Gulf coast of Mississippi. Some visited hotels at Bladon's Springs and Cullom's Springs in Choctaw County, Alabama. Wealthier Mobilians journeyed even farther from home, perhaps to Hot Springs, White Sulphur Springs, Saratoga, or Newport.[8]

The city legislators' long vacations sometimes prevented the board of aldermen and common council from assembling quorums to conduct business during the summer. When rumors circulated that aldermen lacked a quorum during the summer of 1855, the *Mobile Advertiser* still maintained that city legislators had the right to follow the example of their constituents in leaving Mobile at their convenience when they had no pressing business. From 15 July to 28 October 1858, during a yellow fever epidemic, aldermen could not assemble a quorum. On 18 November Newton St. John, president of the board of aldermen, congratulated his fellow legislators that "they were still spared to resume their labours." From 14 August to 11 October 1860, even when no epidemic hit the city, aldermen failed to hold business meetings.[9] When leaders absented themselves from the city, governmental operations slowed to a standstill.

Many of the cotton brokers who fled Mobile each summer for the north favored the Whig party, while many year-round residents preferred the Democratic party.[10] Since voters chose their governor and state representatives in August during the absence of many seasonal residents of the city, Whigs in Mobile stood a better chance of victory in city than in state elections.

Citizens wanted their government to operate in an orderly manner, from conducting elections to providing services. Summer absences of leaders sometimes interfered with the smooth functioning of government. Partisanship also caused disruptions, especially at election time. Although municipal elections in early antebellum Mobile initially proceeded along nonpartisan lines, they developed into heated partisan contests beginning in the late 1830s. Withstanding stiff competition from Democrats, Whigs generally prevailed at the polls in the 1840s. Rivalry sometimes erupted into violence on election days. When politically related street brawls and displays of public drunkenness occurred, newspaper editors implored authorities to maintain the peace. Calm prevailed for some close mayoral elections, even one in 1842 determined by eight votes. The loser in that contest did not sue the winner, but losers in the elections of 1848 and 1850 did file suits against the winners in unsuccessful efforts to overturn vote tallies produced by alleged irregularities.[11]

The annual elections for municipal leaders frequently caused disruptions, which led to lengthening the tenure of officeholders. In 1851 the *Alabama Planter*, a local nonpartisan newspaper, extolled the advantages of extending the terms of office from one to three years: it would reduce the expense of elections by two-thirds, avoid the excitement connected with annual elections, make the offices more important, give officers more time to learn their duties, and increase citizens' interest in elections. An amendment of the city charter approved by the state legislature extended the terms of office for major elected leaders in Mobile to three years beginning in 1852. Under this amendment the mayor, aldermen, and councilmen would serve three-year terms, with the mayor and councilmen running for election every three years and one-third of the aldermen each year. This system for elections would help to keep the public peace and morals, according to the *Alabama Planter*, and thus would enable the city to avoid the great public disturbances caused by annual elections for the mayor, aldermen, and councilmen. Observing officials in office for three years, voters should choose more wisely among candidates for reelection. As the *Planter* observed, "Voters will say that a bad man can do a great deal of harm in a long term and consequently good men great good."[12]

Officeholders who served the first three-year terms won praise from the editor of the *Mobile Advertiser* as "practical businessmen, conversant with the wants of a commercial city, prudent, deliberate and conscientious in their action—never passing a measure without giving it as intelligent, searching, and thorough an examination as circumstances would admit." These officials also reportedly conducted "their deliberations with a courtesy, dignity and decorum, alike creditable to themselves and to the city."[13]

Men considered suitable for local legislative posts often required persuasion to run for office. Although the mayor drew a salary, members of the board of aldermen and the common council received no compensation for their services.[14] Board meetings were usually held after business hours, an arrangement that avoided interference with members' professional duties but took them away from their families and social activities. These circumstances led to what one concerned editor called the "too prevalent unwillingness of competent and proper men to make the personal sacrifice . . . involved in a faithful discharge of the duties devolving upon City Legislators." Potential officeholders actually risked much more by refusing to serve on city boards than by serving, according to the editor. He encouraged "persons permanently interested in the prosperity of the city—the value of whose property and business immeasurably depends upon the management of our municipal affairs" to use their influence for "the election of prudent and intelligent men" and even to take seats in the city councils themselves if the voters elected them.[15] According to the conventional wisdom, men whose personal interests depended on the prosperity of the city made the ideal officials. Almost all (94.6 percent) of the antebellum government leaders listed in the 1860 census owned some local property (see Table 5-1). Nearly half of them claimed estates worth $50,000 or more, which gave them considerable interest in civic affairs that influenced the value of their holdings. Their commercial interests also linked them to city government. Merchants claimed more elective offices than any other occupational group among the urban leaders (see Table 5-2). From the mayoralty and the legislative boards, they determined what improvements would be made and how those improvements would be

Table 5-1. Property Holdings of Government Leaders of Antebellum Mobile

Amount ($)	Real Estate (%)	Personal Estate (%)	Total (%)
None	19.6	5.4	5.4
1-4,999	5.4	12.5	5.4
5,000-24,999	32.1	35.7	21.4
25,000-49,999	19.6	21.4	19.6
50,000-99,999	12.5	12.5	23.2
100,000+	10.7	12.5	25.0
Number of Cases[a]	56.0	56.0	56.0

[a]Those government leaders, counted among the urban leaders described in chapter 3, for whom property holding data appeared in the 1860 census.

Table 5-2. Occupations of Government Leaders of Antebellum Mobile

Occupation	Total[a]	
	N	%
Agriculture	2	1.8
Building	5	4.6
Manufacturing	8	7.3
Transport	1	0.9
Commerce	73	67.0
Professional	14	12.8
Nonprofessional services	2	1.8
Other[b]	4	3.7

[a]Refers to 109 of the urban leaders (described in chapter 3) for whom both government position (mayor, alderman, common councilman) and occupation were known.
[b]Includes categories of semiskilled and unskilled labor, public service, and gentleman. Categories follow those listed in the appendix.

financed to benefit their own interests directly and those of the general public indirectly.

As property owners and taxpayers, leaders wished to keep their tax burden for supporting government low. Property taxes on real estate, slaves, and merchandise in stores generated the largest single source of revenue for the government. Revenue from licenses and rental of city property, mainly the market, provided the next largest sources of funds.[16] The rate of taxation for real and personal property remained virtually constant at 40¢ per $100 of assessed value, the maximum permitted by the charter. Twice during the 1830s the aldermen lowered the rate. In 1832 and 1834, as certain pieces of local real estate had doubled in value from the previous year, the aldermen set the rate of property taxation at 35¢ per $100 value, apparently deciding that a lower tax rate would still generate ample revenue because of the inflated value of property. Not only was inflation raising the value of local property in the mid-1830s, but a building boom was also increasing the amount of property subject to taxation. With the development of new parcels of land and opening of new streets, mechanics worked furiously to construct new houses and stores to meet the demands of new residents. In 1835 the city was one-fourth larger than it had been the previous year.[17] While growth continued at such a pace, taxation rates could remain low and still generate enough revenue to meet the routine expenses of urban government.

Tax revenue normally covered the ordinary expenses of urban government, but major public improvements required considerable additional funds. In the 1830s Mobile's quadrupling population made it one of the fastest growing urban places in the nation. Like other rapidly expanding cities in early nineteenth century-America, Mobile used municipal bond issues to finance public improvement projects. Corporate authorities believed that the past growth of the city warranted these undertakings and that future growth indeed depended on them. Long-term loans arranged by the bond issues spared current taxpayers increased burdens and allowed future generations who would benefit from permanent improvements to share in the cost of acquiring them.[18] City government in effect was speculating in improvements that would boost future property values. Borrowed funds might be repaid by future generations from lower taxes on property that had increased in value as a result of general improvements financed by loans. As long as property taxes produced the main source of funds for city government, urban leaders across the United States justified this speculative strategy for public improvements.

Local officials easily arranged Mobile's first two bond issues for public improvement projects of unquestioned general benefit. In 1830 the mayor and aldermen obtained the city's first major public improvement loan based, according to the *Mobile Register*, "on a desire to advance the permanent improvement of the city while at the same time it is intended to lessen the amount of our City taxes." The $30,000 worth of bonds, issued for twenty years at 8 percent interest, were designated to pay for grading and shelling of streets and obtaining an adequate supply of water for the city. The editor of the *Register* raised no questions regarding the policy of borrowing or the state of city finances. He deemed it "sufficient" that elected representatives had determined the necessity and expediency of the arrangement. Four years after this first municipal bond issue, corporate authorities arranged a much larger one. They borrowed $200,000 through bonds redeemable in thirty years at 6 percent interest to erect a city hall on a lot already owned by the city, to extend the water works, and to make other civic improvements.[19] Like the first loan, the second one apparently sparked no public protest.

During a discussion of another major public improvement project in 1836, disagreements arose over priorities for city spending. The mayor and aldermen decided to purchase a choice downtown block as a site for a city hall. Although they possessed the authority to make the purchase, they apparently hoped to win the citizens' approval at a special public meeting on January 16. A number of people who attended the meeting protested its hasty call and arranged for an adjournment until January 19. In the meantime, the mayor and aldermen held a called meeting January 18 to accept the committee's recommendation to buy the property. A protest signed by 134 residents, including many respected businessmen, objected not only to the apparent overriding of citizens' views but also to the priority attached to the site for a city hall. Protestors argued that other matters required more immediate attention than purchasing the site for a city hall. They specifically listed laying iron water pipes, lighting the city, paving all business streets, and building a powder magazine. Officials nonetheless proceeded to issue $192,000 worth of bonds, redeemable in ten years at 8 percent interest, to buy lots from various individuals on a new site for a city hall.[20]

Tax revenues for the city treasury could not regularly meet interest payments on the loans by the spring of 1836. At that time the city had a bonded indebtedness of $422,000. The city treasurer, J. A. Stuart, expected to receive for the year $70,000 in city taxes, interest of $275 from $15,000 of city bonds loaned to the school commissioners of Mobile County, and nearly $12,000 in notes due to the city. Stuart could not determine how much of the city's anticipated revenue would be spent for any purpose. "There being no regularity in the manner of expending the funds of the city," he reported, "it is impossible to say what bills may be presented for payment." The treasury contained no cash in April 1836 at the time an interest payment was due on the city's loans.[21] Aldermen then resorted to short-term borrowing, authorizing the mayor to borrow $6,000 for ten days from either of the local banks for transmission to New York to pay interest on the city's loans.[22]

Despite the city's financial problems, officials approved still other major expenditures in October 1836. With Mayor George W. Owen casting the tiebreaking vote, the aldermen authorized the city to subscribe for one hundred shares of stock in the Mobile and Cedar Point Railroad, which was projected to transport cotton from the docks to the lower bay for loading onto oceangoing ships. Aldermen also resolved to open a new city graveyard on thirty acres of land owned by a former mayor, Samuel H. Garrow. To pay Garrow $24,000 for his property and to pay for the railroad stock, the city issued $100,000 in bonds paying annual interest of 8 percent for twenty years.[23] This bond issue raised the city's total indebtedness beyond $500,000.

Shortly after approving the loan, the aldermen received a disconcerting committee report regarding haphazard bookkeeping by the city treasurer. The treasurer listed the same deposit twice in the check book, an error that the examining committee thought would have been avoided had the treasurer balanced his cash daily or weekly, neither of which he did regularly. He in fact did not balance his books for over three months in 1836. The committee recommended that the aldermen require the treasurer to submit a statement of receipts and expenditures for each city account at the regular weekly meeting of the board. Of even more concern than slow bookkeeping was the lack of an account on the city ledger for the $200,000 in bonds issued in November 1834. The committee advised that such an account be required for the 1834 and 1836 loans. Finally the committee suggested that clearer records be kept for property owned by the city that was leased out for income.[24] These shoddy bookkeeping practices were not remedied quickly despite the examiners' recommendations, so the city's finances remained in disarray.

Mobile's financial situation grew bleaker as the Panic of 1837 disrupted its economy. Local banks suspended payments of specie on

12 May of that year, after receiving news of earlier suspensions in Montgomery. The fall of cotton prices, depression in the money market, reduction in demand for manufactured goods, and consequent reduction in demand for raw materials plunged Mobile and other American cities, especially in the Southwest, into a severe depression. Banks temporarily suspended payment of specie. The Bank of Mobile managed to weather the panic, but the other local banks—the Planters and Merchants Bank and the Mobile Branch of the Alabama State Bank—never recovered from it. The lack of money in circulation severely thwarted the city's commercial operations.[25]

Speculation in land had materially contributed to inflation before the panic, so losses from real-estate investments loomed ominously large after the panic. Rising merchants and professionals used speculation in land as a way of increasing their fortunes in the 1820s and 1830s. As settlement in Mobile expanded rapidly and real-estate values became inflated, investors profited handsomely from building offices, stores, or homes on their property and renting them to others, from subdividing and reselling tracts of land in the suburbs, or from holding lots for later development or sale. Some who found rents exorbitant tried accumulating funds to purchase their own office space. Philip Phillips, an attorney who moved from Charleston to Mobile in 1835, admitted, "I was more than astonished—I was staggered by what seemed to me an unheard-of-price for a lawyer's office." With just the $5,000 that he had inherited from his father's estate, Phillips paid $1,500 rent on his office for one year. Trying to improve his finances, Phillips committed himself to a $25,000 speculation in building lots. Like many other ambitious men, he made considerable purchases on credit. Like other investors who could not keep up payments on their loans after the onset of the Panic of 1837, Phillips lost his money and property.[26] Some who owned considerable amounts of property could not sell it for one-half or even one-fourth of its value when they needed cash to pay their debts. Debt collection troubled merchants and professionals for a long time. Not enough money circulated even by 1839 to furnish many families with grocery money, much less payments on outstanding bills. Cash was so scarce that one physician could not collect $100 toward the $25,000 to $30,000 outstanding on his books.[27]

With bonded indebtedness of the city government exceeding $500,000, the problems of collecting taxes and making payments on loans considerably overshadowed problems of individuals. Tax revenue dropped not only because of the financial exigencies of individuals but also because of the decline in property values and corresponding decline in property tax revenues that followed the panic. Since Mobile relied so heavily on property taxes for its ordinary income, it faced disaster when that source of revenue decreased substantially. The city defaulted on semiannual interest dividends due on its loans in early 1839.

This muncipal default, the earliest on record among American cities, subjected Mobile to ridicule both in the United States and England. The *London Morning Post* expressed concern both at Mobile's "most unusual" failure to prepare for payment of dividends and at the city's limited provision for payment of the principal at maturity of the bonds. Commenting on Mobile's apparent disregard for its credit reputation, the *Post* remarked, "it must be considered a great reproach to the inhabitants to allow so wealthy and flourishing a place to be less circumspect, in this particular, than the various other cities of the Union, which have likewise contracted loans for the purpose of effecting local improvements." The *Baltimore American* argued that Mobile's failure to make provision for the regular payment of interest due on its municipal bonds held in England discredited not only Mobile but also American securities in general. Only after these articles had appeared in newspapers outside the city did the *Mobile Register* seriously broach the subject of default. The *Register* hoped that evidence of "the disgrace under which this community is living on account of the shameful embarrassments in the city Treasury" would spark some effort to restore the city's good credit rating. "It is time," noted the *Register*, "to redeem our characters from the dishonor which profligacy, ignorance, or criminal negligence somehow has inflicted upon us."[28]

During this crisis of 1839, a yellow fever epidemic and a wave of arson compounded Mobile's financial problems. Yellow fever claimed its first victims in August and caused more deaths from September through November, eventually killing as many as seven hundred people. These deaths and frequent departures of residents for healthier places considerably depleted Mobile's summer population. During the worst of the epidemic, most stores closed their doors, the post office opened only in the morning, and banks opened for only two hours daily.[29] Besides the epidemic, fires threatened Mobilians. Arsonists had destroyed $350,000 to $400,000 worth of property during the first six months of

Fire in 1839 (Courtesy of the Historic Mobile Preservation Society)

1839. On 7, 8, and 9 October incendiaries set blazes that consumed buildings and other property in over twenty-five blocks, one-third of the downtown area. Losses totaled $1,600,000. The debt-ridden city government had to spend capital to deal with fire damages. For instance, the city was forced to construct a new guard house and tower to replace ones destroyed by fire.[30] While city government further overextended itself, its revenues continued to drop along with assessments on property damaged and destroyed by fire and with collections of taxes.

Late in the disastrous fall of 1839 Mobilians held a public meeting to discuss revisions of the city charter to help the fiscal crisis. A citizens' committee drafted and a public assembly approved a proposed amendment to the city charter, which some considered the basic cause of Mobile's financial troubles. As drafted for submission to the state legislature, the amendment suggested provisions to insure the collection and the disbursement of city revenue in a sound and honest manner. The amendment created an elected common council of eight members charged with selecting all the city officers who collected or disbursed municipal funds. The council was to set the amount of security bond required of each city officer for the performance of his duties. Candidates and voters for seats on the common council initially were required to own real or personal property assessed by the city for a tax of at least five dollars. Some residents complained about the undemocratic nature of this property qualification for the common council. The Democratic editor of the *Register* defended the requirement on the grounds that it would reduce the opportunity for corruption: "It needs no argument to prove, that if one class of people, the property holders, *raise* the revenues for the support of an open corporation like the city of Mobile, and another class, who do not pay taxes have the disbursement of it, that an extravagant, injudicious, if not corrupt expenditure of it will be made."[31] Whigs nevertheless succeeded in removing the special propertyholding requirement two years after it was imposed.

The revamping of government provided by the amended charter enacted by the legislature in 1840 failed to solve the city's financial crisis. In 1841 the joint finance committee of the aldermen and councilmen found the city's financial records in complete disarray. The books of the clerk, comptroller, and treasurer reportedly "had but little relation to each other and were almost as distinct and separate as if representing the concerns of so many different corporations." Records of years before 1838 were not indexed, some books were missing, and loose papers were tossed into boxes or piles without any system. While the comptroller's books for 1837 and 1838 were "unbalanced and confused," both the comptroller's and treasurer's ledgers after 1838 were balanced. Rather than spending time sorting out the unbalanced comptroller's books, the legislators' committee decided that it would ascertain the amount of the city's funded indebtedness. The total approached $650,000. In an attempt to work out a means of paying the city's creditors, mainly the holders of the municipal bonds, city property had been turned over to seven trustees who were supposed to make sale or lease arrangements to settle the city's debt. During the depression that followed the Panic of 1837, the sale or lease of city property would have brought so little money that the mayor, aldermen, and councilmen agreed in 1842 to try floating one bond issue to consolidate the total debt from the previous loans. An agreement designed by local authorities and ratified in 1843 by the state legislature provided for a new bond issue of some $706,000 to consolidate the city's total indebtedness.[32]

The legislature extensively amended the charter of Mobile to boost the city's fiscal responsibility. To avoid conflict of interest, the mayor, aldermen, and common councilmen promised to refrain while in office from participating directly or indirectly in any contract for business with the city. Both legislative boards had to approve appropriations of city funds, and their resolutions for spending had to be recorded in books for various departments of government. The comptroller had to keep his books with the double entry system of bookkeeping.[33]

City authorities henceforth might not issue bonds or promissory notes unless the contract arranging the issue specifically provided the means of repayment of the borrowed sums. The amended charter created an annual fund of not less than $10,000 to pay the city's obligation incurred in 1843. Taxes on real estate within the city were pledged to this annual fund, which was to be held by a designated depository. This depository, initially the Alabama Life Insurance and Trust Company, would use the taxes in the annual fund to pay the interest on the debt and to redeem the bonds according to their dates of maturity. The altered charter required the mayor to transfer any surplus in the city treasury at the end of the municipal year to the annual fund for application toward the early redemption of the bonds. The city's creditors agreed to the arrangement to refinance the debt, which meant that no city property had to be sold.[34]

Not only Mobile's credit rating but its national and international image depended upon the regular payment of interest due on the bonds and the successful retirement of the principal of the bond issue according to the set maturation schedules. In the 1850s city government consistently paid annual interest on the bond issue of 1843 in excess of the $10,000 minimum required for the sinking fund account.[35] By 1854, when the first bonds fell due, the city met its obligations to return the principal to the bondholders. Advertisements in the *Mobile Daily Advertiser, New Orleans Picayune, New York Journal of Commerce,* and *Boston Daily Advertiser* notified owners of Mobile municipal bonds to present them for payment to the designated local depository. The mayor boasted, "Not a tinge or suspicion of dishonor rests upon the credit and fair fame of our beloved city."[36] The editor of the *Mobile Advertiser* congratulated city authorities in general for "this gratifying evidence of the skillful management of our city Administration and the auspicious prospect it opens before us in the future."[37]

"Skillful management" improved the city's financial prospects, but so did new taxes. According to the debt settlement, real-estate taxes went toward bond retirement. Unless income from real-estate taxes

Table 5-3. Value of Taxable Property in Mobile, 1820–37

Year	Real Estate ($)	Slaves ($)	Merchandise ($)	Total ($)
1820	493,300	73,300	208,000	774,600
1821	403,200	59,390	383,300	845,890
1822	419,550	85,300	231,300	736,150
1823	989,350	119,300	308,950	1,417,600
1824	832,125	106,575	168,800	1,107,500
1825	1,519,765	218,800	397,500	2,136,065
1826	1,535,640	221,038	535,980	2,292,658
1827	1,408,327	215,750	411,956	2,036,033
1828	1,483,168	232,240	559,678	2,275,086
1829	1,891,760	326,700	500,688	2,719,148
1830	2,162,770	311,555	421,750	2,896,075
1831	1,294,810	274,185	540,449	2,109,444
1832	2,623,110	530,155	975,028	4,128,293
1833	3,377,649	694,805	1,042,400	5,114,854
1834	4,611,950	1,000,350	1,143,725	6,756,025
1835	6,414,425	1,447,000	1,524,160	9,385,585
1836	18,050,080	1,871,100	2,739,050	22,660,230
1837	27,482,961	2,721,300	2,975,250	33,179,511

SOURCE: J. D. B. DeBow, The Industrial Resources, Etc., of the Southern and Western States, 3 vols. (1852), 2:79–80.

rose substantially, the city authorities had to locate other income to meet ordinary expenses of city government. The city charter required tax assessors to appraise real estate according to its "cash value," which did not increase notably after the Panic of 1837.[38] In fact real estate in antebellum Mobile never again equalled its pre-Panic value (see Tables 5-3, 5-4). Property values declined and tax rates remained constant at the maximum of 40¢ per $100 permitted by the charter, so revenue from property taxes dropped precipitously after the Panic of 1837.

Revenue would increase if property-tax rates rose, but taxpayers opposed any increase in their rate of taxation to meet ordinary municipal obligations. When taxpayers in Mobile maintained that they faced heavier taxes than people in other cities, aldermen discovered that the rate of property taxation in Mobile was half or less than half of that in Baltimore, Philadelphia, New York, and Boston. Reports of this aldermanic investigation in 1846 did not win Mobilians' support for raising their property-tax rates. Neither did a plea for increasing the real-estate tax in 1856 to cover a deficit of $28,000 in the city treasury.[39] Without

Table 5-4. Value of Taxable Property in Mobile, 1838-60

Year	Real Estate ($)	Slaves ($)	Merchandise ($)	Other[a] ($)	Total ($)
1838	20,407,435	1,461,200	2,253,286	--	24,121,921
1839	21,098,915	1,225,050	3,156,350	--	25,480,315
1840	13,441,783	1,078,020	1,820,770	--	16,340,573
1841	17,601,950	1,568,900	2,297,600	--	21,468,450
1842	16,138,643	1,667,375	2,477,820	--	20,283,838
1843	14,773,470	1,471,750	1,676,550	--	17,921,770
1844	14,053,056	1,705,845	2,329,976	--	18,088,877
1845	12,622,085	1,428,620	2,442,615	--	16,493,320
1846	12,854,650	1,697,650	2,121,820	71,220	16,745,340
1847	8,638,250	1,323,480	1,760,745	43,515	11,765,990
1848	8,943,810	1,554,350	1,891,750	41,660	12,421,570
1849	9,300,930	1,600,850	1,728,350	14,025	12,644,155
1850	8,577,025	1,345,850	2,041,360	15,820	11,980,055
1851	11,698,045	2,493,845	3,336,656	141,840	17,670,295
1852	11,207,984	2,148,375	3,064,253	70,875	16,420,612
1854[b]	13,051,950	1,927,900	2,745,375	69,350	17,794,575
1855	12,602,145	2,110,550	2,895,550	43,725	17,651,970
1856	13,239,645	2,258,400	3,262,200	448,450	19,208,695
1857	13,404,511	3,580,525	2,917,110	2,368,888	22,271,034
1858	13,402,635	3,494,280	3,123,705	4,434,622	24,455,242
1859	13,511,825	3,582,100	2,710,148	6,952,432	26,756,505
1860	13,967,245	3,989,875	3,553,395	7,652,107	29,163,222

SOURCES: Data for 1838-51 in DeBow, Industrial Resources, 2:79-80; for 1852 and 1859-61 in City of Mobile Property Tax Books, cited in Alan Smith Thompson, "Mobile, Alabama, 1850-61: Economic, Political, Physical, and Population Characteristics" (Ph.D. diss., University of Alabama, 1979), pp. 490-91; for 1854-58 in Hunt's Merchants Magazine 42 (1859): 184-85.
[a]Includes horses and carriages (beginning in 1845); steamboats, plank and shell roads (beginning in 1854); personal property (beginning in 1857); and machinery used in manufacturing, stocks, furniture, plate, frames, watches, clocks, jewelry (beginning in 1858).
[b]Data for 1853 are unavailable.

popular support for heavier taxes, municipal legislators looked to other measures for generating revenue for government.

Rather than increase the rate of real-estate taxes, Mobile, like other debt-ridden American cities, chose to find income from new property taxes and license fees. In addition to real estate, slaves, and merchandise that were already taxed, the list of taxable property expanded to include the value of horses, carriages, wagons, and hacks (1845); steamboats and other watercraft, plank roads, and shell roads (1854); certain per-

Table 5-5. Value of Classes of Taxable Property in Mobile, 1820-37

Year	Real Estate (%)	Slaves (%)	Merchandise (%)	Total ($)
1820	64	9	27	774,600
1821	48	7	45	845,890
1822	57	12	31	736,150
1823	70	8	22	1,417,600
1824	75	10	15	1,107,500
1825	71	10	19	2,136,065
1826	67	10	23	2,292,658
1827	69	11	20	2,036,033
1828	65	10	25	2,275,086
1829	70	12	18	2,719,148
1830	75	11	15	2,896,075
1831	61	13	26	2,109,444
1832	64	13	24	4,128,293
1833	67	14	20	5,114,854
1834	68	15	17	6,756,025
1835	68	15	16	9,385,585
1836	80	8	12	22,660,230
1837	83	8	8	33,179,511

SOURCE: DeBow, Industrial Resources, 2:79-80.

NOTE: Percentages were rounded to nearest whole number.

sonal property (1857); and machinery used in manufacturing, local insurance stock, furniture, plate, watches, clocks, and jewelry (1858). Even income from commission sales, professional services, and foreign companies conducting business locally fell subject to taxation beginning in 1858. In the 1850s the city also collected an annual license tax ranging from five to twenty dollars from persons carrying on a business, trade, or profession within the city limits, with the exceptions of mechanics and journeymen. By the end of the antebellum period these various new taxes provided about one-fourth of the city's tax revenue.[40]

Increases in revenue from other property taxes helped to offset the proportional loss of revenue from real-estate taxes. While real estate had made up 83 percent of the city's taxable property in 1837, it constituted just 51 percent by 1859 (see Tables 5-5, 5-6). In 1858 the state legislature authorized and voters in Mobile approved the assessment of a special tax of 10¢ per $100 of taxable property in addition to the 40¢ per $100 collected then. Receipts from this special tax, which could be levied for only four years, were applied toward the liquidation of city

Table 5-6. Value of Classes of Taxable Property in Mobile, 1838-60

Year	Real Estate (%)	Slaves (%)	Merchandise (%)	Other[a] (%)	Total ($)
1838	85	6	9	–	24,121,921
1839	83	5	12	–	25,480,315
1840	82	7	11	–	16,340,573
1841	82	7	11	–	21,468,450
1842	80	8	12	–	20,283,838
1843	82	8	9	–	17,921,770
1844	78	9	13	–	18,088,877
1845	76	9	15	–	16,493,320
1846	77	10	13	*	16,745,340
1847	74	11	15	*	11,765,990
1848	72	13	15	*	12,421,570
1849	73	13	14	*	12,644,155
1850	72	11	17	*	11,980,055
1851	66	14	19	1	17,670,295
1852	68	13	19	*	16,420,612
1854[b]	73	11	16	*	17,794,575
1855	72	12	16	*	17,651,970
1856	69	12	17	2	19,208,695
1857	60	16	13	11	22,271,034
1858	55	14	13	18	24,455,242
1859	51	13	10	26	26,756,505
1860	48	14	12	26	29,163,222

SOURCES: Data for 1838-51 in DeBow, Industrial Resources, 2:79-80; for 1852, 1859-61 in City of Mobile Property Tax Books, cited in Thompson, "Mobile, Alabama, 1850-61," pp. 490-91; for 1854-58 in Hunt's Merchants Magazine 42 (1859): 184-85.

NOTE: Percentages rounded to nearest whole number.

[a] Includes horses and carriages (beginning in 1845); steamboats, plank and shellroads (beginning in 1854); personal property (beginning in 1857); and machinery used in manufacturing, stocks, furniture, plate, frames, watches, clocks, and jewelry (beginning in 1858).
[b] Data for 1853 are unavailable.
* Less than 1 percent.

debts other than those involved in the bond issues. With efficient tax collection from old and new sources and economical expenditures of revenue, the city treasury contained a surplus balance by the end of the 1859 municipal year.[41]

New fiscal management practices adopted by local officials indicated their assumption of increased responsibilities that came with major public improvement projects, bond issues, and municipal default.

Certainly the accounting procedures required by the amended charter helped financial record keeping. The creation of the common council provided a check on spending resolutions of the board of aldermen and supervision of officials involved in collecting and disbursing city revenue.

Besides making the changes mandated by the amended charter, municipal legislators revamped their committee structure to handle their expanding tasks efficiently. As in other maturing cities across the country, officials in Mobile replaced their ad hoc committees with standing committees to oversee specific areas of government. In the early 1820s aldermen maintained only three committees—streets, accounts, and hospital. Aldermen served three months at a time on one of these committees. They created other committees as necessary. In the 1850s the presidents of the board of aldermen and common council appointed nine to eleven joint standing committees annually, including ones responsible for finance, law, and auditing; fire engines; police; market; streets, pumps, and the like; gas lights; public grounds, property, and so on; hospital; powder magazine; and origin of fires. For the 1856 and 1857 municipal years board members also maintained a standing committee on the special market building. Three aldermen and two councilmen served on each joint committee that considered petitions, ordinances, expenditures, and other matters pertaining to their area of responsibility.[42]

As new management practices and taxes improved the city's financial situation, officials instituted another public improvement project. For a decade after the municipal debt settlement reached in 1844, major public construction was fiscally impossible. The situation changed in 1854 when, at the maturity of the first bond issue from 1844, the city repaid its obligation to its creditors. Prudent management of the sinking fund began to retire debts incurred by municipal bonds. As municipal finances improved, aldermen and councilmen recommended construction of a new markethouse to replace the old one on Government Street that was built in 1823 and declared a nuisance thirty years later.

The Joint Market Committee supported the mayor's recommendation to build two markets, one in the northern and one in the southern part of the city, designed to meet the needs and convenience of Mobile's growing population. First priority was given to the southern market. Rather than propose new taxes to pay for the market, officials

City Hall and New Market in 1857 (University of South Alabama Photographic Archives)

suggested a new bond issue. The state legislature authorized the bond issue if it won voter approval and provided proper means of repayment. Under the municipal boards' plan, money to purchase the site, construct the building, and pay interest on the debt would come entirely from the revenues of the market. Most of the annual rents for stalls in the market would be used for interest payments on the bonds and a sinking fund to retire the bonds at maturity. Voters approved the plan, and in 1855 the city issued $44,000 worth of bonds at 6 percent interest for ten years. Construction began for the new southern market on a site bounded by Royal, Church, Water, and Government streets.[43]

Circumstances soon necessitated additional public construction on the site of the markethouse. In 1855 the mayor and legislative boards held their meetings in a municipal building on the corner of Conti and St. Emanuel streets. This structure had a leaky roof and rotten timbers and floors. The Joint Committee on Public Property suggested adding a second story to the markethouse to accommodate officials who then had offices in the municipal building and those who lacked offices to transact their official business, including the city surveyor, tax assessor, and tax collector. Sale of the dilapidated municipal building should, according to the committee, provide funds to construct the offices. On 27 December 1855 a fire of suspicious origin destroyed the mayor's office and with it all records and vouchers pertaining to the new market. Rather than make major repairs to the fire-damaged municipal building, aldermen and councilmen decided to construct new city offices over the market. In September 1856 city officials hired five prominent local builders to finish construction of the market and city offices. Merchants' stalls in the market and offices in City Hall were occupied in 1857.[44]

A city ordinance designated the second story of the central building of the market fronting on Royal Street as the municipal building of the city. There the mayor or an alderman or councilman daily (except Sunday) held mayor's court regarding violations of local ordinances. Besides the mayor's courtroom, the new City Hall held offices for the mayor, treasurer, clerk, tax collector, tax assessor, and surveyor. It also provided rooms for the city marshal and police officers, city guard, and a holding room for persons in custody awaiting hearings.[45]

Location of municipal offices over the market and within sight of the harbor demonstrated symbolically the close connection between business and government in Mobile. Completion of the municipal buildings and their regular use indicated in a tangible way that government had not only survived its default crisis but had also created a permanent seat of government.[46]

That success must not obscure the precarious condition of the city's finances, which resulted from a host of problems, especially overextension of government for public improvements and poor supervision of fiscal affairs. Influenced by the so-called Alabama fever or Alabama delusion that the boom of the 1830s would usher in widespread prosperity, leaders expected continued increases in urban growth and property values. They initiated costly public improvements financed by anticipated tax revenues. The collapse of real estate values in the Panic of 1837 disrupted speculation in Mobile. Plummeting tax revenues failed to keep up interest payments on a municipal debt of half a million dollars, a large obligation for the population of some 12,000 in Mobile. Compared to total debts and populations of other American cities, including those in the South, Mobile's case was extreme enough to account for the bankruptcy.[47]

After the default the *Mobile Register* raised suspicions about "profligacy, ignorance, or criminal negligence" on the part of elected officials.[48] Hints of corruption persisted even though neither civil nor criminal charges were filed as a result of mismanagement. Municipal officials certainly mishandled finances. Why they did so cannot be determined conclusively. Indirect evidence, however, suggests some problems with conflict of interest for officeholders who did business with the city. Municipal records before the default do not solidly indicate the extent of conflict of interest among the mayor and aldermen. After the crisis the amended charter specifically required the mayor and legislators to pledge not to conduct business directly or indirectly with the city while they held office. That stipulation suggests an effort to deal with a real problem.

Negligence of officials probably contributed as much as anything else to the city's financial crisis. Absorbed with their own economic interests during the cotton boom of the 1830s, the merchants who served in city government neglected to oversee the city's finances as carefully as they supervised their own accounts. Even the legislators who examined the comptroller's books in 1840 and 1841 reported that "they could not have accomplished more without an encroachment upon their business avocations, neither to be expected or required."[49] They did finally insist on double entry bookkeeping, then routine for mercantile operations, after the default crisis. Profiting from their experience with the pitfalls of speculative financing, they slowly guided city government to economic restraint and sound credit. Municipal investments of the 1850s, for instance, had separate accounts and sources of revenue, which made them far more secure than bonds issued in the 1830s.

The debt settlement of 1843 and subsequent bond issues financed major public improvement projects. New taxes generated enough revenue to support city services if officials carefully appropriated funds. No longer could city government expend funds on the speculative basis of the booming 1830s; recovery depended upon fiscal responsibility.

* 6 *

City Services

THE commercial leaders of city government insisted that it provide services to ensure order, protect property, and make Mobile an attractive place for conducting business. They weighed the benefits of services and improvements against their costs to taxpayers. Overextension of municipal finances for major public improvements eventually drove the city into default after the Panic of 1837 and prompted more careful use of funds in the later antebellum years. Not only did city legislators scrutinize expenditures more carefully, but they also used a clause in the city charter as amended in 1843 to justify selective allocation of tax monies.

Urban leaders in America generally preferred expenditures for the downtown business district and residential neighborhoods favored by prominent merchants on the assumption that what helped these areas eventually benefited the whole city. The city fathers of Mobile had followed this unwritten policy since Mobile's earliest days even though the first city charter directed officials to expend funds "for the benefit and improvement of said city, and the comfort, convenience, and safety of the inhabitants."[1] The wording of the charter thus implied no distinction among Mobilians for the allocation of city services. The 1843 amended charter formally rationalized preferential appropriations. According to the charter, in the expenditure of tax funds "the mayor, aldermen and common councilmen shall have a proper regard to the appropriation of the same to the improvement of the different wards of the said city, in proportion to the amount of taxes paid by each ward."[2] In other words, wards that paid the most taxes would receive the most city services. The poorest wards would receive the fewest services. This manner of allocating public services frequently appeared in other American cities, although rarely with the specific sanction of their charters.

Expenditures for city departments remained stable in the 1840s and grew in the 1850s. Total appropriations for the 1840–41 municipal year amounted to $62,531. The city allocated an additional $41,586 toward liquidating its floating debt. While reducing the city's debt took so much of its revenue, municipal legislators kept expenditures for basic services as low as possible. Members of the joint finance committee even reported a decrease of $15,141 in expenditures for the first three quarters of the municipal year of 1842 ($36,546) compared to the same three quarters of 1841 ($51,688).[3] Costs of providing services to the city's ever growing population, of course, rose over the years. The sharpest increases came between 1852 and 1858, when expenditures rose by one-third (see Table 6-1).

Relative expenditures for each of the seven departments changed slightly from year to year, yet basic priorities in spending remained similar for two decades. The government operated without a formal budget, but a year-end account of revenues and disbursements provided much the same information contained in a budget. For the 1840–41 municipal year, salaries for city officers and for guards claimed the two largest portions of total departmentalized expenditures, 23.4 percent and 22.7 percent, respectively.[4] Records of appropriations in the 1850s indicate that the guards, or policemen, generally received the largest share of departmental allocations from authorities concerned with maintaining order in their city. Miscellaneous accounts claimed the next largest portion of monies for everything from gas lights to a reception for a former president. Salaries for officers, such as the mayor and comptroller, usually ranked a close third.

The proportion of the total expenditures allocated to certain departments did not conclusively establish their order of preference, however, because some did not depend exclusively on the city government for their operating funds. The city paid in full salaries for guards, laborers, operators of horses and carts, and officers. In 1852 an average guard earned $35 per month, an owner of a horse and cart $50, and a laborer $31.87 while employed on city services. Municipal support for the fire department, however, consisted primarily of purchasing major pieces of equipment such as fire engines. Individual members of volunteer fire companies paid for most of their own expenses. The city hospital received fees from white patients who were able to pay for their

Table 6-1. Percentages of Annual Expenditures for City Departments, 1852-58

Year	Guards	Laborers	Horses and Carts	Fire Department	Salaries of Officers	Miscellaneous Accounts	City Hospital	Total[a] ($)
1852	28	6	7	5	18	26	11	60,055
1853	26	9	9	4	19	23	10	72,579
1854	21	6	9	11	20	23	11	73,963
1855	23	7	9	6	20	21	13	80,684
1856	23	7	9	3	19	28	11	88,636
1857	29	9	12	3	19	18	10	89,154
1858	31	6	11	3	14	24	11	82,405

SOURCE: Aldermen's Minutes, 16 December 1852, 1 December 1853, 8 December 1854, 13 December 1855, 11 December 1856; Common Council Minutes, 8 January 1858, 14 December 1858, MPL.
NOTES: Percentages rounded to nearest whole number.
[a]Sum of expenditures for city departments exclusive of other expenditures of corporation.

own care and from owners of slave patients as well as head taxes from ship passengers arriving in Mobile from any port except New Orleans.[5] Accounts of city expenditures provide only general ideas of major priorities.

Street improvements, which were financed by assessments on property owners, naturally appeared more often in prosperous rather than poor areas of the city. As in other American cities, local legislators in Mobile authorized paving of streets upon the request of private citizens. After the completion of the work, owners of property fronting the improved streets paid assessments for their shares of the cost of the service to the city treasury. These arrangements took up a good deal of time at municipal board meetings, particularly in the 1830s when the city expanded so rapidly. While the public and private sectors normally cooperated for street improvements, individuals or groups sometimes arranged paving or repairs without government aid. Newspaper editors consistently praised such public-spirited citizens. They suggested that others emulate the example set by butchers on Stone Street, who in 1857, after city authorities had failed for several months to repair rain-damaged roads in their neighborhood, undertook the repairs themselves. This citizens' group expected to complete the repairs in less time and at less expense than if the city had hired its ordinary contractors.[6]

Street improvements contributed materially to the property values and healthfulness of the city. As early as 1822 a local editor lauded the "zealous public spirit" of city government and individuals for filling up holes in the streets and making them passable in the commercial district. In so doing these civic-minded people reportedly contributed to the healthfulness of the place, raised property values, and encouraged further improvements. Thus they indirectly increased the amount of taxable property for the city. As an editor explained the cost-benefit formula used by city authorities in 1858, "Every dollar expended in grading the streets, opening sewers, in even judicious adornment, will repay the expenditure a hundred fold, and attract from abroad population and wealth, which are necessary to give value to real estate."[7] If appeals to financial considerations were not enough, editors and aldermen championed street improvements as ways to reduce the risk of epidemic diseases. Proper grading and construction of gutters along streets should prevent the accumulation of pools of stagnant water, which were believed to have some connection with diseases.[8]

The effectiveness of measures to improve streets varied greatly. Several visitors in the 1830s and 1840s praised the cleanliness and drainage of streets in Mobile.[9] Others who visited during the same period recorded a more unfavorable but probably more accurate picture. They complained of dust polluting the air during dry periods and mud clogging the streets during the winter rainy season. "For fear of being 'mired'" one English traveler in 1857 hired a carriage to take him a few hundred yards from his hotel to the steamer at the dock.[10] Reports of regrading operations in the low-lying business district appeared frequently enough in local newspapers to indicate that street maintenance continually required attention. Commercial areas that were seen first by visitors and frequented by local merchants received the most care, for the benefits of making improvements there seemed to offset the costs.

Provision of police protection further illustrated the selective application of city services. The police department in Mobile, like that in many other antebellum American cities, slowly developed from an amateur toward a professional organization. When Mobile first became an American city, police protection came from a city watch, manned by a rotating group of adult white male citizens whose names were drawn from lists of those eligible for guard duty. Anyone might furnish a substitute or pay a fine if he chose not to report for duty himself. Members of the city watch stopped suspicious people, quelled disturbances, made arrests, and dispersed disorderly gatherings of slaves. In 1825 aldermen authorized the mayor to hire city guards, beginning with seven in August and reducing the number to four the next month. By 1831 the city paid six guards. In 1835 the city guard reorganized to provide a fixed group of paid men—one captain, one lieutenant, and twenty-three privates—to guard property and maintain order. An amendment to the city charter in 1839 abolished the city guard and created a police force responsible to a recorder.[11]

The size of the police force slowly increased to meet influential residents' demands for protection. In 1839 the city guard consisted of one marshal, three deputy marshals, one night sentinel, and thirty privates. In 1842 the maximum number of watchmen jumped to forty-five, and a few years later to fifty-two. By 1856 the efficiency of the police in the central part of the city reportedly prompted disorderly persons to seek safety in remote areas of the city. The joint police committee of aldermen and councilmen complained, "Those of our well disposed citizens whose residences are in the suberbs [*sic*] are, therefore, but the more exposed and their property more endangered by the very measures necessary for the better security of those in the guarded districts." To increase protection for their "well disposed" constituents in residential neighborhoods near the business district, city legislators authorized the mayor to add four watchmen to the nightly patrols.[12] In 1858 the board of aldermen and common council received authority to approve the hiring of any number of policemen deemed necessary by the mayor. In 1859 Mobile employed more policemen for its population of 30,000 than did Richmond for its 38,000 residents. Richmond then employed five day officers and forty night watchmen, while Mobile engaged nearly sixty guards.[13] Neither city, however, had police forces fully adequate for their needs.

Most policemen served night duty. For instance, of the forty-five watchmen employed in 1842, four manned day patrols, and two each served in the guardhouse, powder magazine, and bell tower. The remaining thirty-five acted as night watchmen, serving on one of two shifts that walked the city from dusk to dawn. On either the early or late shift, the foot patrol in 1842 thus included a maximum of eighteen men to guard 150 blocks of the city.[14]

Whatever the number of watchmen employed to guard the city, it never satisfied all residents. Dissatisfaction also resulted from the inefficiency of watchmen on duty. When few or no violators of city ordinances appeared in the mayor's court for several consecutive days, newspaper editors alternately praised the diligence of policemen in thwarting crimes and suggested their failure in enforcement of the law. Evidence of apparent cases of negligence, although harmful to the city's image, occasionally surfaced in local newspaper columns. A "Citizen" asked, "Where Are the Police?" in May 1854 when for several nights in a row "the orgies of half-drunken vagabonds, whose curses and howlings render night hideous" disturbed the sleep of residents along "some of the principal streets, nearly in the heart of the city." This concerned Mobilian inquired, "Should such things be allowed in an *orderly* city?" Frequent, unchecked street brawls indicated the inefficiency of certain night watchmen. Some lack of diligence in law enforcement resulted from policemen's physical exhaustion. As the mayor fired one night watchman for sleeping on duty in 1856, he remarked that "the guard[s] were paid to *watch* and not to *sleep*."[15] Some guards took daytime jobs to supplement their incomes, thus reducing their efficiency as night watchmen. Mobile's problems with moonlighting night watchmen resembled those of Charleston and Savannah, which also paid relatively low salaries to guards.[16]

In addition to the police force's problems with manpower and effective enforcement, the ineffectiveness of penal institutions also hampered efforts to maintain order in the city. Places of incarceration failed to restrain prisoners. In 1822 the city jail reportedly held prisoners "in the daytime, *if well* guarded!" No guardhouse ever proved entirely satisfactory as a means of coercion for lawbreakers. In 1840 Police Recorder Walter Smith observed that, since Mobile had just two small cells, lawbreakers frequently went free even if they refused to pay a fine, to post bail for good behavior, or to leave the city. Smith found three groups of lawbreakers particularly objectionable: "persons of disorderly and riotous habits . . . thrown upon us by the consequence of rigid police elsewhere," vagrants, and "dissolute and disorderly women." These people often proved unable or unwilling to pay fines levied on them. The city required male vagrants and prisoners who did not pay their fines to work on street repairs. Because of public sentiment against women doing street repair work, those who were unable to pay their fines had no ready way to discharge their obligations to the city. Smith suggested repairing the old guardhouse as a workhouse to provide separate lodging for males and females and a workroom where indigent women lawbreakers might be employed in some pursuit useful to the city. City finances did not permit realization of Smith's plan. Calls for a workhouse separate from the guardhouse continued to appear periodically in local papers.[17]

Many lawbreakers arrested in Mobile committed offenses that were commonplace in other southern cities. On the basis of limited police reports and mayor's court records available, it appears that disorderly conduct and slaves' misbehavior accounted for the largest number of arrests. A great deal of violence apparently resulted from drinking. For example, one-third of the 557 arrests made in January 1856 were for disorderly conduct and drunkenness. Slaves' misconduct accounted for another third of the arrests that month. The remaining offenses included several cases of theft and assault and battery as well as a host of violations of various ordinances. Police even apprehended one person for bribing an officer and an officer for accepting a bribe.[18]

Street fights frequently disrupted the peace in Mobile. Groups of tipsy sailors and adventurers wandered about the streets at night reportedly "hunting for the next dram shop or fight, both of which were conveniently at hand."[19] Some residents carried concealed weapons as protection, although in so doing they violated a stringent state law passed in 1839.[20] Personal and political quarrels sparked a large number of brawls among rich and poor. Some of the bitterest affrays resulted from intraparty feuds. Contrary to state law, Mobilians engaged in dueling. In 1830, because of an article in a Tuscaloosa newspaper, one state legislator from the port city fired shots at a fellow legislator in a public street in Mobile. Conflicts over women and points of honor also instigated duels. As public sentiment increasingly turned against dueling, some challenges issued in Mobile were carried out in Mississippi or New Orleans.[21]

Whites demanded that policemen carefully monitor the behavior of blacks, slave and free, in the city. Blacks made up at least three-tenths of the population of antebellum Mobile.[22] The proportion of slaves among all the inhabitants of Mobile dropped from 37 to 26 percent between 1830 and 1860. Yet the number of slaves increased each decade, although at a much slower rate in the later antebellum years. Two factors that contributed to the decline of slavery in other cities, the harmful effects of urban life on the institution and the planters' demand for slaves, affected Mobile to a limited degree. More important, an ample supply of immigrants joined the urban labor force in the 1840s and 1850s, taking over jobs formerly held by slaves.[23]

Since free blacks composed an anomalous element in society, whites feared them out of all proportion to their numbers. The small growth rate of the free black element and its decline in percentage of the total population provide some indication of its tenuous position in Mobile. Despite the awkward place occupied by free blacks in Mobile, the port city attracted the largest concentration of free blacks within the state, 817 in 1860. Their absolute numbers remained small, but their very presence appeared to whites to threaten the racial order.

Mobile's municipal government, like that in other southern cities, assumed responsibility for enforcing the slave code, including its patrol provisions. Shortly after Alabama achieved statehood, its legislature had passed a slave patrol law to be executed by captains of militia companies. In the 1830s the city of Mobile initiated its own slave patrol as a fire preventive measure. Aldermen authorized the mayor to hire any number of persons he deemed necessary to arrest any slave "walking or lurking about the city" after 10 P.M. without a pass from his master.[24] The municipality continued to provide the slave patrol as part of its police protection.

Law-enforcement authorities attempted to curtail trade of any sort with slaves without permission of their masters. A city ordinance prohibited buying from or selling to any slave any commodity without his master's consent. This regulation also forbade giving alcoholic beverages to slaves without their owners' permission. Judging from accounts of violations, it seems that the twenty-dollar fine failed to curb the illegal trade. Authorities staged several concerted attacks on the illegal trade, apparently without much success. In 1854 "A Citizen" informed the *Alabama Planter* that hundreds of slaves were drunk daily, which lowered their value as workers. On Sundays, the citizen reported, bondsmen enjoyed all-day bacchanalian revels in certain districts of the city (particularly in the vicinity of St. Louis Street). Anxious whites used an economic argument against the illegal liquor trade with slaves, maintaining that it ruined the bondsmen's labor and diminished their market value. The vice also allegedly led to dishonesty and other problems, including the most threatening of all—insubordination.[25] This potential evil so concerned Mayor Charles C. Langdon that he devoted most of his 1854 state of the city message to the illegal trade with bondsmen, tracing it to the numerous illegal, white-owned drinking houses where slaves assembled for gambling as well as imbibing. According to the mayor, "the dens of iniquity are managed so adroitly as to almost defy detection and conviction." In 1854 prosecutions of those who sold intoxicants to slaves without their owners' permission increased only slightly. Three years later officials waged another futile assault on the illegal trade. Many of those engaged in the commerce continued to evade police.[26]

As in other southern cities, authorities attempted, with varying degrees of success, to control slave gatherings. Any congregation of four or more slaves off their masters' premises constituted an "unlawful assembly" unless the mayor or an alderman or councilman had granted written permission. Slaves might, however, hold balls on the premises of their owners or employers under their supervision. The city required the manager of any dance or other assembly for slaves to secure a license, which never permitted the gathering to continue past 1 A.M. On Sundays, when masters customarily excused their slaves from labor, extra watchmen patrolled the streets. Although patrols had the power to whip slaves found in some unlicensed assembly, they often merely arrested offenders and detained them for sentencing by the mayor's court. In 1851 the mayor ordered a dozen slaves convicted of singing and dancing without a license "to dance to the tune of ten lashes each."[27]

Two practices that particularly troubled authorities were the hiring-out and living-out systems, since both removed slaves from the direct supervision of their masters. Without supervision, hired-out slaves allegedly resorted to "gambling, drinking, and debauchery of all kinds" to accumulate the monthly payments due their owners.[28] Slaves often abused the hiring-out system by finding their own employment without their masters' consent. The municipal government supervised these arrangements. By 1826 an ordinance prohibited slaves from hiring their own time and the time of other slaves without their masters' approval. Masters complied with the ordinance by recording slaves for hire with the city clerk and purchasing the hired-out slaves badges, which cost five dollars apiece, at the mayor's office or at authorized places in the city where hired slaves received work assignments. This regulation requiring identification badges to be worn conspicuously on the slaves' dress served much more to control the slaves than to bring in revenue for the city. The municipal government also stipulated the length of the work day—from sunrise to sunset, with set breaks for breakfast and dinner. Periodically the magistrates made extra efforts to enforce the regulations on hired-out slaves, often with little success.[29]

To some whites, slaves' hiring themselves out was not nearly as upsetting a practice as slaves' living apart from their masters. An 1847 ordinance forbade living out and required slaves in the city to live within the enclosure of the residence of their owner, owner's agent, or employer. The *Mobile Register* expected the new law to reduce "crime and licentiousness" among slaves, which could be "traced to the great liberty and freedom of restraint allowed them, by over indulgent or avaricious owners, in suffering them to hire their own time, and to rent premises on which to live, where they are entirely free from restraint imposed upon them by the presence of their owners or employers."[30]

After the 1847 ordinance had failed to curb the living-out system, aldermen in 1850 enacted a new law that sanctioned and regulated the separate residential arrangement for slaves. This ordinance permitted separate residence if the slave registered his owner's written permission and paid a five-dollar fee annually. Under the first year of this arrangement, authorities issued 200 permits and arrested 100 bondsmen who failed to obtain them. During 1855 the city also granted about 200 permits, yet Mayor Jones M. Withers estimated that 1,000 slaves actually lived apart from their owners that year. When he urged that the city revoke the privilege of living out, the municipal boards merely tightened the existing laws. The 1856 ordinance required any slaveowner, employer, or agent who allowed a slave to live apart from him to file a complete description of the slave and the precise address of the slave's new residence. Owners or agents of the large numbers of slaves hired by cotton presses particularly wanted to retain the living-out system because it facilitated housing of slaves away from their masters' homes.[31]

Despite the convenience it provided some slaveholders, the living-out system posed serious threats to order within the city. "It is to its influence, more perhaps than to all other causes," Mayor Withers charged in 1856, "that we are indebted for the spirit of insubordination, so manifest and so much complained of in the community." According to the mayor, "a feeling of discontent and rebellion" developed in those servants not privileged to live apart from their masters; and they lost "their cheerful obedience capacity and faithfulness." The living-out system in fact admirably suited "the purposes of abolition emissaries." The easy contact living out fostered between slaves and free blacks frightened whites. "It so blends and mixes up the slave and free colored population," Withers complained, "as to render inoperative the laws for the government of the latter."[32]

Authorities particularly tried to curb the privileges of free blacks, who allegedly exerted a "baneful influence" upon slaves.[33] The state and city governments passed regulations on free blacks in three phases, each expanding the scope of the previous one. In the 1820s laws generally attempted to limit contact between free blacks and slaves. In the next decade they prohibited immigration of free blacks into the city or the state and insisted that newly emancipated freedmen leave the state. Regulations passed in the 1850s required white guardians for free blacks, forbade all emancipations, and provided for voluntary reenslavement of free blacks.[34]

Free blacks selectively abided by laws designed to regulate their behavior. For instance, they persistently defied an 1820 registration ordinance that called for them to file their descriptions, addresses, and length of residence in Mobile annually with the mayor. They were also required to promise to keep the peace and to free the city from their support. "The estimable privilege of dwelling here should cause them readily to comply with the requirements of the law," the *Mobile Register* argued in 1859. Nevertheless, free blacks manifested "stolid indifference and almost determined purpose not to comply with the law."[35] In contrast to the registration ordinance, the Guardian Law, which offered some protection to free blacks, quickly won a considerable measure of obedience. As passed by the state legislature in 1853, the Guardian Law required all free blacks over fourteen years of age to select white guardians who were to submit annual reports on their charges to the county judge of probate. By 1855 more than half of the free blacks in Mobile listed white guardians.[36]

Authorities refused to admit transient free blacks into the city. The Mobile Harbor Law, passed by the state legislature in 1839, sought to prevent free blacks from entering the state by ship. The law required the harbor master to inform the sheriff of Mobile County whenever any vessel carrying free blacks arrived in the port. The sheriff then locked up the free blacks until the vessel left port. The Alabama Anti-Immigration Act of 1832 forbade free blacks to visit the state for more than thirty days and forbade newly emancipated freedmen to remain in the state.[37]

Four free blacks who arrived in Mobile from New York on board the steamer *Warsaw* in 1835 tested local determination to enforce the harbor and anti-immigration laws. At a time when southerners keenly feared the infiltration of abolitionists and their propaganda, these blacks reportedly carried incendiary tracts published by the abolitionist philanthropist Arthur Tappan. Mobilians despised these four agents less than they did "the master spirits of the conspiracy, the Tappans, the Buffums, the Garrisons, and the Thompsons." According to the *Mobile Register*, local officials shipped the blacks back to New York on the *Warsaw* about two weeks after their arrival. *Niles' Register* reported a contradictory story from an unidentified source: whites had lynched one black "on the suspicion of being an agent of mischief." The national weekly praised Mobile's authorities for "following the dictates of their own judgment, upon the evidence before them . . . undeterred by the officious dictation from abroad."[38] In the absence of further documentation, the fate of the *Warsaw* passengers remains in doubt. Harbor laws remained in force in Mobile and other southern ports. Rather than locking up free blacks, Alabama law eventually required that they remain on board vessels anchored in the port or traversing Mobile Bay.[39]

As an old port undergoing rapid resettlement, Mobile perhaps experienced more of certain forms of lawlessness than older southern cities. A resettled city, much like a frontier boom town, attracted an unusually high proportion of vice associated with gamblers, confidence men, and prostitutes. Along with New Orleans and Natchez, Mobile became known as a southern gambling center. Gamblers ousted from the nearby Crescent City frequently stopped in Mobile. During the cotton-marketing season in Mobile, professional gamblers tried to win some of the profits made by visiting planters and their local business agents. While the state legislature held its sessions in Tuscaloosa, which served as the capital from 1826 to 1847, gamblers from Mobile temporarily shifted operations to the capital.[40] As the sessions ended in Tuscaloosa, gamblers resumed business in the port city.

Local and state laws rendered gambling illegal for virtually the entire antebellum period. In 1822 aldermen in Mobile passed an ordinance that declared playing cards, faro, or any other game of chance for money or anything of value illegal and imposed a $50 fine on violators. Two years later the state legislature enacted a bill to raise revenue for the government that included $400 license fees for lotto, keno, or other tables kept for gaming. Aldermen in Mobile soon passed an ordinance providing a $250 annual local license fee for gaming tables.[41] By the end of 1825 Governor Israel Pickens maintained that the provisions of the revenue law licensing gaming tables resulted in "greatly multiplying these nurseries of idleness and dissipation." Admitting that previous antigambling laws "were but too often evaded among the private haunts of vice," he called for tougher legislation.[42] Early in 1826 the legislature complied with his request by passing an act to prohibit further granting of licenses for gaming tables and to provide stiff penalties for violators. The port city's aldermen then reenacted their antigambling ordinance.[43] This ordinance remained in force for the rest of the antebellum era.

Antigambling regulations failed to halt a practice that apparently attracted numerous residents and visitors. In 1826 on a visit to a couple of gaming houses that operated in the backs of coffee houses, Karl Bernhard, the duke of Saxe-Weimar-Eisenach, observed planters who had brought their crops to market gambling alongside sailors. Someone told him "that respectable merchants were in the habit of going there to have an eye over their clerks, and also to observe what mechanics or other small tradesmen, played here, to stop giving credit to such as haunted the resorts of these gentry."[44] A number of buildings along the river housed liquor shops that served as fronts for heavy percentage games like rondo and craps.

By the 1840s Shakespeare's Row in the business district housed the main gambling operations. Built in the style of a Spanish courtyard, the row had two entrances from opposite streets. Merchants' offices, banks, jewelry stores, tailors' shops, money-brokerage firms, coffee houses, billiard saloons, and restaurants occupied the part of Shakespeare's Row that faced the street. All of the twenty-eight rooms opening onto the courtyard were used for gambling. According to a professional gambler, the courtyard of Shakespeare's Row was "one vast gambling-hell, the resort, of evenings, of persons moving in the different upper walks of life." There, he said, "from early candle-light till the break of day, the rattling of faro-checks and the spinning of roulette wheels could be heard without cessation." "Only persons of gentlemanly exterior" found admission to these gambling rooms; "the unclean and disorderly" were turned away by the owners.[45]

Reform efforts to suppress gambling failed as city authorities neglected strict enforcement of antigambling laws. A discussion in the *Mobile Literary Gazette* in 1839 offers clues regarding officials' limited enforcement of ordinances against gambling. The "fashionable and seductive vice" allegedly operated extensively within the city and brought distress to families headed by gamblers. In an appeal to economic considerations, the *Gazette* asked all landlords, businessmen, professionals, and tenants to consider the effect upon rents of the large number of rooms, and even whole buildings, used by gamblers. Landlords, according to the *Gazette*, might temporarily benefit from the exorbitant rents accruing to them from their gambler tenants, but they would lose in the long run from the moral degeneration associated with gambling. "There is no disputing the fact," argued the *Gazette*, "that those parts of the city which are known to be the resorts of gamblers are always avoided by those from whom the honest and industrious tradesman expects his support."[46] Shopkeepers might have denied credit to known gamblers, but landlords who rented to gamblers as well as cotton factors whose clients enjoyed gambling tolerated gaming houses. Since gambling was not a crime against property, it did not particularly trouble civic officials. However, those who committed violent crimes in or near gaming houses threatened public order and safety and often received punishment that gamblers escaped.

Like gambling, prostitution apparently thrived in the port city despite laws against it. Under city ordinances, vagrants, public drunks, "public prostitutes or such as lead a notorious, lewd or lascivious course of life," and keepers of disorderly houses faced fines of fifty dollars. Instead of putting such people in jail, the mayor usually offered them the option of posting good-behavior bonds or leaving the city. Male violators of the ordinance against vagrancy and disorderly conduct perhaps received jail sentences along with other penalties. Women rarely received jail sentences, probably because the guardhouse had no separate accommodations for them.[47]

Cases presented in the mayor's court in 1859 illustrate this pattern. A man reportedly rented a house and "tenanted it with three bawdy women whose behavior and language was such as to shock the sensibilities of all the decent people in the neighborhood." According to the report of the mayor's court published in the *Mobile Advertiser*, "the lowest class men visited the place, and as the house was blindless and curtainless, and the doors or windows seldom closed, passersby and others being near were compelled to see and hear that which is disgusting." The keeper of the disorderly house received a sentence of a twenty-five-dollar fine or twenty-five days in jail plus a hundred-dollar bond for future good behavior, while the female occupants of the house were apparently not sentenced to jail terms. Two women charged with keeping a disorderly house had to post bonds for good behavior or leave town under the stipulations of the vagrancy act.[48]

Brothels that maintained more discreet standards of behavior operated relatively free of interference from the police. Four were located side by side in an outlying ward in 1860.[49] As long as order and public decorum were maintained, authorities apparently tolerated prostitution. From the civic leaders' standpoint, the benefits of efforts to eliminate vice completely would not offset the costs to taxpayers. Since prostitution perpetrated no crime against property, it was a vice that authorities, whose greatest concerns were order and protection of property, accepted within certain bounds.

Fires, the major threat to property, particularly alarmed Mobile's city fathers. As in other American cities, when private efforts at fire fighting failed to keep property destruction to a minimum, residents organized their own volunteer companies. In the 1820s Mobilians and visitors managed to halt some blazes by quick cooperative action. Residents even saved the Mobile Hotel in December 1822, although they acted without coordination or an adequate supply of fire buckets. Municipal officials had apparently neglected to enforce regulations requiring residents to have fire buckets.[50] Emergency bucket brigades could not prevent the destruction by fire of two-thirds of the business district in October 1827. That blaze at last stimulated some ongoing organization of fire-fighting efforts. From 1830 to 1843 residents formed nine volunteer fire companies, one for free black Creoles and eight for whites. In 1838 the amateur fire companies formed the Mobile Fire Department Association to provide aid for ill members and their families.

The city government slowly instituted fire-prevention measures. Aldermen designated fire limits within which they prohibited the construction of wooden buildings. They fined persons who had built wooden structures within the fire zone after 1 January 1829 and had the construction removed at the city's expense as a fire deterrent.[51] To help volunteer fire companies, aldermen periodically contributed municipal funds toward the purchase of equipment.

In 1839 a fresh series of destructive fires emphasized the need for even more concerted actions. During the first six months of the year, fires, mainly due to arson, destroyed an estimated $350,000 to $400,000 worth of property. Insurance agents agreed in June not to issue any more fire-insurance policies until the city improved its protection of property.[52] Outbreaks of arson decreased briefly, but incendiaries resumed their work in October. A series of six blazes, the worst of which occurred on 7, 8, and 9 October, consumed buildings and other property valued at $1,600,000. The first of these began in a workshop on Dauphin Street and proceeded to burn about fourteen blocks, including warehouses, stores, and the City Hotel. The second major fire consumed 500 buildings in eleven blocks from Conception Street to Conti, St. Francis, Joachim, St. Michael, Claiborne, and Franklin streets. The third blaze destroyed the Mansion House, the unfinished Government

Hotel, the Planters and Merchants Bank, and many valuable brick buildings. These fires in October consumed one-third of the downtown area of Mobile. Property losses due to fire in 1839 exceeded $2,000,000.[53]

At the time of the fires in 1839, Mobilians felt sure that incendiaries had set them, but they could not discover who the criminals were. Policemen packed the jail with suspects, mostly vagrants who were arrested while they walked around the city at night without satisfactory explanations of their actions. According to later accounts, people at first suspected "the low Irish population about the harbor" of arson to facilitate plunder. In 1843 some escaped slaves were said to have confessed that slaves had conspired to burn the city in 1839. While many whites had fled town because of the yellow fever epidemic, slaves reasoned that a fire would give them the chance to create confusion during which they could massacre the remaining whites and take over the city. Since residents did not learn of this supposed plot at the time, they did not have an insurrection panic in 1839. Later, however, they did worry about the possibility of another conspiracy of arson. In 1857 the regionally notorious outlaw James Copeland confessed that he and his gang had set the great fire of 1839 in Mobile, although he did not specify which of the great fires. According to Copeland, the outlaws plundered homes and businesses, hid the booty in boats docked at the river, and set the fire as a diversion to ensure their escape. Copeland confessed to the robbery and arson in Mobile shortly before he was hung in Mississippi for crimes committed in that state.[54] Even though his confession cannot be verified, it offers the most plausible explanation for the concentrated episodes of arson in October 1839.

Citizens' dissatisfaction with protection against arson in 1839 led them to organize their own patrols. Believing that they and their property were inadequately protected by municipal authorities, residents of the West Ward enrolled themselves as members of the Volunteer Guard in March. By early October, when fires occurred daily, one Mobilian reported that "every body expect[ed] at night to be burnt before morning."[55] To augment protection by the city guards, a public meeting created a committee of safety. Soon afterward a prominent banker observed, "The city is well guarded at night by the citizens, and as long as the guard can be kept up, we may be safe, but it is hard work to be up night after night." As incidents of arson decreased, citizens disbanded their volunteer watch.[56]

After 1839 city legislators passed new ordinances to improve and to coordinate fire protection. Municipal fire limits were extended to include the entire burned district, thus requiring new construction there to be of brick. In 1843 city authorities provided for the annual election of general officers for the fire department, who would supervise firefighting efforts, inspect equipment, and submit annual reports to the municipal boards. "The qualified white firemen" of the city's eight fire companies elected their own chief engineer, assistant engineers, and eight fire wardens. Fire wardens were required to examine buildings in their districts at least twice a year to check compliance with building codes for the fire zone. A special board composed of city legislators and firemen investigated the origin of all fires.[57]

Legislation provided for new sources of regular financial aid to fire fighters. The city government obligated itself for the first time to appropriate specific sums each quarter to fire companies from unallocated funds. Payments to fire companies, however, fell short of amounts promised them, and members used their own monies for expenses, even the construction of an engine house. Expenditures in the 1850s compared unfavorably with those of Natchez, which used bond issues for construction of fire houses and tax revenues for maintenance and equipment. Natchez spent over $8,000 for fire protection in 1850, while Mobile spent about $3,000 (see Table 6-1). As city finances improved in Mobile, municipal funds paid for new equipment.[58]

Instead of municipal funds, contributions from insurance companies paid many of the operating expenses of the fire department. Each insurance agency operating locally that was not chartered by the state of Alabama was required by state law to contribute $200 annually to the Fire Department Association of Mobile. In both 1854 and 1855 these insurance companies contributed $2,400 to purchase new fire hoses and to repair engines.[59] Friendly relations between insurance agencies and fire companies encouraged speedy responses to fires, which in turn reduced risks for propertyholders and insurance companies and maintained the value of local taxable property.

In the 1850s public and private sectors continued to cooperate in fire fighting. One civic leader argued that the city should assume all necessary expenses of the fire department to relieve the financial burden on volunteer firemen who gave their time and money, and in some cases their lives, in protecting persons and property. Elected officials never obligated the government to pay the total costs of the fire department, although they continued municipal contributions throughout the decade. The Mobile Fire Department, with eight engine companies and one hook-and-ladder company, compiled a successful record of fire fighting. The further extension of the fire limits in 1851 helped to reduce fire hazards by placing new areas under the code against wooden construction. Losses from fires in the departmental reporting year from April 1853 to April 1854 totaled $111,550, a sum that the chief engineer called "trifling compared to former years." Losses dropped to $109,795 in 1855. For the year ending in April 1860, fire losses totaled $327,000, an increase within the decade but still far less than the $2,000,000 loss in 1839. Many fires reportedly resulted from arson rather than negligence on the part of persons responsible for fire protection.[60]

Just as residents expected police and fire protection from their city government, so they expected protection from certain health hazards and epidemics. Animals roaming at large in the city posed sanitation and safety problems never effectively treated by authorities. Complaints in local newspapers from the 1830s through the 1850s indicate that unleashed dogs, hogs, and cows persisted as nuisances. "An innumerable quantity of hogs" reportedly scattered kitchen refuse about the main streets and wallowed in pools of standing water in 1844. A visitor in the 1850s, appalled by the congregation of stray dogs in woods at the ends of main streets, reported, "The press complains—everybody complains—but nobody cares; nobody will obey anybody, or observe any sort of regulation, no matter how good or essential."[61]

Inadequate regulations and methods of enforcement hampered efforts to restrain loose animals. In 1836 the editor of the *Mobile Mercantile Advertiser for the Country* printed a proclamation against unrestrained dogs issued by the mayor of New York City and a copy of an ordinance on the subject passed by city legislators in Baltimore in an unsuccessful attempt to get a similar restriction passed in Mobile. An irate taxpayer in a neighborhood where unrestrained hogs tore up streets in 1853 pleaded to no avail for stringent laws against loose animals.[62] While the position of superintendent of animals remained vacant for a number of weeks in 1854, the city had no one responsible for enforcing even the weak laws against unrestrained animals. According to the *Mobile Advertiser*, "Horses, cows, swine and goats have now emphatically the 'freedom of the city,' and are great annoyances to pedestrians and housekeepers."[63] A petition signed by 249 citizens implored the municipal boards to draft an effective ordinance to keep cattle, horses, and hogs from running at large in the city. The aldermen's police committee drafted such an ordinance, but the board changed it to permit cows to run loose and thus failed to satisfy the petitioners. In 1856 a cow running at large in Dauphin Street tossed and severely bruised a small boy, who later died of the injuries. "We doubt," the *Mobile Register* observed, "if the spectacle of cows, goats and swine wandering at will through streets . . . is exhibited in any other city of the Union."[64] In fact, however, many other cities allowed animals to run loose, so officials in Mobile lacked examples of successful ways to deal with the health hazard, inconvenience, and occasional danger to human lives posed by unrestrained animals. Perhaps because no proof existed that unrestrained animals directly interfered with business or caused disease, officials could not justify the expense of restraint.

Elected officials and physicians agreed, although for different reasons, on the need for cleanliness in the city. Merchants who led city government knew that a clean city favorably impressed visitors. Physicians believed that good sanitation helped to improve public health. As the editor of the *Mobile Advertiser* argued: "Judicious health regulations, cost what they may, are in the end sound economy, as, by the confidence they would give at home and abroad, the trade of the city would be largely augmented, our reputation would be better, and the actual profit from increased business would, doubtless, pay back twice over the entire expense thus incurred—at least, so it seems to us."[65] The expense of routine enforcement remained low; aldermen periodically inspected property within their wards to order the removal of filth and stagnant water, which were believed to cause disease. Ordinances regarding cleanliness of streets, gutters, sidewalks, yards, and vacant lots were usually better enforced during warm weather.[66]

When city officials made special appropriations for sanitation, they kept expenditures low. Sometimes aldermen authorized the mayor to purchase lime as a disinfectant for deposit in various areas of the city. They allocated funds on an ad hoc basis as epidemics threatened Mobile, spending $2,000 in 1839 and $1,000 in 1853.[67] Authorities even directed special efforts toward the eradication of noxious miasmas, gaseous substances emitted from putrid and decaying organic matter. In 1853 Mayor C. C. Langdon arranged for the burning of tar in barrels on street corners in an attempt to dispel the miasma that was popularly supposed to be a cause of yellow fever. The Mobile Gas Light Company donated "that disinfecting agent" coal tar and citizens contributed empty barrels, which policemen placed on street corners, filled with tar, and lit at a set time each night. The only expense to the city in this burning operation came from funds paid to owners of barrels who refused to donate them.[68] In its combination of public and private efforts with minimal public expenditures, the burning experiment reflected an approach to disease prevention common to Mobile and numerous other antebellum cities.

The Board of Health, appointed by the mayor and municipal legislators, officially supervised efforts to remove causes of diseases. As established in 1823, the board consisted of three physicians (one resident, one visiting, and one consulting) and one health officer. Usually late each spring or early each summer the board organized to fulfill its responsibilities. In years when epidemics ravaging other American cities along the Atlantic or Gulf coasts threatened to attack Mobile as well, the board sometimes organized earlier than usual. If Mobile had sustained an epidemic in the summer, city officials sometimes appointed special investigatory committees of physicians in the fall, as they did in 1826, to study the causes of the disease and to recommend suggestions for preventive measures to the Board of Health.[69]

While the Board of Health possessed broad supervisory powers, its accomplishments remained limited by service that usually lasted only from June through November and by its members' deference to the businessmen in city government who made the appointments. From New Orleans to Richmond, boards of health in southern cities functioned under similar constraints. Health officials had to exercise great caution in announcing the existence of an epidemic for fear of alarming citizens and, even more important, disrupting business. The Board of Health customarily issued reassuring statements about the health of the city for as long as possible.[70]

Statements issued by the Board of Health in 1853, when Mobile faced a severe epidemic of yellow fever that ultimately killed one-tenth of the city's summer population, illustrate the board's usual practices. The board made its first statement concerning the presence of the disease on 15 August. "Believing it at all times to be their duty to apprise citizens of the approach or existence of any dangerous disease," the Board of Health noted the recent appearance of several cases of yellow fever in various parts of the city. Yet the board maintained that these cases were not unusually malignant or unmanageable but responsive to early treatment.[71] The next day (16 August) the board decided to publish daily lists of deaths, thus acknowledging the presence of an epidemic in a manner praised as "right and honest and politic" by the *Mobile Advertiser*.[72] At the end of the month published reports from the Board of Health indicated a sharp increase in the number of cases. Not until 27 October did the board halt daily reports of deaths, declaring that yellow fever cases were no longer present in epidemic numbers. An accompanying statement that absentee residents and visitors might safely enter the city signaled not only the official end of the epidemic but also the opening of the business season.[73] At the end of every epidemic the "all-clear" statement by the Board of Health served commercial as well as medical purposes.

Epidemics indicated measures taken to prevent and contain dreaded diseases had failed. Yellow fever troubled officials more than any other pestilence. Before the germ theory of disease, people widely believed that yellow fever developed from miasma. Scientific observation challenged the miasmatic theory because the simultaneous presence of heat, moisture, and decomposing organic material did not routinely result in epidemics. While similar conditions existed each summer in antebellum Mobile, epidemics plagued the city not regularly but sporadically: 1819, 1825, 1837, 1839, 1843, 1853, and 1858. Before some of these epidemics the city had directed intensive sanitary measures supposed to guarantee respite from yellow fever. These precautions obviously failed to accomplish their purpose. As the *New Orleans Daily Delta* exclaimed about yellow fever in 1853, "In clean, salubrious Mobile, on a dry shell bank, with breezes from the sea to blow through her streets, this disease prevails as violently as in our own swamp-girt, filthy, badly-governed city!" Even large expenditures on sanitation projects proved futile. Savannah spent $200,000 on draining lands around the city and placing them in dry cultivation, but epidemics appeared there as often as in other coastal cities.[74]

Neither sanitation campaigns nor quarantines succeeded in preventing epidemics. Although a quarantine was reputed to prevent the outbreak of an epidemic, the application of the measure sparked controversy among government and business leaders. After the yellow fever epidemic of 1853 Dr. William Anderson, president of the Board of

Health, admitted that quarantine was frequently considered in Mobile but rarely enforced up to this time because of worries about the expense of enforcement and the restriction of commerce involved with it. "No one could dislike more than myself," Anderson noted, "to place any restrictions on the commerce of our city." "But commerce brings in nothing but money, and money will not compensate for the loss of our citizens, nor cheer the hearts made desolate by death," he reasoned.[75] After several vessels with yellow fever on board arrived in the port late in August 1854, the Board of Health advised the mayor to enforce the ordinance providing for a quarantine. Dr. E. S. Mordecai, health officer and quarantine physician, inspected all vessels arriving in the harbor and moved persons with yellow fever to the quarantine ship in Mobile Bay. All ships arriving from ports where yellow fever was known to prevail were detained for six days. Inspection fees paid by seventy-two ship captains kept quarantine expenses minimal for city government.[76] Thus officials' reservations about expenses associated with enforcing the quarantine seemed unwarranted.

In 1855, as yellow fever devastated Norfolk and Portsmouth, Virginia, popular demand in Mobile for the establishment of a quarantine overrode medical advice to the city legislators that the practice had no proven scientific merit. The majority report of the joint hospital committee contended that "public opinion in this city demands a quarantine, that nothing short of its establishment will quiet the public mind and relieve it of apprehension." The report maintained that no harm could come from a quarantine, except perhaps expense. Alderman George A. Ketchum, a physician, dissented from the majority report to argue against the quarantine. Declaring that yellow fever was not contagious, Ketchum maintained "the establishment of a quarantine as a protective measure against the disease is worthless" as well as costly and disruptive to commerce. He also argued the impracticability of establishing a perfectly effective system of quarantine. Ketchum favored instead a rigid enforcement of sanitary measures as the "surest precaution" against yellow fever and other epidemic diseases.[77] His fellow aldermen adopted his minority report against the quarantine, while the common councilmen accepted the majority report for the quarantine.[78] After further legislative wrangling, Alderman Ketchum withdrew his minority report and both boards voted for the establishment of a quarantine.

Cholera and smallpox constituted lesser threats to Mobile than yellow fever, but municipal officials took important steps toward their prevention and treatment. Authorities in Mobile adopted measures used in other cities against both threats to public health. By the 1830s, when cholera first appeared in America, physicians generally believed that some local atmospheric conditions caused the disease, but ordinary citizens thought that it was contagious. Thus the public sometimes pressed for quarantines. When news arrived in the United States of the cholera epidemic in Europe in 1831, Atlantic ports began seeking further information about the disease and establishing quarantines for passengers and goods arriving from infected ports of Europe. Municipal governments in large cities along the Atlantic coast, such as New York, Boston, and Philadelphia, led the fight against the disease in their communities. Smaller cities, which were poorly equipped to handle such a threat, sought to adapt the techniques used by larger cities for their own use. American municipal governments sent skilled observers to Atlantic ports where epidemics prevailed in the hope that they might find a curative treatment or preventive measure for cholera.[79] In September 1832 the mayor and aldermen of Mobile sent Dr. Henry S. Levert to Philadelphia to observe the care of cholera patients there. By the time Levert reached Philadelphia, he found few remaining cases of cholera to observe and conflicting recommendations from physicians about the course of treatment. He proceeded to Richmond for another opportunity to observe the disease.[80]

When faced with cases of cholera, city authorities took every precaution thought effective against the disease. Throughout the winter of 1832–33 and spring of 1833, aldermen inspected their wards to see that citizens removed filth and stagnant water, which were believed to contribute to the atmospheric conditions causing the disease. For about two weeks in November 1833, while cholera prevailed in New Orleans and threatened Mobile, the city government prohibited the introduction of oysters, which were believed to carry cholera, into the city limits. Although some deaths resulted from cholera in Mobile, the Board of Health refrained from declaring an epidemic in either 1832 or 1833.[81] Mobile suffered another outbreak of cholera in 1836 and faced an even greater threat in 1848 and 1849 as a major incidence of the disease occurred in American ports entered by a new wave of European immigrants. In December 1848, while New Orleans admitted the presence of cholera, the Board of Health in Mobile issued a standard set of precautions taken against epidemics: maintenance of a clean environment and moderate lifestyle.[82]

Only for smallpox did the city government ultimately assume primary responsibility for both prevention and treatment. To care for victims of smallpox, the city supported a "pest house." Whenever the Board of Health learned about cases of smallpox, it ordered that people with the disease be isolated and cared for at city expense. In 1831 and in 1835 aldermen opened temporary hospitals in the suburbs for smallpox victims. In 1839 the Board of Health advised the corporate authorities to provide a permanent place to care for smallpox patients. In 1839 the government built a new wooden pest house, which burned to the ground two years later. The Joint Hospital Committee of aldermen and common councilmen then suggested construction of a small brick building, but city finances could not support the project then. Municipal records do not indicate that a permanent pest house was erected, although they do note that the corporate authorities paid a physician who cared for smallpox patients at a pest house in 1857 and set rates for the care of patients in the pest house in 1859.[83]

Perhaps thinking that vaccination against the disease might prove less expensive to the city than treatment, officials eventually assumed the cost of preventive efforts against smallpox. In 1858 the government chose to pay physicians ten cents per person for the vaccination of the poor. Aldermen expected that the cost of the vaccination program would be so low that it would not pose a financial burden. In this vaccination program Mobile followed the practice of many other antebellum American cities.[84]

The only publicly supported facility that provided health care on a year-round basis was the City Hospital. In Mobile's early American years the City Hospital consisted of a one-room house "calculated," according to a local physician, "for the uncomfortable accommodation of half a dozen sick without regular nurses."[85] The hospital apparently operated near a workhouse that kept vagrants employed at tending the lot surrounding both buildings. The city maintained an "Irish Hospital" at least in 1825 and 1826, when aldermen approved payment of bills for services and supplies there. Municipal records do not clarify whether the first city hospital and "Irish Hospital" were one and the same, although it seems likely.[86]

In 1830 the city built a permanent hospital on St. Anthony Street at the point of its intersection with Broad Street. By 1837 the facility could accommodate 150 people. Until the United States Marine Hospital was built in 1842, the City Hospital served as a marine hospital under an arrangement between the collector of the port and city authorities. The mayor and aldermen initially directed the management of the hospital by appointing a physician to supervise the medical department, a surgeon to run the surgical department, and a steward to contract for supplies and to police the institution. Corporate officials eventually decided that the hospital could be run more efficiently and economically by contracting out its management to private groups. The Samaritan Society, a nondenominational benevolent association; the Sisters of Charity, Roman Catholic nursing nuns; and the Alabama Medical College, the state medical school in Mobile, consecutively spent several years operating the City Hospital. Each group that contracted to manage the hospital had to agree to admit pauper patients free of charge.[87]

Public health and fire protection both demanded an adequate supply of safe water for the city. A private company initiated service under a monopoly agreement that reverted to the city government when terms of the contract were not fulfilled. After public operation of the water works eventually failed as well, private entrepreneurs resumed the franchise. Whoever administered the water supply, the system used in Mobile followed that in Philadelphia of distributing water from one source through the city by a system of pipes.[88] In 1820 several ambitious businessmen—Lewis Judson, Addin Lewis, Archibald W. Gordon, William H. Robertson, and Francis W. Armstrong—formed the Mobile Acqueduct Company to provide exclusive water service by laying pipes from Three Mile Creek into the city. When the Mobile Acqueduct Company failed to comply with the stipulations of its act of incorporation, the state legislature revoked its charter in 1824 and transferred its rights and powers to the city.[89]

The city government itself then attempted for over a decade to supply fresh water. Bond issues in 1830 and 1834 included funds for extending the water works. The city tried to supply water from a fountain at the foot of Spring Hill through a pipe to the city for distribution to various users. For this purpose the city had about four miles of pipes, including 16,000 feet of iron or log pipes of 3-inch bore and 6,000 feet of 5-inch bore. By the end of 1836 municipal operation of the facility had clearly failed to provide enough safe water for Mobilians. City officials then offered the water works for sale "with the sole idea that in the hands of individuals an ample supply of water would be furnished more surely and promptly than could be hoped for from a corporate body subject to radical change every year."[90]

Henry Hitchcock, a successful attorney and real-estate developer, purchased the water works on a twenty-year lease under which he had to sell the system back to the city in 1856. The city required Hitchcock to introduce an ample supply of water into the city within two years of the agreement in order to retain the lease. After the Panic of 1837 Hitchcock needed investment capital to finance repairs and improvements in the water system, so he revived the Mobile Acqueduct Company in an effort, unfortunately at an unpropitious time, to sell $150,000 worth of stock. By early 1839 neither the lessee nor the city had met contractual obligations outlined in the 1836 agreement.[91]

After Hitchcock died of yellow fever in the fall of 1839, Albert Stein, a German-born hydraulic engineer who had advised Hitchcock on the operation of the Mobile system, contracted with the city to operate the water works himself. While Stein approached his task with much experience in hydraulic engineering for American cities, he still faced obstacles posed by the system that he had assumed from Hitchcock. Before moving to Mobile, Stein had designed and directed the construction of water works for Lynchburg, Richmond, Nashville, and New Orleans. In Mobile he obtained a lease on the water works for twenty years, after which he had to sell the facility back to the city. The final price would be determined by an arbitrator or a committee from Philadelphia if necessary. In return for the city-granted right to collect set fees from individual, family, and commercial users of water, Stein agreed to allow the city free use of certain hydrants for extinguishing fires and cleaning streets. He also agreed to provide water at no cost to the city hospital and guardhouse.[92]

Stein's water system depended upon a pumping plant near the foot of Spring Hill on Three Mile Creek, seven miles west of the city. From there he piped water to an elevated tank on Spring Hill Avenue two miles west of town. Pipelines then distributed water to the downtown area served by Stein's system. Some of the pipes were cast iron, but the majority were bored-out pine logs. Service lines to users were metal. The reservoir that provided the water was only slightly elevated above the city, and the pipes that carried the water into the city were generally only eight inches in diameter. Under these conditions Stein could not provide enough water for all parts of the city. Service within the fire limits was uneven; service extended beyond the fire zone to such public facilities as hospitals. When residents complained about water shortages in the 1850s, Stein attributed them to waste through fire plugs, occasional broken pipes, and inadequate elevation at the reservoir, which kept the pressure low in pipes.[93]

To improve service the municipal boards advocated purchase of the Water Works, pending voters' approval of the financing. In 1854 both the aldermen and councilmen adopted a report calling for the city to purchase the Water Works from the proprietor at his price of $180,000. Municipal bonds, if approved by the voters, would provide the funds. By a more than four to one margin, voters rejected the bond issue for buying the Water Works. After the election the *Mobile Advertiser* attempted to convince Mobilians that "an abundance of water is as necessary to the convenience and safety of a city as buildings are necessary for the convenience and comfort of its inhabitants."[94] Despite the appeal for the city to take over the Water Works, the private contractor retained his lease. Water service remained less than adequate until 1886, when a new private company built a pumping plant on Clear Creek and a reservoir on Moffat Road, from which it piped water to the business and residential areas not reached by Stein's system. After purchasing Stein's system from his heirs in 1898, the city government established a municipal water system in 1900. Seven years later the city purchased the other private water-supply company and connected its lines to those of the city system.[95]

Compared to an adequate supply of safe water, other improvements offered more to enhance the appearance of the city and at a lower cost to taxpayers.[96] Gas lighting brightened the appearance of Mobile as much as any other single improvement. Baltimore, the first American city to provide gas lighting for its streets, made the service a public utility in 1816. Instead of creating a public utility for gas lighting, aldermen in Mobile contracted with the entrepreneur who supplied gas lamps for nearby New Orleans. James H. Caldwell, a theater operator, secured the contract for gas lighting in New Orleans in 1835 and in Mobile the next year. The agreement required Caldwell to supply enough gas to illuminate the city within bounds set by the mayor and aldermen, to furnish lamps similar to those erected in New Orleans, and to maintain the system of lights for thirty years. During the period of his monopoly, Caldwell charged Mobilians the same price for gas that he collected from residents of New Orleans. He initiated service in June 1837 in the downtown retail district. Twenty years later the city had 175 gas lamps, more of which were reportedly owned by private than public customers. The *Mobile Register* claimed that it cost "no more to light the whole city than to pay 13 or 14 night guards" in an apparent effort to stimulate the government into extending gas lighting.[97] While the service did not reach the entire city, it did illumine at public expense the areas frequented by visitors and local merchants.

Once more pressing civic needs were met, officials gave some attention to beautifying their environment. Like most antebellum cities, Mobile had few open spaces downtown. Creating a public square in one of them required expenditures both to acquire and to decorate the property. Leaders eventually justified the cost for beautification by the benefits accruing to the health of citizens, image of the city, and prosperity of business.[98] Development of a public square proceeded slowly, especially in view of the city's shaky financial situation. In the 1830s the city purchased all land in the square bounded by St. Joseph, St. Francis, Conception, and Dauphin streets as a site for a city hall. After the Panic of 1837 officials abandoned their construction plans. When the trustees of city property tried to sell building lots in the square along with other city-owned parcels, they found that some of the city square had been dedicated to public use forever so that it could not be sold. The debt arrangements ratified in 1843 avoided the sale of any lands owned by the city. To provide a little income from land left idle on the city square, municipal authorities leased some of it to the operator of a livery stable.[99]

In the 1850s civic-minded Mobilians initiated efforts to turn the public square into a spot of beauty. As the *Alabama Planter* noted in 1850, the people wanted to see the one vacant spot set aside and "dressed up to gladden the eye with its green trees and herbage and sparkling fountain." That vision differed sharply from the way the square was then used; as the New York journalist Frederick Law Olmsted observed, it was "a horse and hog pasture, and clothes-drying yard."[100] By 1852 a wooden fence constructed around the square by the city had become, according to the *Planter*, "an eye-sore to everybody—dilapidated, liable to be blown down by every gust of wind and withal inadequate to keep out horses, cattle and goats . . . which the pastoral taste of our city fathers tolerates and allows the largest freedom." The *Planter* lauded A. R. Meslier for his drive to get subscriptions for removing the unsightly wooden enclosure and erecting an iron fence in its place. Three people donated $600 each, and others contributed smaller amounts toward the estimated cost of $6,000.[101] Meanwhile the lessee of the livery stable on the square moved to another location, although he still owed the city payments on the unexpired term of his lease. The city trustees could not release him from his obligation unless the municipal government would assume responsibility for the amount of the lessee's notes. Since the square could not quickly be cleared, the contributions for the ornamental iron fence had to be returned to their donors. Shortly after the discontinuation of the beautification drive, municipal authorities proposed using the public square as a site for a markethouse that should produce revenue to help the city free itself of debt. Arguing against this plan, the *Alabama Planter* maintained that the city needed the public square to provide a spot of pure air. In addition, the square, which the city already owned, offered an ideal place for beauty and public recreation that the city might not be able to purchase ten years later. Officials chose to reserve the public square for its designated purpose. In 1853 the city auctioned off the livery stable and its adjoining structures on the square with the requirement that the purchaser demolish the buildings and remove the debris from the site.[102] This action at last cleared the square of all temporary property.

In 1859 citizens finally completed the beautification of the public square, which was named Bienville Square in honor of the founder of Mobile. Augustus R. Meslier and Lewis T. Woodruff had collected nearly $10,000 in donations for an iron fence to replace the wooden one. "This ornament has been the result of public spirit on the part of our citizens," observed the *Mobile Register*, "as it had been accomplished entirely by private subscription." Public funds paid $1,525 for grading and paving sidewalks, constructing a brick base for the fence, and building curbs around the square.[103]

Bienville Square then became a place of general recreation for Mobilians. Municipal officials sponsored two late-afternoon public concerts by brass bands in September. According to the *Mobile Register*, "The City Fathers . . . planned this nice little entertainment for their grateful children." Within less than a week after the city-sponsored concerts several young men hired a brass band to play another concert at the square, fulfilling the hope of officials that private citizens would continue the practice begun by the city. Several women petitioned municipal authorities for permission to erect twelve gas lamps in the square so that the whole park might be lit at night. These women promised to pay the cost of laying the pipes and raising the lamps if the city would buy the gas to light them. This plan, which the *Mobile Register* deemed quite fair, would help to keep unrespectable women from assembling at the square after dark.[104]

The city acquired a second public square as a gift from Archibald W. Gordon, a native of Connecticut who had made his home in Mobile since the 1820s. Gordon prospered in real estate and commercial dealings. In 1850 he donated as a public promenade a tract that he had purchased in 1821. The property was bound by Charles Street on the east, New Hampshire Street on the south, Chatham Street on the west, and Main and Massachusetts streets on the north. While city legislators wanted to name the square after its donor, they yielded to Gordon's wish that the property be called Washington Square. Gordon stipulated that the city enclose the square with a fence and improve it with plantings and walks. The city government fulfilled its obligation by contracting for the planting of both shade and ornamental trees and the laying of walks on Washington Square. Municipal legislators passed an ordinance to ensure that both Washington and Bienville squares would serve the purposes for which they were intended. This ordinance provided fifty-dollar fines for depositing building materials or hanging clothes on the squares, cutting down or injuring trees, shrubs, and flowers on the squares, and turning animals loose in the squares.[105]

The dedication of the squares to public recreation illustrated the maturation of the city. After years spent opening streets and organizing police and fire protection, elected officials responded to public pressure for the aesthetic development of the city. In this process, of course, they welcomed private contributions as they had always had to any public endeavor.

City services above all accommodated commerce. Streets in the business district were paved earlier and repaired more often than those elsewhere in the city. Police concentrated their patrols in the commercial areas. They conveniently ignored gambling houses and brothels unless these places, in themselves illegal, became scenes of rowdiness that spilled over into the public streets. Fire zones initially included the downtown business district and eventually expanded to include adjacent preferred residential neighborhoods. The periphery of the city received little in the way of street improvements or police and fire protection. Unless a service directly aided business interests, city fathers might ignore it until a crisis pushed them to action. Services that promoted sanitation and health in the city, for instance, often were not provided regularly until an epidemic appeared in Mobile or a nearby coastal city. The possibility of undertaking extensive sanitation projects like Savannah's apparently never occurred to Mobile's leaders. For services that only tangentially aided business, city fathers preferred to establish private franchises, such as that for gas lighting. Municipal funds paid for lamplighting only in the commercial district. Beautification efforts attracted municipal support late in the antebellum era and then only after civic-minded residents initiated projects and contributed substantially to them.

In some ways Mobile's legislators may appear stingy, short-sighted, and narrow-minded in their attitudes toward provision of city services. Certainly in this respect they shared the attitudes of their counterparts throughout much of urban America. Yet they also displayed vision about investing city funds in projects to boost property values and increase commerce in the city. Bond issues for these projects, which were initiated unwisely without provisions for repayment of capital, brought financial disaster to the city government. This situation checked expenditures and prompted restraint. The city's poverty and its leaders' concerns about balancing benefits of services to business with their costs to taxpayers explained many of the limits imposed on city services.

* 7 *

Social Services

NINETEENTH-CENTURY Americans, especially urbanites, witnessed an increasingly high incidence of poverty. In rapidly growing cities with large numbers of immigrants in their populations, poverty was far more common than urban leaders cared to admit. Early in the century Americans widely accepted it as a fixed part of the social order, the result of human beings' frailties. Neither the government nor private citizens thought that they had an obligation to help the poor. By the 1830s evangelical Protestants had begun to suggest that poverty could be substantially reduced if Christians assumed social obligations toward poor people who suffered through no fault of their own.[1]

Yet in the South the prevalence of a religious belief that emphasized individual sin and salvation diminished collective efforts to relieve social distress. Social services in southern cities, including Mobile, remained limited throughout the antebellum era.[2] Outpourings of benevolence came primarily from private charities. Governmental funds provided some aid, usually through established institutions, while private philanthropy channeled relief directly to individuals. The essential conservatism of the well-to-do providers of social services, whether they sat on municipal boards or charitable directorates, meant that symptoms of poverty such as hunger and illness received more attention than deeper maladies like unemployment. Only with the public school system did leaders establish an institution that might provide long-term help to improve the lives of poor Mobilians.

From the 1820s through the 1850s local newspaper columns indicated a general acceptance of the existence of poverty, even though its presence harmed the city's sought-after image of prosperity. Editors rarely addressed the subject directly. Their few comments nonetheless reiterated their belief in the inevitability of poverty in their midst. As the *Mobile Argus* observed in 1822, "Our city is rapidly increasing in wealth and numbers, and we must expect a portion of the poorer class of society."[3] "Life-Gatherings among the Poor," a series of columns in the *Mobile Advertiser* in the summer of 1854, attempted to inform readers of the extent of poverty in the city. According to the pastor who wrote the columns, numerous people who attended local churches in the winter and spent the summer at Spring Hill, Cottage Hill, the Eastern Shore, Saratoga, or Newport "would vainly ask, 'Have we real poverty in Mobile?'" He replied, "Christian men and women of our city we have the poor among us. It is right that we should; it is God's order—appointed by His will. . . . They are here: some because of sin; others, of misfortune. They are among us, however, as you may know, if you will trouble yourself with the effort."[4]

In other words, contrary to a widely held belief that poverty resulted from immorality or lack of virtue, neglect or indifference frequently caused poverty. For instance, commercial stagnation in 1855 increased the incidence of poverty as financially troubled businessmen halted construction projects that had given employment to laborers and mechanics. Unemployment forced hundreds of people to depend "for a precarious subsistence upon the charity of kind-hearted individuals, assisted by the county, the charitable societies, and the clergy, all of whose disposable means are enlisted to their full extent," noted a newspaper columnist. Fifty families in the working-class parish of St. John's Episcopal Church, their rector reported, relied completely on charity for their subsistence because they did not have enough food, clothing, and fuel. "No one can doubt," the *Mobile Advertiser* observed, "that this want is directly traceable to circumstances over which the sufferers can have no control."[5]

While some poverty was to be expected, whether as a result of God's will or financial exigencies, government officials sought to reduce the number of public charges. For this purpose they enforced laws against vagrancy and begging. As a port Mobile attracted a sizable number of transients, whom authorities were determined not to support at public expense. An ordinance to regulate ship passengers and transient persons required that captains of vessels entering Mobile Bay submit descriptive passenger lists to the mayor. If the mayor thought that any of the passengers might become a charge to the city, he could demand a $500 bond from the owner or master of the vessel and an agreement to pay all expenses for the public care of that person for one year. A Mobilian who received in his home a stranger "who may be liable to become a charge to the city" had to report the person to the mayor or an overseer of the poor for the county within two days or pay a fine himself if the person became a public charge. The mayor had the power to order persons liable to become public charges to leave the city. Vagrants, beggars, and all persons without visible means of support who remained in the city faced fines or jail terms.[6]

These ordinances against vagrancy and begging, of course, met the purpose for which they were intended only when they were strictly enforced. In November 1857, as transient beggars who frequented Mobile during the business season appeared in stores and homes with their tales of woe, the vigilance of the city marshal reduced their numbers as compared to the previous year.[7]

Municipal authorities in Mobile, as in other American cities, maintained that public aid to the poor should be minimal, for they believed that the primary responsibility for charity lay with private associations. Public funds for poor relief could in fact provide very limited aid. In 1819 voters created a poor fund from an annual poll tax of one dollar for each adult white male. This fund initially supplied monies on an ad hoc basis for the care of the ill poor in the city.[8] Demands for aid could not be met entirely by this fund, which, with numerous exemptions, failed to generate substantial revenue. In 1819 the city had 104 poll taxpayers. The number of men paying poll taxes grew to 1,725 in 1839, then declined for several years, and finally increased in the 1850s.[9] Separate accounts were not maintained for poll taxes expended through the poor fund, so it is difficult to determine how much city revenue financed poor relief.

Public facilities and private charities, rather than municipally subsidized individuals, were the proper agencies for poor relief, according to city officials. Even though they disapproved of outdoor relief, municipal officials occasionally paid it in response to special petitions. For instance, aldermen authorized payment in excess of $100 to a local man who had kept paupers and vagrants in 1826. Aldermen and councilmen paid a woman $70 in 1840 for the support of an orphan child for a year, although they informed her that they would pay no more bills for this purpose.[10]

Municipal funds eventually financed several permanent facilities for the poor, the most significant being the general hospital. In 1822 the editor of the *Mobile Argus* proposed the construction of a general hospital to serve unfortunate laborers, particularly sailors, "who in the late hour of peril [the War of 1812] were not wanting—who contributed to the glory with which our country is encircled." Subscriptions could finance construction costs, and proper management could make the pauper hospital operate on less money than was then expended on an ad hoc basis for the poor ill. "A Subscriber" sent the *Argus* a copy of the report from the trustees of the poor house in Baltimore outlining the system in which the costs of care rendered to paupers was recovered by the paupers' labor.[11]

Mobile adopted the system for a pauper hospital used in Baltimore and other southern cities in the early nineteenth century. In 1824 the city built a hospital and workhouse. These first facilities were crude, but the city paid a physician to treat patients there. The hospital opened in the 1830s contained space for 150 patients, many of whom were paupers. Part of its operating funds came from a head tax on ship passengers entering the port of Mobile. The mayor or a member of the aldermanic hospital committee had to sign an admission permit for each patient unable to pay for his care. As nonpaying patients became convalescent, they were required to perform such work around the hospital as was deemed appropriate by the hospital committee for as long as necessary to pay for their treatment at the rate of one dollar a day.[12]

Besides the hospital, city government contributed to another facility for the poor. The Female Benevolent Society, founded in 1829 to aid indigent widows, initially gave food, clothing, and medical supplies to needy women who had been located by its visiting committee. Soon the society petitioned city officials for funds with which to build a house for the permanent relief of "the most unfortunate, and helpless persons" in the community. According to the petition of Mrs. Henry Hitchcock, president of the Female Benevolent Society, "in a Christian land" poor widows should not be allowed to suffer in "wretched cabins" or be turned out into the street when they could not pay their rent.[13] In 1835 Henry Hitchcock donated a lot and the city government appropriated $5,000 to erect on that lot several small brick houses.[14]

In compliance with a promise to city officials, the Female Benevolent Society raised all of the money to maintain the houses on Widows' Row and to care for their occupants. Throughout 1849 members of the society aided sixteen widows on Widows' Row and a number of families who did not live on Widows' Row, all for a total of less than $300. In 1850 the *Mobile Register* listed the effects of twenty years of donations to the charitable association: "The helpless mother has been cheered, fatherless children cared for, the sufferings of the sick alleviated, and the sorrows of death soothed."[15]

From income of the Mobile County Court of Commissioners of Roads and Revenue, the county government provided a poor house that admitted a number of persons who could not support themselves. Relief to residents of the house suited the preferences of authorities who disapproved of direct public aid to paupers in their own homes. The county poor house was supposed to work toward self-sufficiency by training the occupants who were able to raise their own food.[16] Eighteen paupers, including two elderly blind persons, lived at the poor house in 1860. Of the sixteen who listed a place of birth in the census, nine came from foreign countries. Eight of them came from Ireland, the birthplace of the largest foreign-born element of the population of Mobile.[17]

Private benevolent organizations shouldered much of the responsibility for relieving the suffering of poor Mobilians. Private charity, according to the popular belief, reflected true philanthropy better than public contributions toward poor relief. As the *Mobile Advertiser* argued,

> Private charity speaks of a philanthropic heart—such gifts are the offspring of genuine benevolence. Men may be found who would vote away public funds for charitable purposes, who would not give a dime from their own pockets to clothe the naked or feed the starving—hence we think that the liberal private donations and tender of personal services made by our citizens, reflect much more credit upon the city, than had twice the amount been voted by the corporate authorities.[18]

Yellow fever epidemics in the late 1830s prompted Mobilians to form several charitable societies to care for the afflicted and their orphans. One year after the yellow fever epidemic of 1837 civic leaders organized the Samaritan Society to dispense aid to the ill and destitute in their community. While Samaritans provided aid on a year-round basis, they concentrated their efforts during the summer, when yellow fever threatened the port city. They directed fundraising drives late each spring to prepare for the potentially deadly summer. Expenses often exceeded $1,000 per year. The number of medical cases alone treated through the society in relatively healthy years (June to June) rose from 118 in 1847–48 to 192 in 1859–60. During epidemics the Samaritan Society aided far more people, 346 in 1853 and 258 in 1858, for instance.[19]

During the widespread yellow fever epidemic in 1839, prominent citizens realized that the poor needed extraordinary aid when the few doctors in the city were swamped with patients and the few nurses charged exorbitant fees. Twelve men who lunched together regularly at the Alhambra organized the Can't Get Away Club to care for needy victims of the epidemic. Contributing from their own resources, they raised a relief fund for distribution during outbreaks of yellow fever. Besides money, the Can't Get Away Club members gave their own services as nurses. "Nothing could exceed in pure philanthropy the acts of self-devotion for which every member became distinguished at that fatal epoch [1839]", reported Louis Tasistro, an English actor who visited Mobile shortly after the episode. "Setting aside all personal considerations," each member rushed to tend a neighbor who contracted yellow fever and stayed with his patient through the crisis of the disease or until he caught the fever himself. In that case, another member took his place. Members of the Can't Get Away Club "were seen flying in every direction . . . administering the balm of consolation to all who stood in want of assistance, without regard to the condition, or circumstances of the patient."[20] When the yellow fever outbreak was over, the club terminated its activities until another epidemic appeared in the city. In 1853 the Can't Get Away Club cared for 1,920 patients, 270 of whom were treated in infirmaries opened by the club in a carriage house and a hotel.[21]

Some of the funds to provide these services during epidemics came from liberal subscriptions of members of the societies, but many donations came from residents of other cities. Contributions came to the mayor, who routinely divided them between the Samaritan Society and Can't Get Away Club. In 1853 funds came from residents of Selma,

Linden, Macon, Philadelphia, and Boston. Mobile also received aid from the Howard Association of New Orleans, which dispatched money as well as doctors and nurses to help those suffering in their neighboring city. In 1853 yellow fever perhaps claimed relatively more lives in Mobile than in New Orleans.[22]

Despite the availability of free medical care to poor people afflicted with yellow fever, the disease claimed many lives and left many orphans. Churchwomen founded two orphanages to care for children left without parents by the yellow fever epidemics of 1837 and 1839. In 1838, under the guidance of Bishop Michael Portier, nine women formed the Catholic Female Charitable Society to support and to educate poor orphans and to aid the indigent.[23] Immediately after the disastrous fires and yellow fever epidemic of 1839, a dozen Protestant women formed their own orphan asylum society, calling themselves Protestant, as they said, "not in a spirit of sectarianism or exclusiveness" but in an effort to differentiate themselves from the "successful and highly useful" Catholic association. The Protestant Orphan Asylum Society initially included Episcopal, Presbyterian, Methodist, and Unitarian churchwomen; it later added Baptists. Members took charge of orphans formerly supported by the Episcopal Orphan Society, which was then apparently defunct.[24]

Both orphan aid societies obtained county tax revenue. In 1839 the act of incorporation for the Protestant Orphan Asylum Society permitted the organization to apply to the Mobile County Court of Commissioners of Roads and Revenue for the legal allowance for the support of orphans. It took the society four and one-half years to obtain its first grant from the court. In June 1844 the Protestant Orphan Asylum Society received $688.80 for its charges. Two years later the Catholic Female Charitable Society successfully obtained its first grant of public funds from the County Court of Commissioners of Roads and Revenue. For a number of years thereafter the Catholic association received $500 of county taxes annually toward the support of its homeless children. The Mobile County Court of Commissioners of Roads and Revenue continued annual grants to each of the private orphan aid societies according to the number of children in their care.[25]

County taxes paid only part of the cost of supporting children in the local orphanages, so their sponsoring societies raised additional funds. The Catholic Female Charitable Society cared for a large number of orphans, increasing from 3 when the asylum opened its doors near the Catholic church in 1838 to 182 in separate boys' and girls' homes in 1860. The Sisters of Charity supervised all children when they assumed management of the asylum in 1842, but they relinquished charge of the boys to the Brothers of the Sacred Heart in 1847.[26] The Protestant Orphan Asylum on Dauphin Street admitted both boys and girls, numbering 59 by 1860.[27] To support orphans in their charge, the Catholic and Protestant women's societies used a variety of techniques to raise funds. Beginning in 1839, the Catholic Female Charitable Society sponsored an annual orphans' fair on New Year's Eve and New Year's Day. Mystics who paraded on New Year's Eve sometimes visited the fair in costume to present donations.[28] The Protestant Orphan Asylum Society sponsored other fundraising events such as a concert of sacred music, a strawberry and ice cream party, and a benefit performance of the circus.[29]

Individual philanthropists materially aided the women's orphan aid societies. In 1840 John Dease gave the Catholic Female Charitable Society $5,000. In 1858 the Protestant Orphan Asylum Society received a legacy of $10,000 bequeathed by the late James Battle. Women managers of the society also accepted such practical gifts as suits for the boys from J. L. Weeks, a cow from Duke Goodman, and a dinner each New Year's Day from Israel I. Jones, a Jewish auctioneer who lived near the orphanage.[30]

Yellow fever relief organizations dispensed aid to a broad cross-section of needy Mobilians. Other paternalistic benevolent societies concentrated their efforts toward specific groups such as orphans. Sailors, whose labor materially contributed to the prosperity of the port city, became the particular charitable project of two benevolent associations. The Mobile Port Society, which was organized in 1835, sought primarily to promote the moral and social improvement of seafarers by encouraging the foundation of institutions for their benefit. H. B. Gwathmey, president of the Mobile Chamber of Commerce, led the Mobile Port Society in its formative years. In 1837 the society furnished a place of worship for seamen, or a bethel, in one of the buildings in Hitchcock's Row, located on Government Street near Water Street. By the next year the Port Society was so much in debt that it could not rent another bethel, so the Unitarian minister Henry B. Brewster rented a hall on Commerce Street at the corner of Government, where the bethel had once been located. Brewster established the bethel on a nondenominational basis, but he found that Presbyterian, Baptist, Methodist, and Episcopal clergymen opposed his intention to let Unitarians, along with ministers of other denominations, preach in the mission. Sectarian rivalry thus hampered the bethel.[31] Later, as Unitarians withdrew from active support of the bethel and the general financial situation improved in Mobile, the benevolent association for seamen built its own bethel.

The Ladies of the Bethel Society, which was organized in 1837, raised funds for the mission planned by the Mobile Port Society. The women's group sponsored fundraising fairs for the bethel in 1838, 1841, and 1843. Male trustees of the Seamen's House, whom the state legislature incorporated to manage the interests of the cause of the bethel in Mobile, solicited subscriptions and superintended the building of a church. Late in 1845 representative clergymen from Episcopal, Methodist, and Presbyterian churches dedicated the Bethel Church, located convenient to the docks area on Water Street between Theatre and Monroe streets. A year later the Ladies of the Bethel Society rented a "Sailor's House" on Church Street to provide inexpensive food and lodging to seamen while they were in port. This house served its purpose so well that its sponsoring society looked for another sailors' boarding house to rent in 1849. In the late 1850s, the mission to seamen included a chapel with regular worship services and Sunday school, a sailors' home with a library and reading room, and a floating bethel in Mobile Bay.[32] All of these institutions indicated their sponsors' concern for men "who, by their toil, build up our cities and enrich our citizens."[33]

To supplement the work of major paternalistic organizations, Mobilians formed a host of mutual aid societies. Mutual aid in sickness and death played an integral part in the program of fraternal groups. Indeed, Masonry received public commendation for "the relation a Mason bears to a brother, to the widow and orphan of a brother." A committee of charity of Masons visited and administered relief to all poor and ill members, and widows and orphans of the deceased. Masons belonged, according to the *Mobile Register*, "to that class of philanthropists, who 'do good in secret,' and would blush to find it fame."[34]

Volunteer fire companies also provided aid to their disabled members and to widows and orphans of the deceased. In 1833 the Neptune Engine Company Number 2 formed the first relief fund with appropriations from its treasury and donations from commercial firms. In 1838 the system used by Neptune Company served as the model for the Mobile Fire Department Association formed by eight white companies to provide aid for ill members and their families. Beginning in 1838, this joint benevolent association received a state-levied tax of $200 per year from all insurance agencies in Mobile. Insurance agents like Robert S. Bunker and merchants like John B. Todd had business as well as charitable reasons for serving as officers of the association.[35]

Stevedores and others who worked along Mobile Bay formed their own mutual aid association, the Baymen's Society, in 1851 to relieve members in distress or sickness. About 100 men joined the society in its first year. A. B. Meek, attorney, journalist, and legislator, served as president of the Baymen's Society, an association of what the *Mobile Register* called "one of our largest industrial classes."[36]

In 1855 lay churchmen formed an interdenominational mutual aid society and benevolent association called the Brotherhood of the Church. Closely tied to the Episcopal church, the Brotherhood used Bishop Nicholas Hamner Cobbs, Alabama's first Episcopal bishop, as its ex-officio visitor and counselor. Lay officers, headed by an insurance agent named Robert S. Bunker, accepted applications for aid. The Brotherhood sought to promote Christian fellowship among members through frequent contact, mutual aid, and encouragement in good works. Mutual aid for members included relief to the ill, Christian burial of the dead, and assistance to their families. Members also resolved to provide burial for other churchmen, to aid their families, and to assist the clergy in their ministries to the sick and destitute. Besides these goals, the Brotherhood supported other benevolent causes with its contingency fund.[37]

Ethnic groups maintained their own benevolent organizations. Among immigrant aid groups, the Hibernian Benevolent Society, which was founded in 1822, faced by far the most formidable task because of the large numbers of Irishmen who settled in antebellum Mobile. By 1860 natives of Ireland made up half of the foreign-born population. Many of the Irishmen who arrived in the 1840s and 1850s assumed low-paying jobs that failed to meet their financial needs. The Hibernian Benevolent Society offered "an asylum to every oppressed

Irishman."[38] Each St. Patrick's Day at a ball, dinner, or mass members collected contributions for their Charitable Fund, which provided relief to indigent immigrants, particularly orphans, widows, and the sick in the city.[39]

Since the tasks facing the Hibernian Benevolent Society often overwhelmed its own resources, other charitable associations also ministered to Irish immigrants. A large number of Irish-born Mobilians received medical care and food through the Samaritan Society. Of the 190 cases treated by the society for the last six months of 1846, natives of Ireland accounted for two-thirds of the total.[40] Admissions to the orphanages sponsored by the Catholic Female Charitable Society often included large numbers of Irish-born children. In 1853, the year of the severe yellow fever epidemic, almost half of the children admitted to the boys' and girls' orphanages came from Ireland.[41]

Other ethnic groups, whose native lands had relatively small representation among Mobile's foreign-born, maintained their own benevolent associations. By 1860 just one-seventh of the foreigners, who made up one-quarter of the total free population, hailed from Germany. Smaller fractions came from France and Scotland. Natives of each of these countries formed mutual aid associations. The German Turners Society and the St. Andrews Society for Scotsmen provided relief to ill members and families of deceased members. La Société Francaise de Bienfaisance (The French Benevolent Society) provided medical care to needy members. Henry de St. Cyr and John Hurtel, who were respected in both government and business circles, led the society, which printed its announcements in local newspapers in French.[42]

Benevolent associations, both paternalistic and mutual aid societies, tended to treat the immediate symptoms of poverty such as hunger and illness rather than deeper maladies like unemployment. As a cotton port Mobile routinely had seasonal unemployment during the summer. Furthermore, when cotton prices dropped, people involved in the cotton trade reduced their expenditures for goods and services, which in turn led to unemployment. Creation of jobs for the needy during hard times would have required a commitment that few middle- or upper-class residents cared to make. Like other mid-nineteenth-century Americans, they preferred private charitable aid programs and sporadic outpourings of disaster relief to deal with the poor.[43]

Only one association in antebellum Mobile provided employment for the needy. In 1856 the *Mobile Register* noted that some poor people were so proud that they would prefer jobs to handouts. "It is in seeking out the suffering, and ministering to them, not only in money, but in sympathy that we are deficient," observed the *Register*. As a sympathetic response to the poor who wished employment, the *Register* urged well-to-do ladies to provide employment for needy women.[44] Women eventually sponsored the only job agency in antebellum Mobile. In 1860 prominent churchwomen under the leadership of Mrs. Josiah Nott, the wife of a successful physician, managed the Protestant Episcopal Church Employment Society to furnish sewing jobs to poor women. Managers took orders for items and referred them to seamstresses. The employment bureau kept a supply of clothes for children and servants for sale in its depository on Dauphin Street opposite the Cathedral of the Immaculate Conception.[45]

Charitable associations generally ministered to those whose needs isolated them from society. Any institutions that benevolent societies established tended to isolate the needy even more. In contrast, public schools eventually provided the means for drawing rich and poor alike into the mainstream of society. Social reform might be achieved through the capabilities for indoctrination and discipline available in the institution of public schools.[46] These goals became increasingly desirable as society became more heterogeneous. For Mobile disparities between rich and poor and between native-born and immigrant in the 1850s created underlying conditions suited to the establishment of genuine public schools. Until then indifference and finances hampered the founding of public schools.

Private interests predominated for many years in education in Mobile. In early American Mobile many residents subscribed to the view, common in the Jacksonian era, that governmental activism was undesirable in social services, including education. Some maintained that the state had no duty to establish public schools for all. Moreover, like many southerners, Mobilians who could afford private schools for their children preferred them to public schools on the assumption that an education someone bought was superior to one handed to him by the state.[47]

Early state laws did make some provision for public schools, with much control left at the county level. At the time of Alabama's admission into the Union in 1819, the sixteenth section of each township was reserved to support a school for the township. A state law passed in 1823 provided for the division of authority over sixteenth-section lands between township school commissioners and district school trustees. Commissioners, who were appointed by the county commission, primarily administered income from the sixteenth section. Trustees, whom the citizens in the area served by the school elected, essentially ran the school, hiring and dismissing teachers, choosing texts, and so forth.[48] Moving beyond the state law, Mobilians in 1825 held a public meeting that resolved "a uniform system of education ought now to be adopted." In 1826 the state legislature enacted a bill, which was drafted by Mobile's representative, Willoughby Barton, to incorporate the Mobile County School Commissioners, empowering them to establish and to regulate schools. This bill provided for school revenue in addition to the income from sixteenth-section lands. New sources of revenue included certain fines, penalties, and forfeitures; taxes on auction sales; filing fees from circuit and county courts; license taxes on theatrical performances; and one-fourth of regular county taxes. In addition, the commissioners received the power to raise $50,000 by lottery for the school fund.[49]

Although the state statute had designated these funds for public schools in Mobile, commissioners had difficulty in collecting their revenue. Various county officials apparently withheld monies from the school fund. In 1829 the Alabama legislature ordered Mobile's auctioneers, tax collector, court clerks, and justices of the peace to submit strict accountings of their receipts to the school commissioners. Those who violated this law were subject to stiff fines. Despite this provision, tardy collection of school funds persisted. As a result, in 1836 the state legislature authorized the school commissioners to appoint committees to examine auctioneers' books quarterly. In addition, collectors might attend auctions, demand payment on the spot from auctioneers, and sell property themselves if the auctioneers balked at compliance. Certain provisions of the law contained loopholes that the circuit-court clerk used to avoid surrendering some monies. To increase revenue for Mobile's public schools, the legislature initiated a special tax for the school board in 1836.[50]

With their meager resources, school commissioners chose to distribute funds among private schools rather than establish public schools. They paternalistically arranged for the education of a few poor children at public expense. In 1833 the board of school commissioners took over Eliza Randall's Infant School and retained her as principal. Parents still

Barton Academy (Courtesy of the Museum of the City of Mobile)

paid two dollars per month tuition for each pupil. By augmenting Mrs. Randall's salary, the board arranged for the free instruction of five to ten indigent children. At the same time the board hired two men to teach Latin, Greek, and French to boys and two women to run a female school. School commissioners agreed to pay teachers one dollar per month per child for the education of five to ten pupils from poor homes or orphans, thus establishing their practice of subsidizing private education with public funds.[51] Throughout the state public funds helped to support private schools.[52]

Instructional services taxed the school commissioners' funds far less than the $100,000 cost of constructing a magnificent three-story school building on Government Street. Built in 1835 and 1836, Barton Academy was named for the author of the 1826 bill for public education in Mobile County. Building funds came from a $50,000 state-approved lottery, a city loan of $15,000, and private donations raised by two members of the school board, Henry Hitchcock and Silas Dinsmore.

When construction costs outran the school fund, commissioners had to carry a debt of $12,000 after the completion of the academy.[53] As a result of this burden, the commissioners decided to require tuition temporarily from parents and guardians of children enrolled in classes in the academy. "To insure good instructors," they insisted on tuition rates equal to those in private schools, minus a deduction "equivalent to the rent of a School House."[54] This arrangement, initiated for financial reasons and intended to be temporary, persisted for more than fifteen years.

For a brief period large numbers of poor children attended classes in the tax-supported schools. In 1838 the commissioners organized a department in Barton Academy solely for the instruction of poor boys. There pupils studied spelling, reading, writing, geography, and arithmetic. At first parents had to pay a token charge of $1 per month for each boy. In January 1839 the school commissioners repealed the fee and allowed the instructor to admit any boy whose parents could not afford the tuition in the higher male department (then $5 to $7 per month). Some poor girls also had the chance for a formal education in the Free Female Department, authorized by the school commissioners in February 1839. In lieu of student fees, the board paid the teacher a monthly salary of $2.50 per pupil. The Free Department, Male and Female, attracted a large enrollment, registering 150 out of 350 pupils at Barton Academy in 1839.[55]

Free education ended as the school commissioners faced financial crisis. Debts incurred for the construction of Barton Academy strained the school fund, especially when the Panic of 1837 cut its revenues. To generate more income, the school commissioners in 1838 rented some of the unused rooms in the academy to local clubs like the Franklin Society, Philomathean Society, and Masons' Lodge. Rental income failed to augment the school fund substantially. So, to cut expenses, the school commissioners discontinued both the boys' and girls' free schools in August 1839. In addition, the board demanded rent from private teachers who had formerly used rooms in Barton rent-free. All of these economy measures reduced operating expenses but failed to repay the school commissioners' $12,000 debt. Therefore, they auctioned away Barton Academy in 1840 for $15,000.[56]

In a public-spirited effort civic leaders intervened to buy back Barton Academy. Thomas McGran, who had purchased the building, initially granted the school commissioners sixty days to redeem the property. He eventually extended the redemption period to fifteen years. Two former school commissioners, Samuel P. Bullard and Daniel Chandler, sought office again in 1841 for the sole purpose of saving Barton and liquidating the board's debt. As president of the school board in 1841, Bullard obtained personal notes from six well-to-do men and one business firm to muster enough capital to buy back Barton Academy. Thus, according to Bullard, John A. Campbell, Daniel Chandler, James Innerarity, James Sanford, Solomon Mordecai, Samuel Wallace, and Ledyard, Hatter and Company earned the community's lasting gratitude.[57]

Further actions not only staved off immediate financial disaster, but also provided safeguards against future crises. As a stop-gap measure, the school commissioners increased the rents charged to private teachers who used rooms in Barton Academy. New financial restrictions placed on the school board by the 1843 legislature emphasized solvency at the expense of education. This legislation required that revenues from the school fund first be applied toward the liquidation of the school commissioners' debts. After the debt was repaid, the fund might be applied toward the instruction of children. In addition, the legislature forbade selling or encumbering any school property except to pay previously contracted debts.[58]

After the school commissioners had abolished their own free school, they channeled tax monies into nonsectarian and sectarian charity schools. For instance, in 1844 the commissioners granted fourteen scholarships to the school run by Schuyler Clarke in Barton Academy. The greatest boon to publicly financed education short of a genuine public school system came in the act passed by the Alabama legislature in 1846 to aid free schools in the city of Mobile. According to its provisions, a taxpayer could designate whether his school tax would go to a free school run by his denomination or to the general school fund. The Methodist Free School received the first appropriations under this arrangement. In 1847 the Bethel School (Presbyterian) joined the ranks of tax-aided charity schools. By 1851 Catholic and Episcopal free schools in the county also received benefits. Total sums allocated to denominational free schools remained small ($3,550 for 1851–52).[59] Yet public school funds ensured that some children received an education they might never have had otherwise.

Aldermen in Mobile contributed municipal funds, perhaps totalling $1,500 a year, to the free schools run by various denominations. For some schools municipal aid exceeded support from county school taxes. In 1846 the city paid $35 per month to the Bethel School run by the pastor of the Bethel Church, the Reverend Alexander McGlashan. County school commissioners allocated it $25 monthly. By 1852 the city was contributing to the Presbyterian, Catholic, Episcopal, and Methodist free schools total aid in the sum of $77.50 each month. These subsidies reflected the aldermen's view "that these schools should be fostered and cherished by the City."[60]

Catholic free schools, the oldest in the city, enrolled the largest number of pupils. In the early American years priests occasionally taught children reading, writing, and arithmetic free of charge. The Reverend Gabriel Chalon, for instance, offered classes at the Catholic chapel in 1832. Catholic education began to take permanent form in 1841 when the Sisters of Charity opened both their free and pay schools. Tuition from the pay school financed the free education of the indigent. By 1844 the sisters taught ninety orphans free of charge and sixty girls who paid tuition. In addition, they engaged a lay schoolmaster for forty boys. The Brothers of the Sacred Heart, who moved to Mobile in 1847, ran both a free and a pay school for boys. By 1852 the brothers and sisters enrolled about 400 poor children in their four free schools, exclusive of the orphan schools. (One school enrolled boys; one, girls; one, whites of both sexes; and one, black Creoles of both sexes.)[61]

Protestants also founded free schools, but on a smaller scale than those established by Catholics. Methodists opened the first Protestant free school in cooperation with a Unitarian minister. In 1842 Charles Dall, the Unitarian, taught Sunday school classes in reading to poor children for one hour before worship services. Dall made an arrangement with the pastor of what was then called the Jackson Street Methodist Church to teach twenty poor children five days a week. Classes first met in the Unitarian church building on the corner of Jackson and St. Michael streets, which was rented to the Methodist congregation. After Dall left Mobile, Methodists continued the free school at the Franklin Street Church.[62] In 1846 the Bethel Church (Presbyterian) opened a school to help many boys and girls, some nearly grown, who could not make satisfactory progress toward learning to read in Sunday school. Donations from its sponsoring church, from the Mobile

County School Commissioners, from city government, and from private individuals supported the Bethel School. During its first six months, the school enrolled 223 children, aged five to nineteen. In 1848 214 children attended the Bethel School and its new branch in Orange Grove, an outlying district. The Bethel Free School, the Methodist Free School at the Franklin Street Methodist Church, and the Episcopal Free School at Trinity Church admitted poor children without regard to their religious affiliation.[63]

While most free schools enrolled whites exclusively, some accepted only free blacks of Creole descent. Special educational privileges for black Creoles evolved from provisions in the Louisiana Purchase Treaty of 1803 that had guaranteed to free residents of Louisiana and their descendants the rights, privileges, and immunities of citizens of the United States. The Adams-Onis Treaty by which Spain ceded West Florida (which included Mobile and Baldwin Counties) to the United States in 1819 confirmed that the free inhabitants of that territory had "all privileges, rights, and immunities of the citizens of the United States." This stipulation ensured the educational rights of the descendants of Mobile's free black residents of Creole derivation in 1803. Thus, after the Nat Turner insurrection of 1831 when Alabama, like other southern states, prohibited blacks, free and slave, from being taught to read and write, the "free Colored Creoles" of Mobile won the right to have their own schools. In 1833 the state authorized the mayor and aldermen to issue licenses to people they deemed suitable to instruct the black Creoles. The first teachers who received these licenses for one year were William H. Johnson and A. Sellier, both in 1844.[64]

Churches sponsored the first clearly free schools for black Creoles. In 1849, after his success with the Bethel Free School, the Reverend Alexander McGlashan opened a school for Creoles, which quickly enrolled seventy pupils. Free-will offerings financed this project. Catholics established Creole schools in 1850. That year the Brothers of the Sacred Heart taught twenty Creole boys and the Sisters of Charity enrolled fifty Creole girls.[65] These free schools operated on the profits from the Catholics' pay schools.

Even with the presence of numerous private and parochial schools, some tax-subsidized, a census of school-age children in 1851 showed that nearly 42 percent attended no school. Of the 3,524 school-age white children, only 2,400 were enrolled in school. School commissioners admitted that tuition prices were so high that the ordinary laborer did not earn enough to maintain "one child at a good school, much less . . . several."[66] As the *Mobile Advertiser* noted, "No workingman can afford to send his children to school in Mobile."[67] Fees of five to six dollars per month for the basic curriculum plus two dollars more for instruction in a modern foreign language were indeed beyond the budgets of laborers. Yet many working-class people chose not to admit this problem to charity-school authorities because they preferred not to be labelled as paupers. Poor Mobilians desired an alternative to expensive private schools and to socially stigmatized free schools. One laborer urged immediate action "for the benefit of the most numerous part of our population, whose children are either growing up destitute of the common rudiments of education or else contenting, and deceiving themselves by what little they get from the little charity schools in the city."[68]

The campaign for public education was managed not by the working-class parents most likely to benefit directly from the system but by civic leaders interested in using common schools to create an ordered society. By the early 1850s the population of Mobile was far more heterogeneous than it had ever been, including large numbers of newly arrived immigrants. Columns discussing public schools in local newspapers may not have mentioned the diversity among residents as a sign of the need for increased order, but they did include as a goal for public schools fostering "social intercourse and individual friendship among the different classes of the community."[69] Leading advocates of a public school system in Mobile resembled their counterparts in such places as Beverly, Massachusetts, and Wilmington, Delaware, in that they were well-educated, middle-class men who hoped to promote social order through the schools.[70]

Responding to the increased demand for public education without the stigma of charity, some school commissioners recommended the economically expedient course of expanding the system of public aid to already established free schools. To augment the school fund for this purpose, the committee proposed selling Barton Academy and other school property elsewhere in the county, investing the $40,000 anticipated price, and distributing interest from this capital fund to free schools. Proponents of the sale contended that high-yield investments would produce more revenue than the $1,000 received annually from renting Barton Academy to private schools and clubs. Another faction of the school board opposed the sale of Barton and proposed instead using the building for its original purpose—public schools.[71]

Agitation about selling Barton increased after February 1852, when the Alabama legislature authorized the sale if a majority of voters approved it at the county election in August. According to one school-board member, this act proved "far-reaching in its effects, and much more potent in its influence than its framers had designed, desired, or expected." Mobilians formed parties for and against the proposed sale of Barton.[72] Walter Smith championed forces for the sale. He called the academy useless as a public school and suggested construction of several plain but substantial school buildings in different parts of the city. Arguing that the public wanted only a tax-supported common school education, Smith maintained that Barton Academy would not be used as a high school. Smith contended that the sale of Barton Academy and its lot would bring $30,000 which, when properly invested, would yield $2,400 annual interest for extending the school system.[73]

Mayor Kiah B. Sewall led opponents of the sale who wished to keep Barton Academy and make it the focal point of a three-tiered system of public education. According to Sewall, each of the states with the oldest public school systems operated them on three levels, primary, grammar, and high school, all of which were considered essential. Sewall thought that Mobile should follow examples set by New York, Boston, New Orleans, and Portland in using the three-level system. Centrally located Barton Academy could house one level of the public school program on each of its three floors.[74] A teacher echoed Sewall's argument that Barton Academy could be used advantageously for common schools, accommodating in its classrooms at least 1,000 students who were then being educated in free schools scattered throughout the city. With tax support and minimal tuition charges in the intermediate and high school departments, the school commissioners could finance common schools. "Would it not be better to use thus a noble building for the purposes designed by the public spirited men who planned it," the teacher asked, "than to sacrifice it for one third its value, to be used for such purposes as speculators might think best?"[75]

Following this practical reasoning, someone who signed himself "One Vote" maintained that common schools should be established in the handsome building already available for that purpose instead of selling it when a similar building could not be obtained for the sale price.[76]

In August 1852 Mobilians overwhelmingly voted against the sale of Barton Academy, thus endorsing the organization of a genuine public school system. Large majorities elected each member of the "no sale" ticket of school commissioners, which included prominent merchants and editors.[77]

Northern-born urban leaders were instrumental in organizing the movement for a genuine public school system. In this effort they were perhaps influenced by the example set a decade earlier by the northern-born merchants and lawyers in New Orleans who had organized public schools there.[78] Natives of the North had consistently supported the cause of public education in Mobile; they made up more than one-third (37.3 percent) of the urban leaders elected as school commissioners between 1826 and 1860. Five of the twelve school commissioners elected on the reform ticket in 1852 had moved to Mobile from the North. Probably the two most influential members of the new board were Thaddeus Sanford, the Connecticut-born editor of the *Mobile Register* for many years, and Willis G. Clark, the New Yorker who began editing the *Mobile Advertiser* in the 1850s. Both Sanford and Clark used their newspapers to speak favorably for public education.[79] They were just two of numerous northern-born editors of southern newspapers who took progressive stands for the establishment of public schools.[80]

The economy and efficiency in education available through the public school system definitely appealed to the business leaders who ruled the city. "The main object to be obtained by Public Schools," reported the committee that drafted the plan in 1852, "is to educate the *greatest* number, in the *best* manner, and at the *least* expense." Public schools were designed to arrange pupils' studies systematically so that each teacher could instruct more children than in private schools. Moreover, students in public schools should progress from lower to higher departments on the basis of their qualifications; in the private schools teachers tended to let parental whims influence promotion. Discipline in public schools might be more uniform and disinterested than in private schools.[81] By providing for adequate supervision, the plan for public schools promised improvements over the old system of tax aid to private schools, particularly in regard to management and nonsectarianism.[82]

Advocates of public schools boasted that the new system in its early years of operation produced what every enlightened community had— "a cheap, well-arranged, equitable and republican principle for popular instruction."[83] As established in 1852, the Mobile Public School System included three levels: primary, grammar, and high school, each with separate male and female departments. Later the levels were subdivided to consist of primary, intermediate, junior grammar, senior grammar, and high school. School commissioners of Mobile incorporated some of the distinctive features of northern public school systems suitable for a beginning southern system, features that Willis Clark identified on a visit to New York, Boston, and other northeastern cities in 1853.[84] Textbooks adopted for a number of subjects conformed to ones used in urban public school systems in Massachusetts.[85]

Curriculum in the public schools reflected American preferences for a "thorough English education." This priority meant that ancient and modern languages were available in the high school department only as secondary and incidental courses subject to additional fees.[86] Educational concerns also dictated the reading of the Bible in public schools to acquaint students with American political and social privileges. "As the whole structure of our government," Commissioner Walter Smith argued, "supposed a knowledge of the moral attributes of God, and of the retributions of eternity, which the Bible alone teaches, so it is *right* in the people be instructed on those points." In order to keep public schools free of sectarian or denominational influences, commissioners required that teachers read a chapter from the Bible each morning without inculcating sectarian sentiments. Commissioners also stipulated that teachers "show by precept and example, the benefit and excellence of virtue and morality."[87]

The public school system assumed management of the already established Creole School, thus directly providing tax-supported education for the county's black Creoles. A few years later the school board nearly closed the school. In 1856, after lengthy discussions of the legality and wisdom of continuing a public school for this special class of citizens, school commissioners approved a recommendation from its executive committee chaired by Willis Clark to discontinue the Creole School. Before the opening of the new school term, Thaddeus Sanford requested fellow board members to appoint a special committee to investigate "the propriety and legality of continuing the Creole School." This committee, chaired by Sanford, recommended the expediency of continuing the Creole School "on the principles on which it has heretofore been conducted." The board accepted this recommendation and supported the school until the Civil War. To ensure that it stayed within the law regarding the education of Creoles, the board resolved to have the local committee for the school take a careful census of all school-age children in the district who were descendants of the Creole inhabitants of the territory at the time of cession in 1819. A copy of this list would then be given to the teacher of the Creole School with an order to admit only those children whose names appeared on the list. Enough children attended the Creole School by 1860 to warrant the employment of an assistant teacher.[88] Their education at public expense placed the black Creoles of Mobile in a position that free blacks occupied in virtually no other late antebellum southern city.[89]

Public schools in Mobile and changes in political emphases in the state legislature helped to produce laws that established a statewide system of public education. In the 1850s some legislators began to accept the notion that Whig educational reformers had long argued, that is, ignorant people did not make good citizens who were capable of self-government. The cause of public education became one that politicians adopted in an effort to win popular approval. The session of 1853 established the state's public school system, and the session of 1855 completed the task by providing, through certain license fees and property taxes, sound funding for the schools. Together, the Public Schools Act of 1854 and the Public Schools Amendments Act of 1856 also diminished local autonomy in certain areas by creating the offices of state and county superintendent of education, both of whom were given much administrative discretion.[90]

State legislation altered the administration of public schools in Mobile. From 1852 to 1854 the board of school commissioners formed its own committees to supervise the schools. In 1854 the commissioners hired a superintendent to oversee the administration of the six school districts in the city and the seventeen in the county outside the city. Board members continued to certify the qualifications of teachers and to appropriate funds, but the superintendent assumed responsibility for day-to-day operations. Parents and guardians of school-age children and school taxpayers exercised some control over schools in the county outside the city, for they had the right to elect local committees of trustees who hired teachers subject to approval by the school commissioners. The board filled vacancies on the local committees.[91] In 1859 the commissioners determined that the school system was so well organized that they no longer needed a superintendent. They discontinued the position of superintendent and shifted his duties to the principal of the boys' high school.[92]

New sources of school revenue turned the ledgers toward balanced budgets in Mobile. During the first two years of the public school system, when tax monies and tuition charges failed to cover expenses, the school board met deficiencies by obtaining loans on the personal security of some board members. The 1856 school-tax law brought in new revenues from license fees and property taxes that helped the school commissioners to come close to balancing their budgets late in the decade. School commissioners spent the tax revenues allocated to them at the rate of $4 per school-age white and black Creole child in the district. About $1.30 of this amount came directly from state educational funds.[93]

Public schools eventually attracted a wide cross-section of students, drawing pupils from certain free and pay schools that either closed or lost enrollment. With the opening of public schools, taxes designated for education could no longer be channeled into denominational free schools. Protestant free schools closed, thus releasing students for the public schools. Catholic schools, free and pay, persisted with total enrollment as high as 1,000 in 1857. The most exclusive Catholic school, Visitation Convent, maintained its regular schedule. Yet the convent school declined in size, enrolling ninety-eight girls in 1851 and seventy-three in 1860.[94] Enrollment may have dropped there and in other expensive private schools because parents perceived that the new public schools offered far more than the old free or pauper schools. A statement by Willis Clark suggests this tendency: "The [public] schools attained so high a character, both with regard to discipline and thoroughness of instruction, that the rich soon sought them for their children in preference to sending them to the best private schools the city afforded."[95] More than one-fourth of Mobile's school-age white children in fact attended public schools by 1860.[96] This proportion placed the city ahead of southern (one-seventh) and northern (one-sixth) averages for public school attendance in 1860.[97]

Mobilians liked to believe that their city was progressive in social services. They believed that they contributed generously to charities when the needs of the poor were brought to their attention. In this belief affluent residents contented themselves that urban poverty was kept in check without major expenditures of tax revenues. When the magnitude of poverty in the 1850s belied that notion, civic leaders tended to downplay the problem. Leaders did, however, come to support a public school system that might instill community-wide values and lessons expected of potential voters and taxpayers. Recognizing that some of their fellow southern cities were also establishing public schools, civic leaders in Mobile did not wish to see their own city lag behind in an effort that might attract new people to their city. They patterned their educational system after models developed for advanced northeastern cities on the assumption that progress demanded such imitation.

✳ 8 ✳

Pursuit of Progress

I N the 1850s Mobilians reflected on their pursuit of progress for their city. True, the population had doubled in the 1820s and quadrupled in the 1830s. But the rate of growth had slowed in the 1840s, when the population did not even double from the previous decade. Civic leaders tended to interpret this fact and a host of economic indicators as stagnation. As a way of reversing the trend after the local economy had recovered from the lingering effects of the Panic of 1837, boosters promoted railroads, direct trade, and manufacturing for Mobile. These new enterprises promised to reinvigorate the city by diversifying its economy and in so doing to place the city squarely in the movement for southern commercial independence from northern domination. That offered the only path to genuine progress for Mobile.

"A new era of prosperity is beginning to dawn," maintained *Rowan's Directory* in 1850, "and a bright prospect to the Mobilian, is in full view." After years of depression following the Panic of 1837, Mobile at last exhibited signs of a revitalized economy, with commerce, manufacturing, and construction on the upswing. Householders increased in number by 50 percent in two years as new homes were constructed on formerly vacant lots within the city and its suburbs.[1] Several hundred new buildings, mostly homes, were constructed during the summer of 1850 alone. At that time real estate developers also erected a block of six stores on St. Francis Street and three on Water Street. Local boosters, such as the editor of the *Mobile Advertiser*, interpreted the increase in the value of real estate as "evidence of a healthy prosperity in our city."[2] Throughout the decade spurts of major construction evoked praise from the press. In 1853 large construction projects on Royal Street included the Odd Fellows Hall, County Courthouse, Savings Bank, and the Battle House.[3] By 1859 the *Mobile Register* announced that someone who had left Mobile five years earlier would hardly recognize the city because of the many new buildings necessitated by the increasing commerce of the port. According to the *Register*, the 180 buildings that were constructed during the summer of 1859 "would of themselves make a quite good sized town."[4] This construction indicated to the editor of the *Mobile Advertiser* "the rapid growth of the city, and a healthy tone of financial affairs among us." After recounting a long list of construction projects in the true spirit of urban boosterism, the editor asked, "Who will contend that Mobile is 'the one horse town' that croakers for the last fifteen, twenty or thirty years have persisted in calling it?"[5]

Prospects for Mobile in the 1850s seemed especially bright to older residents who had witnessed the city's development since its American occupation. They took special interest in local history during the decade and contributed the first major columns on the subject to local newspapers. Publication in 1851 of Albert J. Pickett's *History of Alabama* sparked a controversy with longtime residents of Mobile who disagreed with his assertion that the French had originally established the city near the mouth of Dog River. Older Mobilians maintained that stories from their fathers and grandfathers had never mentioned Dog River as the first site of the city. Furthermore, those who lived in the vicinity of the alleged site had found no remains of an early settlement. Believing these local residents and Catholic parish records that disputed Pickett's account, the *Alabama Planter* tried to correct the record by publishing its own findings about the founding of Mobile.[6]

In a lengthy column entitled "The Olden Time," which appeared in the *Mobile Register* in 1856, editor John Forsyth compiled the reminiscences of many of the city's "oldest inhabitants . . . to present a picture of Mobile, as it appeared when it first began to assume any importance as a commercial city." This detailed sketch concentrated on the decade from 1817 to 1827, during which the colonial military town dominated by Fort Charlotte gave way to the bustling commercial port served by steamboats. Streets were opened and stores, homes, and public buildings appeared in the town. Although a yellow fever outbreak in 1819 somewhat stunted the town's growth, development continued until the fire in 1827 destroyed Mobile from Conti to St. Michael streets, "making room for an improved [brick] style of building." "From that time the city went on steadily increasing" until the Panic of 1837, "when the whole community was ruined by the injudicious banking system then in vogue, and the spirit of wild speculation which it had fostered." According to the authors of the column, "Never were the prospects of Mobile brighter than at the present moment" (1856) when the city had the means to capture the trade of the west by new railroads. These rail lines should make Mobile within fifty years become "the largest exporting city on the Gulf."[7]

Railroads provided one of the several avenues to southern independence and urban growth that were suggested by a series of commercial conventions held throughout the South beginning in the late 1830s. Commercial conventions themselves may not have found universal favor, but southern independence evoked such widespread enthusiasm that rival newspapers in Mobile vied with each other to express their loyalty to the cause. When the *Mobile Register* accused the *Mobile Advertiser* of lacking interest in commercial conventions, Willis G. Clark of the *Advertiser* admitted that he thought commercial conventions fruitless. Clark nevertheless reiterated his support for the cause of southern independence, pledging "to arouse our people to the importance of developing home resources, of encouraging home manufactures, of building up home educational institutions and of building up *home* commercial centres." He particularly favored railroads and judicious state aid for internal improvements.[8] "Southron" argued in the *Advertiser* that the South's problems during the Panic of 1857 stemmed mainly from "the close connection and intimate relations existing between the North and South in all business transactions." "Southron" called on southerners to seek new avenues of trade and to handle their own trade. In that way great distribution centers for imports and factories would develop in southern cities.[9] Throughout the decade, Mobilians tried every means to progress suggested by Clark and "Southron."

Like many other southern urbanites, Mobilians concluded that railroads offered the best means of offsetting the declining prosperity of their city. In the 1840s Mobilians perceived their city to be in a slump that placed it farther and farther behind its rival on the Gulf, New Orleans. J. D. B. DeBow, editor of the New Orleans-based commercial journal *DeBow's Review*, found it "melancholy to see that an opinion of her [Mobile's] decline, whether actual or imaginary, exists in the minds of her people." According to DeBow, Mobile was increasingly changing from "one of the most active commercial cities of the South into a mere depot for the storage and transshipment of cotton bales."[10] Mobile had been an entrepot for cotton throughout its American history. However, local citizens slowly came to view that function as inadequate to stimulate necessary growth of their city. During adversity Mobilians could see more clearly than during prosperity "the ruinous fluctuations to which the city is liable [because of] her total dependence for subsistence on influences over which [Mobilians] have no control."[11]

Urban rivalry provided a major stimulus for railroad building as Mobile sought to avoid becoming what the *Mobile Register* called "a mere suburb and outpost of New Orleans."[12] Keenly aware that their city's share of cotton exports remained smaller than that of New Orleans, Mobilians determined to connect the Alabama port with the mouth of the Ohio River, thereby tapping both the trade of the West and cotton districts of Mississippi that normally followed the Mississippi River to New Orleans. The preference for a north-to-south rail line reflected the promoters' conviction that a link between regions with different climates and therefore different products would make a better investment than an east-to-west connection within southern cotton districts. The north-to-south line would not so much supplement or replace river trade as it would open fresh commercial connections.[13]

The vision for the Mobile and Ohio Railroad came from Marshall J. D. Baldwyn, who dreamed of a rail link from Mobile to Cairo, Illinois. Even though Baldwyn had never built a railroad or in fact distinguished himself in any enterprise, his unwavering conviction that his plan would transform Mobile into a great city eventually persuaded such established merchants as Sidney Smith and Duke Goodman. Early in 1847 a public meeting appointed a committee to investigate the proposed railroad. By the end of the year promoters had obtained a preliminary survey of the route and had launched efforts to obtain charters from states along the proposed route and land grants from Congress. Sidney Smith, one of Baldwyn's early converts to his plan, headed the provisional railroad association.[14]

The survey of the route praised Mobile, in the language of urban boosterism, as the logical southern terminus of the trunk railroad projected to the Ohio River valley. Both *DeBow's Review* and *Hunt's Mer-*

chants' Magazine published the engineer Lewis Troost's report on the route, which argued the geographic advantages of Mobile. Not only was Mobile the point on the Gulf of Mexico nearest to the junction of the Mississippi and the Ohio rivers but the city was also best situated of all Gulf ports for trade with Texas, Mexico, and the West Indies. "A central position on the Gulf—an elevated and healthy location—an abundant supply of pure water—the best harbor on the coast," noted *Hunt's Merchants' Magazine*, "all these combine to make Mobile the most favorable point that could be selected for the terminus of a great trunk, like the projected railway to Ohio."[15] According to Troost, the healthiness of Mobile compared favorably with that of any other southern seaport "while during an epidemic, strangers who are only liable to it, can avoid its influence by an hour's drive into the country on the sand-hills, where they are as free from contagion and in as healthy and pleasant climate as the north."[16]

The Mobile and Ohio Railroad Company expected to pay its initial grading costs with local subscriptions for stock. In 1848, with the preliminary survey and charters from Alabama, Mississippi, Tennessee, and Kentucky, the company launched a stock subscription drive for funds to grade the first 120 miles of the line, running from Mobile to the Jackson Railroad in Mississippi. As revolutions in Europe caused financial repercussions in the United States, the economic situation in the spring of 1848 looked "unpropituous" for such an ambitious undertaking as the Mobile and Ohio, nearly 500 miles long. Nevertheless the *Mobile Register* argued that postponement of the project might prove fatal to the city.[17] Enough residents shared that view to subscribe $650,000 of capital stock in the railroad company during the first twenty days of the subscription drive in May. Shareholders then elected thirteen directors of the company, who chose one of their number, Sidney Smith, as president, selected other officers, and began preparations for construction.[18] The charter from Alabama permitted construction to begin when the amount subscribed to the capital stock exceeded $250,000.[19]

The Mobile and Ohio obtained federal grants of public land along its route. On a southern visit in 1849 Senator Stephen Douglas of Illinois consulted in Mobile with officers of the railroad company. He offered to include an application for federal land grants in Alabama and Mississippi for the Mobile and Ohio in his bill for Illinois to secure grants for the Illinois Central in Illinois. Douglas hoped to cement the North and South with this railroad system. The bill to aid the two rail lines that projected continuous connections from the Gulf to the Great Lakes eventually drew the support of congressmen from areas affected by the railroads. As enacted into law in 1850, Douglas's bill obtained grants of alternate sections of public lands in Alabama and Mississippi along the route of the Mobile and Ohio Railroad.[20]

Propertyholders in the city of Mobile voted special tax levies on themselves to aid the Mobile and Ohio Railroad. Since Alabama did not permit home rule on such taxation, each proposal had to be authorized by the state legislature before owners of real estate in Mobile could vote on it. In 1850 propertyowners overwhelmingly (404 to 7) voted for a "railroad tax" of 25¢ per $100 of real estate within city limits to raise $300,000 for the Mobile and Ohio Railroad. Two years later propertyholders in Mobile voted strongly (832 to 6) in favor of a new railroad tax of 2 percent per year on each $100 of real estate within the city for five years.[21] One Mobilian called this special railroad tax, which replaced the earlier one, "the most important measure for this city that has ever happened for its future prosperity."[22] Passage of the tax ensured the completion of the Mobile and Ohio from Mobile to the Mississippi state line.

In contrast to generous contributions from municipal sources of taxation in Mobile, the state of Alabama provided meager aid to the Mobile and Ohio. The city of Mobile ultimately subscribed $1,100,000 from special taxes on real estate to the Mobile and Ohio Railroad, while the state eventually loaned the company only $400,000. Mobile became one of three American cities, along with Louisville and Portland, that spent more than their respective states for railroad promotion.[23]

State-wide internal-improvements conventions, cities, and legislators from districts affected by proposed railroads lobbied extensively for state aid during the 1850s. At the railroad convention held in Talladega in 1849, the president of the convention, Philip Phillips, a state legislator from Mobile, advocated the creation of railroad and river linkages to connect north and south Alabama. For the southern terminus of a railroad southbound from Gunter's Landing on the Tennessee River, he favored Selma because of that town's location on the Alabama River, which connected to Mobile Bay. In 1851 delegates assembled in Mobile for another railroad convention, sponsored by stockholders of the Alabama and Tennessee River and Mobile and Ohio railroads. Senator William R. King presided over the convention, and Philip Phillips presented resolutions on behalf of the committee appointed to draft them. Believing that an internal improvements system offered the best way to develop and to advance the agricultural, mineral, and commercial interests of the state, delegates called for state aid to major projects then underway. Aid should not, they agreed, jeopardize the credit of the state nor create new debts. Railroad promoters at the convention suggested that aid come from the 5 percent of the proceeds of federal land sales in the state reserved for internal improvements by the act of Congress providing for admission of Alabama into the Union. Convention delegates appointed a committee to write an address to the people of Alabama, for publication in newspapers throughout the state, requesting Alabamians to urge their legislators to provide state aid to a system of five railroads, including the Mobile and Ohio and the Alabama and Tennessee River railroads.[24]

Philip Phillips, the author of the committee's address to Alabama, chaired the Alabama House Committee on Internal Improvements during the 1851 session. For that committee he wrote a report calling for state aid to improve transportation systems in the manner recommended by the railroad convention. He asked the legislature to investigate the funds containing the state's 5 percent of the proceeds from the sales of federal lands and to use those funds for internal improvements.[25]

Federal legislation initially gave Alabama control over 3 percent of the trust, while the United States Congress retained control over the remaining 2 percent. The legislature deposited the 3 percent fund in an account in the state bank. When the state bank became insolvent after the Panic of 1837, the state lost the money. Congress maintained control over 2 percent of the trust, with the intention of financing roads entering Alabama from other states. None had been built by 1841, when Congress gave the fund to the state provided that the money would be used to provide north-south and east-west links for the state, that is, to link the Tennessee River with Mobile Bay and to help build a road or a railroad from West Point, Georgia, across Alabama toward Jackson, Mississippi. Alabama legislators eventually appropriated some of this fund in loans to companies that chartered railroads meeting the requirements set by Congress.[26] In this way the state encouraged internal improvements.

In 1854, over Governor John A. Winston's veto, the legislature approved a loan of $400,000 to the Mobile and Ohio Railroad Company. Winston steadfastly opposed state aid to private internal improvement companies on practical and philosophical grounds: he maintained that the state should get out of debt before aiding railroads, and on principle he opposed government interference with private enterprise. He envisioned a simple republican government, certainly far removed from the activist role then demanded by railroad promoters. Railroad supporters prevailed with the legislature, which overrode the governor's veto of the Mobile and Ohio loan, but the terms of the loan left much influence to the governor.[27]

Continuing conflicts between the company and the governor embroiled the company and the state in extended litigation. The company had to furnish collateral for the loan in first mortgage bonds or personal securities sufficient to satisfy the governor that the state's money would be repaid. The company was required to pay interest on the amount of the loan at an annual rate of 6 percent until the principal fell due in two years. At the due date the company requested and won, over another veto by Winston, an extension of the loan. Renewal terms authorized the governor to receive first mortgage bonds or personal securities or both to satisfy him that the state's money was secure.[28] Despite pleas from the directors of the company, Winston demanded personal securities from them for the entire loan and mortgage bonds for $600,000. When the company refused to comply with his terms, Winston advertised the railroad's first mortgage bonds, given the state at the time of the initial loan, for sale. The Mobile and Ohio Railroad Company obtained an injunction against the governor, but state courts eventually upheld the governor's position. A compromise arranged in 1857 and enacted into law in 1858 permitted repayment of the loan in installments beginning in 1860. The company had to continue interest payments at a higher annual rate of 8 percent on the amount of the loan. The legislature later extended the payment arrangement to require the entire principal to be paid in 1862.[29]

The situation that forced the Mobile and Ohio Railroad Company to extend its state loan in 1856 resulted largely from its difficulties in borrowing funds from English financiers during the Crimean War. Sidney Smith, president of the Mobile and Ohio, journeyed to England in 1853 and 1854 trying to arrange loans for iron and other construction needs. Instability in Europe, caused by bad harvests and the

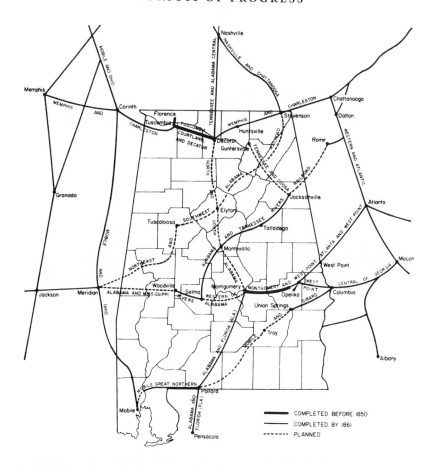

Railroads in Alabama in 1861 (Reprinted by permission of Louisiana State University Press from *Politics and Power in a Slave Society: Alabama 1800–1860* by J. Mills Thornton III, copyright © 1978)

onset of the Crimean War, made British financiers wary of loans to southern railroads from 1853 to 1855. Rumors circulated in England by officers of rival railroads that their competitors were insolvent also hurt the cause of southern railroads. In 1856, when it was $1,500,000 in debt, the Mobile and Ohio issued income bonds and tried to sell its excess public lands at auction in an effort to ward off insolvency.[30] During the company's financial crisis in 1856, stockholders ousted Sidney Smith from the presidency and replaced him with Arthur F. Hopkins, an attorney, to provide new management. Bankers in London eventually agreed to loans that helped to pay for completion of the line. Extension of the state loan also facilitated construction.[31]

These corporate difficulties of the Mobile and Ohio Company seriously delayed work on the railroad. While construction on the southern end of the line from Mobile was halted for a year, builders concentrated on the northern end of the project. Jackson, Tennessee, and Columbus, Kentucky, were joined by 1859. At that time the southern end of the Mobile and Ohio reached 300 miles from Mobile. The remaining 100 miles of the line between northern Mississippi and southern Tennessee required two more years for completion. In the spring of 1861 the northern and southern ends of the Mobile and Ohio were connected, with Marshall J. D. Baldwyn driving a silver spike at the junction in Corinth, Mississippi.[32] Track was never laid from Columbus, Kentucky to Cairo, Illinois, the ultimate destination of the line.

Throughout the construction process local newspaper stories and published annual reports of the Mobile and Ohio Company commented on benefits to the local economy from the railroad. Newspapers ascribed a host of improvements in the city to the railroad. The *Mobile Weekly Herald and Tribune* in 1849 ascribed an increase in population and real estate prices to the Mobile and Ohio, which attracted new enterprise to the city. Two years later the *Mobile Register* also attributed the increase in population, construction, and property values to the railroad project. Residents filled excursion trains on newly opened segments of the line north from Mobile to see progress for themselves.[33]

Annual reports of the company provided evidence of an escalating volume of business conducted by the Mobile and Ohio. By the end of 1854, with some 100 miles of line in operation, the railroad drew "business from sections more remote than were expected to employ it." Counties in Mississippi that had shipped their crops through Vicksburg and the Pearl River to New Orleans began to seek a market in Mobile. By 1858, when the company operated 242 miles of line, the Mobile and Ohio transported over 152,000 bales of cotton to the Alabama port.[34] More than 73,000 passengers rode the line in 1858. The railroad depot in the northern part of Mobile on Royal Street between Lipscomb and Hunt streets became the scene of much activity, especially during the cotton season. Real estate developers built a branch ice depot, a hotel, and two large cotton warehouses near the depot.[35]

Even though these local improvements attributed to the Mobile and Ohio boosted the economy, the city never eclipsed New Orleans, because a competing railroad from the Crescent City to the northern destination of the Mobile and Ohio beat the line from Mobile to its target. Before 1850 businessmen in New Orleans had displayed little interest in railroads. A number of residents apparently thought that the geographic situation of New Orleans would prohibit loss of trade. Those who favored railroads also knew that financing would be difficult because the Louisiana state constitution opposed state aid to railroads and local bankers hesitated to approve loans for railroad promotion. Yet urban boosters in New Orleans came to worry about the commercial future of their city in relation to its southern rivals, especially Mobile. In the late 1840s the share of total cotton exports handled by New Orleans had decreased from 50 to 38 percent. Mobile, which in the late 1840s exported nearly half as much cotton as New Orleans, threatened to increase its share at New Orleans' expense by launching the Mobile and Ohio Railroad project. That line would also capture some of the western trade that New Orleans had long received as a result of its location on the Mississippi River.[36]

To save western trade and to checkmate competition from Mobile, businessmen in New Orleans decided to build their own railroad. Promoters of the New Orleans, Jackson, and Great Northern Railroad admitted that the main inspiration for their line came from the rival project of their "little neighbor" Mobile. *DeBow's Review* even congratulated Mobilians for "the energy, harmonious action, and unflinching perseverance" that they displayed in their railroad enterprise and thanked them "for the example they present for our imitation."[37]

With more successful financing than the Mobile and Ohio, the New Orleans, Jackson, and Great Northern established a direct connection with Columbus, Kentucky, in January 1860, more than a year before its rival. Although both lines received the same aid from Tennessee ($10,000 per mile built in the state), the New Orleans, Jackson, and Great Northern received bonds from Mississippi that amounted to three times the value of the loan that state made to the Mobile and Ohio ($200,000). Louisiana subscribed to the New Orleans line bonds worth four times as much as the loan Alabama granted to the Mobile and Ohio ($400,000). Failure to obtain English loans hurt both lines from 1853 to 1855, but the New Orleans, Jackson, and Great Northern ultimately operated solidly on credit received from the sale of both state and New Orleans municipal bonds. While the company originally had planned its line to extend only as far north as Nashville, financing problems with some counties along that route caused a change in the northern destination, to Jackson, Tennessee. At Jackson the Great Northern reached a point on the Mobile and Ohio that linked it to Columbus, Kentucky.[38] Thus the huge investment of resources that Mobilians had made in the Mobile and Ohio not only failed to bring them their anticipated rewards but ultimately aided their rival Gulf port.

Rivalry with small southern cities prompted Mobilians to support a railroad to connect the Alabama port with the Chattahoochee River and in turn to link the Gulf of Mexico with the Atlantic Ocean. Impetus for the Mobile and Girard Railroad, as it was called, came from capitalists in Columbus, Georgia, whose city depended for its livelihood on the Chattahoochee River. Fearing that the Central of Georgia Railroad would upset their river-based trade patterns, businessmen in Columbus proposed stabilizing their city's future by constructing a railroad to Mobile, thus forging a link from the Gulf to the Atlantic. They also wished to thwart the plans of a Montgomery entrepreneur named Charles T. Pollard, who was attempting to create a railroad network for his city based on trade routes other than rivers. Pollard's plan to connect the Montgomery and West Point Railroad with Mobile would provide a link between the Gulf and the Atlantic that would cut Columbus off from the trade of southeastern Alabama. Mobilians ultimately favored the Girard line over Pollard's Alabama and Florida Railroad because they feared competition from Montgomery's merchants, who had already established direct steamboat connections between their city and New Orleans, thus bypassing Mobile. Spurned by Mobile's railroad promoters, Pollard eventually selected Pensacola rather than Mobile for the southern terminus of the Alabama and Florida.[39]

Mobilians voted liberal support for the Mobile and Girard Railroad. In May 1853 the president of Columbus's railroad company asked a public gathering in Mobile for subscriptions of city bonds for $1,000,000 to construct the line northeast from Mobile to meet the section directed southwestward from Columbus. Several local backers of railroads, including President Sidney Smith of the Mobile and Ohio, endorsed this subscription, arguing that the Mobile and Girard would ensure Mobile's prosperity and greatness. That summer corporate authorities approved a city purchase of 10,000 shares of capital stock in the Mobile and Girard Railroad Company pending approval of propertyholders. Payments on the $1,000,000 subscription would come from city bonds that would be repaid through special taxes approved by propertyowners. As voting day approached, the *Mobile Advertiser* argued that Columbus and Savannah would snatch the trade of eastern Alabama away from Mobile if propertyowners failed to support the Mobile and Girard Railroad. In addition, Pensacola was already forging a rail link with Montgomery. Mobile needed to use the Girard line as a means of making its own rail connection, albeit indirect, with Montgomery and Selma. To boost their own city, propertyowners in Mobile voted overwhelmingly (425 to 33) for the subscription to the Mobile and Girard.[40]

Generous subscriptions of capital from Mobile failed to push the Girard line to completion by 1860. Backers of the Mobile and Girard in Columbus initiated efforts to obtain federal land grants for their railroad in 1851 and succeeded five years later. But the rival Alabama and Florida Railroad also obtained federal land grants in 1856. With financial support from the West Point Railroad, the Alabama and Florida Railroad Company laid tracks much faster than the Mobile and Girard. The owners of the Alabama and Florida and the West Point—largely the same group of investors—even outflanked the Mobile and Girard in 1855 by laying a spur line to connect Columbus to the Montgomery and West Point Railroad at Opelika. By 1860 the Alabama and Florida had completed its line to the Gulf at Pensacola, while the Mobile and Girard had laid tracks only as far as Union Springs.[41] Thus Montgomery thwarted Columbus's effort to become the marketing center for southeastern Alabama. Mobile, of course, also lost out to Montgomery in this round.

Competition for the trade of southern Alabama prompted Mobilians to undertake a connection with the Alabama and Florida Railroad. In 1859 local railroad promoters planned the Mobile and Great Northern Railroad to run from Tensas on the Tensas River in Baldwin County east to Pollard in Conecuh County to intersect with the Alabama and Florida Railroad.[42] In this way the delay in construction of the Mobile and Girard would not completely ruin Mobile's effort to retain the trade of central and southern Alabama.

Mayor Jones M. Withers, a vocal supporter of municipal aid for the Mobile and Great Northern, explained the critical need for the line to offset actions by rival cities: "The earnest, intelligent and persistent efforts being made on either side of us to divert to other ports the large and desirable trade which naturally flows to this, must soon result in an accomplished fact, if nothing be done by us to prevent this dwarfing of our city to the dimensions of a decaying country village." Withers urged Mobilians to "take care of their own interests and build up their own prosperity."[43]

Voters again decided whether municipal aid should be granted to a railroad, this time the Mobile and Great Northern. According to the *Mobile Advertiser*, municipal aid served the general interests of the city better than private investment in the construction of railroads: "If Mobile suffers detriment or retrogrades, private capital can be removed elsewhere and find profitable employment, perhaps, in building up a rival for her own commerce and trade, but the city must remain and suffer the more for the withdrawal of this capital."[44] Voters approved the issuance of municipal bonds to aid the Mobile and Great Northern as sanctioned by the state legislature.[45] The fifty-mile line was completed by 1861.

Mobilians contemplated a rail link with New Orleans, but the low priority project never became a reality. Local promoters of the Mobile and New Orleans Railroad received a state charter late in 1851 for a line to proceed westward from Mobile to the coast of the Gulf of Mexico or the Mississippi state line. According to the charter, construction of the railroad had to begin within two years of legislative approval of the act of incorporation and construction had to be completed within eight years from its start, or the charter would become inoperative. Railroad backers had to rely on private subscriptions since they could not obtain federal land grants or state aid for this project. Authorities in Mobile granted the company the right to enter the city with the railroad as long as it did not reach to Mobile Bay or the Mobile River.[46] Aldermen feared that extending the Mobile and New Orleans Railroad to the docks of Mobile would ruin the city's transshipment business. With all of Mobilians' other commitments to railroads that seemed more promising for their city than the Mobile and New Orleans, it is not surprising that the project failed.

Despite all of the public and private investments and editorial support for railroads, only one major line, the Mobile and Ohio, served Mobile. Certainly it extended Mobile's hinterland, but it maintained the same function as other southern railroads, the transportation of staple crops to seaports.[47] Only a small portion of the line ran through Alabama, thus drawing local investors' attention to distant areas. When the line was completed to its northern terminus in 1861, it faced stiff competition from the rival railroad from New Orleans. Intrastate railroad lines projected to sustain and to enhance Mobile's prosperity by connecting the city to trade inside and outside Alabama failed to materialize before 1860. In summary, railroads failed to expand Mobile's trade significantly. For its major lines of commerce the port still depended on its river system or bay.

Northern shipping interests transported the bulk of imports into Mobile, a situation that advocates of southern independence wished to remedy. As one explained the problem, "Our state of dependence upon the North for our supplier of foreign goods, and even for almost every article that belongs to an everyday use, is a crying shame to us, and cannot be too soon broken."[48] John Forsyth, editor of the *Mobile Register*, asked, "What is Mobile but a commercial outpost of New York?" "Our merchants," he maintained, "are the mere agents of Northern capitalists, and intent only on the calculation of how much of commissions they can obtain thence, and how long it will take to get the productions and importations of New York into their stores."[49] Only by arranging for the direct importation of their goods could local merchants free themselves of their virtual colonial dependence upon the North.

In the 1850s Mobilians launched companies to own and operate ships between Mobile and various Gulf and Atlantic ports, thus breaking their dependence on northern shippers. These actions marked a departure from previous so-called direct trade established by a few local hardware and dry-goods merchants who imported their wares directly from Britain. Another select group directly imported their wines and brandies from France and fruits and coffee from South America.[50] Each of them won praise from local editors, but their examples were not generally emulated. Together, the businessmen who arranged for direct importation of their stock controlled only a small portion of the trade in consumer goods. Furthermore, they did not own the ships that carried their imports. In the 1850s southern patriotism and the acute export-import imbalance in Mobile's trade convinced local businessmen that they had to develop their own shipping interests.

Advocates of direct trade initially focused on establishing service between Mobile and New York, the Alabama port's main source of imports. The New York and Alabama Steamship Company, which was chartered in 1852, owned and operated steam-powered vessels between Mobile and New York. Lucien Mead, a local cotton factor, bank director, and insurance-company president, supplied much of the capital investment. His *Black Warrior* could reach Mobile in eight days from New York and Havana, although the trip often took longer.[51] In 1854 local businessmen tried to improve direct trade by conferring with officers of steamer companies in New York regarding a general plan and requirements for local financing of a new venture. The next year affluent cotton brokers and insurance-company officers organized the Mobile Steamship Company. As chartered by the state legislature in 1856, the company might purchase the steamer *Quaker City* and others to ply the waters between Mobile and New York or any ports on the Atlantic Ocean or Gulf of Mexico deemed expedient by its officers.[52]

Early voyages of the *Quaker City* irritated local investors because the ship did not follow a regular New York to Havana to Mobile and return schedule. On its arrival in New York from Mobile and Havana, the *Quaker City* might then be chartered for a voyage to Liverpool. Editor Willis G. Clark of the *Mobile Advertiser* deemed this charter, while profitable, "unjust" to local merchants who owned stock in the Mobile Steamship Company. "If a steam line to New York is to be of any benefit to Mobile or to become profitable to stockholders," Clark observed, "it must be *reliable* and regular." Merchants in Mobile and in the interior needed solid information about the steamer's arrivals and departures so that they could schedule their purchases and shipments.[53] The Mobile Steamship Company failed to establish regular service to Mobile and in fact had its charter amended in 1858 to permit operations "from any port or ports as it may see fit" without using Mobile as the terminus for voyages.[54]

Local merchants also tried to establish regular steamer service between Mobile and Liverpool. In 1854 Daniel Wheeler and Company announced that a steamer line would operate between the ports for one year and would continue longer if it proved successful. The *Mobile Advertiser* hailed this announcement "as the harbinger of better things in the importing business of Mobile." The line of British steamers carried cargoes ranging from beer to hardware and earthenware consigned to local merchants.[55] This direct trade, like that with New York, ultimately could not be sustained because Mobile lacked adequate exports year round for return cargoes.

Direct trade with Central America drew some interest from merchants in Mobile. Lucien Mead, an important stockholder in the Mobile Steamship Company, Henry O. Brewer, a lumber factor, and Joseph E. Murrell, a direct trade promoter, organized the Mobile and Vera Cruz Mexican Gulf Steamship Company to conduct steamer service between Mobile and Vera Cruz or other Gulf ports. Lumber was expected to account for much of the cargo exported from Mobile. Mobilians also formed the Mobile and Nicaragua Steamship Company in 1858 for steamer service between Mobile and Greytown as well as other Gulf, Caribbean, or Atlantic ports.[56] The demise of filibustering in Nicaragua helped to account for the company's lack of success.

By 1860 direct trade from Mobile remained so insignificant that fifty-two merchants and mercantile firms sponsored a public meeting on southern direct-import trade. The editor of the *Mobile Advertiser* feared that the meeting might give the appearance that no direct trade was then conducted, despite the fact that several local mercantile houses had imported their goods directly from Europe for several years.[57] These merchants made their arrangements individually, while the meeting advocated concerted action. A merchants' committee appointed at the meeting eventually recommended correspondence with the Belge-American Company, which was organized by Robert Livingston, a Mobilian and a respected advocate of direct trade. This committee hoped to change the current situation in which 90 percent of the $10,000,000 of foreign goods that entered Alabama annually came through ports in nonslaveholding states.[58]

In addition to direct trade, Mobilians encouraged industry to diversify their economy. They recognized that manufacturing could create a permanent industrial class to build up the city with purchases of goods and services. The editor of the *Mobile Advertiser* urged in 1850: "Let every Mobilian interest himself in the enterprises which are to benefit his city, and invest his surplus capital in works which shall cause a demand for labor here, and he will have the satisfaction of knowing that his wants are supplied by those who are friendly to his views and principles, and not by those who gladly receive his money, but at the same time, viper like, strive to injure those who benefit them."[59] Editors repeatedly promoted patronage of local manufacturing enterprises for their benefits to the city. For instance, the editor of the *Alabama Planter* urged Mobilians to purchase boots and shoes from local artisans who spent most of their earnings in payments to landlords, grocers, butchers, and other retailers, "all serving to promote the general prosperity of the city and enrich our people."[60]

Home industry also promised independence from northern domination, as manufacturing promoters reminded their potential investors and customers. Editorial puffs for a variety of local manufacturing establishments stressed their quality of workmanship and economy of price in comparison to northern-made competitors. For instance, when Robert J. Walker and James Gannaway opened their Sash and Blind Factory in 1850 to produce window sashes, blinds, and doors, the *Alabama Planter* promised, "The material and workmanship will be equal to any north or south . . . , the prices will be so low as to afford no excuse for builders to send abroad for these articles." After a few months of operation, the factory produced sashes and blinds "said by good judges to be equal to any bought from the North," according to the *Mobile Advertiser*.[61] In promoting local carriagemaker Asa S. Rose, the *Advertiser* directed residents who planned on purchasing carriages or buggies to "look around them and see if their wants cannot as well be supplied by a Mobile mechanic as by those of a foreign state." Even larger vehicles for transportation were manufactured locally. Thanks to its own car factory six miles north of the city in Whistler, the Mobile and Ohio Railroad could make its own coaches more cheaply than it could buy similar models from the North. After a ride on a locally built car, John Forsyth, editor of the *Mobile Register*, praised the coach's springs, woodwork, and seat arrangement. The local model cost $1,600, while a similar one purchased from a northern manufacturer would cost $2,500.[62]

Local pride and economy even dictated the purchase of locally carved tombstones of Alabama marble. Throughout the 1850s Jarvis

Turner operated a marble yard that received marble from quarries near Centerville and Talladega. From the opening of his business, editors promoted it as a way of sustaining a market for Alabama marble. According to the *Mobile Advertiser*, every Alabamian should have enough state pride to direct his executors "to have the slab, intended to mark his last resting place, made from native Alabama marble." "The principle of preferring home industry and native productions against the world," contended the *Advertiser*, "may appropriately be graven on our tombstones, as a legacy to those who may succeed us." "It is the manifestation of patriotism, of that love of country upon which is founded our national prosperity," noted the *Advertiser* in its call for support of local industry. The *Alabama Planter* reminded readers that Jarvis Turner also fashioned church altars quite successfully. He managed to remedy imperfections in an altar ordered from Paris for the Cathedral of the Immaculate Conception. When officials of the cathedral ordered another altar for the sanctuary, they contracted for it directly with Turner for a price 20 percent cheaper than a comparable one available from Paris.[63]

Ironically, some industries most praised for their potential in freeing Mobile from northern domination depended upon the North for managers, workers, or raw materials. The Mobile Manufacturing Company, which was organized in 1849, built a three-story brick factory four miles from the city on Dog River to produce cotton cloth. The company also constructed housing accommodations for fifty operatives.[64] Production of osnaburgs and sheetings began with the aid of twenty-one male and female Irish immigrants, who had been employed in a northern factory that had ceased operations. A director of the Mobile company had hired them on a business trip in the summer of 1851. Other investors purchased the factory in 1852, renaming it the Mobile and Dog River Manufacturing Company. Under new management the factory produced sheetings, osnaburgs, and yarns for the city and country trade. Expansion of operations required the importation of more machines and operatives from the North in 1856. These changes enabled the Mobile and Dog River Factory to produce 8,000 yards of cloth per day in 1857, when its goods were reportedly preferred for appearance and durability in Mobile and New Orleans to those of northern manufacture.[65]

While the cotton factory depended on northern-trained operatives, iron foundries relied on the North for their managers and raw materials. The major local foundry in the 1850s, Skaats and Company, was owned by B. F. Skaats and Charles W. Gazzam, both natives of Pennsylvania. Skaats, an experienced founder, personally supervised operations at his shop. There in 1850 various machines powered by a steam engine could cast all parts of an engine, make engines and boilers, and plane iron. Skaats and Company also included an extensive blacksmith shop.[66] The foundry made many of the castings for machines in Mobile and sold castings in New Orleans. By the end of the decade Skaats and Company produced $150,000 worth of machinery and steam engines. For all of the company's assets, the *Mobile Advertiser* sadly noted, "The iron used is from Pittsburg[h] and Scotland, when it ought to be furnished from the inexhaustible beds of iron ore in Alabama."[67]

Mining mineral resources in north Alabama interested some in Mobile who sought to increase local trade by shipping coal and iron ore through the port. As early as 1848, two Mobilians made arrangements for refueling ships of the Royal Mail Line with Alabama coal as they stopped at Mobile Point on their way from Southampton to Vera Cruz.[68] William Phineas Browne, a former Mobilian, established mines and a rolling mill in Shelby County during the 1850s, but his project remained limited due to difficulties with securing adequate financial backing, numbers of laborers, and transportation lines. The absence of a rail line into the mining district caused such transportation problems as to make mining very costly. After his move to Shelby County, Browne continued to visit Mobile to attend to business regarding his significant commercial propertyholdings. If Mobilians gave Browne any support, editorial or financial, they did so from a desire to increase the port's trade by shipping coal for steamship fuel and home heating. Browne owned an iron foundry in Mobile, but he showed no special inclination toward expanding it or building others to manufacture products from iron ore that he mined in north Alabama.[69] Perhaps his problems with his mining operations limited his plans for processing ore.

For all of the efforts to create industries that would break the domination of the North, the city's economy remained commercially oriented and essentially undiversified. Of the five manufacturing enterprises with the highest value of annual product in 1860, only one provided anything in the way of genuine industrial independence. Foundries that produced machines and steam engines worth $250,000 in 1860 certainly ventured into a new area of manufacturing. Most of the major industries, however, involved processing of agricultural products. Flour mills, grist mills, and a distillery in fact generated products worth more than those of the textile mill (see Table 8-1). In processing agricultural products from the hinterland, these plants remained in the first stage of development toward industrial independence.

The lumber industry provided Mobile County's most valuable manufactures. Saw mills and planing mills produced $434,200 worth of lumber by 1860. Another factory derived $106,000 of rosin oil from pine lumber by 1860. Lumber, both sawed and planed, rosin oil, and turpentine accounted for nearly 44 percent of the industrial products of the county (see Tables 8-1 and 8-2). Almost half of the capital invested in manufacturing was committed to some aspect of the lumber industry.

Mobile's rich timber resources provided ample raw materials for shipbuilding, yet that industry remained very limited. For many years very few vessels were built in Mobile, and many of these were small sloops. Local businessmen had been satisfied to use oceangoing vessels built elsewhere to handle their shipping. Agitation for direct trade sparked fresh interest in local shipbuilding when the Southern Rights Association urged home production of steam-powered vessels in 1850. Three years later Mobile's shipbuilders completed the *William Jones, Jr.*, the first steamboat entirely constructed and fitted in the vicinity of Mobile. For passengers' comfort, this 200-foot-long ship had superbly finished staterooms, a barber's salon, and a ladies' washroom. Nothing of its size was built later in the decade, although shipbuilding did continue on a small scale. In 1860 the one shipbuilding firm in the county employed a dozen men who produced vessels valued at $17,000. Shipbuilding suffered from the limited local supply of mechanics skilled in the work.[70] More important, the industry suffered from having few orders and few substantial backers. Even promoters of direct trade purchased their steamers from the North. Entrepreneurs with investment capital often preferred to put their money into facilities for processing cotton, which yielded quicker and surer profits than industries like shipbuilding.

Mobile County nevertheless served as a model for manufacturing within the state of Alabama. Capital invested in manufacturing in Mobile County by 1860 made it one of only six counties in the state with

Table 8-1. Manufacturing Enterprises in Mobile County, 1860

Enterprise	Number of Establishments	Capital Invested ($)	Number of Employees	Annual Value of Product ($)
Lumber Industry[a]	33	600,625	285	657,675
Machinery[b]	3	233,910	102	250,000
Flour, Meal, Liquor	5	36,700	14	126,500
Other[c]	7	86,250	69	123,200
Textiles	1	100,000	150	120,000
Metal Work[d]	3	17,500	14	92,000
Coal and Gas[e]	16	138,175	54	81,200
Woodworking[f]	5	3,875	22	31,131
Shipbuilding	1	1,500	1	17,000
Boots and Shoes	1	1,500	3	2,100
Total	75	1,219,075	724	1,500,916

SOURCE: Compiled from Eighth Census, Manufacturing, p. 9.

[a]Includes the production of planed lumber, sawed lumber, rosin oil, crude turpentine, distilled turpentine as well as timber cutting for firewood.
[b]Includes those of unspecified type and steam engines.
[c]Includes carving (furniture making), cigar making, marble work, making of plaster ornaments, soap making, and building wagons and carts.
[d]Includes the production of tin, copper, and sheet-iron ware.
[e]Includes the production of gas, charcoal, and refined coal oil.
[f]Includes cooperage and the making of sashes, doors, blinds, and shingles.

Table 8-2. Manufacturing in Mobile County, 1860

Enterprise	Number of Establishments (%)	Capital Invested (%)	Number of Employees (%)	Annual Value of Product (%)
Lumber Industry	44.0	49.3	39.4	43.8
Machinery	4.0	19.2	14.1	16.6
Flour, Meal, Liquor	6.7	3.0	1.9	8.4
Other	9.3	7.1	9.5	8.2
Textiles	1.3	8.2	20.7	8.0
Metal Work	4.0	1.4	1.9	6.1
Coal and Gas	21.3	11.3	7.4	5.4
Woodworking	6.7	0.3	3.0	2.1
Shipbuilding	1.3	0.1	1.5	0.1
Boots and Shoes	1.3	0.0	0.4	0.1
Total (%)	99.9	99.9	99.8	99.8
Total (N)	75	$1,219,075	724	$1,500,916

SOURCE: Compiled from Eighth Census, Manufacturing, p. 9.

NOTES: Percentages were rounded to nearest tenth.

Explanations of enterprises included in each category may be found in table 8-1.

more than $400,000 invested in manufacturing. Annual value of industrial products in Mobile led Alabama in 1860 and placed the county among only nine in the state with an annual value of industrial products exceeding $400,000.[71]

Despite its leadership in manufacturing within the state, Mobile lagged behind rival southern cities, even ones with smaller populations, in industrialization. On the basis of population, capital investment, employment in manufacturing, and value of annual product together, Mobile compiled the second worst record on industrialization among southern cities with populations over 20,000 (see Table 8-3). Only Charleston, where the elite had long refrained from major investment in industry, registered a lesser commitment to manufacturing.[72] Not only did Mobile rate poorly in manufacturing compared with other major southern cities, it also failed to make the most advantageous use of capital invested in industry. Alone among southern cities, Mobile recorded more money invested in manufacturing than produced annually by manufactured goods. Some of this unfavorable financial situation resulted from the late emphasis on manufacturing in Mobile. Initial investment capital could not always quickly generate valuable products. Southern cities like Richmond and Louisville with well-developed manufacturing sectors managed to produce industrial goods valued far in excess of capital invested in industry. Mobile's late start in industrialization combined with the city's continued preoccupation with the cotton trade to produce only limited progress in diversification of the local economy through manufacturing.

The pursuit of progress toward diversification and in turn independence from northern domination extended to educational institutions. In 1855 businessmen from Mobile and Baldwin counties launched a drive to create the College of South Alabama to meet the needs of the growing population of Mobile and its environs. Proponents argued that the college would offset weaknesses in the state's other institutions of higher learning. The University of Alabama in Tuscaloosa allegedly did not maintain educational standards equal to those of schools in the Northeast, which provided models for excellence. Spring Hill College, just outside of Mobile, a Catholic institution founded in 1830, reportedly employed faculty members who were too "sectarian." Until nativism assumed strength locally, Spring Hill College had enjoyed community support, although many of its students came from Louisiana.

Table 8-3. Population and Manufactures of Major Southern Cities, 1860

City	Population	Capital Invested ($)	Hands Employed	Value of Product ($)
New Orleans	168,675	2,693,746	5,062	10,926,135
St. Louis	160,773	9,205,205	9,352	21,772,323
Louisville	68,033	4,967,588	6,679	12,933,092
Washington	61,122	1,630,090	2,373	3,413,372
Charleston	40,522	742,000	852	1,064,715
Richmond	37,910	4,534,615	7,474	12,800,280
Mobile	29,258	1,193,475	664	1,359,936
Memphis	22,623	790,200	892	1,671,498
Savannah	22,292	902,300	639	1,907,367

SOURCE: Statistics of the United States (Including Mortality, Property, &c.,) in 1860; Compiled from the Original Returns and Being the Final Exhibit of the Eighth Census under the Direction of the Secretary of the Interior (1866; reprint ed., New York: Arno Press, 1976), p. xviii.

Promoters of the College of South Alabama maintained that their institution would represent parental values, presumably Protestant, for students from Alabama, Georgia, Mississippi, and Florida. Sponsors urged Mobilians to loan the college money for the "encouragement of humanizing influences." Students' patronage would benefit the local economy.[73] Despite the sponsors' appeals, the College of South Alabama was not established for over a century.

Economic interests, southern patriotism, and urban rivalry all sparked local support for the Alabama Medical College. In 1859 the *Mobile Register* estimated that the 250 Alabamians who attended medical schools out of state spent $200,000 annually for tuition and room and board. Many Alabamians enrolled in the Medical Department of the University of Louisiana; in fact, 69 of the 332 students there in 1859 were from Alabama. More Alabamians attended medical schools in Charleston, Philadelphia, and other cities, thus enriching rivals of Mobile in both the South and North. A local medical school, according to the *Register*, should keep a "vastly greater sum" than $200,000 in Alabama and circulate it in Mobile. The school would, it was hoped, be good enough to keep at home students from Alabama who formerly had to go elsewhere and to attract students from adjacent states. According to the *Register*, Mobile's reputation for scientific investigations, the excellence of the museum established for the college, the talent of the faculty of local physicians, and the personal popularity of Josiah C. Nott, local surgeon and ethnologist who headed the faculty, promised respect for the Medical College of Alabama. With a respectable beginning, the local medical school took "a new step towards rendering us independent from the North." Location of the school at home even offered scientific advantages. According to the *Register*, on-the-spot study of diseases peculiar to the Southwest could not be overrated.[74]

The successful opening term of the new medical college vindicated the hopes of its backers. Mobilians subscribed $25,000 for the school, and the state appropriated $50,000 as the school became incorporated as a department of the University of Alabama, with its own self-perpetuating board of trustees.[75] Dr. Nott used some of the funds to purchase teaching models and medical equipment from England, France, Germany, and Italy. With a reputable museum and faculty, the school offered its first lecture series from November 1859 to March

1860. Classes began with 50 students. The *Mobile Register* boasted, "No other medical college in the United States had begun with so large a number." The Medical School of New Orleans reportedly enrolled only 32 students initially.[76] Of the 111 students who matriculated during the first course of lectures and clinical instruction at the United States Marine Hospital and City Hospital in Mobile, 15 received diplomas in 1860.[77]

Compared to some other ventures promoting southern independence, the medical college required a relatively small outlay of capital. Perhaps that is why it enjoyed early success. Local capital and state aid might finance projects that were not too expensive, but anything requiring large expenditures from either source proved hazardous. State aid never reached substantial proportions for two predominant reasons. Conflicts between intrastate economic divisions, north Alabama using the Tennessee River as its main avenue of commerce and south Alabama using the Alabama-Tombigbee River system that flowed into Mobile Bay, sparked numerous squabbles among legislators who withheld funds from projects Mobilians considered essential to the progress of their city. Sometimes the intrastate economic splits in the legislature resulted from the rural districts' suspicion of the urban districts.

Misunderstandings between planters in the interior and merchants in the port were nothing new, but they grew increasingly sharp, beginning in the late 1840s. Residents of the port knew well its financial value to the state. As the *Alabama Tribune* noted in 1849, the state tax for Mobile County in 1848 amounted to almost one-eighth of the total for the state. "One would suppose from this," the *Tribune* surmised, "that Mobile is of some little value to the state."[78]

Even reporters from other cities in the state maintained that the interior and the port depended on each other for their prosperity. A reporter from the *Huntsville Southern Advocate* rejoiced over improvements in the commercial metropolis in 1853, including construction of buildings, factories, and steam mills, and the Mobile and Ohio Railroad. For Mobile's future, he hoped: "Long may it continue to flourish and grow into a large and magnificent city, and become the pride, ornament and benefactor of the State. Let no mean and pitiful jealousy exist on the part of the interior. Its prosperity is the prosperity of the whole. Its growth is the growth of the whole. It is necessary to the country, and the country is essential to it. Both must rise or fall together."[79] All too often this sentiment seemed absent among state legislators who controlled the purse strings for aid to various internal improvement projects. Unless assistance to benefit the port could be balanced by aid to other parts of the state, it stood little chance of passage. Thus the political effects of intrastate economic cleavages hurt the prospects for state aid to Mobile.

The other obstacle to state aid for internal improvements came from Governor John A. Winston, who served two terms from 1853 to 1857. Not only did he veto bills to aid the Mobile and Ohio Railroad, but he also vetoed a host of bills designed to aid other private internal-improvements companies. Many Alabamians supported Winston's Jacksonian Democratic rationale for his vetoes, even though legislators often mustered the simple majority of votes necessary to override them. Urbanites throughout the state and prominent newspapers, both Whig and Democrat, criticized Winston for interfering with actions designed to integrate the state into the new market economy of the mid-nineteenth century.[80] One Mobilian labeled Winston's determined opposition to state aid for private internal improvements companies "old fogyism."[81]

During Winston's reelection campaign in 1855, his critics in Mobile painted a bleak picture of their city's future if he won another term. Based on the governor's past behavior, "An Old Citizen of Mobile" advised his neighbors not to expect further state aid for internal improvements but to expect instead more taxes on themselves to offset the meager contributions from the state. Cotton merchants should expect further suffering from their dependence upon shipments on rivers that often had low water levels, for the governor would veto bills to aid railroads. Retailers should consider that their customers in the interior would not purchase new clothes, shoes, and special groceries if they could not get their cotton to market. Without railroads to expand trade with the interior, the city's internal economy might not sustain new construction, thus forcing brickmakers, bricklayers, plasterers, carpenters, and painters to seek employment elsewhere.[82] In short, Winston's opposition to state aid for internal improvements spelled continued trouble for Mobile.

Winston's critics urged voters to support his opponent for governor, the Know-Nothing candidate George D. Shortridge. A "liberal and enlightened politician," Shortridge promised support for improvements in the state that would keep pace with projects of neighboring states and benefit every part of Alabama.[83] Shortridge, a circuit judge and a former Democrat who had embraced the new American party, led the polls in Mobile, but Winston won reelection from the state-wide returns. As predicted, Winston continued his opposition to state aid to railroads, some of which promised benefits to Mobile, where he, interestingly enough, maintained a cotton-factorage business throughout the 1850s and a residence after his retirement from the governorship.[84]

Increased state aid undoubtedly would have hastened the completion of Mobile's projects designed to contribute to urban growth and southern commercial independence, yet the sum of all those projects, even if realized, would not restore the rate of growth that the city had maintained during its formative American years or secure economic freedom from the North. For all of the optimism associated with advocates of railroads, direct trade, and manufacturing, pessimism also influenced them. Much of their energy and money went toward a major rail line, which failed in its visionary purpose of enabling Mobile to eclipse the domestic commerce of New Orleans. Furthermore, promoters of direct trade registered no sustained success in increasing Mobile's share of the nation's import business. Industrialists launched several laudable enterprises in the 1850s, yet they could not make the city independent of the North for any manufactured items. Thus, no matter what their accomplishments, in terms of their own stated goals boosters of southern commercial independence failed in antebellum Mobile. Among their fellow citizens they found neither the interest nor the capital necessary to change the direction of Mobile's economy substantially. The city remained devoted to commerce, especially in cotton, which sold well during peaks of international demand in the 1850s. In its concentration on the cotton trade, Mobile remained essentially in a colonial relationship with the North. Acute realization of this fact in the 1850s prompted some Mobilians not only to try to alter their position within the economic system but also to hold the northern-born residents among them personally liable for the system.

* 9 *

Test of Loyalty

IN the 1850s many Mobilians decided that their city could best pursue progress only with its political leaders firmly committed to the South. Southern loyalty had not received such emphasis in Mobile's early American years, when citizens had chosen their governmental leaders on the basis of their contributions to urban development. By the 1850s, however, a substantial number of voters demanded from their elected officials devotion to the region. Evidence of loyalty included not only investment in and support for internal improvements projects but also birth in the South. Important political officeholders, who often had lobbied for internal improvements and other projects ostensibly to promote southern independence, suddenly attracted suspicion if they had moved to Mobile from the North.

As sectional tensions of the 1850s pushed the South closer to secession, Mobilians, like other urbanites, had to choose between regional and commercial loyalties. Their city had grown because of its economic links to the North as a marketing and financing agent for the cotton trade. Thus the severance of those ties promised major disruption in Mobile. Wary about Mobile's future in the event of an extremist's victory in the presidential contest of 1860, voters registered preferences for moderate candidates. Southern loyalty nevertheless soon encouraged separation from the North, as agitation for secession began in earnest after Abraham Lincoln's election to the presidency. Local Unionists ultimately failed to stem the tide of rising support for disunion. Even cooperationists could not dampen support for immediate secession.

Advocates of southern independence, whatever their partisan affiliations, raised questions about the regional loyalty of any local decision maker who supported unionist positions, particularly one who was born outside the South. What counted most for the success of a local politician in the crisis-laden 1850s was his reputation for loyalty to the South and its institutions. His political record might not necessarily determine the public's reaction to him if opponents charged that his birth outside the South raised suspicions about his regional loyalties. Ironically, almost no one raised the issue of benefits Mobile in particular and the South in general had received from membership in the Union, especially the regional specialization within the economy. Those who maintained Unionist positions throughout the decade might exhibit true concern for Mobile and its development, yet extremists denied that.

The first major test of loyalty to the South came in response to the Compromise of 1850 and the Nashville Convention. Three hundred Mobilians, Whigs and Democrats, assembled before the Nashville Convention to express their support for the convention as a means of indicating resistance to northern aggression. The *Mobile Register* urged Mobilians to remain true to their obligations both to the Union and southern rights.[1] During the spring and summer political leaders in Mobile looked among themselves for signs of disloyalty to the South, particularly from northern-born politicians.

Connecticut-born Charles C. Langdon, mayor and editor of the Whig *Mobile Advertiser*, bore the brunt of this witch hunt for antisouthern politicians. Prominent members of his own party, who called themselves the Twenty-Seven, accused Langdon of disloyalty to the South for his support of moderation during the crisis provoked by the Compromise of 1850. Resolutions affirming southern rights within the Union and reserving the right to judge actions taken by Congress appealed to local Southern Rights Democrats and even to some Whigs, including Langdon, but other Whigs, including the Twenty-Seven, argued among themselves about loyalty to the South. Disenchanted Whigs labeled Langdon as "an enemy of the South, a Free-soiler, an Abolitionist."[2] Langdon rebutted these and other charges in a series of editorial letters published in the *Advertiser*.

One of Langdon's supporters, who signed himself "Pinckney" in letters to the editor of the *Advertiser*, defended Langdon with his own record: "The editorials of the Advertiser for years past were a sufficient guarantee that you would uphold to the extent of your ability the rights of the South and had no sympathy with the unjust claim of the North, and that if the worst should come to the worst, would throw aside the pen and buckling on the sword bravely fight in defence of our trodden down liberties."[3] "Pinckney" particularly criticized Whigs who viewed the "mere fact of his [Langdon's] having been born at the North" as "evidence of treason."[4]

Although he was born in Connecticut, by 1850 Langdon had lived in Alabama for twenty-five years. Langdon was the son of a veteran of the Revolution who became a farmer and a member of the Connecticut legislature. After his education at common schools and an Episcopal academy near his hometown, Langdon taught school for several years. In 1825, at the age of twenty, he moved to Alabama with his brother, who owned a dry-goods business in Marion in Perry County. In 1834 Langdon established a cotton commission house in Mobile in partnership with a man from Perry County. After their business failed in the Panic of 1837, Langdon embarked on a political career as editor of the Whig newspaper, the *Mobile Advertiser*. He also represented Mobile County in the state legislature for the 1839 and 1840 terms. In 1848 and 1849 voters elected Langdon mayor of Mobile.[5]

Critics who hoped to ruin Langdon's political career in 1850 failed as Mobilians registered support for the Union and its advocate at the *Advertiser*. In December Langdon squeaked to reelection as mayor with only twelve more votes than his Democratic opponent.[6]

Langdon's luck in the mayoral race of 1850 failed to hold for the congressional election of 1851. In a bitter campaign that made an issue of Langdon's northern birth, voters chose John Bragg, a Southern Rights Democrat. Bragg believed in the principle of secession, although he opposed immediate exercise of the option. Langdon ran as an unconditional Unionist. Accusations made against Langdon in 1850 resurfaced to harm his candidacy for Congress.[7]

By 1852 the Democrats' split into the Southern Rights and National factions helped Langdon to win election to the first three-year mayoral term.[8] Langdon's retirement from the *Advertiser* also helped him in municipal politics. Arguing that his health was failing from the rigors of editorial work, Langdon sold the *Advertiser* in October 1852 to Willis G. Clark, a native of New York, whom he described as a "sound conservative Whig."[9] Langdon then established a vineyard north of the city, devoting his attention to his agricultural pursuits and later to his duties as mayor.

Like Langdon in 1851, the next northern-born candidate for the First District seat in Congress found his birth in the North and loyalty to the South made campaign issues. Opposing candidates in 1853 were both two-term state legislators from Mobile: Elihu Lockwood, a Whig born in New York who represented Mobile County in the 1847 and 1849 terms of the General Assembly, and Philip Phillips, a Democrat born in South Carolina, who represented Mobile in the 1844 and 1851 sessions.[10] Both candidates had resided in Alabama since the 1830s. Lockwood had to counter rumors circulating through the district that his birth in New York made him suspect in his support for slavery. The *Mobile Advertiser* informed readers that Lockwood had moved to Alabama as a boy, was a descendant of slaveholders, and had owned slaves for a long time. After practicing law in Wilcox County and earning a "high reputation" there, Lockwood had settled in Mobile in 1840. Most of Lockwood's property was located in the congressional district, so he had "the strongest interest in securing the welfare of its citizens."[11]

Partisan newspapers debated the support given to internal improvements by Lockwood and Phillips. During Lockwood's first term he helped to win passage of the bill to charter the Mobile and Ohio Railroad. In both terms he delivered speeches advocating internal improvements for the state, but Phillips received more credit for supporting internal improvements because he chaired the House Committee on Internal Improvements. The *Register* and *Advertiser* specifically disputed the political and financial support given by Lockwood and Phillips for the Mobile and Ohio Railroad. According to the *Advertiser*, Lockwood subscribed to five times the number of shares to which Phillips had subscribed, and Phillips had, moreover, failed to make installment payments on his shares and forfeited them. Lockwood not only retained shares in the Mobile and Ohio Railroad, but he also owned stock in the Mobile and Girard Railroad, Battle House, Point Clear Hotel, and the Mobile and New York Steamship Company.[12] He probably committed more money to internal improvements companies than Phillips, but Phillips managed to convince the public that he was the true champion of the internal improvements cause. Phillips won the election to Congress. Whig newspapers explained Lockwood's defeat as a result of Whigs defecting to Phillips when Phillips promised to support legislation to improve the harbor of Mobile.[13]

In the mid-1850s local politicians shifted their suspicions of non-southerners in their midst away from the northern-born to the foreign-born, especially Catholics. By this time Catholics formed a numerical majority of church members in a community where Protestants controlled major business, government, and editorial offices. The affiliations of many foreign-born Mobilians with the Catholic church particularly troubled leaders who saw in this relationship a combination that might at some time challenge their power. After all, the foreign-born made up 24 percent of the city's total population, 34 percent of whites, and 50 percent of the free labor force.[14] Furthermore, large numbers of foreign-born men had become naturalized citizens whose votes might sway the outcomes of local elections. From 1840 through 1854, 744 men became naturalized citizens in Mobile. Of these, 369 (47.7 percent) came from Ireland and 121 (15.6 percent) came from Germany, the two most frequently listed places of birth.[15]

Capitalizing on native-born residents' resentment of foreigners, many politicians, whose first consideration was officeholding, cooperated with the nativistic American party. The party quickly gained followers in the port city, where it made its first appearance in the state. Many Whigs flocked to the new party, apparently as a means of regaining power.[16]

Catholic management of City Hospital provided the first test of the American party's strength in 1854. The Sisters of Charity had administered the hospital under contract since 1852, when aldermen had praised them for their "prompt, faithful and unremitted attention." In April 1854, after receiving complaints from Protestant clergymen, some aldermen accused the nuns of a multitude of offenses, the most important being that they tried to induce Protestant patients to embrace the Catholic faith. Sister Mary Hilary Brawner, superior of the hospital, denied the allegations. After an investigating committee found the charges untrue, Mayor Charles C. Langdon nevertheless recommended a change in hospital administration, not because of hostility toward Catholics, he said, but because of his opposition to any sectarian management. Meanwhile, the Sisters of Charity had resigned as administrators of City Hospital, saying that their services were "no longer appreciated or desired." Aldermen then transferred authority over the hospital to a committee of municipal board members.[17]

After this display of strength against the Catholic nuns, the American party gained followers rapidly. Members in Mobile reportedly numbered 678 in June and 3,000 by December. The American party made a clean sweep of the Mobile County elections in August, the first races entered by the new party in Alabama.[18]

As American partisans prepared for municipal elections in the fall, the *Mobile Advertiser*, their political press, praised the national, rather than sectional, concerns of the party. Countering the claims of the Democratic press that the American party was antisouthern, the *Advertiser* maintained that the principles of the party seemed as applicable to the South as to the North. Furthermore, the American party took a conservative position on the slavery issue.[19]

Protestant values influenced the local government, which was composed of an ever increasing number of American partyites. Mayor Langdon, by this time a Know-Nothing, called for an ordinance to ensure proper observance of the Christian Sabbath. "Open desecration" of Sunday by shopowners who opened their stores for business as usual troubled the mayor. He specifically listed as offenders Jewish grocers on Dauphin Street and saloonkeepers, even some Catholic ones, throughout the city. According to the mayor, native Americans rarely opened stores on Sundays. He maintained that foreign-born merchants should conform to the community mores of Mobile. "An Ordinance for the better observance of the Christian Sabbath" won the overwhelming support of aldermen in 1855. This ordinance prohibited worldly labor, business sales (including those at bars and sports events), dray hauling, disturbances of church services, and unnecessary employment of slaves on Sunday. The provisions of the ordinance did not apply to steamboats or trains, ice houses, livery stables, milkmen, newsboys delivering papers, barbers, and employees of the gas works.[20] Supporters of the ordinance, of course, risked political opposition from people directly affected by its prohibitions and from others, mainly foreign-born, who resented its implications.

As the American Party gained strength, antiforeign sentiment appeared openly and violently in 1855 before several elections. Late in April, shortly before the election for probate judge, American partisans displayed their clout by demolishing a shanty on the northwest corner of St. Michael and Dearborne streets, known as the "Wood Pile." Irishmen who occupied the shanty put up little resistance against the large crowd of attackers. Apparently those who demolished the "Wood Pile" and another unidentified building, both places of ill repute, escaped arrest, for their actions reflected the views of the city's decision makers.

"Americans in this city are numerous enough and powerful enough," noted the *Advertiser*, "to be magnanimous and forbearing towards the foreign element." To avoid repetition of violence, the *Advertiser* urged that both Americans and "well disposed naturalized citizens among us and there are many such estimable, orderly and industrious—take care to discourage whatever tends to inflame the passions."[21]

In May four men attacked Father Nachon, a Jesuit teacher from Spring Hill College, while he was riding to the Dog River Factory to conduct Sunday services for Irish-born operatives living in company housing there. The *Advertiser* initially described the attackers as "Romanist Irishmen" who beat the priest for "an abuse of his sacred office." Soon the *Advertiser* admitted that no evidence sustained its early report that the attackers were Catholic Irishmen. Democrats blamed the Americans for the beating.[22] The identity of the attackers and the motive for their action remained a mystery.

That summer and fall, despite concerted opposition from Anti-American (Democratic) forces, the American party scored its biggest triumphs at the polls in Mobile. Anti-Americans reportedly harassed naturalized citizens who supported the American party, people whom the *Mobile Advertiser* called "considerate and respectable persons who have some stake in the country, who have an American family" as distinct from "the rabble of foreigners who have recently invaded . . . our shores."[23] Some immigrants, mostly Germans, formed a chapter of Sag Nichts, a national political association composed mainly of foreign-born, to oppose the American party. Democrats appealed to Sag Nichts by claiming that Americans wanted to degrade foreign-born citizens. A letter to the editor of the *Mobile Advertiser* denied that charge, maintaining that the American party merely sought to purify government of corrupt influences that the old party organizations used to win elections by manipulating the bloc votes of the foreign-born. This writer urged naturalized citizens to support the American party at the county and state elections in August.[24] Gangs attacked some foreigners in the southern part of the city a few days before the election. Despite the preelection violence, polling day passed quietly as Americans elected their Congressional candidate, Percy Walker, formerly a Democrat, who won with the combined support of the American party, Southern Rights Democrats, and supporters of state aid to railroads.[25]

"Anti-Americanism *withers* in Mobile," reported the *Mobile Adver-*

tiser after the municipal elections in December 1855, when the American party slate for mayor, aldermen, and common councilmen won throughout the city.[26] The new mayor, elected for a three-year term, was Jones M. Withers, a native Alabamian and a Democrat. Withers, at the time a state legislator from Mobile, was elected while attending a legislative session in Montgomery. Elected mayor "without his knowledge or consent," Withers obtained a leave of absence from the state legislature to qualify in Mobile for the office after his election. Soon he attended to unfinished legislative business, resigned his seat, and returned to assume his duties as mayor.[27] The outgoing mayor, Charles C. Langdon, who by this time edited the independent *Mobile News*, won election to Withers's seat in the state legislature.[28]

As the first native Alabamian elected mayor of Mobile, Jones M. Withers suited the preferences of the American party. His birth in Alabama, in the public's perception, tied him more closely than Langdon to the interests of the state and its port. Langdon had actually lived in Mobile longer than Withers, but the native southerner exemplified a combination of vocations admired by southerners. Born in Huntsville in 1814 to a planter who had moved there from Virginia, Withers attended Greene Academy in Huntsville until he entered the United States Military Academy at West Point. Following his graduation in 1835, he served briefly in the army. In 1838 Withers became a lawyer and moved to Tuscaloosa. Relocating in Mobile in 1841, he worked as both an attorney and a commission merchant. Withers made Mobile his home, except for a short residence in Lowndes County in 1846. For a brief period he edited the *Mobile Tribune*.[29] Not incidentally to his political prominence, Withers was a brother-in-law of Governor Clement Comer Clay and an uncle of Senator Clement Claiborne Clay.

In 1856 Withers and a number of other prominent officeholders renounced the American party for various political reasons. Withers believed that the party broke its pledges of loyalty to southern rights. Congressman Percy Walker, who had won election on the American ticket, stumped the Mobile district condemning the American party's principle of religious proscription. Walker retained his congressional seat, but Withers resigned as mayor in July when he broke with the party. Aldermen and councilmen, a majority of whom were elected as Americans, nonetheless reelected Withers mayor. Withers resumed his ties with Democrats and ran successfully in 1858 for another three-year term as mayor.[30]

As partisan agitation of nativism subsided, financial troubles facing Mobile in the mid-1850s, which culminated in the Panic of 1857, sparked new attacks on nonsoutherners. Compared to its past rapid growth, the city indeed stagnated in the 1850s. Editors and other city boosters tried a number of measures to entice enough fresh investment capital into local projects to spur new growth. When these efforts failed, editors chided affluent residents in general for their reluctance to invest in somewhat risky ventures. Later they singled out northern-born merchants as the worst offenders.

Risk capital was extremely difficult to raise in Mobile, as in many other southern cities. Periodically during the 1850s local editors published columns that commented sarcastically on wealthy men who withheld investment funds from anything not in their own line of business. Someone who signed himself "Anti-Croaker" wrote the *Mobile Advertiser* regarding the class of "croakers" who cursed the city. According to the author, croakers complained frequently about the decline of the city, yet they never thought of doing anything to reverse the trend. They were "generally men possessing wealth—mostly men in active business—who have never invested a dollar outside of their business, without satisfactory security, and with the certainty of its paying them a large interest." Lacking public spirit, they refused to invest in some enterprise for the public good. Railroads, for instance, did not interest these businessmen because they did not produce immediate dividends. Editor Willis G. Clark of the *Mobile Advertiser* agreed with "Anti-Croaker's" impatience with those who saw a poor future for the city yet did nothing to prevent it. He favored "the go-ahead-thriving, hopeful spirit" required for success. "The maxim 'Where there's a will there's a way,'" he observed, "would never better apply than in our case." As Clark reminded readers, Mobile had faced some croakers at every phase of her development. Overcoming such persons in the past, Mobile should check such "pecuniary suicides" in the future.[31]

Critics of wealthy merchants who hesitated or refused to invest in internal improvements projects like railroads implied that these merchants lacked genuine interest in local development because the profits from their trade depended largely on prices of cotton set in world, rather than local, markets. The accusations might not directly mention birthplace outside the South as a factor in reducing willingness to make local investments, but the implication was clear. For instance, when the

Mobile Register worried about local apathy toward building a railroad northeast from Mobile, it implored "the men of wealth and substance, who are enjoying the rich harvest of our present trade to shell out some of the enormous gains which they miserly hoard up . . . , to invest them in the means of necessary transportation." To appeal to local pride and southern patriotism, the editor felt, would be in vain. He concluded, "The [municipal] corporation—the poor—the indebted corporation is our only resource. The laboring poor must build roads for these 'merchant princes'." City funds, it is true, frequently backed ventures that lacked adequate financing from private or other governmental sources.[32] But large municipal pledges to railroads in particular taxed the resources of a government that was still struggling to overcome bankruptcy.

Accusations against reluctant local investors peaked in 1858 when the *Mobile Register* sought an explanation for the city's stagnation. As the newspaper noted, the city's population growth had failed to keep pace with the increase in cotton bales received by the port. In 1813 the town had 5,000 people and received 7,000 bales of cotton for export. By 1856 the port accepted nearly 600,000 bales, or nearly eighty-five times the number handled during the first year of American occupation. Yet the population in 1856 was only five times greater than that in 1813. This difference between growth rates in population and cotton receipts represented stagnation to the *Register*. Editor John Forsyth blamed stagnation on the fact that most of the proceeds from the cotton trade were not spent locally. By the late 1850s the cotton business amounted to $30,000,000 annually and generated $1,800,000 annually in commissions to sellers, buyers, brokers, and weighers. According to Forsyth, northern-born cotton merchants bore the blame for limited local development because of their reluctance to reinvest their profits in Mobile. "While they do not condemn, perhaps they even sympathize, with our institutions," the *Register* observed, "they do not regard them as stable, and are constantly apprehensive of change." To put it more directly, "they deem property insecure, and by fears of this sort are deterred from making investments there." These cotton traders from outside Mobile allegedly sustained interests in the city only insofar as they supported the cotton trade. During the summers they reportedly left the city and took their profits from the cotton trade with them for investment elsewhere.[33]

When the city was not booming, particularly during financial panics and sectional controversies, Mobilians tended to denigrate the civic leaders who came from outside the South as exploiters who were not doing enough to foster growth. As one disgruntled Mobilian later remarked about the northern- and foreign-born cotton buyers: "They came like birds of passage with the earliest frost and fed fat upon wild celery and other spice berries in the season of their maturity, not greedily and voraciously . . . , but always willing to leave some pickings behind for the native stay-at-home, like courteous gentlemen as they were."[34]

These accusations against the nonsouthern cotton merchants involved some complicated issues. After the Panic of 1857 the *Register* castigated northerners for failing to invest enough of their cotton profits locally. Another advocate of southern rights had once charged that northerners owned half of the real estate and seven-eighths of the bank and insurance stock in the city. Northerners in fact faced accusations both of not investing enough money locally and of investing too much. Available evidence on propertyholding in the city does not substantiate the charge of excessive control of real estate and stocks by northerners, even though their money was clearly welcome because it contributed to the development of the city.[35] Mobilians proved "very willing" that eastern capitalists invest, for instance, in the Mobile and Ohio Railroad.[36] When that project or some other internal improvement venture moved along more slowly than desired, city boosters blamed financial problems on northerners in their midst.

At such times critics ignored the fact that nonsouthern urban leaders had in many ways contributed materially to local progress. They helped to establish town government and adapt it to the needs of a growing city. They opened business links with major northeastern and foreign firms for shipping, insuring, and marketing the cotton that became the major export of Mobile. They spearheaded both the Mobile and Ohio Railroad and the public school system as ways to strengthen the city's future prospects. They served in a variety of charitable activities to ease the suffering of the poor. They even organized the beautification of Bienville Square. Contributions like these were forgotten as critics focused on the stereotype of the outside capitalists who came to the South only to exploit it for their own purposes.

In the early antebellum years southerners had nurtured every eco-

nomic tie to the North that would not compromise the South.[37] No-
where did this occur on a greater scale in proportion to the size of the
city than in Mobile. Lacking almost any established export-import
firms at the time of the American takeover, settlers welcomed businessmen from outside the South, including many from New York, who
opened trading relationships with northern and foreign firms.[38] Regional specialization, with the South providing the cotton and exporting facilities and the North providing the bulk of financial, insurance,
and shipping services, made the cotton trade profitable for both regions.

When the relationship became severely imbalanced in the 1850s,
southerners agitated for parity. By this time, however, the system
was so well entrenched that substantive changes in it were impossible. Southern merchants, who by the hundreds visited northern
wholesalers and bankers, still maintained huge accounts in the North.
Southern tourists, who journeyed north by the thousands, frequently
preferred to take vacations at northern resorts and to purchase northern-
made or northern-imported goods in northern stores rather than trade
with fellow southerners. In 1860 Thomas P. Kettell estimated that the
South's trade imbalance in favor of the North exceeded $200,000,000.
Regardless of how much southerners criticized the imbalance and
passed resolutions to alter the situation, circumstances still placed the
South in a state of colonial dependency.[39] Since Mobile was the southern port most dependent on New York for its imports, residents keenly
experienced the frustrations inherent in their economic subserviency to
the North. Criticism of northern-born businessmen or politicians in
Mobile vented some of these frustrations.

Representation of native northerners in local commerce and politics in fact declined somewhat in the 1850s. In 1850 natives of northern
states made up slightly more than 18 percent of the city's American-
born free population, a proportion unequaled in other Lower South
cities except New Orleans, where northerners' representation only
barely exceeded that in Mobile. Of Mobile's free adult males, who constituted the major component of the free work force, 19.5 percent hailed
from the North in 1850. By 1860, however, only 16.0 percent came from
the North. Northerners' representation declined notably in commercial, public service, and professional occupations. Late in the decade
southern-born men took northerners' places in some of these activities,
especially in highly visible political offices such as the mayoralty. Cer-

tainly by 1860 northern-born men retained strength, both in numbers and influence, in local affairs, but their power was reduced from 1850. Southerners remained determined to increase their own commercial and political power locally and nationally as they vied with northerners and foreigners in their midst.[40]

Secession provided the ultimate expression of southerners' wish for independence from northern domination. Because secession would disrupt their city's profitable trade patterns, Mobilians moved only cautiously toward that action. Public meetings had discussed secession in the wake of the Nashville Convention in 1850, yet they raised the subject only sporadically for a number of years afterward. Beginning in 1858 Mobilians raised the issue of secession more frequently, although they rarely considered publicly the adverse effects that the action might have on their city.

In Mobile commercial independence provided a rationale for the southern rights movement that found favor in urban as opposed to nonurban areas of the South. John Forsyth, Democratic editor of the *Mobile Register*, delivered a public address in 1858 in which he stated widely held local views about the benefits of disunion for the South: "I have no more doubt that the effect of separation would be to transfer the energies of industry, population, commerce, and wealth, from the North to the South, than I have that it is to the Union with us, the wealth-producing States, that the North owes its great progress in material prosperity. . . . The Union broken, we should have what has been so long the dream of the South—direct trade and commercial independence."[41] Forsyth's speech failed to explain how, in view of obstacles to the accumulation of risk capital in the South, the region's dreams of commercial independence might be realized.

The rising political power of the new Republican party threatened to thwart these dreams of urban and commercially minded southerners. Some who had been partisan enemies united against this threat. As Republicans gained electoral strength, Forsyth praised former Whigs in Mobile who joined the Democatic party, "the only one which can be depended on to save the South from the rule of Black Republicanism."[42] As the election of 1860 approached, while others in his party campaigned for the Southern Democratic ticket, Forsyth supported the National Democratic ticket. Prospects of imminent secession and personal loyalties prompted Forsyth to manage the presidential campaign in Alabama of his friend, the National Democratic candidate Stephen A. Douglas.

Mobile's vote in the presidential election, in keeping with the trend in many other southern cities, reflected the moderate preferences of city voters. Seventy-one percent of voters in the city of Mobile voted for moderate candidates, Constitutional Unionist John Bell or National Democrat Stephen Douglas. Of major southern ports, only New Orleans with its 80 percent vote for Bell and Douglas exceeded Mobile's support for moderates. Like Mobile, other southern cities dominated by business leaders valued the Union enough to oppose extremists during the presidential campaign of 1860.[43] Rural voters in southern states provided most of Breckinridge's support.

In Mobile voters' preferences in 1860 related to their ties to the cotton trade, their nativity, and their slaveholding status. With editorial support from the *Mobile Register*, Douglas attracted a plurality of 38 percent of the city's vote, coming strongly from businessmen and artisans, with the northern- and foreign-born prominent among them. Foreign-born voters favored Douglas rather than Bell in reaction to the American party's attacks on them in the 1850s. Bell, who polled 33 percent of the city's vote, attracted much support from middle-class, northern-born merchants and slaveholders. Cotton factors, brokers, and buyers favored Douglas and Bell over Breckinridge out of concern for maintaining financial ties between the North and the South. Many businessmen who represented northern capital in southern markets favored above all keeping sectional tensions from blocking their access to northern financial institutions. Breckinridge, who garnered 29 percent of the vote, claimed his greatest following among slaveholding attorneys and farmers.[44]

As the returns came in on the night of 6 November 1860, Mobilians began shifting their sympathies from moderation to secession. That night in John Forsyth's office at the *Register*, Stephen A. Douglas learned that he had led the polls in Mobile but lost the state and nation. Anticipating Abraham Lincoln's victory, Forsyth had written an editorial endorsing a call for a state convention to decide Alabama's response. He showed it to Douglas, who voiced his disapproval. Forsyth argued that the only way to control the secession tendency was to pretend to acquiesce to it and to elect Unionists to manage the convention. Douglas warned Forsyth that if Unionists could not prevent the convention from meeting they could not control it when it assembled in Montgomery. Forsyth nevertheless insisted on printing his editorial. Unable to dissuade his friend from an action that he felt would only encourage secession, Douglas retired to his lodgings at the Battle House.[45]

Shortly after the presidential election, while political activists pondered secession, cotton factors wished the South would remain in the Union at least long enough to allow them to market that season's crop. "Our market is unsettled by the election news," admitted one cotton merchant two days after Lincoln's victory. He hoped "in a few days that confidence will be restored and things will move on as before." Cautiously he advised a client, "We presume that any secession movement in the South will not take effect before the inauguration of Lincoln, which will allow time for the disposal of the cotton crop in the regular way." His predictions about the timing of secession, at least for states in the Lower South, proved inaccurate as support mounted for early disunion.[46]

In Mobile popular support for secession increased in the weeks after the election as Alabama prepared for a state convention. Early in December the women's auxiliary of the Young Men's Secession Association staged a gala at which the women presented the association with a banner reading "Alabama the Time Has Come." When news arrived on 20 December of South Carolina's passage of an ordinance of secession, local secessionists fired a 100-gun salute, staged a military parade, and rang bells. As hundreds thronged the streets, many citizens delivered impromptu speeches. Fireworks lit the city. In short, according to resident Kate Cumming, "everything was done to prove that Mobile, at least, approved of what South Carolina had done."[47]

In the campaign before the election of delegates to Alabama's secession convention, both major newspapers in Mobile adopted cooperationist stands. Cooperationists emphasized that their program of united action by southern states offered conservatives the chance for a smooth transition of power with minimal disruption. Southerners had only two choices for action, argued the *Mobile Register*. They might follow "a mere hurrah movement . . . in which frenzied appeals will take place of reason," fragmenting the South and weakening it. Or, southerners might model themselves on the patience and wisdom of the Founding Fathers "so that we have at least a firm foundation laid for a new edifice ere the old one is razed to the ground." These arguments promoted by the *Register* found support in the *Mobile Advertiser* as both newspapers explained their rationales for supporting cooperation rather than immediate secession.[48]

Many voters in Mobile rejected their newspapers' pleas for moderation. Former Whigs among the cooperationists, hopeful that they could influence the convention, ignored public opinion in urging the election of unpledged delegates. Secessionists, who ran pledged delegates, scored a resounding victory in Mobile. In the convention election Mobile's voters favored secessionist delegates by a two-to-one majority. Cooperationists lost all seven wards. Native southerners, especially slaveholders, provided many votes for secessionists, while nonslaveholders born in the North gave important support to cooperationists. Among cooperationists slaveholding merchants from the North provided the most consistent support.[49]

Mobile's urban politics in 1860 depended a great deal upon the birthplaces of its activists. Politically active men who were born outside the slave South, especially nonslaveholders and merchants, proved to be the group least likely to favor secession. They defended slave society, but they had not internalized its values enough to wish immediate disunion.[50]

Business interests in Mobile, as in other southern cities, lost some influence for moderation both in local elections for delegates to secession conventions and in the conventions themselves. Mobile's delegates included only 1 merchant, who served along with 2 attorneys and 1 physician. Of the 100 delegates at the Alabama convention, only 9 directly represented the business class, and 4 of them favored secession while only 5 favored cooperation. Delegates from Mobile voted with the majority for an ordinance of secession 11 January 1861. Mississippi's convention had no merchant or businessman among its 100 delegates. Numbered among the 169 delegates at South Carolina's convention were only 16 businessmen, all of whom voted for secession. Throughout the South mercantile interests changed their public posture as they recognized increasing popular support for secession.[51]

Public celebrations marked receipt in Mobile 11 January of the news that Alabama had adopted an ordinance of secession that day and Florida had taken the same action the previous day. People thronged the streets, gathering around what they called a "secession pole" at the foot of Government Street to raise a southern flag. Citizens fired 100 guns for Alabama and 15 for Florida. To the tune of the "Southern Marseillaise," the crowd marched away from the "secession pole" to reassemble at the Customs House, where a lone-star flag waved from the balcony. More people delivered speeches from the steps of the building. Two militia companies, the Mobile Cadets and Independent Rifles, paraded in the streets. That night a fireworks display illumined Bienville Square with crowd-pleasing patterns like the "Southern Cross" and "Lone Star."[52]

Public demonstrations marked news of other states' ordinances of secession, notably that of Virginia shortly after the Confederate capture of Fort Sumter at Charleston had prompted President Lincoln to call for volunteers to defend the Union. As Mobilians heard of Virginia's secession, the city became, according to Kate Cumming, "delirious with joy as boom after boom for 'Virginia out' rent the air." Seth Roberts closed the shutters of his drug store and wrote boldly in chalk, "Virginia out, nuff said." Some Mobilians wept for happiness. Others set off displays of fireworks.[53]

These celebrations might create the impression that Mobilians uniformly supported secession, yet that was not true. Residents who disapproved of secession simply avoided disclosing their views publicly. Northern-born businessmen, who had learned through years of practice to accommodate themselves to local mores, particularly took care about expressing regrets regarding secession. William Rix, a merchant from Vermont, absented himself from the public celebration of Virginia's secession, "as it would have been almost equivalent to treason," he said, "to have passed through the streets without joining in the demonstration of frantic joy that seemed to have deposed every other emotion in the people." He concerned himself with "how to manage the responsibilities involved in citizenship in a state in rebellion against its government."[54]

Southern loyalty for secessionists, whether enthusiastic or reluctant, eventually overrode unionist sentiment, both patriotic and economic. City-wide celebrations of secession, albeit contrived, presented Mobilians both to themselves and to outsiders as more unified than they had ever been in their history. Mobilians supported the Confederacy hoping that it would, among other things, end their colonial relationship to the North and spur urban growth in their city.

Niles' Register had predicted in 1822 that Mobile would become one of the most populous southern cities. By 1860 Mobile had instead become the least populous of major southern cities, ranking seventh in the region and twenty-seventh among all American cities.[55] In many respects, Mobile remained the second-class port, in comparison to New Orleans, that the *Louisiana Gazette* had labeled it in 1822. Explanations both for the growth that propelled Mobile into national prominence and for its subsequent failure to achieve its full potential revolved around the colonial nature of Mobile's commerce. Under its French, British, and Spanish colonial rulers, Mobile had served as an export-oriented trading center, and it maintained that same function under American control. Colonial dependency, the condition that Mobile's commercially minded citizens wished so desperately to change in the war for southern independence, in fact would continue to plague the city until long after the end of that conflict. Mobile, like a number of other southern cities, was to remain economically dependent on the North for many years to come. Mobile never again achieved as much regional or national prominence among America's cities as it had in 1860 when cotton was king.

Appendix

CLASSIFICATION OF OCCUPATIONS

AGRICULTURE
Farmer
FISHING
Fisherman
Oysterman
BUILDING
Bricklayer
Carpenter
Caulker
Contractor
Mason
Painter
Plasterer
MANUFACTURING
Food
  Baker
  Confectioner
  Cook
  Miller
Jewelry
  Watchmaker
Print and Art
  Musician
  Portrait Painter
  Printer
Metal
  Blacksmith
  Tinsmith
Transport Trades
  Sailmaker
  Ship Carpenter
Clothing
  Bonnet Bleacher

Shoemaker
Tailor
Homefurnishing
  Cabinet Maker
  Finisher
  Mattress Maker
  Upholsterer
Mechanic
  Boiler Maker
  Engineer
  Machinist
  Wheelwright
Building Material
  Brick Maker
  Lumberman
  Sawyer
Other Trades
  Carriage Maker
  Cigar Maker
  Saddler
  Soapmaker
TRANSPORT
Brakeman
City Express Man
Pilot
Sailor/Mariner
Ship Chandler
Steamboatman
COMMERCE
Proprietor Level ($500+ property)
  Broker
  Businessman
  Commission Merchant

APPENDIX

Cotton Factor
Landlord
Merchant (varied types)
President of Insurance Company
Speculator
Wharfinger
EMPLOYEE LEVEL
Agent
Auctioneer
Bar Keeper
Bank Officer
Bookkeeper
Clerk
Cotton Sampler
Market Man
Officer of Insurance Company
Tradesman/Storekeeper
PROFESSIONS
Attorney
Clergyman
Editor/Publisher
Judge
Physician

NONPROFESSIONAL SERVICES
Barber
Butcher
Druggist
Telegraph Manager
SEMISKILLED LABOR
Bayman
Cab Driver
Drayman
Stevedore
Steward
Waterman
Woodcutter
UNSKILLED LABOR
PUBLIC SERVICE
Constable
Inspector
Lamplighter
Policeman
Public Official
Watchman
GENTLEMAN

NOTE: This system follows the one suggested for mid-nineteenth-century pre-industrial cities by Michael B. Katz in "Occupational Classification in History," *Journal of Interdisciplinary History* 3 (1972): 63–88. All occupations listed for both the leaders and sample are included.

Notes

ABBREVIATIONS

ASDAH Alabama State Department of Archives and History, Montgomery, Alabama

BA Mobile County School Board Offices, Barton Academy, Mobile, Alabama

BL Baker Library, Graduate School of Business Administration, Harvard University, Cambridge, Massachusetts

CMA City of Mobile Archives, Mobile, Alabama

Duke William R. Perkins Library, Duke University, Durham, North Carolina

HMPSA Historic Mobile Preservation Society Archives, Oakleigh, Mobile, Alabama

MPL Special Collections Division, Mobile Public Library, Mobile, Alabama

NYHS New-York Historical Society, New York City, New York

SHC Southern Historical Collection, University of North Carolina Library, Chapel Hill, North Carolina

INTRODUCTION

1. Hiram Fuller, *Belle Brittan on a Tour, at Newport, and Here and There* (New York: Derby & Jackson, 1858), p. 112.

2. David R. Goldfield, "The Urban South: A Regional Framework," *American Historical Review* 86 (1981): 1009–34.

3. Robert Greenhalgh Albion, *The Rise of New York Port [1815–1860]* (New York: Charles Scribner's Sons, 1939), pp. 103–4.

4. Leonard P. Curry, "Urbanization and Urbanism in the Old South: A Comparative View," *Journal of Southern History* 40 (1974): 60.

5. David R. Goldfield and Blaine A. Brownell, *Urban America: From Downtown to No Town* (Boston: Houghton Mifflin, 1979), p. 20.

6. Goldfield, "Urban South," p. 1012.

CHAPTER 1

1. *Niles' Register* 22 (1822): 96. *Niles' Weekly Register* became *Niles' National Register* in 1839, but it will be cited consistently here as *Niles' Register*. See also *Mobile Register*, 7 February 1822. The *Register* changed its title slightly several times during the antebellum period, but the citation will remain the same here.

2. Solomon Mordecai to Ellen Mordecai, 20 August 1829, Mordecai Family Papers, SHC.

3. Karl Bernhard, Duke of Saxe-Weimar-Eisenach, *Travels Through North America During the Years 1825 and 1826*, 2 vols. (Philadelphia: Carey, Lea & Carey, 1828), 2:39.

4. Clarence E. Carter, ed., *The Territorial Papers of the United States, vol. 18, The Territory of Alabama, 1817–1819* (Washington: Government Printing Office, 1952), p. 124.

5. Adam Hodgson, *Remarks during a Journey through North America in the Years 1819, 1820, and 1821, in a Series of Letters*, ed. Samuel Whiting, 2 vols. (New York: Samuel Whiting, 1823), 1:151–52.

6. Welcome Arnold Greene, *The Journals of Welcome Arnold Greene: Journeys in the South*, ed. Alice E. Smith (Madison: State Historical Society of Wisconsin, 1957), p. 228; and *Rowan's Mobile Directory and Commercial Supplement for 1850–51* (Mobile: Strickland & Benjamin, 1850), pp. 15–16.

7. Peter Joseph Hamilton, *Colonial Mobile: An Historical Study Largely from Original Sources, of the Alabama-Tombigbee Basin and the Old South West from the Discovery of the Spiritu Santo in 1519 until the Demolition of Fort Charlotte in 1821*, rev. ed. (Boston: Houghton Mifflin, 1910; reprint ed., Mobile: First National Bank, 1952), pp. 479, 390; *Mobile Register*, 7 February 1822; and Karl Bernhard, Duke of Saxe-Weimar-Eisenach, *Travels*, 2:39.

8. Edward Pessen, *Jacksonian America: Society, Personality, and Politics*, rev. ed. (Homewood, Ill.: Dorsey Press, 1978), chap. 2; Hodgson, *Remarks*, 1:152–53; and Margaret Hall, *The Aristocratic Journey: Being the Outspoken Letters of Mrs. Basil Hall Written during a Fourteen Months' Sojourn in America, 1827–1828*, ed. Una Pope-Hennessy (New York: G. P. Putnam's Sons, 1931), pp. 246, 248.

9. *Mobile Register*, 6 July 1856; and Hamilton, *Colonial Mobile*, p. 446.

10. *Mobile Register*, 2 December 1822.

11. *Niles' Register* 39 (1830): 156.

12. Bernard Reynolds, *Sketches of Mobile, from 1814 to the Present Time* (Mobile: B. H. Richardson, 1868), p. 21.

13. David Ward, *Cities and Immigrants: A Geography of Change in Nineteenth-Century America* (New York: Oxford University Press, 1971), p. 29.

14. Solomon Mordecai to Ellen Mordecai, 8 December 1823, Mordecai Family Papers, SHC.

15. Solomon Mordecai to Ellen Mordecai, 2 February 1825, 19 December 1823, Mordecai Family Papers, SHC.

16. Greene, *Journals*, p. 228.

17. Solomon Mordecai to Ellen Mordecai, 2 February 1825, Mordecai Family Papers, SHC.

18. James C. Parker, "Blakeley: A Frontier Seaport," *Alabama Review* 27 (1974): 39, 41; and Hamilton, *Colonial Mobile*, p. 449. Hamilton explains (p. 407) that "Blakeley" sometimes appears incorrectly in records without the second *e*. When that happens in titles or quotations cited here, *sic* will not be added.

19. Stuart Seely Sprague, "Alabama Town Promotion during the Era of Good Feelings," *Alabama Historical Quarterly* 37 (1974): 19–20; Parker, "Blakeley," pp. 42–43; Carter, *Territorial Papers*, 18:498; Harry A. Toulmin, *A Digest of the Laws of the State of Alabama* (Cahawba, Ala.: Ginn and Curtis, 1823), pp. 796–98; and *Mobile Argus*, 5 December 1822.

20. Hodgson, *Remarks*, 1:151–52.

21. James C. Parker, "The Development of the Port of Mobile, 1819–1836" (M.A. thesis, Auburn University, 1968), p. 119.

22. Parker, "Blakeley," pp. 49–50.

23. Ibid.; and Peter A. Brannon, *Lilies, Lions, and Bag-pipes: A Tale of Other Days in Alabama* (Montgomery: Paragon Press, 1934), p. 25.

24. Parker, "Blakeley," pp. 46, 50; and Reynolds, *Sketches of Mobile*, p. 10.

25. Parker, "Blakeley," p. 51; *New York American*, quoted in *Niles' Register* 24 (1823): 295; Allan R. Pred, *Urban Growth and the Circulation of Information: The United States System of Cities, 1790–1840* (Cambridge, Mass.: Harvard University Press, 1973), p. 225; and Ward, *Cities and Immigrants*, p. 13.

26. "The Sea-Ports in the Gulf of Mexico," *Louisiana Gazette* (New Orleans), quoted in *Mobile Argus*, 30 December 1822.

27. Jay Higginbotham, *Old Mobile: Fort Louis de la Louisiane, 1702–1711* (Mobile: Museum of the City of Mobile, 1977), pp. 24–25; Hamilton, *Colonial Mobile*, pp. 83–84; and Peter Joseph Hamilton, *Mobile of the Five Flags: The Story of the River Basin and Coast about Mobile from the Earliest Times to the Present* (Mobile: Gill Printing Co., 1913), pp. 44–48, 78, 116.

28. Higginbotham, *Old Mobile*, pp. 21–22n.

29. Hamilton, *Mobile of Five Flags*, p. 61; and David R. Goldfield and Blaine A. Brownell, *Urban America: From Downtown to No Town* (Boston: Houghton Mifflin, 1979), pp. 13–14, 27.

30. Weymouth T. Jordan, "Ante-Bellum Mobile: Alabama's Agricultural Emporium," *Alabama Review* 1 (1948): 181; and Hamilton, *Mobile of Five Flags*, pp. 96, 68.

31. Hamilton, *Colonial Mobile*, p. 251; and Jordan, "Ante-Bellum Mobile," p. 181.

32. Hamilton, *Colonial Mobile*, p. 332; U.S. Bureau of the Census, *The Seventh Census of the United States: 1850* (Washington: Robert Armstrong, Public Printer, 1853), p. liii; and *Mobile Register*, 7 February 1822.

33. Clement Eaton, *A History of the Old South*, 2d ed. (New York: Macmillan, 1966), pp. 200–201; and Thomas P. Abernethy, *The South in the New Nation, 1789–1819* (Baton Rouge: Louisiana State University Press, 1961), chap. 13.

34. Abernethy, *South in the New Nation*, chap. 13.

35. Hamilton, *Colonial Mobile*, pp. 410–13.

36. Toulmin, *Digest of Laws*, pp. 780–82; and Hamilton, *Colonial Mobile*, pp. 439–41.

37. Toulmin, *Digest of Laws*, pp. 780–81; and Hamilton, *Colonial Mobile*, pp. 442–45.

38. Toulmin, *Digest of Laws*, pp. 784–93. According to an 1820 clarification of the act of incorporation, property was not taxable past one-half mile west of the easternmost street in the city. Subsequent acts passed in 1820 and 1821 dealt with surveying land, opening, widening, extending, and regulating streets, and keeping records.

39. Hamilton, *Colonial Mobile*, pp. 478–81.

40. Ibid., p. 473; and Hamilton, *Mobile of Five Flags*, p. 219.

41. *Niles' Register* 33 (1827): 182–96; and *Mobile Register*, 6 July 1856, 19 January 1828.

42. [Edouard Delius], *Wanderungen eines jungen Norddeutschen durch Portugal, Spanien, und Nord-Amerika in dem Jahren 1827–1831*, ed. Georg Lotz, 4 vols. (Hamburg: Herold-schen Buchhandlungen, 1834), 4:111; Thomas Hamilton, *Men and Manners in America* (Philadelphia: Carey, Lea & Blanchard, 1833), p. 328; and Carl David Arfwedson, *The United States and Canada in 1832, 1833, and 1834*, 2 vols. (London: Richard Bentley, 1834), 2:44.

43. *Mobile Register*, quoted in *Niles' Register* 45 (1833): 165.

CHAPTER 2

1. Joseph Holt Ingraham, ed., *The Sunny South; or, The Southerner at Home, Embracing Five Years' Experience of a Northern Governess in the Land of the Sugar and the Cotton* (Philadelphia: G. G. Evans, 1860), pp. 507–8. As an Episcopal priest, Ingraham often masked his authorship of secular works.

2. Charles Mackay, *Life and Liberty in America; or, Sketches of a Tour in the United States and Canada, in 1857–8* (New York: Harper & Brothers, 1859), p. 180.

3. Charles S. Davis, *The Cotton Kingdom in Alabama* (Montgomery: Alabama State Department of Archives and History, 1939), pp. 42–43.

4. Ibid., p. 25.

5. Robert Greenhalgh Albion, *The Rise of New York Port [1815–1860]* (New York: Charles Scribner's Sons, 1939), p. 105.

6. Davis, *Cotton Kingdom in Alabama*, p. 21; *Mobile Advertiser*, 22 March 1856; Peter Joseph Hamilton, *Colonial Mobile: An Historical Study Largely from Original Sources, of the Alabama-Tombigbee Basin and the Old South West from the Discovery of the Spiritu Santo in 1519 until the Demolition of Fort Charlotte in 1821*, rev. ed. (Boston: Houghton Mifflin, 1910; reprint ed., Mobile: First National Bank, 1952), p. 471n; and *Mobile Register*, 1 December 1846. The *Mobile Advertiser* altered its name slightly during the antebellum years, but the citation will remain the same here.

7. Davis, *Cotton Kingdom in Alabama*, p. 129.

8. *Niles' Register* 29 (1825): 147; Albion, *Rise of New York Port*, pp. 107–10; and Robert Greenhalgh Albion, *Square-Riggers on a Schedule: The New York Sailing Packets to England, France, and the Cotton Ports* (Princeton, N.J.: Princeton University Press, 1938), pp. 60–61, 70, 134, 290, 302–3, 310.

9. Allan R. Pred, *Urban Growth and the Circulation of Information: The United States System of Cities, 1790-1840* (Cambridge, Mass.: Harvard University Press, 1973), pp. 119, 122-23; and *Urban Growth and City-Systems in the United States, 1840-1860* (Cambridge, Mass.: Harvard University Press, 1980), pp. 115-16, 167.

10. *Hunt's Merchants' Magazine* 13 (1845): 417-18, 19 (1848): 593.

11. Ingraham, *Sunny South*, p. 502; John W. Oldmixon, *Transatlantic Wanderings; or, A Last Look at the United States* (London: George Routledge, 1855), p. 152; J. W. Hengiston [Siras Redding], "Mobile, Pensacola, and the Floridas: Cotton Barque to Cape Cod, along the Gulf Stream," *New Monthly Magazine* 98 (1853): 366; and John S. C. Abbott, *South and North; or, Impressions Received during a Trip to Cuba and the South* (New York: Abbey & Abbot, 1860), pp. 91-92.

12. *Mobile Register*, 9 January, 4 and 11 March, 9 April, 10 August 1835; William H. Brantley, *Banking in Alabama, 1816-1860*, 2 vols. (Birmingham: Oxmoor Press, 1961-67), 1: 307-8; Peter Joseph Hamilton, *Mobile of the Five Flags: The Story of the River Basin and Coast about Mobile from the Earliest Times to the Present* (Mobile: Gill Printing Co., 1913), pp. 247-48; James C. Parker, "The Development of the Port of Mobile, 1819-1836" (M.A. thesis, Auburn University, 1968), pp. 103-4; and Robert S. Cotterill, "The Beginnings of Railroads in the Southwest," *Mississippi Valley Historical Review* 8 (1922): 324.

13. U.S. Congress, 29th Congress, 1st Session, House Document 156, Committee on Commerce, Joint Memorial of the Legislature of Alabama, 9 March 1846; and Hamilton, *Mobile of Five Flags*, pp. 270-71.

14. Parker, "Development of Port of Mobile," pp. 44-45; Hamilton, *Colonial Mobile*, p. 473; *Hunt's Merchants' Magazine* 13 (1845): 417, 24 (1851): 266; T. C. Fay, *Mobile Directory or Strangers' Guide for 1839* (Mobile: R. R. Dade, 1839); *Directory for the City of Mobile, 1859* (Mobile: Farrow & Dennett, 1859); and Hamilton, *Mobile of Five Flags*, p. 270.

15. *Hunt's Merchants' Magazine* 24 (1851): 266; and Parker, "Development of Port of Mobile," pp. 46-47.

16. Ralph W. Haskins, "Planter and Cotton Factor in the Old South: Some Areas of Friction," *Agricultural History* 39 (1955): 1; and Duke Goodman Circular, 7 June 1832, Singleton Family Papers, SHC.

17. Alfred H. Stone, "The Cotton Factorage System of the Southern States," *American Historical Review* 20 (1915): 561; Harold D. Woodman, *King Cotton and His Retainers: Financing and Marketing the Cotton Crop of the South, 1800-1925* (Lexington: University of Kentucky Press, 1968), p. 53; Thomas P. Abernethy, *The Formative Period in Alabama, 1815-1828* (1922; rpt. ed., University, Ala.: University of Alabama Press, 1965), p. 107; and Haskins, "Planter and Factor," p. 2.

18. Davis, *Cotton Kingdom in Alabama*, pp. 149-50.

19. David R. Goldfield and Blaine A. Brownell, *Urban America: From Downtown to No Town* (Boston: Houghton Mifflin, 1979), pp. 129-30; Robertson & Barnewall to Ogden Day & Co., 11 May 1821, Peters & Stebbins to Ogden Day & Co., 14 March, 7 April 1821, R. Stebbins & Co. to Ogden Ferguson & Co., 10 April 1830, Ogden Ferguson & Day Papers, NYHS; Brown Brothers & Co. to McLoskey & Hagan, 8 November 1825, Brown Brothers & Co. to John Boyd & Co., 26 July, 19 December 1826, Brown Brothers & Co. Letter Book, Brown Broth-

ers Harriman & Co. Historical File, NYHS; John Killick, "Risk Specialization and Profit in the Mercantile Sector of the Nineteenth Century Cotton Trade: Alexander Brown and Sons 1820–80," *Business History* 16 (1974): 5; N. W. Collet to Stewart Brown, 10 September 1858, Brown, Shipley & Co. to Brown Brothers & Co., 12 May 1859, Brown Brothers Harriman & Co. Historical File, NYHS; John R. Killick, "The Cotton Operations of Alexander Brown and Sons in the Deep South, 1820–1860," *Journal of Southern History* 43 (1977): 181; and Edwin J. Perkins, *Financing Anglo-American Trade: The House of Brown, 1800–1880* (Cambridge, Mass.: Harvard University Press, 1975), p. 97.

20. Davis, *Cotton Kingdom in Alabama*, p. 153; and R. G. Dun & Co. Credit Reports, Alabama, 17:230, 180, 66, BL.

21. Frederic Cople Jaher, "Antebellum Charleston: Anatomy of an Economic Failure," in *Class, Conflict, and Consensus: Antebellum Southern Community Studies*, ed. Orville Vernon Burton and Robert C. McMath, Jr. (Westport, Conn.: Greenwood Press, 1982), p. 212.

22. William Garrett, *Reminiscences of Public Men in Alabama for Thirty Years* (Atlanta: Plantation Publishing Company's Press, 1872), pp. 726–27; Thomas McAdory Owen, *History of Alabama and Dictionary of Alabama Biography*, 4 vols. (Chicago: S. J. Clarke Publishing Co., 1921), 4:1790, 3:78–79; and Bernard Reynolds, *Sketches of Mobile, from 1814 to the Present Time* (Mobile: B. H. Richardson, 1868), p. 38.

23. Haskins, "Planter and Factor," pp. 7, 2; *Alabama Planter*, 5 September 1853. Other Alabama cities besides Mobile published newspapers called the *Alabama Planter*, but the only *Alabama Planter* cited here will be the one published in Mobile.

24. *Acts of Alabama*, Session of 1857–58, pp. 58–60; *Senate Journal*, Session of 1857–58, pp. 251, 302, 306, 322; and *House Journal*, Session of 1857–58, pp. 537, 544.

25. Haskins, "Planter and Factor," pp. 2, 4, 7.

26. Ibid., p. 7; and Hengiston, "Mobile, Pensacola, and the Floridas," p. 363. The latter citation contains the quotation.

27. R. K. Hinton to Joel W. Jones, 13 and 21 October 1857, and James Eddins to John A. Winston & Co., 28 October 1857, Parham-Winston Collection, ASDAH. The first citation contains the quotation.

28. Duke W. Goodman to Richard Singleton, 4 September 1841, Singleton Papers, SHC.

29. *House Journal*, Session of 1832–33, pp. 37, 76, 89, 96–97; *Senate Journal*, Session of 1832–33, pp. 77, 100, 159; and *Niles' Register* 43 (1833): 319.

30. *Acts of Alabama*, Session of 1837, pp. 12–13, 33–35.

31. *House Journal*, Session of 1837, pp. 116–17. See also *House Journal*, Session of 1837, pp. 16, 21–22, 26, 47–48, 56, 69, 77, 86, 89, 92–94; and *Senate Journal*, Session of 1837, pp. 20, 40, 70, 75, 106–8, 127.

32. Garrett, *Reminiscences*, pp. 44–46.

33. Haskins, "Planter and Factor," p. 5; and *Mobile Advertiser*, 28 March 1855.

34. Haskins, "Planter and Factor," p. 11; and *Mobile Register*, 7 January 1837.

35. Brantley, *Banking in Alabama*, 1:53–54, 58, 79, 276, 289.

36. *Mobile Register*, 11 July 1884; Brantley, *Banking in Alabama*, 2:244; and *Mobile Register*, 25 April 1848. The last citation contains the quotation.

37. *Acts of Alabama*, Session of 1852, p. 37.

38. R. G. Dun & Co. Credit Reports, Alabama, 17:309, BL.

39. Brantley, *Banking in Alabama*, 1:179–80, 184, 228, 234, 288; *Niles' Register* 45 (1833): 165, 44 (1833): 220; and Weymouth T. Jordan, "Antebellum Mobile: Alabama's Agricultural Emporium," *Alabama Review* 1 (1948): 191.

40. Brantley, *Banking in Alabama*, 1:184–85, 249–53, 262–63, 269, 288, 296; and *Mobile Register*, 6 June, 21 and 26 September 1832.

41. Davis, *Cotton Kingdom in Alabama*, pp. 34–35; A. Barclay to Benjamin Fitzpatrick, 11 February 1842, Governors' Correspondence: Fitzpatrick, State Branch Bank File, ASDAH; *Alabama Planter*, 13 June 1853; and *Mobile Advertiser*, 24 February 1859.

42. Brantley, *Banking in Alabama*, 1:310, 321, 325, 472, and 2: 45, 218; *Mobile Register*, 15 October 1835, 12 February 1836, 28 October, 15 December 1842, 31 January 1846; and *Acts of Alabama*, Session of 1850, pp. 126–27.

43. *Mobile Register*, 15 and 26 February 1850, 3 March 1860; *Alabama Planter*, 30 June 1851; *Rowan's Mobile Directory and Commercial Supplement for 1850–51* (Mobile: Strickland & Benjamin, 1850), p. 21; *Acts of Alabama*, Session of 1851–52, pp. 277–78; *Acts of Alabama*, Session of 1853–54, pp. 371–72; *Mobile Advertiser*, 21 October, 8 December 1854; and *Acts of Alabama*, Session of 1857–58, pp. 17, 26, 27.

44. *Bankers' Magazine*, cited in *Hunt's Merchants' Magazine* 18 (1848): 326.

45. Woodman, *King Cotton and His Retainers*, p. 122.

46. R. G. Dun & Co. Credit Reports, Alabama, 17:21, BL; Charles D. Dickey to Stewart A. Brown, 5 March 1858, Mobile Agency Envelope, Brown Shipley & Co. to Brown Brothers & Co., 16 March 1858, Brown Brothers Harriman & Co. Historical File, Morrell & Dickey to Brown Brothers & Co., 14 January 1851, 16 January 1852, Mobile Agency Envelope, Charles D. Dickey to Brown Brothers & Co., 5 June 1851, 4 December 1855, 1 February 1858, Mobile Agency Envelope, Brown Brothers Harriman & Co. Historical File, NYHS; Killick, "Cotton Operations," pp. 184, 193; and Perkins, *Financing Anglo-American Trade*, p. 41.

47. Charles D. Dickey to Brown Brothers & Co., 19 December 1855, Mobile Agency Envelope, Brown Brothers Harriman & Co. Historical File, NYHS.

48. Charles D. Dickey to Brown Brothers Harriman & Co., 1 February 1858, Mobile Agency Envelope, Brown Brothers Harriman & Co. Historical File, NYHS.

49. Charles D. Dickey to Stewart Brown, 22 November 1859, Mobile Agency Envelope, Brown Brothers Harriman & Co. Historical File, NYHS.

50. Charles D. Dickey to Stewart Brown, 18 November 1859, Mobile Agency Envelope, Brown Brothers Harriman & Co. Historical File, NYHS; and Killick, "Risk Specialization and Profit," pp. 8–9.

51. *Alabama Planter*, 12 January 1852. See also *Mobile Register*, 2 March 1829, 3 June 1830, 3 June 1833, 10 November 1836, 8 September 1848, 19 December 1849, 19 November 1858, 13 May 1852; *Acts of Alabama*, Session of 1849–50, pp. 302–6, 309–10; *Acts of Alabama*, Session of 1851–52, pp. 119–26; *Acts of Alabama*, Session

NOTES TO PAGES 41−45

of 1853–54; pp. 403–4, 406, 427–28, 473; *Acts of Alabama*, Session of 1857–58, pp. 105–10, 118–21; and *Acts of Alabama*, Session of 1859–60, pp. 161–63, 494–95.

52. *Mobile Register*, 16 May 1833, 21 March 1845, 13 May 1852, 11 April 1853, 13 September 1855, 17 April 1860; and Edwin T. Wood, *Mobile Directory, and Register, for 1844, Embracing the Names of Firms, the Individuals Composing Them, and House-holders Generally within the City Limits, Alphabetically Arranged* (Mobile: Dade & Thompson, 1844), pp. 39–41.

53. Clement Eaton, *The Growth of Southern Civilization, 1790–1860* (New York: Harper & Brothers, 1961), p. 217; and *Rowan's Directory 1850–51*, p. 21.

54. *Mobile Mercantile Advertiser*, 1 January 1824, and *Mobile Register*, 12 December 1840, cited in Paul Wayne Taylor, "Mobile, 1818–1859, As Her Newspapers Pictured Her" (M.A. thesis, University of Alabama, 1951), p. 27; *Mobile Register*, 23 October 1837; *Hunt's Merchants' Magazine* 4 (1841): 274–75; and A. Barclay to Benjamin Fitzpatrick, 11 February 1842, Governors' Correspondence: Fitzpatrick, State Branch Bank File, ADSAH.

55. *Acts of Alabama*, Session of 1853–54, p. 270; and *Mobile Daily Advertiser*, 11, 16, and 17 March, 7 April 1854.

56. *Mobile Advertiser*, 16 March 1854.

57. Ibid., 13 November 1857.

58. William R. Robertson, *The Comprehensive Mobile Guide and Directory Referring to the Business Locations for 1852* (Mobile: Carver & Ryland, 1852), p. ii; and *Mobile Advertiser*, 8 April 1854.

59. Aldermen's Minutes, 18 February, 4 March 1858, 21 February 1859, MPL; and *Mobile Register*, 11 August 1858.

60. *Mobile Register*, 22 January 1846.

61. Daniel Boorstin, *The Americans: The National Experience* (New York: Random House, 1965), p. 143; and Karl Bernhard, Duke of Saxe-Weimar-Eisenach, *Travels through North America during the Years 1825 and 1826*, 2 vols. (Philadephia: Carey, Lea & Carey, 1828), 2:39.

62. Margaret Hall, *The Aristocratic Journey: Being the Outspoken Letters of Mrs. Basil Hall Written during a Fourteen Months' Sojourn in America, 1827–1828*, ed. Una Pope-Hennessy (New York: G. P. Putnam's Sons, 1931), pp. 245–46; *Rowan's Directory 1850–51*, p. 17; *Niles' Register* 49 (1835): 241; James S. Buckingham, *The Slave States of America*, 2 vols. (London: Fisher, Son, 1842), 1:283; and *Mobile Register*, 6 April 1836, 28 February 1840.

63. *Mobile Register*, 23 November 1842, 1 August 1843, 8 November 1845; Francis S. Bronson, *Bronson's Travelers' Directory, from New York to New Orleans, Embracing All the Most Important Routes, with a Condensed Outline of the Country through Which They Pass* (La Grange, Ga.: American Star Book Store, 1845), p. 20; and J. G. Warriner to Edward A. Greene, 13 March 1842, Mobile Letters, SHC. The last citation contains the quotation.

64. Alexander Mackay, *The Western World; or, Travels in the United States in 1846–47*, 3 vols. (London: Richard Bentley, 1849), 3:281; *Mobile Advertiser*, 20 July, 15 August, 2 October 1850; *Rowan's Directory 1850–51*, p. 22; and Oldmixon, *Transatlantic Wanderings*, p. 153.

65. *Mobile Register*, 13 December 1852, 13 May 1859; *Acts of Alabama*, Session of 1851 – 52, pp. 256 – 58; and Boorstin, *The Americans*, pp. 136 – 37.

66. Amelia Matilda Murray, *Letters from the United States, Cuba, and Canada* (New York: G. P. Putnam, 1856), p. 309; Jane M. E. Turnbull and Marion Turnbull, *Photographs*, 2 vols. in 1 (London: J. C. Newly, 1859), 2 : 62; *DeBow's Review* 25 (1859): 112; Caldwell Delaney, *Remember Mobile*, 2d ed. (Mobile: Haunted Book Shop, 1969), p. 154; and *Mobile Register*, 3 February 1853, 5 January 1858.

67. *Mobile Advertiser*, 15 October 1853.

68. Mary Morgan Duggar, "The Theatre in Mobile in 1822 – 1860," (M.A. thesis, University of Alabama, 1941), pp. 203 – 4; *Alabama Planter*, 6 November 1854.

69. *Mobile Register*, 14 August 1840; and *Alabama Tribune* (Mobile), 27 September 1849.

70. James H. Dormon, *Theater in the Antebellum South, 1815 – 1861* (Chapel Hill: University of North Carolina Press, 1967), pp. 114 – 15, 117 – 19; Noah M. Ludlow, *Dramatic Life As I Found It: A Record of Personal Experience* (St. Louis: G. I. Jones, 1880), pp. 260 – 61, 332 – 35, 343 – 44; Frances Margaret Bailey, "A History of the Stage in Mobile, Alabama, from 1824 to 1850" (M.A. thesis, State University of Iowa, 1934), p. 25; and *Mobile Register*, 28 April 1834.

71. Dormon, *Theater in Antebellum South*, pp. 123 – 24, 188, 195; Ludlow, *Dramatic Life*, pp. 508, 511 – 12; *Mobile Register*, 21 November 1838; Subscription List for a New Theatre in Mobile, 2 March 1839, Ludlow-Fields-Maury Collection, Missouri Historical Society, St. Louis; Louis Fitzgerald Tasistro, *Random Shots and Southern Breezes, Containing Critical Remarks on the Southern States and Southern Institutions, with Semi-serious Observations on Men and Manners*, 2 vols. (New York: Harper & Brothers, 1842), 1 : 250 – 51; and Duggar, "Theatre in Mobile," pp. 233, 237 – 39.

CHAPTER 3

1. David Goldfield, *Urban Growth in the Age of Sectionalism: Virginia, 1847 – 1861* (Baton Rouge: Louisiana State University Press, 1977), p. 31; and Walter S. Glazer, "Participation and Power: Voluntary Associations and the Functional Organization of Cincinnati in 1840," *Historical Methods Newsletter* 5 (1972): 151 – 68. Some of these findings were previously published in Harriet E. Amos, "'Birds of Passage' in a Cotton Port: Northerners and Foreigners Among the Urban Leaders of Mobile, 1820 – 1860," in *Class, Conflict, and Consensus: Antebellum Southern Community Studies*, ed. Orville Vernon Burton and Robert C. McMath, Jr. (Westport, Conn.: Greenwood Press, 1982), pp. 232 – 62.

2. Contemporary newspapers available on microfilm in several repositories include the *Mobile Register*, published under slightly variant titles from 1821 to the present; the *Alabama Planter*, published from 1846 through 1854; and the *Mobile Advertiser*, published under slightly variant titles from 1833 to 1861. Scattered issues of several other Mobile newspapers are available on microfilm in the Amelia Gayle Gorgas Library, University of Alabama at Tuscaloosa, University, Alabama.

The main sources of information on government organizations include, in Mobile, the Minutes of the Aldermen and the Common Councilmen, virtually complete from 1820 through 1860 and available on microfilm in the Mobile Public Library, and Minutes of the Board of School Commissioners, virtually complete from 1836 through 1860 and available in the School Board Offices in Barton Academy.

Also helpful are city directories: *Mobile Directory Embracing Names of the Heads of Families and Persons in Business, Alphabetically Arranged for 1837* (Mobile: H. M. McGuire & T. C. Fay, 1837); *Mobile Directory or Strangers' Guide for 1838* (Mobile: R. R. Dade, 1839); R. P. Vail, *Mobile Directory or Strangers' Guide, for 1842* (Mobile: Dade & Thompson, 1842); Edwin T. Wood, *Mobile Directory, and Register for 1844* (Mobile: Dade & Thompson, 1844); *Rowan's Mobile Directory and Commercial Supplement for 1850–51*: (Mobile: Strickland & Benjamin, 1850); William R. Robertson, *The Comprehensive Mobile Guide and Directory, Referring to the Business Locations, for 1852* (Mobile: Carver & Ryland, 1852); *Mobile Directory and Commercial Supplements for 1855–6* (Mobile: Strickland, 1855); *Daughdrill & Walker's General Directory for the City and County of Mobile, for 1856* (Mobile: Farrow, Stokes & Dennett, 1856); *Directory for the City of Mobile, 1859* (Mobile: Farrow & Dennett, 1859); and *Directory for the City of Mobile for 1861* (Mobile: Farrow & Dennett, 1861).

Biographical information was gathered from the Original Returns of the United States Census for 1830 through 1860 (Mobile was not included in the 1820 census), Free Population and Slave Schedules, available on microfilm from the National Archives. Financial and biographical information was located in the Credit Reports of R. G. Dun & Co., housed in the Baker Library, Graduate School of Business Administration, Harvard University (BL). Alabama vols. 17 and 18 pertain to Mobile County from 1846 to 1883. Useful comments regarding these credit reports as historical sources are available in James H. Madison, "The Credit Reports of R. G. Dun & Co. as Historical Sources," *Historical Methods Newsletter* 8 (1975): 128–31; and J. W. Lozier, "Uses of Nineteenth Century Credit Reports: A Researcher's Review of the Dun and Bradstreet Collection, 1845–1890," typed, undated MS, 5 pp., BL.

Published biographical sources include W. Brewer, *Alabama* (Montgomery: Barrett & Brown, 1872); William Garrett, *Reminiscences of Public Men in Alabama for Thirty Years* (Atlanta: Plantation Publishing Company's Press, 1872); and Thomas McAdory Owen, *History of Alabama and Dictionary of Alabama Biography*, 4 vols. (Chicago: S. J. Clarke Publishing Co., 1921).

3. Invaluable assistance in the design and execution of the computer program for analyzing data from the 1860 census was provided by Henry F. Inman of the University of Alabama in Birmingham.

4. On the associational activity of other urban leaders, see Goldfield, *Urban Growth*, pp. 32–33; and Glazer, "Participation and Power," pp. 151–68.

5. Bernard Reynolds, *Sketches of Mobile, from 1814 to the Present Time* (Mobile: B. H. Richardson, 1868), pp. 12–13; Brewer, *Alabama*, p. 399; *Eighth Census*, Free Population Schedule, Alabama, microcopy 653, roll 17, p. 343; Aldermen's Minutes, 2 June 1824, 7 December 1824, 9 July 1825, MPL; *Mobile Register*, 9 August 1825,

30 December 1835, 10 November 1836, 2 June 1837, 29 January 1838, 28 February 1838, 10 January 1839, 6 January 1840, 14 February 1840, 5 January 1841, 1 April 1841, 16 and 21 December 1841, 15 March 1842, 3 and 5 January 1843, 14 March 1843, 21 March 1858; *Alabama Planter*, 7 August 1852; and School Board Minutes, 6 September 1852, 10 August 1859, BA.

6. R. G. Dun & Co. Credit Reports, Alabama, 17:100, BL; *Eighth Census*, Free Population Schedule, Alabama, microcopy 653, roll 17, p. 384; *Mobile Register*, 2 November 1836, 31 January 1850, 13 March 1851, 13 May 1852, 11 April 1853, 13 September 1855, 16 March 1856, 22 April 1856, 27 April 1857, 15 January 1858, 23 February 1859, 17 April 1860; William H. Brantley, *Banking in Alabama*, 2 vols. (Birmingham: Oxmoor Press, 1961–67), 2:332; *Mobile Weekly Advertiser*, 26 August 1854; School Board Minutes, 4 March 1845, BA; and *Mobile Advertiser*, 21 July 1855.

7. R. G. Dun & Co. Credit Reports, Alabama, 18:390, BL; *Eighth Census*, Free Population Schedule, Alabama, microcopy 653, roll 17, p. 370; *Mobile Register*, 4 and 23 January 1832, 1 January 1833, 16 May 1833, 21 January 1834, 29 June 1835, 12 February 1836, 10 November 1836, 2 June 1837, 2 January 1838, 28 February 1838, 8 January 1839, 6 January 1840, 17 February 1840, 5 and 6 January 1841, 3 and 4 January 1842, 3 January 1843, 14 March 1843, 8 November 1843, 3 January 1844, 18 March 1844, 21 March 1845, 7 January 1846, 6 January 1847, 10 and 11 January 1848, 10 December 1849, 31 January 1850, 13 March 1851, 13 May 1852, 4 January 1853, 12 May 1853, 13 September 1855, 16 March 1856, 22 April 1856, 27 April 1857, 15 January 1858, 27 February 1858, 23 and 25 February 1859, 17 April 1860; *Alabama Planter*, 8 January 1849, 13 January 1851, 10 February 1851, 21 February 1852, 9 January 1854, 13 March 1854; *Mobile Weekly Advertiser*, 26 August 1854; Brantley, *Banking in Alabama*, 2:332, 1:213; Aldermen's Minutes, 4 December 1851; and School Board Minutes, 28 February 1846, BA.

8. Joyce Maynard Ghent and Frederic Cople Jaher, "The Chicago Business Elite, 1830–1930: A Collective Biography," *Business History Review* 50 (1976): 301; and Frederic Cople Jaher, *The Urban Establishment: Upper Strata in Boston, New York, Charleston, Chicago, and Los Angeles* (Urbana: University of Illinois Press, 1982), p. 456.

9. William W. Chenault and Robert C. Reinders, "The Northern-Born Community of New Orleans in the 1850s," *Journal of American History* 51 (1964): 232–47; William O. Lynch, "Westward Flow of Southern Colonists before 1861," *Journal of Southern History* 9 (1943): 316–17; Goldfield, *Urban Growth*, pp. 41–42, 53; Michael B. Chesson, *Richmond after the War, 1865–1900* (Richmond: Virginia State Library, 1981), p. 8; and Jaher, *Urban Establishment*, p. 338.

10. Michael H. Frisch, *Town into City: Springfield, Massachusetts, and the Meaning of Community, 1840–1880* (Cambridge, Mass.: Harvard University Press, 1972), pp. 33–34.

11. Erwin Craighead, *Mobile: Fact and Tradition, Noteworthy People and Events* (Mobile: Powers Printing Co., 1930), p. 355; and *Mobile Register*, 4 May 1829. The latter citation contains the quotation.

12. R. G. Dun & Co. Credit Reports, Alabama, 17:243, BL.

13. Ibid., 17:59; and Owen, *History of Alabama*, 3:328, 331, 336, 339.

14. The mayor was the only paid official of those included among the urban leaders. His annual salary grew from $1,000 in 1826 to $4,000 in 1860. See Aldermen's Minutes, 1826, p. 197; and 1858, p. 117, MPL.

15. Karl Bernhard, Duke of Saxe-Weimar-Eisenach, *Travels through North America during the Years 1825 and 1826*, 2 vols. (Philadelphia: Carey, Lea & Carey, 1828), 2:39; and Jaher, *Urban Establishment*, p. 318. Regarding kinship network of Boston's upper class, see Jaher, *Urban Establishment*, pp. 73–75.

16. R. G. Dun & Co. Credit Reports, Alabama, 17:21, 10, 125, 230, 242, BL. The count excludes six other possible sets of men with the same surname and place of birth who could not be positively identified as brothers.

17. Historical Activities Committee, *Alabama Portraits Prior to 1870* (Mobile: National Society of the Colonial Dames of America in the State of Alabama, 1969), p. 146; *Mobile Register*, 10 January 1822, 7 August 1823, 7 January 1824, 6 June 1860, 11 July 1884; *Mobile Argus*, 6 January 1823; and Brantley, *Banking in Alabama*, 1:55, 78–79, 127.

18. R. G. Dun & Co. Credit Reports, Alabama, 17:74, BL.

19. Goldfield, *Urban Growth*, pp. 34–36, 50.

20. Joseph Holt Ingraham, ed., *The Sunny South; or, The Southerner at Home, Embracing Five Years' Experience of a Northern Governess in the Land of the Sugar and the Cotton* (Philadelphia: G. G. Evans, 1860), pp. 506–7.

21. See Michael B. Katz, "Occupational Classification in History," *Journal of Interdisciplinary History* 3 (1972): 63–88; and the classification system used for this study, adapted from Katz and listed in the appendix.

22. Edward Pessen, *Jacksonian America: Society, Personality, and Politics*, rev. ed. (Homewood, Ill.: Dorsey Press, 1978), p. 81; and Jaher, *Urban Establishment*, pp. 713, 202, 68, 71.

23. The value of property in the county was the sum of real estate, $16,863,030, and personal property, $24,667,845, listed in U.S. Bureau of the Census, *Statistics of the United States including Mortality, Property, etc. in 1860* (Washington: Government Printing Office, 1866), p. 296. Total value of property held in the city in 1860 was $29,163,222. See City Property Tax Books, 1860, CMA. The leaders' total wealth was the sum of their real estate, $3,301,200, and personal property, $4,395,300. A detailed study of wealth holdings for Mobile in the 1850s may be found in Alan Smith Thompson, "Mobile, Alabama, 1850–1861: Economic, Political, Physical, and Population Characteristics" (Ph.D. diss., University of Alabama, 1979), pp. 282–344.

24. Solomon Mordecai to Ellen Mordecai, 7 August 1836, Mordecai Family Papers, SHC; and *Mobile Register*, 30 September 1835, 7 September 1859. Regarding real-estate speculation by the elite of Chicago during its growth boom in the 1830s, see Jaher, *Urban Establishment*, p. 457.

25. Regarding the prevalence of small-sized slaveholdings in New Orleans during the 1850s, see Robert C. Reinders, "Slavery in New Orleans in the Decade before the Civil War," in *Plantation, Town, and Country: Essays on the Local History of American Slave Society*, ed. Elinor Miller and Eugene D. Genovese (Urbana: University of Illinois Press, 1974), p. 369.

26. *Eighth Census*, Free Population Schedule, Alabama, microcopy 653, roll 17, pp. 756, 680, 660, and Slave Schedule, roll 33, pp. 13, 73–74, 32–34, 29–30.

27. Goldfield, *Urban Growth*, pp. 38–39.

28. Joseph Karl Menn, "The Large Slaveholders of the Deep South, 1860" (Ph.D. diss., University of Texas, 1964), pp. 437–38. Birthplaces were listed in the 1860 census for fourteen of the eighteen large slaveowners.

29. Fletcher M. Green, *The Role of the Yankee in the Old South* (Athens: University of Georgia Press, 1972), pp. 4–5.

30. Daniel R. Hundley, *Social Relations in Our Southern States*, ed. William J. Cooper, Jr. (Baton Rouge: Louisiana State University Press, 1979), pp. 104–5; and Frederick Law Olmsted, *A Journey in the Seaboard Slave States, with Remarks on Their Economy* (New York: Dix & Edwards, 1856), p. 567. See also Carl N. Degler, *The Other South: Southern Dissenters in the Nineteenth Century* (New York: Harper & Row, 1974), pp. 88–89.

31. *Mobile Register*, 17 August 1856; *Mobile Advertiser*, 17 August 1856, 28 September 1856; and Kate Upson Clark, "The Affair of Strickland and Company," Kate Upson Clark Papers, Sophia Smith Collection (Women's Archive), Smith College, Northampton, Mass. See also Caldwell Delaney, "The Banishment of Strickland," in *A Mobile Sextet: Papers Read before the Alabama Historical Association 1952–1971* (Mobile: Haunted Book Shop, 1981), pp. 151–79.

32. Don Harrison Doyle, "The Social Functions of Voluntary Associations in a Nineteenth-Century Town," *Social Science History* 1 (1977): 338, 342–43, 345.

33. *Mobile Register*, 10 April 1848; and Caldwell Delaney, *The Phoenix Volunteer Fire Company of Mobile, 1838–1888* (Mobile: Mission Press, 1967), pp. 1, 5.

34. Caldwell Delaney, ed., *Craighead's Mobile, Being the Fugitive Writings of Erwin S. Craighead and Frank Craighead* (Mobile: Haunted Book Shop, 1968), pp. 62–63; *Mobile Register*, 1 January 1829, 3 April 1858; Peter Joseph Hamilton, *Mobile of the Five Flags: The Story of the River Basin and Coast about Mobile from the Earliest Times to the Present* (Mobile: Gill Printing Co., 1913); and *Deep South Genealogical Quarterly* 1 (1963): 35–42, 9 (1972): 27–35, 10 (1973): 172.

35. Leonard P. Curry, "Urbanization and Urbanism in the Old South: A Comparative View," *Journal of Southern History* 40 (1974): 57; and Stuart Blumin, *The Urban Threshold: Growth and Change in a Nineteenth-Century American Community* (Chicago: University of Chicago Press, 1976), p. 183.

36. *Mobile Register*, 20 January 1856. Charities are discussed in chapter 7.

37. Wayne Dean, *Mardi Gras: Mobile's Illogical Whoop-De-Doo, 1704–1970* (Chicago: Adams Printing Co., 1971), pp. 9–10, 13–15.

38. Solomon Mordecai to Ellen Mordecai, 2 January 1824, Mordecai Family Papers, SHC; Jones Fuller to Anna Thomas, 1 January 1846, Mrs. Jones Fuller to Mrs. Ann Thomas, 8 January 1852, Fuller-Thomas Papers, Fuller Division, Duke; and Clitherall Books, 3:42–43, SHC.

39. Dean, *Mardi Gras*, p. 27.

40. Ibid., pp. 27, 29, 220, 222; *Mobile Register*, 31 December 1852, 4 January 1847; *Alabama Planter*, 4 January 1847; and *Mobile Advertiser*, 3 January 1851.

41. Erwin Craighead, *From Mobile's Past: Sketches of Memorable People and Events* (Mobile: Powers Printing Co., 1925), p. 141; Corine Chadwick Stephens, "Madame Octavia Walton Le Vert" (M.A. thesis, University of Georgia, 1940), p. 81; Thomas Cooper De Leon, *Belles, Beaux, and Brains of the 60's* (New York: G. W. Dillingham, Co., 1907), p. 183; Louis Fitzgerald Tasistro, *Random Shots and Southern Breezes, Containing Critical Remarks on the Southern States and Southern Institutions, with Semi-serious Observations on Men and Manners*, 2 vols. (New York: Harper & Brothers, 1842), 1:232; Thomas Low Nichols, *Forty Years of American Life*, 2 vols. (London: J. Maxwell, 1864), 1:225; Caldwell Delaney, *Remember Mobile*, 2d ed. (Mobile: Haunted Book Shop, 1969), pp. 189−90; Frederika Bremer, *The Homes of the New World: Impressions of America*, trans. Mary Howitt, 2 vols. (New York: Harper & Brothers, 1853), 2:215; and Virginia Tatnall Peacock, *Famous American Belles of the Nineteenth Century* (Philadelphia: J. B. Lippincott 1901), pp. 110−11.

42. De Leon, *Belles*, pp. 186−87, 181−82.

43. William E. Dodd, *The Cotton Kingdom: A Chronicle of the Old South* (New Haven, Conn.: Yale University Press, 1921), p. 99; Edward Pessen, *Riches, Class, and Power before the Civil War* (Lexington, Mass.: D. C. Heath, 1973), p. 244; and David R. Goldfield and Blaine A. Brownell, *Urban America: From Downtown to No Town* (Boston: Houghton Mifflin, 1979), pp. 160−61.

44. The major sources of data about the leaders' religious affiliations were the following, all in Mobile: Lois D. Mitchell, comp., Parish Records of Christ Episcopal Church, vol. 1 (1832−39), MPL; Lucille Mallon and Corrine Lee, comps., Parish Records of Christ Episcopal Church, vols. 2 (1846−56) and 3 (1856−84), MPL; Records, St. Paul's Episcopal Church; Parish Register, Trinity Episcopal Church; Official Membership and Church Records of St. Francis Street Methodist Church, 1840−1912, St. Francis Street Methodist Church; Minutes of Church Meetings of First Baptist Church, vols. 1 (1835−48) and 2 (1845−75), First Baptist Church; Government Street Presbyterian Church Register, Government Street Presbyterian Church; Session Book of the Second Presbyterian Church, vols. 1 (1842−55) and 2 (1855−68), and Records of Third Presbyterian Church, 1853−68, Central Presbyterian Church.

45. Alabama State Census, 1855, Mobile County, pp. 133−34, ASDAH.

46. Oscar Hugh Lipscomb, "The Administration of Michael Portier, Vicar Apostolic of Alabama and the Floridas, 1825−1829, and First Bishop of Mobile, 1829−1859" (Ph.D. diss., Catholic University of America, 1963), pp. 295−96, 307−8.

47. Solomon I. Jones and Israel I. Jones, English-born auctioneers and urban leaders, operated the "Best Jewhouse in Mobile" and held "a good position in society," according to R. G. Dun & Co. Credit Reports, Alabama, 17:121, BL. See also Bertram Wallace Korn, *The Jews of Mobile, Alabama, 1763−1841* (Cincinnati: Hebrew Union College Press, 1970).

48. Pessen, *Jacksonian America*, p. 96; and Thompson, "Mobile, Alabama, 1850−1861," pp. 182−247.

49. Hundley, *Social Relations*, pp. 156−57.

50. See chapter 5 regarding the bankruptcy and responses to it.

51. Names and partisan affiliations came from *Alabama Planter*, 11 December 1848; *Mobile Advertiser*, 29 March 1848, 4 December 1849, 2 July, 4 and 17 December 1850, 8 December 1852; *Mobile Register*, 17 January 1848, 1 and 4 December 1849, 4 April, 21 November, 3, 4 and 16 December 1850, 26 May, 16 and 28 July 1851, 7 May, 25 October, 1 and 9 December 1852, 7 and 31 May, 8 July 1853; Aldermen's Minutes, 4 December 1851, MPL; and Thompson, "Mobile, Alabama," pp. 130, 133, 144, 147. Alan Thompson graciously shared some information about political identification with the author. City Property Tax Books are located in CMA.

52. See Thomas B. Alexander et al., "Who Were the Alabama Whigs?" *Alabama Review* 16 (1963): 14. Median value of the real estate holdings of Mobile's political leaders of 1850 closely resembles that for state legislators of 1849, $4,000. See J. Mills Thornton III, *Politics and Power in a Slave Society: Alabama, 1800−1860* (Baton Rouge: Louisiana State University Press, 1978), p. 297.

53. Alexander et al. find slaveholdings of a sample of Whigs and Democrats quite similar in "Who Were the Alabama Whigs?" p. 15. For legislators of 1849, Thornton (*Politics and Power*, p. 297) finds Whigs' median slaveholding (16) almost double that of Democrats (8.5).

54. Alexander et al. find no substantial age differences between party leaders in their sample in "Who Were the Alabama Whigs?" p. 13.

55. Grady McWhiney, "Were the Whigs a Class Party in Alabama?" *Journal of Southern History* 23 (1957): 518−19. For legislators in 1849, Thornton (*Politics and Power*, p. 299) finds 59 percent farmers and 26 percent lawyers.

56. McWhiney, "Were Whigs a Class Party?" pp. 516−17.

57. For state politicians, see McWhiney, "Were Whigs a Class Party?" p. 521.

58. Jaher, *Urban Establishment*, p. 471.

59. *Mobile Advertiser*, 27 November 1855.

60. Jaher, *Urban Establishment*, pp. 455−56, 73, 204−5.

61. A. B. Meek to William Gilmore Simms, 23 November 1851, A. B. Meek Papers, ASDAH; and *Rowan's Directory 1850−51*, p. 22.

62. Craighead, *From Mobile's Past*, pp. 75−76; and *Mobile Register*, 30 January 1844, 15 November 1845, 28 March 1846, 22 January 1848, 5 January 1850, 20 January 1853, 24 March 1853, 21 January 1858, 23 February 1858. Admissions into the Franklin Society appear in *Deep South Genealogical Quarterly* 11 (1974): 40−44, 64.

63. *Mobile Advertiser*, 9 March 1855.

64. William H. Willis, "A Southern Traveler's Diary, 1840," *Publications of the Southern History Association* 8 (1904): 136−37.

CHAPTER 4

1. John A. Eisterhold, "Mobile: Lumber Center of the Gulf Coast," *Alabama Review* 26 (1973): 90−91; Frederick Law Olmsted, *A Journey in the Seaboard Slave States, with Remarks on Their Economy* (New York: Dix & Edwards, 1856), p. 566; and *Mobile Register*, 14 October 1835. The last citation contains the quotation.

2. Carville V. Earle, "Interpreting the Size of Cities and City Systems: Agricultural Economy and Urban Labor in the Chicago and Mobile Urban Systems during the 1850s" (Paper read to the Social Science History Association, November 1979), p. 9; J. W. Hengiston [Siras Redding], "Mobile, Pensacola, and the Floridas: Cotton Barque to Cape Cod, along the Gulf Stream," *New Monthly Magazine* 98 (1853): 369; John W. Oldmixon, *Transatlantic Wanderings; or, A Last Look at the United States* (London: George Routledge, 1855), p. 155; and *Rowan's Mobile Directory and Commercial Supplement for 1850−51* (Mobile: Strickland & Benjamin, 1850), pp. 16−17.

3. Solomon Mordecai to Ellen Mordecai, 3 March 1823, Mordecai Family Papers, SHC; and Gustavus Horton to Eliza Horton, 12 August 1838, Eliza Horton to Gustavus Horton, Jr., 10 July, 26 July 1852, Horton Family Papers, in the possession of Edith Richards, Mobile. The quotation comes from the letter of 10 July 1852.

4. Charles Lyell, *A Second Visit to the United States of America*, 2 vols. (New York: Harper & Brothers, 1849), 2:62.

5. Solomon Mordecai to Ellen Mordecai, 3 March 1823, Mordecai Family Papers, SHC; and Olmsted, *Journey*, p. 567.

6. *Mobile Advertiser*, 29 November 1851.

7. Stuart Blumin, *The Urban Threshold: Growth and Change in a Nineteenth-Century American Community* (Chicago: University of Chicago Press, 1976), p. 69.

8. *Mobile Register*, 16 February 1839.

9. Ibid.

10. Ibid., 6 November 1840.

11. *Mobile Argus*, 5−19 December 1822; and *Mobile Register*, 13 December 1837, 9 July 1838.

12. *Alabama Planter*, 6 March 1854.

13. *Mobile Advertiser*, 31 October 1854.

14. George A. Tracy, *History of the Typographical Union* (Indianapolis: International Typographical Union, 1913), pp. 151, 165, 83−86. According to Tracy (pp. 169, 172, 175, 184), a representative of the Mobile union served on the national executive committee of the union in the late 1850s.

15. *Alabama Planter*, 13 February 1854; and Robert C. Reinders, "Slavery in New Orleans in the Decade before the Civil War," in *Plantation, Town, and Country: Essays on the Local History of American Slave Society*, ed. Elinor Miller and Eugene D. Genovese (Urbana: University of Illinois Press, 1974), p. 370.

16. Frederic Bancroft, *Slave-Trading in the Old South* (Baltimore: J. H. Furst, 1931), p. 298; Charles S. Davis, *The Cotton Kingdom in Alabama* (Montgomery: Alabama State Department of Archives and History, 1939), p. 76; James Benson Sellers, *Slavery in Alabama* (University: University of Alabama Press, 1950), pp. 160−61, 153−54; Peter Joseph Hamilton, *Mobile of the Five Flags* (Mobile: Gill Printing Co., 1913), p. 284; and Richard C. Wade, *Slavery in the Cities: The South, 1820−1860* (New York: Oxford University Press, 1964), p. 205.

17. Kenneth M. Stampp, *The Peculiar Institution: Slavery in the Antebellum South* (New York: Vintage Books, 1956), pp. 253−54; *Niles' Register* 32 (1827): 100; Lewy Dorman, "The Free Negro in Alabama from 1819 to 1861" (M.A. thesis, University of Alabama, 1916), p. 10; and Sellers, *Slavery in Alabama*, p. 161.

18. Laura A. White, "The South in the 1850's As Seen by the British Consuls," *Journal of Southern History* 1 (1933): 38.

19. Emma Langdon Roche, *Historic Sketches of the South* (New York: Knickerbocker Press, 1914), pp. 71–72, 94–97; Harvey Wish, "The Revival of the African Slave Trade in the United States, 1856–1860," *Mississippi Valley Historical Review* 27 (1941): 584–85; and Erwin Craighead, *Mobile: Fact and Tradition, Noteworthy People and Events* (Mobile: Powers Printing Co., 1930), p. 357.

20. Alfred Witherspoon to Tariffa Witherspoon, 1 February 1859, Harrison Henry Cocke Papers, SHC.

21. J. I. Johnson to William A. J. Finney, 30 October 1859, William A. J. Finney Papers, Duke.

22. *Mobile Register*, 8 November 1859; and Philip Thomas to William A. J. Finney, William A. J. Finney Papers, Duke.

23. Slave ownership for 1830, 1840, and 1860 was computed by the author from *Fifth Census*, Slave Schedule, Alabama, microcopy 19, roll 33, pp. 361–71; *Sixth Census*, Slave Schedule, Alabama, microcopy 432, roll 22, pp. 1–81; and *Eighth Census*, Slave Schedule, Alabama, microcopy 653, roll 33, pp. 25–74. For this study the number of individual slaveholders was divided by the total free population to determine the extent of slave ownership. Calculations for 1850 are those of Alan Smith Thompson, "Mobile, Alabama, 1850–1861: Economic, Political, Physical, and Population Characteristics" (Ph.D. diss., University of Alabama, 1979), p. 306. His 8.6 percent is lower than Richard Wade's 11 percent in his *Slavery in the Cities*, p. 20.

24. *Eighth Census*, Slave Schedule, Alabama, microcopy 653, roll 33, pp. 25–74.

25. Thompson, "Mobile, Alabama," p. 306.

26. Solomon Mordecai to Ellen Mordecai, 21 March 1826, 6 January 1828, 16 November 1828, 4 February 1830, Mordecai Family Papers, SHC. The quotations come from the first and last citations.

27. Garrit S. Mott to S. C. Mott, 24 December 1835, Mott Family Papers, NYHS; A. M. Blair to Edwin Blair, 30 November 1843, Blair Letter, University of Alabama Library, University, Alabama; Receipt Book, 15 and 27 June 1853, John D. Dunn Papers, Duke; and Alfred Witherspoon to Tariffa Witherspoon, 1 February 1859, Harrison Henry Cocke Papers, SHC.

28. Thompson, "Mobile, Alabama," p. 318.

29. Colin J. McRae to Mrs. C. M. McRae, 25 September 1858, McRae Family Papers, Old Monterey, Mobile; Sellers, *Slavery in Alabama*, p. 210; *Mobile Register*, 21 May 1833, 9 January 1844, 3 June 1845; and George H. Fry to Rebecca Robinson, 8 November 1848, Fry-Robinson Collection, HMPSA. The quotation comes from the first citation.

30. Colin J. McRae to Mrs. C. M. McRae, 25 September 1858, McRae Family Papers, Old Monterey, Mobile; and Solomon Mordecai to Ellen Mordecai, 22 July 1848, Mordecai Family Papers, SHC.

31. *Mobile Advertiser*, 5 November 1851, 15 December 1854; Aldermen's Minutes, 25 March 1852, 17 January, 9 October, 27 November 1856, MPL; *Mobile Register*, 18 April 1860; and Wade, *Slavery in the Cities*, pp. 65–66, 69, 188.

32. *Alabama Planter*, 3 March 1851; and Robert Russell, *North America: Its Agriculture and Climate* (Edinburgh: Adams & Charles Black, 1857), p. 281.

33. Thompson, "Mobile, Alabama," p. 255.

34. Dorman, "Free Negro," p. 23; Sellers, *Slavery in Alabama*, pp. 383–85; and Ira Berlin, *Slaves without Masters: The Free Negro in the Antebellum South* (New York: Pantheon Books, 1974), pp. 131–32.

35. Marilyn Mannhard, "The Free People of Color in Antebellum Mobile County, Alabama" (M.A. thesis, University of South Alabama, 1982), pp. 5–6; Diane Lee Shelley, "The Effects of Increasing Racism on the Creole Colored in Three Gulf Coast Cities between 1803 and 1860" (M.A. thesis, University of West Florida, 1971), p. 22; Berlin, *Slaves without Masters*, pp. 278, 108–9; Melvin Lee Ross, Jr., "Blacks, Mulattoes, and Creoles in Mobile during the European and American Periods" (M.A. thesis, Purdue University, 1971), pp. 45–46; Dorman, "Free Negro," p. 24; and Sellers, *Slavery in Alabama*, pp. 385–86.

36. Ross, "Blacks, Mulattoes, and Creoles," pp. 77–78.

37. *Alabama Planter*, 28 August 1848. Chastang's emancipation receives mention in Ulrich Bonnell Phillips, *American Negro Slavery: A Survey of the Supply, Employment, and Control of Negro Labor as Determined by the Plantation Regime* (New York: D. Appleton, 1918), p. 428; and John Hope Franklin, *From Slavery to Freedom: A History of Negro Americans*, 3d ed. (New York: Alfred A. Knopf, 1967), p. 215.

38. Dorman, "Free Negro," p. 11; Sellers, *Slavery in Alabama*, pp. 133, 237; *Mobile Register*, 25 December 1844; and Henry G. Connor, *John Archibald Campbell, Associate Justice of the United States Supreme Court 1853–1861* (Boston: Houghton Mifflin, 1920), p. 71.

39. T. C. Fay, *Mobile Directory or Strangers' Guide for 1839* (Mobile: R. R. Dade, 1839), pp. 45–100. See Ross, "Blacks, Mulattoes, and Creoles," pp. 48–49; and Mannhard, "Free People of Color," p. 24.

40. Thompson, "Mobile, Alabama," pp. 275–76; Benjamin Joseph Klebaner, "Public Poor Relief in Charleston, 1800–1860," *South Carolina Historical and Genealogical Magazine* 45 (1954): 213; Clement Eaton, *Growth of Southern Civilization, 1790–1860* (New York: Harper & Brothers, 1961), p. 147; Blake McKelvey, *American Urbanization: A Comparative History* (Glenview, Ill.: Scott, Foresman, 1973), p. 34; Eugene D. Genovese, *Roll, Jordan, Roll: The World the Slaves Made* (New York: Pantheon Books, 1974), p. 405; Wade, *Slavery in the Cities*, pp. 274–75; and Ira Berlin and Herbert G. Gutman, "Natives and Immigrants, Free Men and Slaves: Urban Workingmen in the Antebellum American South," *American Historical Review* 88 (1983):1175–1200. Breakdown on the nativity of the labor force is Thompson's.

41. John S. C. Abbott, *South and North; or, Impressions Received during a Trip to Cuba and the South* (New York: Abbey & Abbott, 1860), pp. 112–13.

42. Alice Kessler-Harris, *Out to Work: A History of Wage-Earning Women in the United States* (New York: Oxford University Press, 1982), pp. 70–72, 46–47, 50.

43. Fay, *Mobile Directory or Strangers' Guide for 1839*, pp. 44–102; William R. Robertson, *The Comprehensive Mobile Guide and Directory* (Mobile: Carver & Ryland, 1852), pp. 12–34; and *Mobile Directory and Commercial Supplement, for 1855–56* (Mobile: Strickland, 1855), pp. 39–114.

44. *Seventh Census*, Manufactures, Alabama, pp. 339–43, ASDAH.

45. *Seventh Census*, Free Population Schedule, Alabama, microcopy 432, roll 11, pp. 310, 367, 378, 388.

46. Thompson, "Mobile, Alabama," pp. 355–56.

47. Ibid., pp. 355–57; Eaton, *Growth of Southern Civilization*, p. 147; Hengiston, "Mobile, Pensacola, and the Floridas," p. 369; Oldmixon, *Transatlantic Wanderings*, p. 155; and *Eighth Census*, Free Population Schedule, Alabama, microcopy 653, roll 17, pp. 318–20.

48. *Eighth Census*, Free Population Schedule, Alabama, microcopy 653, roll 17, pp. 750–52. See Kessler-Harris, *Out to Work*, p. 58. Based on Herbert Gutman's unpublished research, Kessler-Harris notes that women in Nashville drifted in and out of prostitution as their economic conditions changed. This pattern may have occurred in Mobile, but the port city was expected to have a regular supply of prostitutes.

49. Thompson, "Mobile, Alabama," p. 351. In 1850 the census reported employment for 174 persons under eighteen years of age.

50. Protestant Orphan Asylum Society Minutes, 2 March, 2 May, 7 December 1840, 6 and 14 May 1844, HMPSA; and *Acts of Alabama*, Session of 1857–58, p. 144.

51. *Mobile Advertiser*, 22 December 1855; and *Eighth Census*, Free Population Schedule, Alabama, microcopy 653, roll 17, pp. 390–93.

52. Earle, "Interpreting the Size of Cities," pp. 20–21, 24–25, 28.

53. U.S. Bureau of the Census, *Seventh Census of the United States, 1850: Mortality* (Washington: A.O.P. Nicholson, 1855), 2:38–39; and U.S. Bureau of the Census, *Eighth Census of the United States, 1860: Population* (Washington: Government Printing Office, 1866), 1:xxxi.

54. *Mobile Register*, 20 November 1850.

55. Eisterhold, "Mobile: Lumber Center," pp. 90–92; and Stampp, *Peculiar Institution*, p. 427.

56. *Alabama Planter*, 20 June 1853.

57. Mannhard, "Free People of Color," pp. 24–25.

58. Caroline Plunkett to Ellen Mordecai, 2 August 1854, Mordecai Family Papers, SHC.

59. Note that table 4-6 samples the free white female heads of household, including every third one.

60. *Mobile Register*, 8 January 1859. See Ulrich Bonnell Phillips, *Life and Labor in the Old South* (Boston: Little, Brown, 1929), p. 172.

61. Thompson, "Mobile, Alabama," pp. 182–83, 187.

62. Ibid., pp. 207, 210.

63. Ibid., pp. 192, 198, 211–12.

64. Ibid., p. 228.

65. Ross, "Blacks, Mulattoes, and Creoles," p. 61; Thompson, "Mobile, Alabama," p. 220; and Mannhard, "Free People of Color," pp. 16–19.

66. Aldermen's Minutes, 2 December 1829, 21 April 1830, MPL. Some evidence indicates that the company was formed in two stages, temporarily in 1819 and permanently in 1830. The Creole Fire Company originally served as an adjunct to Nep-

tune Company Number 1, which was founded in 1819. Calling the Creole Company the "ancestor" of the fire department, the *Mobile Register* of April 28, 1853 listed the company's organizational date as 1819. However, neither the Neptune nor Creole companies survived into the 1820s. Contemporary newspapers count anniversaries of the Creole Fire Company from 1830, which should be accepted as its founding date. Neptune Fire Company reformed shortly afterward, receiving the number 2.

67. Creole Fire Company Number 1 Constitution Book, Museum of the City of Mobile.

68. Creole Fire Company Number 1 Constitution Book, 3 November 1851, Museum of the City of Mobile; Berlin, *Slaves without Masters*, p. 388; and Mannhard, "Free People of Color," p. 36. Shelley implies ("Effects of Increasing Racism," p. 70) that the resolution requiring dismissal from the fire company of members caught associating with slaves passed, but this was not the case.

69. *Alabama Tribune*, 28 April 1849; *Alabama Planter*, 6 May 1850; and *Mobile Register*, 8 December 1857.

70. *Alabama Tribune*, 24 August 1849.

71. Creole Fire Company Number 1 Constitution Book, 17 May 1852, Museum of the City of Mobile.

72. *Alabama Planter*, 1 May 1848; *Mobile Advertiser*, 25 April 1852; *Mobile Register*, 28 April 1853, 30 April 1856; and Creole Fire Company Number 1 Constitution Book, 4 September 1848, 3 May 1852, 4 September 1850, 7 February 1853, Museum of the City of Mobile.

73. Roster in *Deep South Genealogical Quarterly* 9 (1972): 27–35; and *Mobile Register*, 13 April 1860.

74. Mannhard, "Free People of Color," pp. 36–37; *Mobile Argus*, 20 March 1823; Caldwell Delaney, ed., *Craighead's Mobile, Being the Fugitive Writings of Erwin S. Craighead and Frank Craighead* (Mobile: Haunted Book Shop, 1968), pp. 62–63; *Mobile Register*, 12 January 1829; Hamilton, *Mobile of Five Flags*, p. 276; and *Deep South Genealogical Quarterly* 10 (1973): 172.

75. *Mobile Register*, 1 December 1857, 2 and 19 June 1858.

76. Ibid., 2 May 1856, 2 May 1857, 2 and 5 May 1858, 29 April 1859.

77. Ibid., 26 and 30 March 1858.

78. Ibid., 22 September, 14 October, 12 November 1859.

79. R. P. Vail, *Mobile Directory, or Strangers' Guide, for 1842* (Mobile: Dade & Thompson, 1842), p. 69; *Mobile Argus*, 20 March 1823; *Mobile Register*, 19 March 1824, 19 March 1833, 19 March 1834, 18 March 1836, 16 November 1837, 20 March 1838, 13 February 1839, 11 May 1839, 18 March 1842; and *Mobile Tribune*, 16 March 1851, cited in Minnie Clare Boyd, *Alabama in the Fifties: A Social Study* (New York: Columbia University Press, 1931), p. 221. The quotation comes from the first citation.

80. Thomas Low Nichols, *Forty Years of American Life*, 2 vols. (London: Maxwell, 1864), 1:224. For more information on local churches and their social roles, see Harriet E. Amos, "Social Life in an Antebellum Cotton Port: Mobile, Alabama, 1820–1860" (Ph.D. diss., Emory University, 1976), pp. 223–59.

81. Francis B. Clark to W. F. Clark, 1 January 1844 (typewritten copy), Personal files of Melton McLaurin, University of North Carolina-Wilmington; Oscar Hugh

Lipscomb, "The Administration of Michael Portier, Vicar Apostolic of Alabama and the Floridas, 1825–1829, and First Bishop of Mobile, 1829–1859" (Ph.D. diss., Catholic University of America, 1963), pp. 294–96, 174–75, 178–79, 182, 185–87.

82. Walter Claiborne Whitaker, *History of the Protestant Episcopal Church in Alabama, 1763–1891* (Birmingham: Roberts, 1898), pp. 12–13, 18–19, 64, 136–37; and J. A. Massey, D.D., Sermon on his thirtieth anniversary as rector of Trinity Parish, 31 March 1879, in Parish Record, Trinity Episcopal Church, Mobile.

83. Massey, Sermon; Hamilton, *Mobile of Five Flags*, p. 251; *Mobile Register*, 20 July 1856; and Lucy Green Nelson, ed., *St. John's Church, Mobile: A History Compiled from the Minutes of the Vestries and the Church Registers* (Mobile: n.p., 1963), pp. 11–12, 15–16, 19.

84. George Lewis, *Impressions of America and American Churches, from the Journal of the Reverend G. Lewis* (Edinburgh: W. P. Kennedy, 1845), p. 171.

85. Anson West, *A History of Methodism in Alabama* (Nashville: Privately printed, 1893), pp. 27–29, 249–53, 257, 264, 258–60, 262–63, 578, 580; A. C. Sherman, "The Historic Memories of the St. Francis Street Methodist Church, Mobile, Alabama, Written to Commemorate Its 120th Anniversary, 1840–1960," pp. 13–17, St. Francis Street Methodist Church, Mobile; and Mobile Writers' Workshop, *Historic Churches of Mobile*, 2d ed. (Mobile: Privately printed, 1971), p. 31.

86. Mobile Writers' Workshop, *Historic Churches*, p. 16; *Mobile Register*, 24 January 1844; and Sherman, "Historic Memories," pp. 22–23.

87. James William Marshall, "The Presbyterian Church in Alabama," MS, 9:4426, 4571, 4576, ASDAH; and Charles D. Bates, ed., *The Archives Tell a Story of the Government Street Presbyterian Church, Mobile, Alabama* (Mobile: Gill Printing Co., 1959), p. 110.

88. *Mobile Register*, 18 November 1834, 1 April 1840; Avery Hamilton Reid, *Baptists in Alabama: Their Organization and Witness* (Montgomery: Alabama Baptist State Convention, 1967), p. 51; Minutes, 1:34, 84, 2:1–2, 45–46, 59, and "History of First Baptist Church, Mobile, Ala., for Its First One Hundred Years, 1845–1945," pp. 16–17, 22, First Baptist Church, Mobile; and Benjamin Franklin Riley, *A Memorial History of the Baptists in Alabama; Being an Account of the Struggles and Achievements of the Denomination from 1808 to 1923* (Philadelphia: Judson Press for the Alabama Baptist State Convention, 1923), pp. 93, 137. Despite the title of the First Baptist Church history manuscript, the church dates its founding as 1835.

89. Clarence Gohdes, "Some Notes on the Unitarian Church in the Ante-Bellum South: A Contribution to the History of Southern Liberalism," in *American Studies in Honor of William Kenneth Boyd*, ed. David Kelly Jackson (Durham, N.C.: Duke University Press, 1940), pp. 363–64; Clement Eaton, *Freedom of Thought in the Old South* (New York: Peter Smith, 1951), pp. 297, 300; and Herbert C. Peabody to ——— St. John, 15 January 1859, Herbert C. Peabody Letters, SHC.

90. Bertram Wallace Korn, *The Jews of Mobile, Alabama, 1763–1841* (Cincinnati: Hebrew Union College Press, 1970), pp. 11–12, 23–24, 32, 38–53; Bertram Wallace Korn, *Jews and Negro Slavery in the Old South, 1789–1865* (Philadelphia: Reform Congregation Keneseth Israel, 1961), pp. 15–16; Jacob Rader Marcus, ed., *Memoirs of American Jews, 1775–1865*, 3 vols. (Philadelphia: Jewish Publication Society of Amer-

ica, 1955−56), 2:79; Alfred G. Moses, "A History of the Jews of Mobile," *Publications of the American Jewish Historical Society* 12 (1904):122; and *Mobile Register*, 12 March 1853, 13 May 1858.

91. Regarding the use of French, see *Mobile Register*, 27 May 1822; Peter Joseph Hamilton, *Colonial Mobile: An Historical Study Largely from Original Sources, of the Alabama-Tombigbee Basin and the Old South West from the Discovery of the Spiritu Santo in 1519 until the Demolition of Fort Charlotte in 1821*, rev. ed. (Boston: Houghton Mifflin, 1910; reprint ed., Mobile: First National Bank, 1952), p. 441; Arthur Augustus Thurlow Cunynghame, *A Glimpse at the Great Western Republic* (London: Richard Bentley, 1851), p. 238; Josiah C. Nott to James McKibbin Gage, 28 July 1836, James McKibbin Gage Papers, SHC; Alexander Beaufort Meek Diary, 28 February 1836, Alexander Beaufort Meek Papers, Duke; and *Mobile Advertiser*, 30 November 1851. The quotation comes from the Meek Diary.

92. Mannhard, "Free People of Color," p. 43; and Lipscomb, "Administration of Portier," p. 286.

93. Records, pp. 7, 9, 11, 13, 15, 17, 27, Government Street Presbyterian Church, Mobile; Session Book, Second Presbyterian Church, 1:31, 2:56−57, Central Presbyterian Church, Mobile; and Bates, *Archives Tell a Story*, p. 157.

94. Christ Church Records, 1:5−6, 16, 41, 2:279, MPL; Massey, Sermon; Trinity Parish Record, Trinity Episcopal Church, Mobile; Whitaker, *History of Episcopal Church in Alabama*, pp. 81−83; and Mobile Writers' Workshop, *Historic Churches*, p. 80.

95. Minutes, 1:10−11, 23, 35, 54−55, 127−28, 133−34, 2:109, 140, First Baptist Church, Mobile; and *Mobile Register*, 5 June 1845. The quotations come from Minutes, 1:54−55, First Baptist Church; *Mobile Register*, 5 June 1845; and Minutes, 1:128, 2:140, First Baptist Church, Mobile, respectively. See Sellers, *Slavery in Alabama*, pp. 300−301.

96. West, *History of Methodism in Alabama*, pp. 262, 599, 709−10; Mobile Writers' Workshop, *Historic Churches*, pp. 48−49, 16, 84−85; *Alabama Planter*, 2 May 1853; Sellers, *Slavery in Alabama*, pp. 301, 304. The quotation comes from Lewis, *Impressions of America*, p. 171.

97. Genovese, *Roll, Jordan, Roll*, p. 261; Wade, *Slavery in the Cities*, pp. 84, 256; *Mobile Register*, 1 June 1843; Petition from L. C. Roberts and others to Mayor and Aldermen, 6 September 1832, Letter from Jefferson Hamilton and others to Mayor and Aldermen, 1840, CMA. The quotation comes from the last citation.

CHAPTER 5

1. Harry A. Toulmin, *A Digest of the Laws of the State of Alabama* (Cahawba, Ala.: Ginn & Curtis, 1823), pp. 784−85; Erwin Craighead, *Mobile: Fact and Tradition, Noteworthy People and Events* (Mobile: Powers Printing Co., 1930), p. 129; and *Mobile Register*, 24 March 1826. See Leonard P. Curry, "Urbanization and Urbanism in the Old South: A Comparative View," *Journal of Southern History* 40 (1974):

52; and David R. Goldfield, "Pursuing the American Dream: Cities in the Old South," in *The City in Southern History: The Growth of Urban Civilization in the South*, ed. Blaine A. Brownell and David R. Goldfield (Port Washington, N.Y.: Kennikat Press, 1977), p. 67.

2. Toulmin, *Digest of Laws*, pp. 784–85; and Alexander McKinstry, *The Code of Ordinances of the City of Mobile, with the Charter and an Appendix* (Mobile: S. H. Goetzel, 1859), pp. 6–7, 191, 112. See Goldfield, "Pursuing the American Dream," pp. 67–68.

3. *Mobile Argus*, 20 December 1822; *Mobile Register*, 12 March 1833, 17 December 1833, 29 March 1842; Craighead, *Mobile*, p. 129; and McKinstry, *Code*, pp. 6–7.

4. In the early 1820s voters chose aldermen in December. From 1826 to 1842 city elections occurred in March. In November 1842 voters went to the polls for a second city election in the year, which was necessitated by a modification of the charter, and they also chose their leaders in November 1843. From 1844 through 1861 municipal elections occurred in December.

5. On the seasonal population shifts, see Charles S. Davis, *The Cotton Kingdom in Alabama* (Montgomery: Alabama State Department of Archives and History, 1939), p. 133; John Shaw, *A Ramble through the United States, Canada, and the West Indies* (London: J. F. Hope, 1856), p. 215; Albert C. Koch, *Journey through a Part of the United States of North America in the Years 1844 to 1846*, trans. and ed. Ernst A. Stadler (Carbondale: Southern Illinois University Press, 1972), p. 109; [Edouard Delius], *Wanderungen eines jungen Norddeutschen durch Portugal, Spanien und Nord-Amerika in dem Jahren 1827–1831*, ed. Georg Lotz, 4 vols. (Hamburg: Heroldschen Buchhandlungen, 1834), 4:113; Mrs. Jones Fuller to Mrs. Ann Thomas, 14 June 1847, Fuller-Thomas Papers, Fuller Division, Duke; and *Mobile Register*, 6 July 1838.

6. J. W. Hengiston [Siras Redding], "Mobile, Pensacola, and the Floridas: Cotton Barque to Cape Cod, along the Gulf Stream," *New Monthly Magazine* 98 (1853): 370.

7. Jones W. Withers to Francis J. Levert, 18 June 1850, Levert Family Papers, SHC.

8. See J. H. Schroebel to Thomas P. Miller, 22 August 1843, Schroebel Papers, J. L. Bedsole Library, Mobile College, Mobile; James F. Sulzby, Jr., *Historic Alabama Hotels and Resorts* (University, Ala.: University of Alabama Press, 1960), pp. 136–37; Ruth Irene Jones, "Ante-Bellum Watering Places of Louisiana, Mississippi, Alabama, and Arkansas" (M.A. thesis, University of Texas, 1954), pp. 120–28, 86, 141–43, 153, 157, 132–33; *Alabama Tribune*, 21 July 1849; Juliana Dorsey to Mrs. Coupland, 13 July 1848, Juliana Dorsey to Coupland Dorsey, 21 June 1848, Dorsey and Coupland Papers, Earl Gregg Swem Library, College of William and Mary, Williamsburg, Va.; Joseph Holt Ingraham, ed., *The Sunny South* (Philadephia: G. G. Evans, 1860), p. 503; *Mobile Advertiser*, 25 June 1851; *Mobile Register*, 9 June 1848, 11 July 1857, 2 May 1844; and Mrs. George Fry to Rebecca Robinson, 22 July, 11 August, 29 August, 5 September 1849, Fry-Robinson Collection, HMPSA.

9. *Mobile Advertiser*, 12 September 1855; and Aldermen's Minutes, 1858, pp. 98–104, 1860, pp. 372–73, MPL.

10. See J. Mills Thornton III, *Politics and Power in a Slave Society: Alabama, 1800–1860* (Baton Rouge: Louisiana State University Press, 1978), p. 42.

11. *Mobile Mercantile Advertiser*, 26 March 1839; *Mobile Register*, 23 March 1841, 29 March 1842, 8 November 1842, 7 December 1847, 19 December 1848, 31 December 1850. For more information on competitive local politics, see *Mobile Register*, 18 January, 12 and 22 May, 7, 9, and 14 July, 3, 5, and 7 August, 11 November 1840, 18 March 1841, 8 and 22 November 1848.

12. *Alabama Planter*, 1 December 1851, 25 September 1852.

13. *Mobile Advertiser*, 18 November 1855.

14. Ibid. The mayor's annual salary grew from $500 in 1825 to $4,000 in 1860. See Aldermen's Minutes, 21 April 1825, 16 February 1826, 3 June 1826, 23 May 1834, 9 December 1858, MPL.

15. *Mobile Advertiser*, 18 November 1855.

16. Since revenue data before the Panic of 1837 are not available, these conclusions about the relative importance of specific revenue sources come from analysis of the city's year-end balance sheets for 1840–41, 1851–52, 1852–53, and 1853–54 municipal years. Property taxes accounted for 56 percent of revenue in 1840–41, 61 percent in 1851–52, 59 percent in 1852–53, and 63 percent in 1853–54. Licenses generated 24, 14, 17, and 15 percent of revenues in these years, respectively. Rents produced 14, 15, 14, and 13 percent of revenues for the same years, respectively. Balance sheets are found in Aldermen's Minutes, 3 April 1841, 16 December 1852, 1 December 1853, MPL; and *Mobile Advertiser*, 8 December 1854. See also Goldfield, "Pursuing the American Dream," p. 82; and McKinstry, *Code*, pp. 324–25.

17. Aldermen's Minutes, 28 January 1829, 3 February 1830, 27 March 1856, MPL; *Mobile Register*, 26 February, 18 October 1834, 30 September 1835; and Corporation Proceedings, 25 February 1832, box 18001, envelope 3, folder 4, Corporation Proceedings, 12 April 1842, box 18005, envelope 4, folder 3, CMA.

18. Albert M. Hillhouse, *Municipal Bonds: A Century of Experience* (New York: Prentice-Hall, 1936), p. 31. For an example of this speculative strategy, see Sherry H. Olson, *Baltimore: The Building of an American City* (Baltimore: The Johns Hopkins University Press, 1980), pp. 79–80.

19. *Mobile Register*, 31 August 1830, 23 May 1834.

20. *Mobile Register*, 28 January 1836.

21. Ibid., 23 April 1836.

22. Ibid., 26 April 1836.

23. Ibid., 7 and 13 October 1836. The Mobile and Cedar Point Railroad Company went bankrupt as a result of the Panic of 1837. See chap. 2.

24. *Mobile Register*, 24 October 1836.

25. Allan R. Pred, *Urban Growth and the Circulation of Information* (Cambridge, Mass.: Harvard University Press, 1973), p. 248; *Mobile Register*, 2 October 1837; William H. Brantley, *Banking in Alabama, 1816–1860*, 2 vols. (Birmingham: Oxmoor Press, 1961–67), 2:10, 18.

26. Philip Phillips, "Philip Phillips: Southern Unionist," in *Memoirs of American Jews, 1775–1865*, ed. Jacob Rader Marcus, 3 vols. (Philadelphia: Jewish Publication Society of America, 1956), 3:144, 146.

27. Henry S. Levert to Francis J. Levert, 18 January, 1 May, 30 December 1839, Levert Family Papers, SHC.

28. Hillhouse, *Municipal Bonds*, p. 39; and *Mobile Register*, 16 May 1839.

29. *Mobile Register*, 2 and 7 September 1839; *Niles' Register* 57 (1839): 32; Edwin T. Wood, *Mobile Directory and Register for 1844* (Mobile: Dade & Thompson, 1844), pp. 10, 19, 23, 26; and *Mobile Advertiser*, quoted in *Niles' Register* 57 (1839): 81, 117, 118.

30. *Mobile Register*, 24 June, 1 July 1839; Weymouth J. Jordan, "Ante-Bellum Mobile: Alabama's Agricultural Emporium," *Alabama Review* 1 (1948): 194; *Niles' Register* 57 (1839): 117; Hillhouse, *Municipal Bonds*, pp. 88–89; and Peter Joseph Hamilton, *Mobile of the Five Flags: The Story of the River Basin and Coast about Mobile from the Earliest Times to the Present* (Mobile: Gill Printing Co., 1913), p. 235. For more information on the arson, see chap. 6 below.

31. *Mobile Register*, 16–17 December 1839; and *Acts of Alabama*, Session of 1839–40, pp. 53–58.

32. McKinstry, *Code*, pp. 318–19, 333, 336, 346.

33. Ibid., pp. 8, 321–23.

34. Ibid., pp. 346, 26–29; and Hamilton, *Mobile of Five Flags*, p. 236.

35. See year-end accounting sheets in Aldermen's Minutes, 16 December 1852, 1 December 1853, 8 December 1854, 13 December 1855, 11 December 1856, and Common Council Minutes, 8 January 1858, 14 December 1858, both in MPL. Interest payments on the city's 1844 bonded indebtedness ranged from a low of $16,259 in 1852 to a high of $47,861 in 1857.

36. *Mobile Advertiser*, 8 December 1854.

37. Ibid., 30 December 1854.

38. McKinstry, *Code*, p. 32.

39. Aldermen's Minutes, 20 March 1846, MPL; and *Mobile Advertiser*, 20 April 1856.

40. David R. Goldfield, *Urban Growth in the Age of Sectionalism: Virginia, 1847–1861* (Baton Rouge: Louisiana State University Press, 1977), p. 176; Alan Smith Thompson, "Mobile, Alabama, 1850–1861: Economic, Political, Physical, and Population Characteristics" (Ph.D. diss., University of Alabama, 1979), pp. 286–87, 491; McKinstry, *Code*, pp. 31, 201–8; Goldfield, "Pursuing the American Dream," p. 82; and *Mobile Advertiser*, 8 December 1854.

41. *Acts of Alabama*, Session of 1857–58, p. 52; *Mobile Register*, 29 November 1859; and *Mobile Advertiser*, 13 April 1860.

42. Goldfield, "Pursuing the American Dream," p. 68; Aldermen's Minutes, 9 December 1824, 15 December 1853, 11 December 1856, 29 December 1859, MPL; and *Mobile Advertiser*, 19 December 1857.

43. Aldermen's Minutes, 27 July, 12 August, 1854, MPL; *Mobile Advertiser*, 26 and 29 September, 1 and 3 October 1854; and Elizabeth B. Gould, "The History of City Hall," *Landmark Letter* 15 (1981): 14–15.

44. Gould, "History of City Hall," 15–16; and Aldermen's Minutes, 1 and 8 February 1855, 10 January 1856, MPL.

45. McKinstry, *Code*, pp. 164–67.

46. Although the markethouse ceased to be used for that purpose, City Hall remained in continuous use for governmental operations until September 1979, when Hurricane Frederic seriously damaged the building. Municipal offices relocated temporarily to other quarters while repairs were made to City Hall. Late in 1982 municipal officials reoccupied City Hall.

47. Hillhouse, *Municipal Bonds*, p. 33.

48. *Mobile Register*, 16 May 1839. For comparable charges made against city officials in antebellum Memphis, see Gerald M. Capers, Jr., *The Biography of a River Town, Memphis: Its Heroic Age* (Chapel Hill: University of North Carolina Press, 1939), pp. 127–30.

49. Aldermen's Minutes, 3 April 1841, MPL.

CHAPTER 6

1. Harry A. Toulmin, *A Digest of Laws of the State of Alabama* (Cahawba, Ala.: Ginn & Curtis, 1823), p. 790.

2. Alexander McKinstry, *The Code of Ordinances of the City of Mobile, with the Charter and an Appendix* (Mobile: S. H. Goetzel, 1859), p. 29.

3. Aldermen's Minutes, 3 April 1841, MPL; and McKinstry, *Code*, p. 327.

4. Aldermen's Minutes, 3 April 1841, MPL.

5. Aldermen's Minutes, 18 November 1852, MPL; McKinstry, *Code*, pp. 37, 151. According to the *Mobile Advertiser* for 8 December 1854, the city's miscellaneous accounts fund paid $882.47 for a reception to honor Millard Fillmore on his visit to Mobile.

6. David R. Goldfield, "Pursuing the American Dream: Cities in the Old South," in *The City in Southern History: The Growth of Urban Civilization in the South*, ed. Blaine A. Brownell and David R. Goldfield (Port Washington, N.Y.: Kennikat Press, 1977), p. 76; McKinstry, *Code*, p. 32; and *Mobile Register*, 20 April, 10 May 1833, 13 January 1853, 16 July 1857.

7. *Mobile Register*, 7 February 1822, 5 February 1858.

8. *Mobile Advertiser*, 19 June 1841; and *Mobile Register*, 7 March, 20 April 1858.

9. *Niles' Register* 45 (1833): 132; G. W. Featherstonhaugh, *Excursion through the Slave States from Washington on the Potomac to the Frontier of Mexico, with Sketches of Popular Manners and Geological Notices* (New York: Harper & Brothers, 1844), p. 143; Tyrone Power, *Impressions of America, During the Years 1833, 1834, and 1835*, 2 vols. (London: Richard Bentley, 1836), 2:223–24; and Henri Herz, *My Travels in America*, trans. Henry Bertram Hill (Madison: Department of History, University of Wisconsin, 1963), p. 95.

10. Louis Fitzgerald Tasistro, *Random Shots and Southern Breezes*, 2 vols. (New York: Harper & Brothers, 1842), 1:230–31; Henry Benjamin Whipple, *Bishop Whipple's Southern Diary*, ed. L. B. Shippee (Minneapolis: University of Minnesota Press, 1937), pp. 86–87, 92; J. W. Hengiston [Siras Redding], "Mobile, Pensacola, and the Floridas: Cotton Barque to Cape Cod, along the Gulf Stream," *New*

Monthly Magazine 98 (1853): 367; and James Stirling, *Letters from the Slave States* (London: John W. Parker & Son, 1857), pp. 178–79. The quotation comes from Stirling.

11. Goldfield, "Pursuing the American Dream," p. 73; Edward Pessen, *Jacksonian America: Society, Personality, and Politics* (Homewood, Ill.: Dorsey Press, 1969), pp. 68–69; Leonard P. Curry, "Urbanization and Urbanism in the Old South: A Comparative View," *Journal of Southern History* 40 (1974): 53; Peter Joseph Hamilton, *Mobile of the Five Flags: The Story of the River Basin and Coast about Mobile from the Earliest Times to the Present* (Mobile: Gill Printing Co., 1913), p. 276; Aldermen's Minutes, 16 August, 15 September 1825, 7 September 1831, MPL; and *Mobile Register*, 7 February 1826, 16 April 1835, 23 April 1838, 16 December 1839, cited in Paul Wayne Taylor, "Mobile, 1818–1859, As Her Newspapers Pictured Her" (M.A. thesis, University of Alabama, 1951), pp. 91–92, 144.

12. Aldermen's Minutes, 4 June, 3 July 1839, MPL; *Mobile Register*, 5 May 1842, cited in Taylor, "Mobile As Her Newspapers Pictured Her," pp. 93–94; Common Council Minutes, 27 November 1857, MPL; and Aldermen's Minutes, 27 March, MPL. The last citation contains the quotation.

13. Common Council Minutes, 27 November 1857, MPL; and Ira Berlin, *Slaves without Masters: The Free Negro in the Antebellum South* (New York: Pantheon Books, 1974), p. 330. See also Michael B. Chesson, *Richmond after the War, 1865–1900* (Richmond: Virginia State Library, 1981), pp. 13–14.

14. *Mobile Register*, 5 May 1842, cited in Taylor, "Mobile As Her Newspapers Pictured Her," pp. 93–94.

15. *Mobile Advertiser*, 9 July 1850, 3 June 1855, 10 May 1854, 27 May 1856.

16. Berlin, *Slaves without Masters*, p. 331.

17. *Mobile Register*, 7 February 1822, reprinted in *Register*, 30 November 1848, cited in Taylor, "Mobile As Her Newspapers Pictured Her," p. 96; Walter Smith to Mayor, Aldermen, and Common Councilmen, 27 April 1840, in Corporation Proceedings, 28 April 1840, box 18023, CMA; and *Mobile Advertiser*, 2 August 1856.

18. Goldfield, "Pursuing the American Dream," p. 73; and *Mobile Advertiser*, 9 February 1856.

19. [John O'Connor], *Wanderings of a Vagabond: An Autobiography*, ed. John Morris (New York: Privately printed, [1873]), p. 462.

20. *Niles' Register* 46 (1839): 48; and Whipple, *Whipple's Southern Diary*, pp. 86–87.

21. O'Connor, *Wanderings of a Vagabond*, p. 462; Mrs. George Fry to Rebecca Robinson, 11 June 1848, Fry-Robinson Collection, HMPSA; Henry S. Levert to Francis J. Levert, 29 July 1830, Levert Family Papers, SHC; Aunt ——— to Rebecca Robinson, 19 May 1850, Fry-Robinson Collection, HMPSA; William A. Witherspoon to Henry Lee Reynolds, 7 September 1855; and *Mobile Register*, 16 March, 16 April, 3 June 1858.

22. See table 4–4.

23. See Claudia Dale Goldin, "A Model to Explain the Relative Decline of Urban Slavery," and Harold D. Woodman, "Comment," both in *Race and Slavery in the Western Hemisphere: Quantitative Studies*, ed. Stanley L. Engerman and Eugene D. Genovese (Princeton, N.J.: Princeton University Press, 1975), pp. 427–54.

24. *Niles' Register* 18 (1820): 113–14; and Aldermen's Minutes, 10 April 1830, MPL. The latter source contains the quotation.

25. McKinstry, *Code*, p. 171; and *Alabama Planter*, 13 February 1854.

26. Richard C. Wade, *Slavery in the Cities: The South, 1820–1860* (New York: Oxford University Press, 1964), pp. 86, 151–52; and James Benson Sellers, *Slavery in Alabama* (University: University of Alabama Press, 1950), pp. 233–34. Quotation comes from *Mobile Evening News*, 9 December 1854, cited in Wade, *Slavery in the Cities*, pp. 151–52. See also James Benson Sellers, *The Prohibition Movement in Alabama, 1702–1943* (Chapel Hill: University of North Carolina Press, 1943), p. 29.

27. McKinstry, *Code*, pp. 171–72; *Mobile Register*, 7 February 1826; *Mobile Advertiser*, 13 March 1835, 14 November 1851 (the latter citation contains the quotation); and Wade, *Slavery in the Cities*, p. 90. For comparative information see Robert C. Reinders, "Slavery in New Orleans in the Decade before the Civil War," in *Plantation, Town, and Country: Essays on the Local History of American Slave Society*, ed. Elinor Miller and Eugene D. Genovese (Urbana: University of Illinois Press, 1974), p. 374.

28. *Mobile Register*, 10 July 1847.

29. McKinstry, *Code*, pp. 173–74; *Mobile Register*, 22 October 1831, 27 August 1841; Wade, *Slavery in the Cities*, pp. 40–42; and Aldermen's Minutes, 15 January 1847, MPL.

30. Aldermen's Minutes, 1 July 1847, MPL; and *Mobile Register*, 10 July 1847.

31. McKinstry, *Code*, pp. 172–73; *Mobile Advertiser*, 21 May 1850; Taylor, "Mobile As Her Newspapers Pictured Her," p. 104; Aldermen's Minutes, 24 and 31 January 1856, MPL; *Mobile Advertiser*, 6 January 1856; and Wade, *Slavery in the Cities*, pp. 70–71.

32. Aldermen's Minutes, 17 January 1856, MPL.

33. *Mobile Register*, 8 January 1859.

34. Lewy Dorman, "The Free Negro in Alabama from 1819 to 1861" (M.A. thesis, University of Alabama, 1916), pp. 19–20.

35. McKinstry, *Code*, pp. 119–20; and *Mobile Register*, 28 January 1859.

36. Dorman, "Free Negro," p. 17.

37. Ibid., pp. 12–13; and Sellers, *Slavery in Alabama*, pp. 368–69.

38. *Mobile Register*, 21 August, 2 September 1835 (the latter citation contains the quotation); *Niles' Register* 49 (1835): 74; Dorman, "Free Negro," p. 11; and Sellers, *Slavery in Alabama*, p. 368. Both Dorman and Sellers accept the uncorroborated account in *Niles' Register*.

39. McKinstry, *Code*, p. 120.

40. Herbert Asbury, *Sucker's Progress: An Informal History of Gambling in America from the Colonies to Canfield* (New York: Dodd, Mead, 1938), pp. 128, 130–31; Henry Chafetz, *Play the Devil: A History of Gambling in the United States from 1492 to 1955* (New York: C. N. Potter, 1960), pp. 184–85; and Alexander Beaufort Meek Diary, 23 February 1836, Alexander Beaufort Meek Papers, Duke.

41. *Mobile Register*, 24 January 1822, 6 May 1825; and *Acts of Alabama*, Session of 1824, p. 53.

42. *House Journal*, Session of 1824, p. 12.

43. *Acts of Alabama*, Session of 1825, p. 9; *Acts of Alabama*, Session of 1826, p. 52; and McKinstry, *Code*, p. 121.

44. Karl Bernhard, Duke of Saxe-Weimar-Eisenach, *Travels through North America during the Years 1825 and 1826*, 2 vols. (Philadelphia: Carey, Lea & Carey, 1828), 2 : 50–51.

45. O'Connor, *Wanderings of a Vagabond*, pp. 460–61. See also Asbury, *Sucker's Progress*, p. 130; and Chafetz, *Play the Devil*, p. 186.

46. *Mobile Literary Gazette* 1 (1839): 161.

47. McKinstry, *Code*, p. 209.

48. *Mobile Advertiser*, 15 May 1859; and *Mobile Register*, 15 October 1859.

49. *Eighth Census*, Free Population Schedule, Alabama, microcopy 653, roll 17, pp. 750–52.

50. Goldfield, "Pursuing the American Dream," pp. 74–75; Pessen, *Jacksonian America*, p. 69; Curry, "Urbanization and Urbanism," p. 53; *Mobile Register*, 7 March 1822; and *Mobile Argus*, 5 December 1822.

51. McKinstry, *Code*, p. 43.

52. *Mobile Register*, 24 June, 1 July 1839.

53. *Niles' Register* 47 (1839): 117; and Caldwell Delaney, ed., *Craighead's Mobile, Being the Fugitive Writings of Erwin S. Craighead and Frank Craighead* (Mobile: Haunted Book Shop, 1968), pp. 81–84.

54. Delaney, ed., *Craighead's Mobile*, p. 81; and George Lewis, *Impressions of America and American Churches, from the Journal of the Reverend G. Lewis* (Edinburgh: W. P. Kennedy, 1845), p. 173. Lewis's account of the slave conspiracy actually confused two distinct plots allegedly made by slaves. According to the *Mobile Register* for 1 June 1843, slaves abandoned the first plan to murder whites in favor of a scheme to set fire to the city.

55. *Mobile Register*, 13 March 1839; and Josiah C. Nott to Joseph W. Lesesne, 9 October 1839, Lesesne Papers, SHC. The latter source contains the quotation.

56. *Mobile Register*, 16 and 25 October 1839; and William R. Hallett to Arthur P. Bagby, 23 October 1839, Governor's Correspondence: Bagby, State Branch Bank Folder, ASDAH. The letter contains the quotation.

57. Bernard Reynolds, *Sketches of Mobile, from 1814 to the Present Time* (Mobile: B. H. Richardson, 1868), p. 22; and McKinstry, *Code*, pp. 112–19.

58. Franklin G. Horton to Gustavus Horton, Jr., 16 April 1852, Horton Family Papers, in the possession of Edith Richards, Mobile; D. Clayton James, *Antebellum Natchez* (Baton Rouge: Louisiana State University Press, 1968), pp. 81–82; and Goldfield, "Pursuing the American Dream," pp. 74–75.

59. McKinstry, *Code*, pp. 374–77; and *Mobile Advertiser*, 12 April 1854, 10 April 1855.

60. *Alabama Planter*, 10 April 1852; and *Mobile Advertiser*, 29 October 1851, 12 April 1854, 8 December 1854, 10 April 1855, 28 April 1860.

61. *Mobile Register*, 4 May 1844; and Hengiston, "Mobile, Pensacola, and the Floridas," p. 370.

62. Curry, "Urbanization and Urbanism," pp. 54–55; *Mobile Mercantile Advertiser for the Country*, 11 June, 16 July 1856; and *Mobile Advertiser*, 8 October 1853.

63. *Mobile Advertiser*, 16 February 1854.

64. Ibid., 23 May 1854; and *Mobile Register*, 22 July 1856.

65. David R. Goldfield, "The Business of Health Planning: Disease Prevention in the Old South," *Journal of Southern History* 42 (1976): 560; and *Mobile Advertiser*, 9 June 1855.

66. *Mobile Register*, 21 April 1836, 19 August 1839, 21 May 1840, 28 July 1853.

67. Aldermen's Minutes, 23 July 1825, 11 August 1839, MPL; *Mobile Register*, 2 September 1839; and *Mobile Advertiser*, 16 August 1853. On the rationale for limited spending for sanitation, see Goldfield, "Business of Health Planning," p. 559; Goldfield, "Pursuing the American Dream," pp. 68–70, 72; and David R. Goldfield and Blaine A. Brownell, *Urban America: From Downtown to No Town* (Boston: Houghton Mifflin, 1979), pp. 174–75.

68. *Mobile Register*, 22 August 1853; *Mobile Advertiser*, 21, 23 and 24 August 1853 (quotation on 23 August); and *Alabama Planter*, 29 August 1853.

69. *Mobile Register*, 9 October 1823, 28 June 1825; and Aldermen's Minutes, 7 October 1826, MPL. See also McKinstry, *Code*, p. 122.

70. John Duffy, *The Sword of Pestilence: The New Orleans Yellow Fever Epidemic of 1853* (Baton Rouge: Louisiana State University Press, 1966), p. 22; Goldfield, "Business of Health Planning," pp. 564–65; and Goldfield, "Pursuing the American Dream," p. 71.

71. *Mobile Advertiser*, 17 August 1853.

72. Ibid., 21 August 1853.

73. Ibid., 30 August, 28 October 1853. See *Mobile Register*, 9 November 1858 for another "all-clear" statement.

74. Charles Lyell, *A Second Visit to the United States of America*, 2 vols. (New York: Harper & Brothers, 1849), 2:87; Duffy, *Sword of Pestilence*, pp. 9, 147 (quotation on p. 147); and David R. Goldfield, *Cotton Fields and Skyscrapers: Southern City and Region, 1607–1980* (Baton Rouge: Louisiana State University Press, 1982), p. 41.

75. Goldfield, "Business of Health Planning," p. 562; and *Mobile Advertiser*, 5 September 1854.

76. *Mobile Advertiser*, 29 August, 19 November 1854.

77. Ibid., 28 April 1855.

78. Ibid., 20 May, 8 June, 21 July 1855.

79. Charles E. Rosenberg, *The Cholera Years: The United States in 1832, 1849, and 1866* (Chicago: University of Chicago Press, 1962), pp. 1, 74–75, 81, 172, 13–15, 17, 91, 21.

80. *Mobile Register*, 5 September 1832; Henry S. Levert to John Stocking, Jr., 28 September 1832, box 18008, CMA; and Solomon Mordecai to Ellen Mordecai, 6 October 1832, Mordecai Family Papers, SHC.

81. Solomon Mordecai to Ellen Mordecai, 4 December 1832, Mordecai Family Papers, SHC; and *Mobile Register*, 7 November 1832, 1 January, 11 April, 17 May, 22 June 1833.

82. *Mobile Register*, 23 September 1836, 19 December 1848.

83. Aldermen's Minutes, 23 March 1831, MPL; *Mobile Register*, 18 June 1831, 11 March 1835; Aldermen's Minutes, 5 July 1839, 12 October 1841, MPL; Petition of

Dabney Herndon, M.D., 25 June 1857, box 18037, CMA; and Aldermen's Minutes, 29 December 1859, MPL.

84. Aldermen's Minutes, 18 February 1858, MPL; and Curry, "Urbanization and Urbanism," p. 57.

85. Solomon Mordecai to Ellen Mordecai, 8 April 1823, Mordecai Family Papers, SHC.

86. Aldermen's Minutes, 8 December 1825, 8 May 1826, MPL.

87. *Mobile Directory Embracing Names of the Heads of Families and Persons in Business, Alphabetically Arranged for 1837* (Mobile: H. M. McGuire & T. C. Fay, 1837), p. 65; and Aldermen's Minutes, 5, 12 and 24 February 1852, 8 April 1852, 4 November 1852, 20 October 1859, 29 December 1859, MPL.

88. Goldfield and Brownell, *Urban America*, p. 176; and Curry, "Urbanization and Urbanism," pp. 55—56.

89. Toulmin, *Digest of Laws*, pp. 793—96; and McKinstry, *Code*, pp. 378—83.

90. O. C. Saunders, "Historical Facts on Mobile Water Supply," p. 1, in Mobile—Waterworks File, MPL; and *Mobile Register*, 31 August 1830, 23 May 1834, 14 February 1839. The quotation comes from the last issue.

91. McKinstry, *Code*, pp. 383—95; and *Mobile Register*, 14 February 1839.

92. *Mobile Register*, 14 February 1839; Hamilton, *Mobile of Five Flags*, p. 231; Erwin Craighead, *From Mobile's Past: Sketches of Memorable People and Events* (Mobile: Powers Printing Co., 1925), pp. 219—20; McKinstry, *Code*, pp. 395—405.

93. Saunders, "Mobile Water Supply," pp. 1—2; and *Mobile Advertiser*, 23 November 1851, cited in Taylor, "Mobile As Her Newspapers Pictured Her," p. 152.

94. *Mobile Advertiser*, 3 and 8 June, 21 September 1854 (quotation on 21 September 1854). See also issues for 19, 20, and 22 September.

95. Saunders, "Mobile Water Supply," pp. 1—2.

96. David R. Goldfield, *Urban Growth in the Age of Sectionalism: Virginia, 1847—1860* (Baton Rouge: Louisiana State University Press, 1977), p. 151.

97. Goldfield, "Pursuing the American Dream," p. 76; Craighead, *From Mobile's Past*, p. 81; Curry, "Urbanization and Urbanism," p. 54; McKinstry, *Code*, pp. 405—8; and *Mobile Register*, 10 June 1837, 16 June 1857.

98. Goldfield and Brownell, *Urban America*, p. 185; and Goldfield, "Pursuing the American Dream," p. 78.

99. Erwin Craighead, *Mobile: Fact and Tradition, Noteworthy People and Events* (Mobile: Powers Printing Co., 1930), p. 185; Caldwell Delaney, *Remember Mobile*, 2d ed. (Mobile: Haunted Book Shop, 1969), pp. 153—54; and *Alabama Planter*, 10 April 1852.

100. *Alabama Planter*, 26 August 1850; *Mobile Register*, 6 May 1851; and Frederick Law Olmsted, *A Journey in the Seaboard Slave States, with Remarks on Their Economy* (New York: Dix & Edwards, 1856), p. 565.

101. Craighead, *Mobile*, p. 185; and *Alabama Planter*, 10 April 1852.

102. *Alabama Planter*, 19 June, 4 September, 16 October 1852; Aldermen's Minutes, 1 July 1852, 3 March, 14 July 1853, MPL.

103. Craighead, *Mobile*, p. 186; Aldermen's Minutes, 10 January 1859, MPL; and *Mobile Register*, 26 March 1859.

104. *Mobile Register*, 23 June, 2, 7, 11, and 21 September 1859. The quotation comes on September 2.

105. Aldermen's Minutes, 16 October 1850, 16 January 1851, MPL; *Alabama Planter*, 1 September 1851; and McKinstry, *Code*, pp. 165–66.

CHAPTER 7

1. Ronald G. Walters, *American Reformers, 1815–1860* (New York: Hill & Wang, 1978), pp. 174–77, 179, 194–95.

2. David R. Goldfield, "The Urban South: A Regional Framework," *American Historical Review* 86 (1981): 1021, 1025.

3. *Mobile Argus*, 5 December 1822.

4. *Mobile Advertiser*, 25 June, 2, 9, 16, 23, and 30 July 1854. The quotation comes from the first citation.

5. Ibid., 1 March 1855.

6. Alexander McKinstry, *The Code of Ordinances of the City of Mobile, with the Charter and an Appendix* (Mobile: S. H. Goetzel, 1859), pp. 152–53.

7. Ibid., p. 209; and *Mobile Advertiser*, 8 November 1857.

8. *Mobile Gazette and Commercial Advertiser*, 23 June 1819, cited in Paul Wayne Taylor, "Mobile, 1818–1859, As Her Newspapers Pictured Her" (M.A. thesis, University of Alabama, 1951), p. 5; and Peter Joseph Hamilton, *Colonial Mobile: An Historical Study Largely from Original Sources, of the Alabama-Tombigbee Basin and the Old South West from the Discovery of the Spiritu Santo in 1519 until the Demolition of Fort Charlotte in 1821* (Boston: Houghton Mifflin, 1910; reprint ed., Mobile: First National Bank, 1952), p. 448.

9. *DeBow's Review* 11 (1851): 338.

10. Aldermen's Minutes, 2 September 1826, MPL; Petition of Catherine Dailey to Mayor and Aldermen, 24 September 1839, box 18008, Common Council Proceedings, 10 and 31 January 1840, box 18023, CMA.

11. Ibid., 24 February 1823.

12. David R. Goldfield, "Pursuing the American Dream: Cities in the Old South," in *The City in Southern History: The Growth of Urban Civilization in the South*, ed. Blaine A. Brownell and David R. Goldfield (Port Washington, N.Y.: Kennikat Press, 1977), p. 79; Aldermen's Minutes, 6 January 1825; Sherry H. Olson, *Baltimore: The Building of an American City* (Baltimore: Johns Hopkins University Press, 1980), p. 91; and McKinstry, *Code*, p. 133.

13. Petition of L. Hitchcock to Mayor and Aldermen, 5 February 1831, box 18023, CMA.

14. *Mobile Register*, 4 September 1835.

15. Ibid., 30 January 1850; and Eliza Horton to Gustavus Horton, Jr., 25 April 1852, Horton Family Papers, in the possession of Miss Edith Richards, Mobile.

16. David R. Goldfield and Blaine A. Brownell, *Urban America: From Downtown to No Town* (Boston: Houghton Mifflin, 1979), p. 182; and Robert H. Bremner,

The Public Good: Philanthropy and Welfare in the Civil War Era (New York: Alfred A. Knopf, 1980), p. 26. See also Benjamin Joseph Klebaner, "Public Poor Relief in Charleston, 1800–1860," *South Carolina Historical and Genealogical Magazine* 45 (1954): 210–11, 218.

17. *Eighth Census*, Free Population Schedule, Alabama, microcopy 653, roll 17, pp. 96–97.

18. *Mobile Advertiser*, 12 September 1855. The *Advertiser* cited an undated issue of the *News*.

19. *Mobile Register*, 3 June 1840, 20 July 1842, 2 June 1848, 24 October 1858, 16 June 1860, 19 December 1858; and *Alabama Planter*, 10 July 1854.

20. Erwin Craighead, *Mobile: Fact and Tradition, Noteworthy People and Events* (Mobile: Powers Printing Co., 1930), pp. 253–54; and Louis Fitzgerald Tasistro, *Random Shots and Southern Breezes, Containing Critical Remarks on the Southern States and Southern Institutions, with Semi-Serious Observations on Men and Manners*, 2 vols. (New York: Harper & Brothers, 1842), 1:235.

21. *Alabama Planter*, 10 July 1854; and *Mobile Advertiser*, 14 October, 17 November 1853. See also *Alabama Planter*, 5, 12, and 26 September 1853.

22. *Mobile Advertiser*, 13 September 1853; *Alabama Planter*, 19 and 26 September 1853; and John Duffy, *The Sword of Pestilence: The New Orleans Yellow Fever Epidemic of 1853* (Baton Rouge: Louisiana State University Press, 1966), pp. 125–27.

23. Dorothy J. Loughran, *History of St. Mary's Home, 1838 to 1963* (Mobile: Mission Office Press, 1965), pp. 1–2.

24. Protestant Orphan Asylum Society Minutes, vol. 1, 2 and 8 December 1839, vol. 2, 13 January 1845, HMPSA. The quotation comes from a copy of the petition to the legislature filed after the 8 December 1839 minutes.

25. Protestant Orphan Asylum Society Minutes, vol. 1, 2 April 1840, 13 December 1843, and unidentified newspaper clipping, 4 June 1844, HMPSA; Loughran, *History of St. Mary's Home*, p. 6; and *Mobile Register*, 18 December 1846, 14 October 1855.

26. Loughran, *History of St. Mary's Home*, pp. 3–6; and *Eighth Census*, Free Population Schedule, Alabama, microcopy 653, roll 17, pp. 390–93, 543–45.

27. Protestant Orphan Asylum Society Minutes, vol. 4, 31 March 1846, HMPSA; *Mobile Register*, 22 April, 16 May 1846; and *Eighth Census*, Free Population Schedule, Alabama, microcopy 653, roll 17, pp. 598–600.

28. Loughran, *History of St. Mary's Home*, p. 4; *Mobile Register*, 31 December 1840, 29 December 1841, 31 December 1844, 3 January 1848; and *Alabama Planter*, 10 January 1848.

29. *Mobile Register*, 3 March 1842, 16 May 1846, 9 February 1847.

30. Loughran, *History of St. Mary's Home*, p. 5; *Mobile Register*, 27 November 1857; and Protestant Orphan Asylum Society Minutes, vol. 4, 6 April 1858, 6 January 1846, 4 January 1859, 16 December 1859, HMPSA.

31. *Mobile Register*, 25 April 1835, 25 November 1837, 11 February 1842; and Henry B. Brewster to Henry W. Bellows, 23 November 1838, 7 January 1839, AUA Letters, Andover-Harvard Theological Library, Harvard University, Cambridge, Mass.

32. *Mobile Register*, 5 January 1844, 7 February 1845, 20 December 1845, 4 December 1846; *Mobile Advertiser*, 7 June 1849, cited in Taylor, "Mobile As Her Newspapers Pictured Her," p. 156; and Charles D. Bates, ed., *The Archives Tell a Story of the Government Street Presbyterian Church, Mobile, Alabama* (Mobile: Gill Printing Co., 1959), pp. 115, 122–23.

33. *Mobile Register*, 15 January 1850.

34. Manuscript By-Laws of Mobile Lodge Number 10 Presented to Mobile Lodge Number 40 by F. G. Kimball, in the possession of Fred Clarke, Jr., historian of the lodge, Mobile; and *Mobile Register*, 26 December 1848.

35. *Mobile Register*, 20 June 1833, 23 May 1839, 15 April 1846, 14 April 1847, 13 April 1853; and Peter Joseph Hamilton, *Mobile of the Five Flags: The Story of the River Basin and Coast about Mobile from the Earliest Times to the Present* (Mobile: Gill Printing Co., 1913), p. 233.

36. *Alabama Planter*, 7 February 1852, 29 November 1852; and *Mobile Register*, 20 and 30 November 1852. The quotation comes from the latter issue. See also *Mobile Advertiser*, 27 September 1852.

37. Walter Claiborne Whitaker, *History of the Protestant Episcopal Church in Alabama, 1763–1891* (Birmingham: Roberts, 1898), p. 138; and *Mobile Register*, 9 September 1855.

38. *Mobile Register*, 19 March 1833.

39. Ibid., 17 March 1843, 15 March 1851.

40. Ibid., 19 March 1847; and *Alabama Planter*, 31 May 1847.

41. St. Mary's Catholic Orphan Asylum Record Book, vol. 1, St. Mary's Home, Mobile; *Eighth Census*, Free Population Schedule, Alabama, microcopy 653, roll 17, pp. 390–93, 543–45; and Oscar Hugh Lipscomb, "The Administration of Michael Portier, Vicar Apostolic of Alabama and the Floridas, 1825–1829, and First Bishop of Mobile, 1829–1859" (Ph.D. diss., Catholic University of America, 1963), p. 256.

42. *Mobile Register*, 9 April 1839, 23 November 1839, 7 March 1846, 21 September 1847.

43. See Bremner, *Public Good*, p. 17.

44. *Mobile Register*, 20 January 1856.

45. Ibid., 6 March 1860.

46. Walters, *American Reformers*, p. 206.

47. Francis Butler Simkins and Charles Pierce Roland, *A History of the South*, 4th ed. (New York: Alfred A. Knopf, 1972), p. 171; and J. Mills Thornton III, *Politics and Power in a Slave Society: Alabama, 1800–1860* (Baton Rouge: Louisiana State University Press, 1978), pp. 294–95, 301–2.

48. Thornton, *Politics and Power*, p. 300.

49. *Mobile Register*, 24 May 1825; and Albert Burton Moore, *History of Alabama and Her People*, 3 vols. (Chicago: American Historical Society, 1927), 1:322–23.

50. Harriet B. Ellis, "Mobile Public School Beginnings and Their Background" (M.A. thesis, Auburn University, 1930), pp. 16–17; and Willis G. Clark, *History of Education in Alabama, 1702–1889* (Washington: Government Printing Office, 1889), p. 220.

51. Moore, *History of Alabama*, 1:323; and *Mobile Register*, 18 March 1833, 28 October 1833.

52. Thornton, *Politics and Power*, pp. 293–94.

53. Ellis, "Mobile Public School Beginnings," p. 18; Clark, *History of Education in Alabama*, p. 220; *Mobile Advertiser*, 13 March 1835; and Nita Katharine Pyburn, "Mobile Public Schools before 1860," *Alabama Review* 11 (1958): 177.

54. School Commissioners' Minutes, vol. 1, undated entry preceding that for 23 August 1836, BA.

55. School Commissioners' Minutes, vol. 1, 31 October 1838, 2 January, 26 February, 12 December 1839, 31 July 1840, BA.

56. Ibid., 31 October 1838, 8 June, 8 July, 21 August 1839, 4 November, 14 February 1840; and Ellis, "Mobile Public School Beginnings," p. 24.

57. Ellis, "Mobile Public School Beginnings," pp. 24–25; Pyburn, "Mobile Public Schools," pp. 181–82; and School Commissioners' Minutes, vol. 1, 31 March 1843, BA.

58. Pyburn, "Mobile Public Schools," p. 182; Ellis, "Mobile Public School Beginnings," p. 27; and Clark, *History of Education in Alabama*, p. 220.

59. School Commissioners' Minutes, vol. 1, 3 December 1844, BA; Moore, *History of Alabama*, 1:323; School Commissioners' Minutes, vol. 2, 12 January, 3 March 1847, 12 October 1848, 23 April 1851, BA; and Minnie Clare Boyd, *Alabama in the Fifties: A Social Study* (New York: Columbia University Press, 1931), p. 130.

60. Aldermen's Minutes, 4 June 1844, 7 August 1846, 6 and 13 February 1851, 19 February 1852, MPL (quotation comes from 6 February 1851).

61. *Mobile Register*, 29 February 1832; Lipscomb, "Administration of Portier," pp. 228–30; Brothers of the Sacred Heart, *A Century of Service for the Sacred Heart in the United States, 1847–1947* (n.p., n.d.), p. 118; and *Alabama Planter*, 5 January 1852. See also Loughran, *History of St. Mary's Home*, pp. 4–7.

62. C. H. A. Dall to Charles Briggs, 2 February 1842, AUA Letters, Andover-Harvard Theological Library, Cambridge, Mass.; Daniel Edward Slagle, "A Rational Insight: Unitarianism as an Alternative in the Ante-Bellum South" (M.A. thesis, Auburn University, 1977), pp. 94–95; and *Mobile Register*, 5 December 1846.

63. *Mobile Register*, 17 November 1846, 12 May 1848.

64. *Acts of Alabama*, Session of 1833–34, p. 68; John G. Aiken, *Digest of the Laws of the State of Alabama to 1843* (Philadelphia: Alexander Tower, 1843), p. 397; Carter G. Woodson, *The Education of the Negro Prior to 1861* (New York: Arno Press and the *New York Times*, 1968), p. 166; and Aldermen's Minutes, 15 October, 26 November 1844, MPL. A. Sellier's petition to the mayor, aldermen, and councilmen and a list of children he proposed to teach are filed with the Corporation Proceedings, 26 November 1844, box 18006, envelope 7, folder 3, CMA.

65. *Alabama Planter*, 30 April 1849, 6 May 1850; and Lipscomb, "Administration of Portier," pp. 231–32.

66. School Commissioners' Minutes, vol. 2, 6 November 1851, BA.

67. *Mobile Advertiser*, 21 November 1851.

68. Boyd, *Alabama in the Fifties*, pp. 124–25; and *Alabama Planter*, 18 August 1851.

69. *Mobile Advertiser*, 15 August 1852.

70. Michael B. Katz, *The Irony of Early School Reform: Educational Innovation in Mid-Nineteenth Century Massachusetts* (Cambridge, Mass.: Harvard University

Press, 1968), pp. 1, 19, 40, 213; and Carol E. Hoffecker, *Wilmington, Delaware: Portrait of an Industrial City, 1830–1910* (Charlottesville, Va.: University Press of Virginia for the Eleutherian Mills-Hagley Foundation, 1974), p. 87.

71. Bama Wathan Watson, *The History of Barton Academy* (Mobile: Haunted Book Shop, 1971), p. 24; and Clark, *History of Education in Alabama*, pp. 221–23. Regarding early public meetings on the proposed sale, see *Mobile Advertiser*, 9 and 12 December 1851.

72. Clark, *History of Education in Alabama*, p. 221.

73. *Alabama Planter*, 24 July 1852; and Stephen B. Weeks, *History of Public School Education in Alabama* (Washington: Government Printing Office, 1915), p. 44.

74. *Mobile Advertiser*, 29 July 1852; and Weeks, *History of Public School Education*, p. 44.

75. *Alabama Planter*, 31 July 1852.

76. *Mobile Advertiser*, 1 August 1852.

77. *Mobile Advertiser*, 31 July 1852; Clark, *History of Education in Alabama*, p. 223; and Ellis, "Mobile Public School Beginnings," p. 36.

78. William P. Vaughn, *Schools for All: The Blacks and Public Education in the South, 1865–1877* (Lexington: University Press of Kentucky, 1974), chap. 3; Fletcher M. Green, *The Role of the Yankee in the Old South* (Athens: University of Georgia Press, 1972), p. 61; and Robert C. Reinders, "New England Influences in the Formation of Public Schools in New Orleans," *Journal of Southern History* 30 (1964): 181–95.

79. Harriet E. Amos, "'Birds of Passage' in a Cotton Port: Northerners and Foreigners among the Urban Leaders of Mobile, 1820–1860," in *Class, Conflict, and Consensus: Antebellum Southern Community Studies*, ed. Orville Vernon Burton and Robert C. McMath, Jr. (Westport, Conn.: Greenwood Press, 1982), p. 248.

80. Clement Eaton, *The Growth of Southern Civilization, 1790–1860* (New York: Harper & Row, 1961), pp. 266–68.

81. School Commissioners' Minutes, vol. 2, 21 September 1852, BA. For a very similar economic argument for public education used in Baltimore, see Olson, *Baltimore*, p. 128.

82. *Mobile Advertiser*, 15 August 1852.

83. *Mobile Register*, 3 June 1853.

84. Clark, *History of Education in Alabama*, p. 224; and School Commissioners' Minutes, vol. 3, 23 July 1853, BA.

85. School Commissioners' Minutes, vol. 2, 30 October 1852, BA; and John A. Nietz, *The Evolution of American Secondary School Textbooks* (Rutland, Vt.: Charles E. Tuttle, 1966), pp. 16–18, 50, 53, 101–2, 118, 166, 240–42.

86. School Commissioners' Minutes, vol. 3, 3 May 1854, 18 November 1852, 5 January 1853, vol. 4, 5 January 1859, BA. The quotation comes from the first citation.

87. *Alabama Planter*, 20 January 1851; and School Commissioners' Minutes, vol. 2, 26 October 1852, BA.

88. School Commissioners' Minutes, vol. 3, 8 December 1852, 2 February 1853, 4 June 1856, 18 August 1856, 3 September 1856, vol. 4, 7 March 1860, BA.

89. When Simkins and Roland write in *A History of the South*, "The region's public schools were for whites only" (p. 174), they overlook the Creole School in Mobile. See Ira Berlin, *Slaves without Masters: The Free Negro in the Antebellum South* (New York: Pantheon Books, 1974), pp. 305–6, regarding whites' tendency to bar free blacks from public schools in southern cities.

90. Thornton, *Politics and Power*, pp. 294–95, 300–301.

91. Clark, *History of Education in Alabama*, p. 225; School Commissioners' Minutes, vol. 3, 17 August 1854, 9 January 1855, vol. 4, 7 July 1858, 28 July 1858, BA. Compare *Digest of the Laws Now in Force Relative to the School Commissioners of Mobile County* (Mobile: Mobile Evening News Job Office Print, 1853) with *Organization of the Board of Mobile School Commissioners, and Regulations of the Public Schools, for the City and County of Mobile* (Mobile: Farrow & Dennett, 1860).

92. Clark, *History of Education in Alabama*, p. 228; and Thornton, *Politics and Power*, pp. 301–2.

93. Clark, *History of Education in Alabama*, pp. 227–29; and School Commissioners' Minutes, vol. 3, 29 October 1856, vol. 4, 3 November 1859, BA.

94. School Commissioners' Minutes, vol. 2, 9 October 1852, BA; Lipscomb, "Administration of Portier," pp. 328, 251; and *Eighth Census*, Free Population Schedule, Alabama, Microcopy 653, Roll 17, pp. 117–20.

95. Clark, *History of Education*, p. 226.

96. School Commissioners' Minutes, vol. 3, 24 October 1856, vol. 4, 3 November 1858, 1 June 1859, BA; and *Mobile Register*, 21 March 1858, 3 June 1859.

97. Russel Blaine Nye, *Society and Culture in America, 1830–1860* (New York: Harper & Row, 1974), p. 380. For notes regarding early public school systems in other southern cities, see Leonard P. Curry, "Urbanization and Urbanism in the Old South: A Comparative View," *Journal of Southern History* 40 (1974): 53; and John McCardell, *The Idea of a Southern Nation: Southern Nationalists and Southern Nationalism, 1830–1860* (New York: W. W. Norton, 1979), p. 179.

CHAPTER 8

1. *Rowan's Mobile Directory and Commercial Supplement for 1850–1851* (Mobile: Strickland & Benjamin, 1850), pp. 5, 21–22. The quotation comes from p. 5.

2. *Mobile Advertiser*, 4 October 1850.

3. Ibid., 20 October 1853.

4. *Mobile Register*, 7 September 1859.

5. *Mobile Advertiser*, 22 May 1859.

6. *Alabama Planter*, 4 and 11 September 1852. On 6 July 1856 the *Mobile Register* maintained incorrectly that Mobile was originally located at the mouth of Dog River.

7. *Mobile Register*, 6 July 1856.

8. *Mobile Advertiser*, 17 January 1855. See John McCardell, *The Idea of a Southern Nation: Southern Nationalists and Southern Nationalism, 1830–1860* (New York: W. W. Norton, 1979), pp. 126–27.

9. Ibid., 5–8 November 1857. The quotation comes from 5 November.

10. *DeBow's Review* 4 (1847): 121.

11. *Alabama Planter*, 8 May 1848. See also Grace Lewis Miller, "The Mobile and Ohio Railroad in Ante Bellum Times," *Alabama Historical Quarterly* 7 (1945): 38–39; and *Hunt's Merchants' Magazine* 19 (1848): 580.

12. *Mobile Register*, 27 November 1847.

13. Robert S. Cotterill, "Southern Railroads, 1850–1860," *Mississippi Valley Historical Review* 10 (1924): 396.

14. Peter Joseph Hamilton, *Mobile of the Five Flags: The Story of the River Basin and Coast about Mobile from the Earliest Times to the Present* (Mobile: Gill Printing Co., 1913), p. 248; Erwin Craighead, *Mobile: Fact and Tradition, Noteworthy People and Events* (Mobile: Powers Printing Co., 1930), pp. 189–90; and *Mobile Register*, 15 January 1847.

15. *Hunt's Merchants' Magazine* 19 (1848): 582–83.

16. *DeBow's Review* 3 (1847): 331.

17. *Mobile Register*, 26 February, 28 April, 1, 3, and 9 May 1848. The quotation comes from 28 April.

18. *Hunt's Merchants' Magazine* 19 (1848): 584.

19. *Acts of Alabama*, Session of 1847–48, pp. 225–26.

20. Robert W. Johannsen, *Stephen A. Douglas* (New York: Oxford University Press, 1973), pp. 310–11; George Fort Milton, *The Eve of Conflict: Stephen A. Douglas and the Needless War* (Boston: Houghton Mifflin, 1934), pp. 10–11; Carter Goodrich, *Government Promotion of American Canals and Railroads, 1800–1890* (New York: Columbia Unversity Press, 1960), p. 171; and William Elejuis Martin, *Internal Improvements in Alabama*, Johns Hopkins University Studies in Historical and Political Science, vol. 20, no. 4 (Baltimore: Johns Hopkins University Press, 1902), p. 67.

21. *Mobile Register*, 1 March 1850; *Mobile Weekly Herald and Tribune*, 28 February 1850; *Mobile Advertiser*, 28 February 1850, 15 February 1852; and Aldermen's Minutes, 20 February 1852, MPL. For enabling legislation see *Acts of Alabama*, Session of 1849–50, pp. 150–52.

22. William Anderson to John Bragg, 17 February 1852, John Bragg Papers, SHC.

23. Goodrich, *Government Promotion*, pp. 156–58, 162–63; and Cotterill, "Southern Railroads," p. 396.

24. David T. Morgan, "Philip Phillips and Internal Improvements in Mid-Nineteenth-Century Alabama," *Alabama Review* 34 (1981): 86; *Mobile Register*, 5, 7, 9, 29, and 31 May 1851; and *Hunt's Merchants' Magazine* 25 (1851): 759–60.

25. Morgan, "Philip Phillips," pp. 88–90.

26. Ibid.

27. *Acts of Alabama*, Session of 1853–54, p. 36; and Albert Burton Moore, *History of Alabama and Her People*, 3 vols. (Chicago: American Historical Society, 1927), 1:377.

28. *Acts of Alabama*, Session of 1855–56, pp. 10–11.

29. Cotterill, "Southern Railroads," pp. 399–400; J. C. Rupert et al. to John A. Winston, 25 February 1857, Governor's Correspondence: Winston, ASDAH; and *Acts of Alabama*, Session of 1857–58, p. 268, Session of 1859–60, p. 292.

30. Cotterill, "Southern Railroads," pp. 398–99, 405n.

31. Ibid., p. 400n; and *Mobile Register*, 4 and 8 March 1856.

32. Cotterill, "Southern Railroads," pp. 399–400.

33. *Mobile Weekly Herald and Tribune*, 4 November 1849; *Mobile Register*, 11 April 1851; J. W. Hengiston [Siras Redding], "Mobile, Pensacola, and the Floridas: Cotton Barque to Cape Cod, along the Gulf Stream," *New Monthly Magazine* 98 (1853): 371; *Alabama Planter*, 26 June 1854; and *Mobile Advertiser*, 6 July 1854.

34. *Mobile Advertiser*, 27 February 1855, 22–23 February 1859. See also Charles S. Davis, *The Cotton Kingdom in Alabama* (Montgomery: Alabama State Department of Archives and History, 1939), p. 132.

35. Ibid., 26 November 1854, 7 March 1856; and *Mobile Register*, 26 June 1859.

36. Merl E. Reed, *New Orleans and the Railroads: The Struggle for Commercial Empire, 1830–1860* (Baton Rouge: Louisiana State University Press, 1966), pp. 65, 75–77.

37. Goodrich, *Government Promotion*, p. 159; *DeBow's Review* 19 (1855): 335. See also Robert C. Reinders, *End of an Era: New Orleans, 1850–1860* (New Orleans: Pelican Publishing Co., 1964), p. 47; Thomas D. Clark, *A Pioneer Southern Railroad from New Orleans to Cairo* (Chapel Hill: University of North Carolina Press, 1936), pp. 63–64; and David R. Goldfield, "Pursuing the American Dream: Cities in the Old South," in *The City in Southern History: The Growth of Urban Civilization in the South*, ed. Blaine A. Brownell and David R. Goldfield (Port Washington, N.Y.: Kennikat Press, 1977), p. 55.

38. Cotterill, "Southern Railroads," pp. 397–98, 400–401.

39. J. Mills Thornton III, *Politics and Power in a Slave Society: Alabama, 1800–1860* (Baton Rouge: Louisiana State University Press, 1978), pp. 274–75.

40. *Mobile Register*, 12 May 1853; Aldermen's Minutes, 7 July 1853, MPL; *Alabama Planter*, 11 July 1853; *Mobile Advertiser*, 24 July 1853, 16 August 1853; and *Mobile Register*, 26 July 1853.

41. *DeBow's Review* 15 (1853): 209–10; *Alabama Planter*, 4 September 1854; and Thornton, *Politics and Power*, pp. 275–76.

42. Alan Smith Thompson, "Mobile, Alabama, 1850–1861: Economic, Political, Physical, and Population Characteristics" (Ph.D. diss., University of Alabama, 1979), pp. 92–93.

43. *Mobile Advertiser*, 25 January 1859.

44. Ibid., 13 March 1859.

45. *Mobile Register*, 22 March 1859.

46. *Acts of Alabama*, Session of 1851–52, pp. 155, 159; and Thompson, "Mobile, Alabama," pp. 94–95.

47. Clement Eaton, *The Growth of Southern Civilization, 1790–1860* (New York: Harper & Brothers, 1961), p. 210; and Allan Pred, *Urban Growth and City-Systems in the United States, 1840–1860* (Cambridge, Mass.: Harvard University Press, 1980), pp. 116, 45–47.

48. Peter Hamilton to Henry W. Collier, 5 November 1851, Governor's Correspondence: Collier, ASDAH.

49. John Forsyth, "The North and the South" (speech delivered to the Franklin Society of Mobile), reprinted in *DeBow's Review* 17 (1854): 377.

50. *Mobile Register*, 17 December 1835, 14 March 1842; and *Alabama Planter*, 3 November 1851.

51. *Acts of Alabama*, Session of 1851–52, pp. 148–49; and *Mobile Advertiser*, 7 September 1852.

52. *Mobile Advertiser*, 15 September 1854, 16 December 1855; and *Acts of Alabama*, Session of 1855–56, pp. 247–49.

53. *Mobile Advertiser*, 21 February 1856.

54. *Acts of Alabama*, Session of 1857–58, p. 192.

55. *Mobile Advertiser*, 5 December 1854, 9 March 1855. The quotation comes from the former citation.

56. *Acts of Alabama*, Session of 1851–52, pp. 145–46, Session of 1857–58, pp. 216–17.

57. *Mobile Register*, 24 April 1860; and *Mobile Advertiser*, 25 April 1860.

58. *Mobile Register*, 10 May 1860.

59. *Mobile Advertiser*, 26 November 1850.

60. *Alabama Planter*, 27 October 1851.

61. Ibid., 11 August 1851; and *Mobile Advertiser*, 18 November 1851.

62. *Mobile Advertiser*, 26 May 1852; and *Mobile Register*, 14 February 1858.

63. *Alabama Tribune*, 25 March 1849; *Mobile Advertiser*, 12 June 1850; and *Alabama Planter*, 25 September 1852. As noted in the *Mobile Register* on 21 January 1859, Turner used either American or Italian marble or some combination of them in fashioning monuments.

64. *Alabama Tribune*, 3 May 1849, 8 June 1850; and *Mobile Register*, 6 December 1850.

65. *Mobile Advertiser*, 29 November 1851; *Alabama Planter*, 29 May 1852, 17 January 1853; and *DeBow's Review* 22 (1857): 111.

66. *Mobile Advertiser*, 30 May 1850, 26 September 1851. Skaats was sometimes spelled Skates. According to the *Mobile Register*, 26 October 1833, an early foundry owned by Asa Prior employed as manager a founder with experience in a reputable northern establishment.

67. *Mobile Advertiser*, 26 September 1851.

68. *Mobile Register*, 4 November 1848.

69. Jonathan M. Wiener, *Social Origins of the New South: Alabama, 1860–1885* (Baton Rouge: Louisiana State University Press, 1978), p. 162; Thornton, *Politics and Power*, pp. 290–91; and Virginia Estella Knapp, "William Phineas Browne, A Yankee Business Man of the South" (M.A. thesis, University of Texas, 1948), pp. 19–21, 23–24, 29, 42–45, 53.

70. James C. Parker, "The Development of the Port of Mobile, 1819–1836" (M.A. thesis, Auburn University, 1968), pp. 52–53; Weymouth T. Jordan, *Rebels in the Making: Planters' Conventions and Southern Propaganda* (Tuscaloosa, Ala.: Confederate Publishing Co., 1958), p. 33; Minnie Clare Boyd, *Alabama in the Fifties: A Social Study* (New York: Columbia University Press, 1931), pp. 55–56; *Eighth Census, Manufacturing*, p. 9; and Frederick Law Olmsted, *A Journey in the Seaboard Slave States, with Remarks on Their Economy* (New York: Dix & Edwards, 1856), p. 567.

71. Weymouth T. Jordan, "Ante-Bellum Mobile: Alabama's Agricultural Emporium," *Alabama Review* 1 (1948): 195; and Thornton, *Politics and Power*, pp. 288–89.

72. Frederic Cople Jaher, *The Urban Establishment: Upper Strata in Boston, New York, Charleston, Chicago, and Los Angeles* (Urbana: University of Illinois Press, 1982), p. 356.

73. *Mobile Advertiser*, 22 November 1855.

74. *Mobile Register*, 11 November, 2 October 1859 (the quotations come from the latter issue); and *Mobile Advertiser*, 17 November 1855.

75. *Mobile Register*, 11 November 1859; and Howard L. Holley, "Medical Education in Alabama," *Alabama Review* 7 (1954): 251. Names of trustees appear in the *Mobile Register*, 8 April 1859. See also William Frederick Norwood, *Medical Education in the United States before the Civil War* (Philadelphia: University of Pennsylvania Press, 1944), p. 376.

76. Holley, "Medical Education in Alabama," p. 251; and *Mobile Register*, 16 November 1859.

77. *Mobile Register*, 8 March 1860.

78. *Alabama Tribune*, 13 July 1849.

79. *Huntsville Southern Advocate*, quoted in *Mobile Advertiser*, 21 June 1853.

80. Moore, *History of Alabama*, 1:271–72.

81. *Mobile Advertiser*, 5 August 1855.

82. Ibid.

83. Ibid.

84. Parham-Winston Collection, ASDAH.

CHAPTER 9

1. *Mobile Register*, 20 April 1850.

2. Charles C. Langdon to Hillary Foster, *Mobile Advertiser*, 30 May 1850. Names of the Twenty-Seven appear in *Mobile Advertiser*, 2 July 1850.

3. *Mobile Advertiser*, 2 June 1850.

4. Ibid., 5 June 1850.

5. Thomas McAdory Owen, *History of Alabama and Dictionary of Alabama Biography*, 4 vols. (Chicago: S. J. Clarke Publishing Co., 1921), 4:1008, 1011; W. Brewer, *Alabama: Her History, Resources, War Record, and Public Men from 1540 to 1872* (Montgomery: Barrett & Brown, 1872), pp. 397–98; William Garrett, *Reminiscences of Public Men in Alabama, for Thirty Years, with an Appendix* (Atlanta: Plantation Publishing Company's Press, 1872), pp. 184–85; and Alexander McKinstry, *The Code of Ordinances of the City of Mobile, with the Charter and an Appendix* (Mobile: S. H. Goetzel, 1859), p. 289.

6. Alan S. Thompson, "Southern Rights and Nativism as Issues in Mobile Politics, 1850–1861," *Alabama Review* 35 (1982): 133.

7. Lewy Dorman, *Party Politics in Alabama from 1850 through 1860* (Wetumpka, Ala.: Wetumpka Printing Co., 1935), p. 55; Henry Mayer, "'A Leaven of Disunion': The Growth of the Secessionist Faction in Alabama, 1847–1851," *Alabama Review* 22 (1969): 113; and J. Mills Thornton III, *Politics and Power in a Slave Society: Alabama, 1800–1860* (Baton Rouge: Louisiana State University Press, 1978), p. 193.

8. Thompson, "Southern Rights and Nativism," p. 135.

9. *Mobile Advertiser*, 30 September 1852.

10. McKinstry, *Code*, p. 292.

11. *Mobile Advertiser*, 22 June 1853.

12. Ibid., 22 June, 27 July 1853.

13. Dorman, *Party Politics*, p. 87; *Mobile Advertiser*, 3 August 1853; and David T. Morgan, "Philip Phillips and Internal Improvements in Mid-Nineteenth-Century Alabama," *Alabama Review* 34 (1981): 92.

14. Population figures come from U.S. Bureau of the Census, *Eighth Census of the United States, 1860: Population* (Washington: Government Printing Office, 1864), pp. xxxii, 9. Figures on the labor force come from Alan Smith Thompson, "Mobile, Alabama, 1850–1861: Economic, Political, Physical, and Population Characteristics" (Ph.D. diss., University of Alabama, 1979), pp. 275–76.

15. Figures compiled from An Indexed Catalogue of Minute Entries concerning Naturalization in the Courts of Mobile County, Alabama, 1833–1907, prepared from the Original Records by the Municipal Court Records Project of the Works Progress Administration, MPL.

16. Thompson, "Mobile, Alabama," p. 167.

17. Aldermen's Minutes, 1852, p. 265; 1854, pp. 463, 489–91, 507, MPL; and Oscar Hugh Lipscomb, "The Administration of Michael Portier, Vicar Apostolic of Alabama and the Floridas, 1825–1829, and First Bishop of Mobile, 1829–1859" (Ph.D. diss., Catholic University of America, 1963), pp. 261–63, 265.

18. W. Darrell Overdyke, *The Know-Nothing Party in the South* (Baton Rouge: Louisiana State University Press, 1950), p. 63.

19. *Mobile Advertiser*, 26 November, 3 and 5 December 1854.

20. Ibid., 21 December 1854, 28 January, 2 and 10 February 1855. The quotations come from the 21 December and 10 February issues.

21. Ibid., 22 and 24 April 1855. The quotations come from the latter issue.

22. Ibid., 16 and 17 May 1855.

23. Ibid., 6 and 20 July 1855. The quotation comes from the latter issue.

24. Ibid., 21 and 25 July, 1 August 1855.

25. Ibid., 7 August 1855.

26. *Mobile Advertiser*, 4 December 1855. See also *Mobile Register* of the same date for Democrats' comments.

27. William M. Dowell to F. I. Levert, 8 December 1855, Levert Family Papers, SHC. *Mobile Register* of 1 December 1858 confirms that Withers entered office as mayor unpledged to a party.

28. *Mobile Advertiser*, 9 November 1855; and McKinstry, *Code*, p. 292.

29. James Edward Saunders, *Early Settlers of Alabama with Notes and Genealogies* (New Orleans: L. Graham and Sons, 1899), p. 517; Owen, *History of Alabama*, 4: 1792–93; Brewer, *Alabama*, p. 417; and Garrett, *Reminiscences*, pp. 125–26.

30. Dorman, *Party Politics*, p. 126; Overdyke, *Know-Nothing Party*, p. 125; Aldermen's Minutes, 15 July 1856, MPL; and *Mobile Register*, 2 and 16 July 1856, 1, 3, and 4 December 1858.

31. *Mobile Advertiser*, 2 February 1854.

32. *Mobile Register*, 26 January 1859.

33. Ibid., 5 February 1858.

34. Paul Ravesies, *Scenes and Settlers of Alabama* (Mobile: n.p., 1885), p. 37.

35. Harriet E. Amos, "'Birds of Passage' in a Cotton Port: Northerners and Foreigners among the Urban Leaders of Mobile, 1820–1860," in *Class, Conflict, and Consensus: Antebellum Southern Community Studies*, ed. Orville Vernon Burton and Robert C. McMath, Jr. (Westport, Conn.: Greenwood Press, 1982), p. 252.

36. *Alabama Tribune* (Mobile), 21 March 1849.

37. John Hope Franklin, *A Southern Odyssey: Travelers in the Antebellum North* (Baton Rouge: Louisiana State University Press, 1976), p. 82.

38. Robert Greenhalgh Albion, *The Rise of New York Port [1815–1860]* (New York: Charles Scribner's Sons, 1939), p. 103.

39. Franklin, *Southern Odyssey*, pp. 109, 112.

40. U.S. Bureau of the Census, *Seventh Census of the United States, 1850: Mortality* (Washington: A. O. P. Nicholson, 1855), 2:38–39; and Thompson, "Mobile, Alabama," pp. 33, 265, 277–79. His computations of nativity for 1850 and 1860 come from the Free Population Schedules of the *Seventh Census* and *Eighth Census*.

41. Forsyth is quoted in Robert Royal Russell, "Economic Aspects of Southern Sectionalism, 1840–1861, Part II," *University of Illinois Studies in the Social Studies* 11 (1923): 197.

42. *Mobile Register*, 2 September 1859.

43. Clement Eaton, *The Mind of the Old South*, rev. ed. (Baton Rouge: Louisiana State University Press, 1967), pp. 85–88.

44. William Barney, *The Secessionist Impulse: Alabama and Mississippi in 1860* (Princeton, N.J.: Princeton University Press, 1974), pp. 128–29, 97–99, 74–75; and Thornton, *Politics and Power*, p. 409.

45. George Fort Milton, *The Eve of Conflict: Stephen A. Douglas and the Needless War* (New York: Houghton Mifflin, 1934), p. 500; and Robert W. Johannsen, *Stephen A. Douglas* (New York: Oxford University Press, 1973), pp. 801, 803. The 1859 legislature had required the governor to call such a convention if a Republican won the presidency in 1860.

46. Walker, Mead and Co. to R. H. Adams, 8 November 1860, Faunsdale Plantation Papers, Adams Family Division, Richard Henry Adams Correspondence, box 1, folder 1, Birmingham Public Library Archives, Birmingham, Alabama.

47. H. E. Sterkx, *Partners in Rebellion: Alabama Women in the Civil War* (Cranberry, N.J.: Associated University Presses, 1970), p. 28; Frank Moore, ed., *The Rebellion Record: A Diary of American Events with Documents, Narratives, Illustrative Incidents, Poetry, etc.* (New York: D. Van Nostrand, 1861), pt. 1, Diary of Events, p. 4; and Kate Cumming, *Gleanings from the Southland: Sketches of Life and Manners of the People of the South before, during and after the War of Secession, with Extracts from the Author's Journal and an Epitome of the New South* (Birmingham: Roberts & Son, 1895), pp. 20–21.

48. Barney, *Secessionist Impulse*, pp. 241–42. The quotation comes from *Mobile Register*, quoted in *Weekly Montgomery Confederation*, 23 November 1860.

49. Barney, *Secessionist Impulse*, pp. 253, 283.

50. Ibid., pp. 283–84.

51. Eaton, *Mind of the Old South*, p. 88; and Peter Joseph Hamilton, *Mobile of the Five Flags: The Story of the River Basin and Coast about Mobile from the Earliest Times to the Present* (Mobile: Gill Printing Co., 1913), p. 293. Mobile's delegates were H. G. Humphries, a merchant; John Bragg and Edmund S. Dargan, attorneys; and George A. Ketchum, a physician.

52. Caldwell Delaney, *Remember Mobile*, 2d ed. (Mobile: Haunted Book Shop, 1969), pp. 193–94.

53. Cumming, *Gleanings*, p. 21.

54. [William Rix], *Incidents of Life in a Southern City during the War* (Mobile: n.p., [1880]), p. 5.

55. *Eighth Census, Population*, pp. xxi–xxxii.

Essay on Sources

PRIMARY SOURCES

Manuscript Collections

A wealth of helpful information comes from the Original Returns of the United States Censuses for 1830 through 1860, both Free Population and Slave Schedules, available on microfilm from the National Archives. The U.S. census schedules of manufactures for Alabama in 1850 and 1860, found in the library of the Alabama State Department of Archives and History, provide data on manufacturing enterprises in the city and county of Mobile.

State censuses for 1850 and 1855 provide enumerations of the inhabitants of Mobile County, available in the library of the Alabama State Department of Archives and History.

The Southern Historical Collection in the University of North Carolina Library at Chapel Hill contains the richest body of personal papers for this study. The Mordecai Family Papers are the single best source of information, containing letters written by Dr. Solomon Mordecai to his relatives in North Carolina from 1823 to 1860 (with some gaps in the late 1830s and the 1840s). Letters written by Solomon's sister Ellen Mordecai to her brother, found in this collection and in the Jacob Mordecai Papers in the William R. Perkins Library of Duke University in Durham, North Carolina, augment the information in Dr. Mordecai's correspondence.

Other especially useful collections in the Southern Historical Collection are the Levert Family Papers, Herbert C. Peabody Papers, and Eliza Carolina (Burgwin) Clitherall Books. The Levert Papers contain letters written between 1829 and 1858 by the Mobile physician Henry Levert to his brother, a merchant in Huntsville. The Herbert C. Peabody Papers include the personal and business correspondence of Peabody, a cotton broker, from 1845 to 1859. Eliza Clitherall, a widow who lived with her wealthy son-in-law John A. M. Battle in Spring Hill in the 1850s, describes the religious and social activities of the elite in the last eight volumes of her diary. (Typewritten copies of these volumes are available.) Other sets of papers in the Southern Historical Collection that contain informative notes include the Henry Lee Reynolds Papers, the John Bragg Papers, and the Joseph W. Lesesne Papers.

Several collections in the William R. Perkins Library of Duke University shed further light on antebellum Mobilians. In addition to the Jacob Mordecai Papers, these collections include the Theophilus Clark Papers and the Fuller Division of the Fuller-Thomas Papers.

The Alabama State Department of Archives and History houses several collections that are useful for this project. In the Maps and Manuscripts Division, the Octavia Walton Levert Diary, with entries from 1846 to 1852, provides the largest available body of material relating directly to Mobile, mainly copies of letters or poems, written by the city's most famous woman in the antebellum period. The Alexander Beaufort Meek Papers contain some of his correspondence, drafts of some of his published speeches and poems, and his unpublished history of Alabama. Unfortunately, most of the private papers of these two well-known Mobilians, A. B. Meek and Octavia Levert, have not been preserved. Correspondence of individual governors in the Civil Archives Division of the Alabama State Department of Archives and History includes letters regarding politics and finance in Mobile.

The Missouri Historical Society in St. Louis holds three helpful collections: the Hitchcock, the Ludlow-Field-Maury, and the Sol Smith collections. Correspondence in the Hitchcock Papers sheds light on the personal financial crisis and religious faith of Henry Hitchcock, an attorney and land developer, during the 1830s. Letters written by theater managers Noah Ludlow and Sol Smith, found in the other two collections mentioned, provide notes not only about business affairs during their long partnership but also about the support given them by prominent Mobilians.

Manuscript collections in still other repositories contain some useful material. These include the Yuille Papers, Amelia Gayle Gorgas Library, University of Alabama, University, Alabama; the Dorsey and Coupland Papers, Earl Gregg Swem Library, College of William and Mary, Williamsburg, Virginia; the Innerarity (John) Papers, Louisiana State University Library, Baton Rouge, Louisiana; and the Kate Upson Clark Papers, Sophia Smith Collection (Women's History Archive), Allan Neilson Library, Smith College, Northampton, Massachusetts.

Various repositories and private individuals in Mobile hold useful manuscript collections. The family papers of the cotton broker Gustavus Horton, held by Miss Edith Richards, include letters dealing with childrearing, education, and the Government Street Presbyterian Church. The Fry-Robinson Collection, found in the Historic Mobile Preservation Society Archives at Oakleigh, contains letters describing the social activities and travels of the George Frys of Mobile. The Jacob Henry Schroebel Collection in the J. L. Bedsole Library of Mobile College includes letters written during the yellow-fever epidemic of 1843. The Bedsole Library also holds the Phoenix Fire Company Number 6 Records (Minute Book), 1841–59, and Merchants Fire Company Number 4 Record Book, 1838–60. At the Museum of the City of Mobile are records of two fire companies: Creole Fire Company Number 1 Constitution Book and Minutes, 1846–53, and Torrent Fire Company Number 5 Records, 1855–61. Fred Clarke, Jr., maintains the Manuscript By Laws of Mobile [Masonic] Lodge Number 10.

Records of elected organizations include, in Mobile, the Minutes of the Aldermen and the Common Councilmen, virtually complete and available on micro-film in the Mobile Public Library, and the Minutes of the Board of School Com-missioners, virtually complete from 1836 and available in the School Board Offices in Barton Academy. In addition, assorted municipal records, such as petitions and letters to city officials, stored in the City of Mobile Archives contain much helpful information. Data on charities are found in the Minutes (1839–60) of the Protes-tant Orphan Asylum Society, in the Historic Mobile Preservation Society Archives at Oakleigh, and the Record Book (1838–60) of St. Mary's Catholic Female Or-phan Asylum, in St. Mary's Home. No list of admissions to the Protestant Asylum or minutes of the Catholic Female Orphan Asylum Society apparently have been preserved.

Records of various churches shed light on their members and occasionally on their doctrines and disciplinary policies. Copies of the Parish Records of Christ (Episcopal) Church are available in the Mobile Public Library in three volumes (1832–39, 1846–56, and 1856–84). Other antebellum records are found in Trinity Episcopal Church (Parish Register), St. Francis Street Methodist Church (Official Membership and Church Record), and Government Street Presbyterian Church (Church Register). In the Central Presbyterian Church are the complete (1842–68) Session Books of the Second Presbyterian Church and the Third Presbyterian Church (1853–68), which include both lists of members and minutes of the ses-sions. The First Baptist Church holds the minutes of the churches that formed it. Early documents in St. Paul's Episcopal Church are very sketchy. No local records exist of the Unitarian congregation, and none of the Jewish congregation in its antebellum years. Baptismal and marriage records from the Catholic churches are available through the archdiocesan chancery. Early records of the black congrega-tions of various denominations, if they ever existed apart from the records of their white sponsoring churches, have apparently not been preserved.

Credit Reports of R. G. Dun & Company, housed in the Baker Library, Gradu-ate School of Business Administration, Harvard University, Cambridge, Massa-chusetts, contain useful financial and personal information regarding local busi-nessmen. Alabama volumes numbers 17 and 18 pertain to Mobile County from 1846 to 1883.

Highly valuable business information comes from the papers of two large firms in the New-York Historical Society, New York City: Brown Brothers Harriman & Company Historical File, and Ogden Ferguson & Day Papers.

Government Documents

Among the most important reference works are the published reports of the Fifth through the Eighth Census of the United States. These include *Fifth Census; or Enumeration of the Inhabitants of the United States, 1830* (Washington: Duff Green, 1832); *Sixth Census or Enumeration of the Inhabitants of the United States, as Corrected at the Department of State, in 1840* (Washington: Blair and Rives, 1841); *The Seventh Census of the United States: 1850* (Washington: Robert Armstrong, 1853); and *Popula-*

tion of the United States in 1860; Compiled from the Original Returns of the Eighth Census, Under the Direction of the Secretary of the Interior (Washington: Government Printing Office, 1864). Also helpful are the U.S. Secretary of the Treasury, *Reports on Commerce and Navigation, 1815–1860.*

Journals of the Alabama House and Senate and acts passed by the General Assembly published at the conclusion of each session document the relationship between the state and city.

Mobile's charters appear in Harry A. Toulmin, *A Digest of the Laws of the State of Alabama* (Cahawba, Ala.: Ginn and Curtis, 1823); and Alexander McKinstry, *The Code of Ordinances of the City of Mobile, with the Charter and an Appendix* (Mobile: S. H. Goetzel, 1859).

Contemporary Books and Articles

A variety of helpful information appears in city directories: *Mobile Directory Embracing Names of the Heads of Families and Persons in Business, Alphabetically Arranged for 1837* (Mobile: H. M. McGuire & T. C. Fay, 1837); *Mobile Directory, or Strangers' Guide for 1838* (Mobile: R. R. Dade, 1839); R. P. Vail, *Mobile Directory, or Strangers' Guide, for 1842* (Mobile: Dade & Thompson, 1842); Edwin T. Wood, *Mobile Directory, and Register for 1844* (Mobile: Dade & Thompson, 1844); *Rowan's Mobile Directory and Commercial Supplement for 1850–51* (Mobile: Strickland & Benjamin, 1850); William R. Robertson, *The Comprehensive Mobile Guide and Directory, Referring to the Business Locations, for 1852* (Mobile: Carver & Ryland, 1852); *Mobile Directory and Commercial Supplements for 1855–6* (Mobile: Strickland, 1855); *Daughdrill & Walker's General Directory for the City and County of Mobile, for 1856* (Mobile: Farrow, Stokes & Dennett, 1856); *Directory for the City of Mobile, 1859* (Mobile: Farrow & Dennett, 1859); and *Directory for the City of Mobile for 1861* (Mobile: Farrow & Dennett, 1861).

Several autobiographical works or reminiscences by Mobilians contain valuable insights. Theater managers Sol Smith and Noah M. Ludlow include many choice observations on all aspects of theatrical life in Mobile in their autobiographies— Smith's *Theatrical Management in the West and South for Thirty Years* (New York: Harper & Brothers, 1868), and Ludlow's *Dramatic Life As I Found It* (St. Louis: G. I. Jones, 1880). (Ludlow often attempts to correct what he considers errors in Smith's book.) Useful sketches of Mobilians also appear in Paul Ravesies, *Scenes and Settlers of Alabama* (Mobile: n.p., 1885), and [Bernard Reynolds], *Sketches of Mobile* (Mobile: B. H. Richardson, 1868).

Travel accounts by American and foreign visitors to Mobile frequently provide helpful observations on a wide range of subjects, depending upon the background and taste of the traveler and the length of time he spent in the city. The definitive guide to travel literature is Thomas D. Clark, *Travels in the Old South: A Bibliography*, vol. 3: *Cotton, Slavery, and Conflict* (Norman: University of Oklahoma Press, 1959). Several hitherto hard-to-obtain articles by travelers are reprinted in Eugene L. Schwaab and Jacqueline Bull, eds., *Travels in the Old South, Selected from*

Periodicals of the Times, 2 vols. (Lexington: University Press of Kentucky, 1973). Of book-length accounts by Americans, the most penetrating observations of Mobile are found in John S. C. Abbott, *South and North* (New York: Abbey & Abbot, 1860); Joseph Holt Ingraham, ed. [actually the author], *The Sunny South* (Philadelphia: G. G. Evans, 1860); [John O'Connor], *Wanderings of a Vagabond*, ed. John Morris (New York: privately printed, [1873]); Frederick Law Olmsted, *A Journey in the Seaboard Slave States* (New York: Dix & Edwards, 1856); and Henry Benjamin Whipple, *Bishop Whipple's Southern Diary*, ed. L. B. Shippee (Minneapolis: University of Minnesota Press, 1937).

Highly useful foreign travelers' accounts of visits during the 1820s come from Karl Bernhard, Duke of Saxe-Weimar-Eisenach, *Travels through North America during the Years 1825 and 1826*, 2 vols. (Philadelphia: Carey, Lea & Carey, 1828), and Adam Hodgson, *Remarks during a Journey through North America in the Years 1819, 1820, and 1821*, 2 vols. (New York: Samuel Whiting, 1823). An upper-class British couple, Basil and Margaret Hall, record interesting, critical stories: Basil Hall, *Travels in North America in the Years 1827 and 1828*, 2 vols. (Philadelphia: Carey, Lea & Carey, 1829), and Margaret Hall, *The Aristocratic Journey*, ed. Una Pope-Hennessy (New York: G. P. Putnam's Sons, 1931).

Men from the British Isles have left helpful descriptions of their visits to Mobile in the 1830s and 1840s. These appear in G. W. Featherstonhaugh, *Excursion through the Slave States* (New York: Harper & Brothers, 1844), Thomas Hamilton, *Men and Manners in America* (Philadelphia: Carey, Lea & Blanchard, 1833), and Tyrone Power, *Impressions of America*, 2 vols. (London: Richard Bentley, 1836). The most useful accounts of Mobile during the 1840s come from George Lewis, *Impressions of America and American Churches* (Edinburgh: W. P. Kennedy, 1845), and Louis Fitzgerald Tasistro, *Random Shots and Southern Breezes*, 2 vols. (New York: Harper & Brothers, 1842).

Good descriptions of Mobile in the 1850s emerge from Frederika Bremer, *The Homes of the New World*, trans. Mary Howitt, 2 vols. (New York: Harper & Brothers, 1853); Hiram Fuller, *Belle Brittan on a Tour, at Newport, and Here and There* (New York: Derby & Jackson, 1858); J. W. Hengiston [Siras Redding], "Mobile, Pensacola, and the Floridas," *New Monthly Magazine* 98 (1853): 362–78; and John W. Oldmixon, *Transatlantic Wanderings* (London: George Routledge, 1855).

Contemporary Newspapers and Periodicals

Contemporary newspapers are the single most valuable source of information for this study. As many as five newspapers were published at one time during some antebellum years. Few of them survive in extended runs. The longest running file is that of the Democratic *Mobile Register*, published from December 1821 to the present day under slightly variant titles. Microfilm copies made through the Library of Congress and filed in the Mobile Public Library and other repositories cover all of the antebellum years except parts of 1825, 1827, 1829–31, 1835, 1837, 1844, 1849–50, 1851–53, 1855–57, 1860, and all of 1854.

The Whig *Mobile Advertiser*, published under slightly variant titles from 1833 to 1861, is available on microfilm from 1840 to 1860, with some gaps, in the Amelia Gayle Gorgas Library of the University of Alabama. Scattered issues of several other Mobile newspapers are found on microfilm in the Gorgas Library. They include the *Merchants and Planters Journal, Mobile Argus, Mobile Gazette, Mobile Gazette and Commercial Advertiser, Mobile Herald and Tribune,* and *Mobile Literary Gazette.*

The Library of Congress preserves issues of the *Mobile Argus* (1822–23), *Mobile Courier* (1835), *Mobile Mercantile Advertiser for the Country* (1836), and *Alabama Tribune* (1849).

Some of the gaps in newspapers can be filled by the complete run of the *Alabama Planter* from December 1846 through November 1854. (This newspaper, which refrained from choosing political sides, simply gave a new name to the *Mobile Weekly Herald and Tribune*, a compilation of the daily *Herald and Tribune.*) The *Planter* is available on microfilm in the Robert W. Woodruff Library for Advanced Studies, Emory University, Atlanta, Georgia.

Three contemporary periodicals contain much useful information, often in articles reprinted from other sources. These are *Niles' Register* (1820–39), published in Baltimore first as *Niles' National Register*, then as *Niles' Weekly Register*; *Hunt's Merchants' Magazine* (1840–49), published in New York; and *DeBow's Review* (1846–60), published in New Orleans.

SECONDARY WORKS

Books and Articles

The standard work for background on antebellum America is Edward Pessen's *Jacksonian America: Society, Personality, and Politics*, rev. ed. (Homewood, Ill.: Dorsey Press, 1978). J. Mills Thornton III presents the most comprehensive study of antebellum Alabama from a political perspective in his *Politics and Power in a Slave Society: Alabama, 1800–1860* (Baton Rouge: Louisiana State University Press, 1978). Weymouth T. Jordan's *Antebellum Alabama, Town and Country* (Tallahassee: Florida State University Press, 1957) provides useful information. Selected phases of this era are satisfactorily examined by Thomas Perkins Abernethy in *The Formative Period in Alabama, 1815–1828* (1922; reprint ed., University: University of Alabama Press, 1965) and by Minnie Clare Boyd in *Alabama in the Fifties: A Social Study* (New York: Columbia University Press, 1931). Other helpful state histories include W. Brewer, *Alabama: Her History, Resources, War Records, and Public Men from 1540 to 1872* (Montgomery: Barrett & Brown, 1872); Albert Burton Moore, *History of Alabama and Her People*, 3 vols. (Chicago: American Historical Society, 1927); Marie Bankhead Owen, *Alabama: A Social and Economic History of the State* (Montgomery: Dixie Book Co., 1938); and Thomas McAdory Owen, *History of Alabama and Dictionary of Alabama Biography*, 4 vols. (Chicago: S. J. Clarke, 1921). James Benson Sellers studies "the peculiar institution" in *Slavery in Alabama* (University: University of Alabama Press, 1950).

A number of excellent studies of nineteenth-century urbanization with careful attention to the South have appeared within the last decade. Leonard P. Curry investigates the comparative perspective in "Urbanization and Urbanism in the Old South: A Comparative View," *Journal of Southern History* 40 (1974): 43–60. David R. Goldfield presents instructive syntheses in "Pursuing the American Dream: Cities in the Old South," in *The City in Southern History: The Growth of Urban Civilization in the South*, ed. Blaine A. Brownell and David R. Goldfield (Port Washington, N.Y.: Kennikat Press, 1977), pp. 52–91; "The Urban South: A Regional Framework," *American Historical Review* 86 (1981): 1009–34; and *Cotton Fields and Skyscrapers: Southern City and Region, 1607–1980* (Baton Rouge: Louisiana State University Press, 1982). Goldfield and Brownell offer a fresh approach to the survey of urban history in *Urban America: From Downtown to No Town* (Boston: Houghton Mifflin, 1979). Allan R. Pred examines urbanization in the pre- and posttelegraphic eras in *Urban Growth and the Circulation of Information: The United States System of Cities, 1790–1840* (Cambridge, Mass.: Harvard University Press, 1973) and *Urban Growth and City-Systems in the United States, 1840–1860* (Cambridge, Mass.: Harvard University Press, 1980). Helpful analysis of immigration appears in David Ward, *Cities and Immigrants: A Geography of Change in Nineteenth-Century America* (New York: Oxford University Press, 1971). Useful methodological and interpretive approaches to the study of southern communities appear in *Class, Conflict, and Consensus: Antebellum Southern Community Studies*, ed. Orville Vernon Burton and Robert C. McMath, Jr. (Westport, Conn.: Greenwood Press, 1982).

Several studies of southern cities are particularly helpful for this project. These include David R. Goldfield, *Urban Growth in the Age of Sectionalism: Virginia, 1847–1861* (Baton Rouge: Louisiana State University Press, 1977); D. Clayton James, *Antebellum Natchez* (Baton Rouge: Louisiana State University Press, 1968); Sherry H. Olson, *Baltimore: The Building of an American City* (Baltimore: Johns Hopkins University Press, 1980); and Robert C. Reinders, *End of an Era: New Orleans, 1850–1860* (New Orleans: Pelican Publishing Co., 1964). Richard C. Wade's observations in *Slavery in the Cities: The South 1820–1860* (New York: Oxford University Press, 1964) have validity for Mobile.

Monographs on several northern cities and towns present insights useful for this study. They include Stuart Blumin, *The Urban Threshold: Growth and Change in a Nineteenth Century American Community* (Chicago: University of Chicago Press, 1976); Don Harrison Doyle, *The Social Order of a Frontier Community: Jacksonville, Illinois, 1825–70* (Urbana: University of Illinois Press, 1978); Michael H. Frisch, *Town into City: Springfield, Massachusetts, and the Meaning of Community, 1840–1880* (Cambridge, Mass.: Harvard University Press, 1972); and Sam Bass Warner, Jr., *The Private City: Philadelphia in Three Periods of Its Growth* (Philadelphia: University of Pennsylvania Press, 1968).

Mobile lacks a full scholarly history. Helpful insights and information appear in

Peter Joseph Hamilton, *Mobile of the Five Flags: The Story of the River Basin and Coast about Mobile from the Earliest Times to the Present* (Mobile: Gill Printing Co., 1913). More popular works include Caldwell Delaney's *Remember Mobile*, 2d ed. (Mobile: Haunted Book Shop, 1969) and his *The Story of Mobile* (Mobile: Haunted Book Shop, 1981) and Jay Higginbotham's *Mobile: City by the Bay* (Mobile: Azalea City Printers, 1968). A useful bibliographic essay comes in Melton McLaurin and Michael Thomason, *Mobile: The Life and Times of a Great Southern City* (Woodland Hills, Calif.: Windsor Publications, 1981). Stories and anecdotes by Erwin Craighead are found in *From Mobile's Past: Sketches of Memorable People and Events* (Mobile: Powers Printing Co., 1925), *Mobile: Fact and Tradition, Noteworthy People and Events* (Mobile: Powers Printing Co., 1930), and *Craighead's Mobile, Being the Fugitive Writings of Erwin S. Craighead and Frank Craighead*, ed. Caldwell Delaney (Mobile: Haunted Book Shop, 1968). Caldwell Delaney's *A Mobile Sextet: Papers Read before the Alabama Historical Association, 1952–1971* (Mobile: Haunted Book Shop, 1981) includes some interesting specialized essays.

Scholarly studies of early Mobile appear in Jay Higginbotham, *Old Mobile: Fort Louis de la Louisiane, 1702–1711* (Mobile: Museum of the City of Mobile, 1977), and Peter Joseph Hamilton, *Colonial Mobile: An Historical Study Largely from Original Sources, of the Alabama-Tombigbee Basin and the Old South West from the Discovery of the Spiritu Santo in 1519 until the Demolition of Fort Charlotte in 1821* (Boston: Houghton Mifflin, 1910; reprint ed., Mobile: First National Bank, 1952). James C. Parker presents an excellent analysis of Mobile's early rival in "Blakeley: A Frontier Seaport," *Alabama Review* 27 (1974): 39–51.

Mobile's cotton trade receives attention in Weymouth T. Jordan, "Ante-Bellum Mobile: Alabama's Agricultural Emporium," *Alabama Review* 1 (1948): 180–202; and Charles S. Davis, *The Cotton Kingdom in Alabama* (Montgomery: Alabama State Department of Archives and History, 1939). Robert Greenhalgh Albion examines Mobile's relationship to New York and American commerce in *The Rise of New York Port [1815–1860]* (New York: Charles Scribner's Sons, 1939). Solid analysis of financing the cotton trade appears in studies of Brown Brothers and Company: Edwin J. Perkins, *Financing Anglo-American Trade: The House of Brown, 1800–1880* (Cambridge, Mass.: Harvard University Press, 1975); John R. Killick, "Risk Specialization and Profit in the Mercantile Sector of the Nineteenth Century Cotton Trade: Alexander Brown and Sons, 1820–80," *Business History* 16 (1974): 1–16; and John R. Killick, "The Cotton Operations of Alexander Brown and Sons in the Deep South, 1820–1860," *Journal of Southern History* 43 (1977): 169–94. Excellent general studies of cotton factors are Alfred H. Stone, "The Cotton Factorage System of the Southern States," *American Historical Review* 20 (1915): 557–65; and Ralph W. Haskins, "Planter and Cotton Factor in the Old South," *Agricultural History* 39 (1955): 1–14. Harold D. Woodman provides the most comprehensive treatment of the entire cotton factorage system in *King Cotton and His Retainers: Financing and Marketing the Cotton Crop of the South, 1800–1925* (Lexington: University of Kentucky Press, 1968). The standard work on banking is William Henderson Brantley, *Banking in Alabama*, 2 vols. (Birmingham: Oxmoor Press, 1961–67). A well-researched study of the lumber trade is John A. Eisterhold, "Mobile: Lumber Center of the Gulf Coast," *Alabama Review* 26 (1973): 83–104.

Numerous studies of urban leaders or elites influenced this analysis of Mobile's city fathers. In addition to previously mentioned articles and monographs on urbanization, articles contributing insights on the process of leadership selection include Richard S. Alcorn, "Leadership and Stability in Mid-Nineteenth Century America: A Case Study of an Illinois Town," *Journal of American History* 61 (1974): 685–702; Don Harrison Doyle, "The Social Functions of Voluntary Associations in a Nineteenth-Century Town," *Social Science History* 1 (1977): 333–56; Walter S. Glazer, "Participation and Power: Voluntary Associations and the Functional Organization of Cincinnati in 1840," *Historical Methods Newsletter* 5 (1972): 151–68; and Edward Pessen, "The Egalitarian Myth and the American Social Reality: Wealth, Mobility, and Egality in the 'Era of the Common Man,'" *American Historical Review* 76 (1971): 989–1034. Pessen's *Riches, Class, and Power before the Civil War* (Lexington, Mass.: D. C. Heath, 1973) presents a detailed analysis of elites in four northeastern cities. Frederic Cople Jaher's work on elites sets a model for thoroughness. His works include "The Boston Brahmins in the Age of Industrial Capitalism," in *The Age of Industrialism in America: Essays in Social Structure and Cultural Values*, ed. Frederic Cople Jaher (New York: Free Press, 1968), pp. 188–262; *The Urban Establishment: Upper Strata in Boston, New York, Charleston, Chicago, and Los Angeles* (Urbana: University of Illinois Press, 1982); and, with Joyce Maynard Ghent, "The Chicago Business Elite, 1830–1930: A Collective Biography," *Business History Review* 50 (1976): 288–328.

City government's financial problems are set in perspective by Albert M. Hillhouse, *Municipal Bonds: A Century of Experience* (New York: Prentice-Hall, 1936). The relationship between city services and financial limitations receives particular attention in disease prevention as examined in David R. Goldfield, "The Business of Health Planning: Disease Prevention in the Old South," *Journal of Southern History* 42 (1976): 557–70; John Duffy, *The Sword of Pestilence: The New Orleans Yellow Fever Epidemic of 1853* (Baton Rouge: Louisiana State University Press, 1966); and Charles E. Rosenberg, *The Cholera Years: The United States in 1832, 1849, and 1866* (Chicago: University of Chicago Press, 1962).

Social services and the constraints upon them are examined in Robert H. Bremner, *The Public Good: Philanthropy and Welfare in the Civil War Era* (New York: Alfred A. Knopf, 1980). Helpful studies of particular social services include Benjamin Joseph Klebaner, "Public Poor Relief in Charleston, 1800–1860," *South Carolina Historical and Genealogical Magazine* 45 (1954): 210–20; Michael B. Katz, *The Irony of Early School Reform: Educational Innovation in Mid-Nineteenth Century Massachusetts* (Cambridge, Mass.: Harvard University Press, 1968); Robert C. Reinders, "New England Influences on the Formation of Public Schools in New Orleans," *Journal of Southern History* 30 (1964): 181–95; and Willis G. Clark, *History of Education in Alabama 1702–1889* (Washington: Government Printing Office, 1889).

Mobilians' efforts toward progress through commercial independence illustrate concepts discussed in John McCardell, *The Idea of a Southern Nation: Southern Nationalists and Southern Nationalism, 1830–1860* (New York: W. W. Norton, 1979). Helpful studies of railroad promotion include Robert S. Cotterill, "Southern Railroads, 1850–1860," *Mississippi Valley Historical Review* 10 (1924): 396–405; Carter

Goodrich, *Government Promotion of American Canals and Railroads, 1800–1890* (New York: Columbia University Press, 1960); Grace Lewis Miller, "The Mobile and Ohio Railroad in Ante Bellum Times," *Alabama Historical Quarterly* 7 (1945): 37–59; David T. Morgan, "Philip Phillips and Internal Improvements in Mid-Nineteenth Century Alabama," *Alabama Review* 34 (1981): 83–93; and Merl E. Reed, *New Orleans and the Railroads: The Struggle for Commercial Empire, 1830–1860* (Baton Rouge: Louisiana State University Press, 1966).

The following studies present insights into the late antebellum sectional tensions within Mobile: Harriet E. Amos, "'Birds of Passage' in a Cotton Port: Northerners and Foreigners among the Urban Leaders of Mobile, 1820–1860," in *Class, Conflict, and Consensus: Antebellum Southern Community Studies,* ed. Orville Vernon Burton and Robert C. McMath, Jr. (Westport, Conn.: Greenwood Press, 1982), pp. 232–62; William W. Chenault and Robert C. Reinders, "The Northern-Born Community of New Orleans in the 1850s," *Journal of American History* 51 (1964): 232–47; Fletcher M. Green, *The Role of the Yankee in the Old South* (Athens: University of Georgia Press, 1972); Lewy Dorman, *Party Politics in Alabama from 1850 through 1860* (Wetumpka, Ala.: Wetumpka Printing Co., 1935); W. Darrell Over-dyke, *The Know-Nothing Party in the South* (Baton Rouge: Louisiana State University Press, 1950); and Alan S. Thompson, "Southern Rights and Nativism as Issues in Mobile Politics, 1850–1861," *Alabama Review* 35 (1982): 127–41. Secession is best explained by Thornton's previously mentioned *Politics and Power in a Slave Society* and William L. Barney, *The Secessionist Impulse: Alabama and Mississippi in 1860* (Princeton, N.J.: Princeton University Press, 1974).

Unpublished Materials

Of the master's theses and doctoral dissertations about Mobile, several provide helpful information for this study. Harriet E. Amos presents the most comprehensive study of antebellum Mobile in "Social Life in an Antebellum Cotton Port: Mobile, Alabama, 1820–1860" (Ph.D. diss., Emory University, 1976).

Two theses that rely almost exclusively on newspapers contain a wealth of data; they are Paul Wayne Taylor, "Mobile, 1818–1859, As Her Newspapers Pictured Her" (M.A. thesis, University of Alabama, 1951); and Robert L. Robinson, "Mobile in the 1850's: A Social, Cultural and Economic History" (M.A. thesis, University of Alabama, 1955). Two quantitatively oriented studies offer useful analyses of wealth and economic structure of late antebellum Mobile. They are Barbara Joan Davis, "A Comparative Analysis of the Economic Structure of Mobile County, Alabama, before and after the Civil War, 1860 and 1870" (M.A. thesis, University of Alabama, 1963); and Alan Smith Thompson, "Mobile, Alabama, 1850–1861: Economic, Political, Physical, and Population Characteristics" (Ph.D. diss., University of Alabama, 1979).

Three master's theses examine free blacks in antebellum Mobile. By far the best study is Marilyn Mannhard, "The Free People of Color in Antebellum Mobile County, Alabama" (University of South Alabama, 1982). Also helpful are Melvin

Lee Ross, Jr., "Blacks, Mulattoes and Creoles in Mobile during the European and American Periods" (Purdue University, 1971); and Diane Lee Shelley, "The Effects of Increasing Racism on the Creole Colored in Three Gulf Coast Cities between 1803 and 1860" (University of West Florida, 1971).

Several studies provide information on more specialized topics. James C. Parker presents an excellent analysis of the early American port in "The Development of the Port of Mobile, 1819–1836" (M.A. thesis, Auburn University, 1968). Oscar Hugh Lipscomb comprehensively studies Catholic activities in "The Administration of Michael Portier, Vicar Apostolic of Alabama and the Floridas, 1825–1829, and First Bishop of Mobile, 1829–1859" (Ph.D. diss., Catholic University of America, 1963). Mary Morgan Duggar presents a helpful history of theatrical activities that amused cotton traders in "The Theatre in Mobile, 1822–1860" (M.A. thesis, University of Alabama, 1941).

Index

Abbott, John S. C., 92
Adams-Onis Treaty, 13, 185
African Baptist Church, 111
African Missions (Methodist), 112
Alabama: statehood, 1; 1850s cotton production, 20; intrastate sectionalism, 20, 219
Alabama and Florida Railroad, 204, 205
Alabama and Tennessee River Railroad, 199
Alabama Life Insurance and Trust Company, 127
Alabama Life Insurance Company, 40
Alabama Medical College: management of City Hospital, 161; effort at southern independence in education, 218; opening term, 218–19
Alabama Mutual Insurance Company, 40
Alabama Planter, 97, 144, 194, 210, 211; on packing fraud, 31; on insurance coverage, 40; on printers' strike, 84; on Pierre Chastang, 91; as nonpartisan, 117–18; on beautifying public square, 164–65
Alabama River, 22, 24
Alabama State Bank (Mobile Branch), 36, 37, 123
Alabama Tribune, 46, 103, 219
Alexander Pope and Son, 29
American Hotel, 44
American Party, 220, 221, 226–27, 228, 229
American Revolution, 11
Ancient Order of Hibernians, 104

Anderson, William, 157
Anti-Immigration Act of 1832, 85, 147
Armstrong, Francis W., 161
Austill and Marshall, 33
Auxiliary Tract Society, 17

Baker, Robert A., 30
Baldwin, Marshall J. D., 196
Baltimore American: criticism of Mobile's default, 124
Bankers, private, 38–39, 40
Bankers' Magazine: comment on shortage of local banking capital, 38
Bank of Mobile: initial charter, 34; outstanding credit rating under Hallett's presidency, 35; limited capital for major export center, 38; competition with private bankers, 39; presidency of Sanford, 50; survivor of the Panic of 1837, 123
Banks, 30–40 passim, 50, 54, 123
Baptists: few wealthy members, 109; black congregations, 111; support for Bethel, 176
Baring Brothers, 39
Barnes, Sarah, 88
Barton, Willoughby, 180
Barton Academy, 181–89 passim
Bates, Joseph, Jr., 33
Battle, James, 45, 175
Battle, John A. M., 45
Battle, Samuel, 45
Battle House, 45, 46, 94
Baymen's Society, 97, 177
Bee Hive Methodist Church, 108
Belge-American Company, 209
Bell, John, 234

Belmont, August, 38
Bernhard, Karl, duke of Saxe-Weimar-
  Eisenach, 44, 149
Bernody, Regis, 90
Bethel (Seamen's House), 175–76
Bethel Free School, 183, 184
Bibb, William Wyatt, 20
Biddle, Nicholas, 35
Bienville Square, 165, 166
Biloxi, 11
Black Belt, 20
Black Warrior (steamship), 208
Blakeley: founding, 4; demise, 5–6
Blakeley Sun, 4
Bloch, Jacob, 106
Board of Health, 156–57
Boeuf Gras Society, 64
Bonapartists, 105
Bond issues: 1830, 1834, 120–21; 1836,
  121–22; recordkeeping problems,
  122; 1843, 126; new regulations, 127;
  for new markethouse, 132, 133; for
  water supply, 161; financial disaster
  to city, 167
Boykin and McRae, 29
Bragg, John, 224
Brawner, Mary Hilary, 226
Breckinridge, John: local support for
  in 1860, 235
Brewer, Henry O., 209
Brewster, Henry B., 175
Brotherhood of the Church, 177
Brothers of the Sacred Heart, 175,
  184, 185
Broun, Harleston, 30
Brown, J. Purdy, 47
Brown Brothers and Company, 54; in-
  ternational merchant banking house,
  30; operations as private bankers,
  38, 39
Browne, William Phineas, 212
Bullard, Samuel P., 183
Bunker, Robert S., 43, 177
Business directories, 43

Caldwell, James, 47
Campbell, John A., 91
Can't Get Away Club, 173
Cathedral of the Immaculate Concep-
  tion, 107
Catholic Female Charitable Society:
  organization, 174; fundraising
  efforts, 175; orphanages, 178
Catholic Orphan Asylums, 95
Catholics: churches, 17, 106–7; nuns,
  93, 94; orphanages, 95, 178; French
  and Spanish heritage, 107; Irish af-
  filiation, 107; schools, 183, 184, 185,
  191, 226
Central of Georgia Railroad, 204
Chalon, Gabriel, 184
Chamber of Commerce. *See* Mobile
  Chamber of Commerce
Chandler, Daniel, 183
Charities. *See* Poor relief
Charleston, 20, 142; decline in rank as
  cotton exporter, 20; limited commit-
  ment to manufacturing, 216
Chastang, Jean, 90
Chastang, Pierre, 90, 91
Chaudron, P., 33, 34
Choctaw Pass, 5
Cholera, 159–60
Christ (Episcopal) Church, 50, 67, 107
Churches: in 1820s, 17; leaders' prefer-
  ences, 50, 67; Catholic, 17, 107; Bap-
  tist, 109, 111; Episcopal, 50, 67, 107,
  110, 169; Presbyterian, 67, 108, 185;
  Methodist, 67, 108, 111, 112; Unitarian, 109; for blacks, 110, 111, 112;
  sponsors of free schools, 183, 184,
  185. *See also* Bethel, and listings
  under individual churches and
  denominations
Church of the Good Shepherd, 111
City charter: 1819, 1826 revision, 114;
  1842, 1852 revisions, 115; 1852 revision,
  117; 1839 revision, 125–26, 140; 1843
  revision, 127, 136

City government: urban leaders' participation and priorities, 75; organization and municipal boards, 114; increase in number of wards and aldermen, 115; requirements for voting, 115; creation of city court judgeship, 115; terms of officeholding, 117; leaders' stake in government, 118; property tax revenues, 120; revenue shortages and indebtedness, 122, 125; bonded indebtedness, 124, 126; creation of Common Council, 126; new revenue sources, 128, 129; organization of municipal boards, 132; post-default finances and fiscal responsibility, 134–35; preferential allocation of city services, 136; spending priorities, 137; supervision of hiring out system, 145; supervision of living out system, 145–46; accommodation to commerce, 166; governmental rationale for services, 167. *See also* City Hall, City Hospital, Fires and fire protection, Police

City Hall: controversy over proposed site, 121; dilapidated building, 133; construction of new building, 134

City Hospital, 137, 219, 226; early facilities, 160; permanent facility, 161; care for the poor, 171

City Insurance Company, 40

Clark, Francis B., 54

Clark, George, and Company, 54

Clark, Willis G.: editor of *Mobile Daily Advertiser*, 54, 188, 189, 191, 208, 224, 230

Clarke, Schuyler, 183

Clay, Clement Claiborne, 229

Clay, Clement Comer, 229

Clotilde, 87

Cobbs, Nicholas Hamner, 177

College of South Alabama: proposal for, 216

Collins, Auguste, 90

Collins, Honore, 90

Collins, Polite, 97

Colonial rule: French, 7–11; British, 11; Spanish, 12

Columbus, Georgia, 204

Comprehensive Mobile Guide and Directory (1852), 43

Compromise of 1850: use to test for southern loyalty, 223

Copeland, James, 152

Cotton trade: critical to urban development, 1, 18–47 passim; Cotton Kingdom expansion, 1, 62; cotton production in hinterland for Mobile, 20; ocean and river transportation of bales, 20, 22; export-import imbalance, 22, 24; wharves, 26; presses and warehouses, 28; factors, 28–34; efforts at regulation, 32–33; seasonal unemployment, 178; effects of dependency, 196; rail transportation of cotton in 1850s, 202, 203; annual profits in 1850s, 231; benefits of regional economic specialization, 233; effort to avoid disruption of trade by secession, 236. *See also* Factors

Cowbellion de Rakin Society, 65

Cox, Brainerd and Company, 26

Creole Fire Company, 101, 103, 104

Creole Free School, 104, 185, 189, 190

Creoles, black, xv, 2, 90; fire company, 101, 103, 104; educational privileges, 185, 190

Crime, 142, 143. *See also* Police

Crimean War: effect on financing of railroads, 200, 201

Cumming, Kate, 236, 238

Dabney, John, 87

Dall, Charles, 184

Daniel Wheeler and Company, 30, 209

Darling, A. B., 45

Dauphin Island, 24

Dawson, William, 80

Dease, John, 175
DeBow, J. D. B., 195–96
DeBow's Review, 196, 203
De Leon, Thomas C., 67
Democrats, 117, 224, 228, 234
Dickey, Charles D., 30, 38–40, 54
Dinsmore, Silas, 181
Direct trade: effort for southern inde-
  pendence, 207; early ventures, 207–
  8; steamship companies, 208–9;
  with Central America, 209; impetus
  for local shipbuilding, 213; limited
  accomplishments, 221
Dog River, 26, 194
Douglas, Stephen A.: aid to Mobile
  and Ohio Railroad, 197; presidential
  campaign, 235, 236
Dubroca, Hilaire, 90
Dueling, 143
Duke of Saxe-Weimar-Eisenach. *See*
  Bernhard, Karl
Duncan Sherman and Company, 38
Durette, Nanette, 90

Education. *See* Schools, public
Elections, local and state, 116, 117
Emanuel, Jonathan, 50, 87
Epidemics. *See* Yellow fever
Episcopalians: white churches, 67, 107,
  169; black churches, 110; support for
  Bethel, 176; mutual aid association,
  177; free school, 183, 184, 185
Episcopal Orphan Society, 174
Eslava, Miguel, 13, 26
Eustis, O., 33, 34

Factors: definition, 28; commissions,
  28; business firms, 29, 30, 32, 33,
  50; northern-born factors, 29;
  southern-born factors, 30; problems
  with planters, 31–33; business expenses, 34
Factors Cotton Press, 88
Farmar, Robert, 11
Fearn, Marv Walker, 67

Fearn, Richard Lee, 67
Female Benevolent Society: organization, 17; aid to indigent widows,
  171, 172
Firemen's Insurance Company, 40
Fires and fire protection: fire in 1827,
  16, 81, 151; formation of early fire
  companies, 17; meetings, 63; Mobile
  Fire Department, 103; Mobile Fire
  Department Association, 103, 151, 153,
  176–77; ethnic and occupational exclusivity of fire companies, 104; fires
  in 1839, 124–25, 151–52, 154; fire in
  1855; 143; volunteer basis of fire protection, 151; comparison to Natchez,
  153; extension of fire limits, 154; fire
  zones, 167. *See also* listings under individual fire companies
First Baptist Church, 109, 111
Florida: British West Florida, 11–12,
  13; East Florida (Spanish), 13
Florida Treaty. *See* Adams-Onis Treaty
Forsyth, John, 106; local history column, 194; critic of economic dependency on North, 207; praise for rail
  car factory, 210; explanation for economic stagnation in 1850s, 231; support for Northern Democratic ticket
  in 1860, 234, 235; editorial on state
  secession convention, 235–36
Fort Charlotte, 12, 15
Fort Condé, 11, 12
Fort Louis de la Louisiane, 11
Forts: Louis de la Louisiane, 11;
  Condé, 11, 12; Charlotte, 12, 15
Fourth Presbyterian Church, 108
Franklin Society, 78
Franklin Street Methodist Church:
  sponsors black mission, 112
Free blacks: jobs, xv, 89, 91; Creole
  and non-Creole backgrounds, 90;
  manumission, 90–91; dependency
  on white patronage, 97–98; resi-
  dences, 101; Creole Fire Company,
  101, 103, 104; population growth,

143; regulations of conduct, 146–48; *Warsaw* incident and Mobile Harbor Law, 147
French and Indian War, 11
Fuller, Hiram, xiii
Fulton Insurance Company, 40

Gage, C. P., 27
Gambling, 148–50
Gannaway, James, 210
Garrett, William, 33
Garrow, Samuel H., 13, 122
Gascoigne, Charles, 112
Gas lighting: operation as private franchise, 163, 164, 167
Gazzam, Charles W., 212
George Martin and Company, 30
German Dramatic Association, 105
German Fusiliers, 64, 105
German (Methodist) Mission, 108
German Turners Society, 105, 178
Goetzel, S. H., 106
Goldthwaite, Eliza, 88
Goodman, Duke W., 112; wharfinger, 27; commission merchant, 30; attitude toward merchant-planter relationship, 32; slaveholdings, 61, 88; charitable donations, 175; railroad supporter, 196
Gordon, Archibald W., 161
Government Street Presbyterian Church: prestige of membership, 50, 67, 108
Gracie, Archibald, 39
Greene, Welcome Arnold, 2
Gulf of Mexico, 24
Gwathmey, Forbes and Company, 30
Gwathmey, H. B., 175

Hall, Basil, 44
Hall, Margaret (Mrs. Basil), 3, 44
Hallett, Thomas, 6, 55, 80
Hallett, William R., banker: 26, 35, 37, 56; early career and marriage, 55–56
Hamilton, Jefferson, 94, 112

Hartwell Davis, 29
Haviland, Clark and Company, 88
Hibernian Benevolent Society, 17, 106, 177–78
Hitchcock, Henry, 37, 172; water works lessee, 162; school board member, 181
Hitchcock, Mrs. Henry, 171
Hitchcock's Row, 175
Hodgson, Adam, 2
Hogan, John B., 22
Hopkins, Arthur F., 202
Horton, Gustavus: cotton dealer, 81; slaveowner, 87
Hotels: scarcity from 1820s through 1840, 44; Battle House, 45–46, 94; destruction by fires, 151
Hundley, Daniel, 75
Hunt's Merchants' Magazine, 28, 196–97
Huntsville Southern Advocate, 219
Hurlburt, Elisha D., 22
Hurtel, John, 178

Illinois Central Railroad, 198
Immigrants: changes in ethnic makeup over antebellum era, xv; English, Irish, and Scottish in 1817, 2; ethnic militia companies, 64, 104–5; Irish, 81, 91–92; German, 91–92; single male predominance, 96; employment of Irish women, 98; German Schiller Festival, 105–6; Irish St. Patrick's Day celebration, 106; labor competition with slaves, 143; Irish arson suspects, 152; Irish residents of Poor House, 172; Irish indigent aid, 177–78; German, French, Scottish aid societies, 178; Irish textile factory workers, 211; religious affiliations, 226; political concerns about naturalized citizens, 226; proportion of population and labor force, 226; German political activity, 228
Independent Rifles, 238

Indians, 7, 11
Innerarity, James, 13, 183
Insurance companies: local, 40; non-local, 40, 153
Irish Benevolent and Naturalization Society, 106
Irish Independent Greens, 64, 104

Jackson Street (Methodist) Church, 108
James Crawford, 29
Jews: organization of congregation, 109–10
John A. Winston and Company, 32
John Boyd and Company, 30
John Forbes and Company, 13
Johnson, William H., 185
Jones, Israel I., 109, 175
Jones, Joel W., 32
Jones, Solomon I., 109
Judson, Catherine Susan, 56
Judson, Lewis, 13, 22, 161

Kennedy, Joshua, 91
Ketchum, George A., 158
King, William R., 199
Know-Nothing Party. *See* American Party
Krafft, Michael, 65
Krebs, Joseph, 26

Laborers: shortages of skilled laborers and high wages, 80–81; patronage difficulties and effect on indus-trialization, 81; furniture makers, 81; dressmakers, 81, 98; tailors protest wage cuts, 81–82; carpenters protest importation of cheap competition, 82–83; printers' association and strike, 84; slaves as unskilled and semiskilled labor, 85; free blacks, 91; immigrant competition, 91–92; white female laborers and high wages, 93–94; child laborers, 95; im-migrant competition with native

whites and blacks, 96; competition in carpentry trades, 97; washers and ironers, 97–98; residence patterns, 99, 101; associational activities, 101–12, 177; role in city, 113; wages of city laborers, 137
Ladies of the Bethel Society, 176
Lafayette Guards, 64, 105
L'Andre, Simon, 90
Langdon, Charles C.: mayor, 144, 155; political problems in 1850s, 223, 226, 229
La Société Francaise de Bienfaisance, 178
Laurendine, Joseph, 103
Ledyard, Hatter and Company, 183
Ledyard, William John, 50
Le Moyne, Jean-Baptiste de Bienville, 64, 164; founded Fort Louis de la Louisiane, 11
Le Moyne, Pierre, d'Iberville, 7
Levert, Henry S., 65, 159
Levert, Octavia Walton, 65, 67
Lewis, Addin, 161; first mayor of American Mobile, 53
Livingston, Robert, 209
Lockwood, Elihu, 225
London Morning Post: criticism of Mobile's default, 124
Louisiana: capitals under the French, 11
Louisiana Gazette, 7, 239
Louisiana Purchase: boundary dispute, 11–12
Louisville: development of manufac-turing in, 216
Ludlow, Noah Miller, 46
Lumber: valuable industry, 213

McGlashan, Alexander, 184, 185
McGran, Thomas, 182–83
Mackay, Alexander, 44
McLoskey, Patrick, 91
McLoskey, Philip, 26
McLoskey Hagan and Company, 30

McRae, Colin J., 29, 89
Magee, Jacob, 42
Malone and Foote, 29
Mansion House (Hotel), 44
Manufacturing: dependence on North, 81, 211–12; as means of diversification of economy, 209–10; for southern independence, 210; sash and blind, carriage, and railroad car factories, 210; textile factory, 211; iron foundries, 212; limitations, 212; lumber industry, 213; Mobile in comparison to Alabama, 213; in comparison to other southern cities, 216
Mardi Gras. See Mystic societies
Marine Dock and Mutual Insurance Company, 40
Martin, George, 30
Masons: social activities, 4; charitable activities, 176
Massacre Island, 7
Mastin, Claude, 67
Mead, Lucien, 209
Meaher, Timothy, 87
Mechanics Fire Company Number 7, 104
Mechanics Savings Company (later Mobile Savings Company), 37
Meek, A. B.: poet, historian, and editor, 78; president of Baymen's Society, 177
Merchants' Exchange, 42, 43
Merchants Fire Company Number 4, 64
Merchants Insurance Company, 40
Meslier, Augustus, R., 165
Methodists: elite membership, 67; mission success, 108; black affiliation, 111, 112; Bethel ministry, 176; free school, 183, 184, 185
Militia companies: social functions, 63–64; guard activities, 83; ethnic exclusivity, 104
Mitchell, Frank, 90

Mitchell, William, 90
Mobile: occupation of, 2; frontier appearance in 1820s, 2–4; foundation for growth, 7; origin of name, 7; colonial rule, 7–12; American territorial organization, 13; incorporation charter, 14; 1820s, 15–16; port and harbor facilities, 24; slave trading center, 85; free black population center, 90; boundaries of city, 99, land development in 1850s, 99, 101; residential patterns, 99; land speculation in 1820s and 1830s, 123; credit rating, 127; gambling center, 148; history columns, 194
Mobile Acqueduct Company, 161, 162
Mobile and Cedar Point Railroad Company, 26, 122
Mobile and Dog River Manufacturing Company, 211
Mobile and Girard Railroad, 204, 205
Mobile and Great Northern Railroad, 205–6
Mobile and New Orleans Railroad, 206
Mobile and Nicaragua Steamship Company, 209
Mobile and Ohio Railroad Company, 210, 232; organization, 196–97; federal land grants, 197–98; special local railroad tax, 198; state aid controversy, 198–200, 220; revenue problems, 200–1; limited achievement of goals, 204, 207; issue in congressional campaign, 225
Mobile and Vera Cruz Mexican Gulf Steamship Company, 209
Mobile Argus, 7, 115; on poverty, 169; on sailors' needs for relief, 171
Mobile Bay, 4, 7, 24
Mobile Bible Society, 17
Mobile Cadets, 238
Mobile Carpentry and Joiners' Mutual Benefit Society, 97

Mobile Chamber of Commerce, 41, 42, 175
Mobile City Directory for 1855–56, 6
Mobile County Court of Commissioners of Roads and Revenue: funds for poor relief, 172; funds for care of orphans, 174
Mobile County School Commissioners: incorporation, 180. *See also* Schools, public
Mobile Daily Advertiser, 54, 78, 116, 118, 127, 194, 205, 209, 210, 211, 223, 227, 230; on printers' strike, 84; on unrestrained animals, 154; on health regulations, 155; on yellow fever epidemic, 157; on municipal takeover of water service, 163; on extent of poverty in Mobile, 169; on private charity, 172; on municipal aid for Mobile and Great Northern Railroad, 206; on Alabama iron ore, 212; on Unionism, 224–25; on Democratic party, 228–29; on secession, 237
Mobile Daily Register, 16, 34, 45, 46, 56, 65, 103, 105, 108, 145, 147, 155, 194, 197, 223, 225, 232, 234–35; advice to merchants, 3; lauds Mobile as winter resort, 44; Democratic views, 49; anniversary celebrations, 63; on labor protest, 82–83; on printers' strike, 84; on two-class society, 99; on Schiller festival, 106; on 1830 bond issue, 121; Democratic editor's views, 126; on mismanagement of city finances, 134; on *Warsaw* incident, 147; on unrestrained animals, 155; on Bienville Square, 165–66; on charities, 172, 176; on Baymen's Society, 177; on the indigent, 178–79; on Thaddeus Sanford, 188; rivalry with New Orleans, 196; on local medical education, 218–19; on city's stagnation, 231; on secession, 236–37
Mobile Fire Department, 103. *See also* Fires and fire protection
Mobile Fire Department Association, 103, 151, 153; mutual aid functions, 177
Mobile Gas Light Company, 156
Mobile Grenadiers, 64, 104
Mobile Hotel, 151
Mobile Journal of Commerce, Letter Sheet Price Current, 28
Mobile Literary Gazette, 149
Mobile Literary Society, 78
Mobile Manufacturing Company (later Mobile and Dog River Manufacturing Company), 211
Mobile Marine Railway and Insurance Company, 40, 50
Mobile Mercantile Advertiser for the Country, 154
Mobile Navigation and Mutual Insurance Company, 40
Mobile News, 229
Mobile Point, 26
Mobile Port Society, 175
Mobile River, 7, 24
Mobile Savings Company. *See* Mechanics Savings Company
Mobile Steamship Company, 208, 209
Mobile Theatre, 47
Mobile Tribune, 229
Mobile Typographical Association, 84, 85
Mobile Weekly Herald and Tribune: on economic benefits of Mobile and Ohio Railroad, 202
Montgomery: as slave trade center, 85; as urban rival, 204–5
Montgomery and West Point Railroad, 204, 205
Moore, Gabriel, 35
Mordecai, E. S.: health officer and quarantine physician, 158
Mordecai, Solomon, 4, 183; hiring out slaves, 88, 89
Murphy, John, 35
Murrell, Joseph E., 209
Mystic societies, 64, 65

Nachon, Father: victim of nativism, 228

Nashville Convention, 223

Natchez, 153

National Typographical Union, 85

Nativism, 226, 227, 228–29. *See also* American Party

Neptune Engine Company Number 2, 177

Neptune Number 1 Creole Fire Company. *See* Creole Fire Company

New Orleans: Mobile's secondary position in relation to, 7, 20; capital of French Louisiana, 11; Mobile's commerce with, 24; rivalry in 1840s, 195–96; rivalry in 1850s, 204

New Orleans Daily Delta, 157

New Orleans, Jackson, and Great Northern Railroad, 204

New York American, 6

New York and Alabama Steamship Company, 208

Niles' Register, 1, 17, 239; on cotton trade regulation, 32; on *Warsaw* incident, 147

Nott, Josiah C., 218

Nott, Mrs. Josiah, 179

Ogden Day and Company, 29

O'Hara, Theodore, 67

Olmsted, Frederick Law, 164

Orphanages: and child labor, 95; public support, 174; private support, 174, 175; prevalence of Irish-born children, 178

Owen, George W., 122

Panic of 1819, 6

Panic of 1837, xv, 26, 30, 33, 162, 164, 193, 195, 199; effect on state bank, 36; effect on wages of hired slaves, 88; real estate losses, 123; debt collection problems, 122; effect on property values, 126, 127

Panic of 1857, 32, 230, 232

Peabody, Herbert C., 109

Perdido River, 11–12

Peters and Stebbins, 29

Phillips, Philip, 94; land speculator in 1830s, 123; advocate of railroads, 198–99; congressional candidate, 225

Pickens, Israel, 148

Pickett, Albert J.: author of *History of Alabama*, 194

Planters and Merchants Bank: charter, 37; failure, 123

Plunkett, Caroline, 97

Police: major departmental expenditure, 137; paid guards, 140; size of force, 140; complaints on effectiveness, 141, 142; enforcement of slave code, 143, 144; citizen patrols, 152; protection of commercial areas, 166. *See also* Crime

Political leaders: property ownership, age, occupation, 76; nonsouthern representation, similarities across party lines, 77

Pollard, Charles T., 204

Poor relief, 192; leaders' affiliations with charities, 64; attitudes toward poverty, 168; theories of causes of poverty, 169; poor fund and charities, 170; outdoor relief, 170–71; private organizations' aid, 172; yellow fever relief, 173–74; seamen's relief, 175–76; mutual aid associations, 176–77, 178; tendency to treat immediate problems of poverty, 178; employment aid society, 178–79

Pope, Alexander, 29

Population: general growth, xiii, 1; disproportionate male-female ratio in 1820s, 3; growth 1785–1813, 11; growth of foreign-born element in 1850s, 96; effect of seasonal shifts on local government, 116

Portier, Bishop Michael, 174

Presbyterians, 108, 185; elite membership, 67; support of bethel, 176; free school, 183, 184

Prostitution, 150

Protestant Episcopal Church Employment Society, 179
Protestant Orphan Asylum, 175
Protestant Orphan Asylum Society, 95, 174, 175
Public improvements: in 1830s, 114, 120, 121; of streets, 139, 140; of public squares, 165, 166
Public schools. See Schools, public
Public Schools Act of 1854, 190
Public Schools Amendments Act of 1856, 190
Public squares: Bienville Square, 164–66; Washington Square, 166

Quaker City, 208
Quarantines, 157, 158

Railroads: Mobile and Cedar Point Railroad, 26, 122; as means to southern independence, 195–96; Mobile and Ohio Railroad, 196–204, 207, 210, 225, 232; New Orleans, Jackson, and Great Northern Railroad, 203–4; Mobile and Girard Railroad, 204–5, 206; Montgomery and West Point Railroad, 204, 205; Alabama and Florida Railroad, 204, 205; Mobile and Great Northern Railroad, 205–6; Mobile and New Orleans Railroad, 206–7; collective failure to achieve set goals, 207, 221
Randall, Eliza, 180–81
Residence patterns: in 1850s, 99, 101
Reynolds, Bernard, 6
R. G. Dun and Company, 35
Richmond: economy, 56; manufacturing, 216
Ripley, Center and Company, 22
Rives, Battle and Company, 29
Rix, William, 87, 238
Roberts, Seth, 238
Robertson, William R., 26, 43, 161

Robertson and Barnewall, 29
Rogers, Isaiah, 45
Roman Catholic Church. See Catholics
Rose, Asa S., 210
Rottenstein, George: head of German Mission, 108
Rowan's Directory, 37, 41, 193
Royal Street Theatre, 47
Ryland, Allen H.: slaveholdings, 61, 88

Sag Nichts, 228
St. Andrew's Society, 178
St. Anthony Street Baptist Church, 109, 111
St. Cyr, Henry de, 178
St. Francis Street Methodist Church, 67, 108; African mission, 112
St. John, Newton, 116; banker, 38–40
St. John, Powers and Company, 38–39
St. John's Episcopal Church, 107, 169
St. Joseph's (Catholic) Church, 107
St. Mary's (Episcopal) Church, 107
St. Paul's (Episcopal) Church, 107
St. Vincent de Paul: parish formed, 107
Salomon, David, 110
Salomon, Ezekiel, 110
Salons, 65
Samaritan Society, 173, 178
Sanford, James, 183
Sanford, Thaddeus, 189; urban leader, 49; slaveowner, 87; editor of *Mobile Register*, 188
Sanitation measures, 167; problem with unrestrained animals, 154–55; enforcement priorities and expenditures, 155, 156; quarantines, 157
Saunders, James E., 61, 188
Savannah, 20, 58, 142; sanitation project, 157
Schlesinger, J., 106
Schlesinger, S., 106
Schools, public: as social service, 168;

early opposition to, 179; early state enabling laws, 179–80; incorporation of county system, 180; revenue problems, 181; construction of Barton Academy, 181; free sectarian schools, 153; public funds to charity schools, 183, 184; for black Creoles, 185; alternative to pauper schools, 186; effort to sell Barton Academy property, 186; establishment of genuine public school system, 188–89; Creole School, 189–90; new revenue sources and enrollment, 191

Schroeder, H. A., 94

Seamen's House. *See* Bethel

Secession: developing crisis, xvi; increasing tensions, 222, 234; 1860 presidential election, 235; state convention, 235–37; Cooperationists, 236–38; influence of nativism, 237

Second (St. Francis Street) Baptist Church, 109, 111

Second Bank of the United States Branch in Mobile, 35, 36

Second Presbyterian Church, 108

Sectionalism: north-south, xiv, xvi; northerners as urban leaders, 53; benefits of commercial ties to North, 222–23; criticism of investments of northerners, 230–33; suppressed Unionism, 238. *See also* Southern independence

Sellier, A., 185

Sewall, Kiah B., 187

Shaari Shomayim U-Maskil el Dol, 109

Shakespeare's Row: gambling district, 149

Shanklin, Abraham, 91

Shipbuilding, 213

Shortridge, George D.: gubernatorial candidacy, 220, 221

Singleton, Richard, 32

Sisters of Charity, 184, 226; care of orphans, 175; teaching of black Creoles, 185; controversy in management of City Hospital, 226

Skaats, B. F., 212

Skaats and Company, 212

Slaveholding: prevalent among urban leaders, 61; sign of accommodation to southern mores, 62; small proportion of population, 87; varied backgrounds of owners, 87–88; support for widows, 88–89; occasional manumissions, 91

Slaves: population in 1830s and 1840s, 85; effect of Nat Turner revolt, 85; prices, 87; hiring arrangements, 88–89, 145; living out system, 89, 145, 146; misconduct, 142; proportion of population, 143; enforcement of slave code, 143, 144, 145, 146; arson suspects, 152

Slave trade: domestic, 85; illicit foreign, 87; effect of price increases in 1850s, 87

Smallpox, 160

Smith, Murray, 67

Smith, Phoebe Desha, 67

Smith, Sidney: merchant, 196, 197; president of Mobile and Ohio Railroad, 200, 205

Smith, Sol, 47

Smith, Walter, 142, 187, 189

Smooth's Hotel, 44

Southern Bank of Alabama, 37

Southern independence: quest for, xvi; avenues to, 195; to offset dependence on New York for imports, 208; manufacturing for, 210; education movement for, 216; Alabama Medical College, 218; effort to counter colonial dependency, 221, 239; advocates of, 222; southern rights movement, 223, 234. *See also* Direct trade, Manufacturing, Railroads

Southern Insurance Company, 40

Southern Rights Association, 213

South Ward Mission (Wesley Chapel), 108
Spanish Mystic Society, 64
Spanish River, 24
Spring Hill: suburb, 70
Spring Hill College, 216, 228
Stein, Albert: slaveowner, 87; operator of water system, 162–63
Stevens, Paran, 45
Stickney, Henry, 16
Strickland, William, 62, 94
Strikers Independent Society, 65
Stuart, J. A., 121
Sunday observance: issue of American party, 227

Tappan, Arthur, 147
Tasistro, Louis, 173
Temperance Society, 17
Tensaw River, 4, 6, 24
Theaters: economic value of, 46; public subscription for construction, 46–47
Third Presbyterian Church, 108
Three Mile Creek, 161, 163
Todd, John B., 177
Tombigbee River, 22, 24
Treaty of Paris of 1763, 11
Treaty of Paris of 1783, 11
Trinity (Episcopal) Church, 107
Troost, Lewis, 197
Turner, Jarvis, 210–11
Turners Society, 105, 178

Unionists, 222, 223, 224, 238
Unitarians: organization, 109; Bethel support, 176; free school, 184
United States Marine Hospital, 161, 219
University of Alabama, 216
Upson, Edwin, 62
Urban leaders: selection and definition, 48–49; commercial preoccupation, 51; geographic or ethnic backgrounds, 51; diverse origins, 52; fluidity, 54; kinship ties, 55; self-made, 56; occupations, 56; property-holding, 58, 59, 61; voluntary associations, 62, 63; religious affiliations, 67; residential patterns, 68; family situations and values, 70; business and government leaders, 75; partisan political leaders, 75; summer vacations, 78; northern-born and public schools, 188; contributions of non-southerners, 232
Urban rivalry: with New Orleans, 195–96; with Montgomery, 204–5; in manufacturing, 216

Vagrancy, 169–70
Visitation Convent, 191
Voluntary associations: fraternal, 4, 176; fire companies, 17, 63, 103, 104; ethnic associations, 17, 104, 105, 106; women's benevolent societies, 17, 171, 172, 174, 175, 176, 178, 179; militia companies, 63–64, 105, 238; mystic societies, 64, 65; poor relief for yellow fever victims, seamen, and other indigent, 172–78

Wallace, Samuel, 183
Walker, Percy, 228, 229
Walker, Robert J., 210
Walton, Sarah, 89
Waring, Moses, 56
War of 1812: American occupation of Mobile, xv, 12
Warrior River, 22
Washington Square, 166
Water supply: early private franchise, 161; lease to Hitchcock, 161; lease to Stein, 162–63; continued private management, 163
Waverly Hotel, 44
Weeks, J. L., 175
Wesley Chapel. See South Ward Mission
West Florida, 13

West Ward, 101, 108; citizen patrol in, 152
Whigs, 117, 126, 223, 224–25; affiliation with American Party, 226
Widows' Row, 172
Wilkinson, James, 12
William Jones, Jr., 213
Winston, John A., 67; commission merchant, 30–31; governor opposed to state aid for internal improvements, 199–200, 220, 221
Withers, Jones M.: mayor, 146, 206, 229
Witherspoon, Alfred, 87
Women: benevolent activities, 17, 171, 172, 174, 175, 176, 178, 179; employment of, 93; wages, 94; white domestics, 94; prostitutes, 94–95; racial competition among laborers, 97–98; indigent widows, 171, 172
Woodruff, Lewis T., 165

Yellow fever: 1819, 90; 1858, 116; 1839, 124–25, 152; 1826, 156; 1853, 156–57; miasmatic theory and preventive measures, 157; 1854, 1855, 158; 1837, 1839, 1853, 173; 1853, 174, 178; 1819, 194
Young Men's Secessionist Association, 226
Yuille, Ann, 87